LEARNING AND
SOCIAL BEHAVIOR

LEARNING AND SOCIAL BEHAVIOR

Barry McLaughlin

UNIVERSITY OF CALIFORNIA, SANTA CRUZ

 THE FREE PRESS, NEW YORK
Collier-Macmillan Limited, London

Fig. 2-2 reprinted from *Behaviorism* by John B. Watson; by permission of W. W.
Norton & Company, Inc.; copyright 1924, 1925 by John B. Watson; copyright 1930,
Revised Edition by W. W. Norton & Company, Inc., and renewed © 1958 by John B.
Watson. Fig. 2-3 reprinted from H. C. Blodgett, University of California Press publica-
tion in Psychology 1929, Vol. 4, p. 120; reprinted by permission of The Regents of the
University of California. Fig. 3-4 reprinted from N. Chomsky, *Syntactic Structures*
(1957), p. 27; reprinted by permission of Mouton & Co., Publishers, The Hague. Figs. 3-5
and 3-6 reprinted from D. Berlyne, *Structure and Direction in Thinking* (1965), pp. 90
and 191; reprinted by permission of John Wiley and Sons, Inc. Fig. 4-1 reprinted from
N. Miller and J. Dollard, *Social Learning and Imitation* (1941), p. 96; reprinted by permission of Yale University Press. Fig. 6-1 reprinted from J. Dollard and N. Miller, *Personality and Psychotherapy* (1950), p. 223; reprinted by permission of McGraw-Hill
Book Co. Fig. 6-3 reprinted from Lovaas, Schaeffer, and Simmons, *Journal of Experimental Research in Personality* (1965), Vol. 1, p. 103; reprinted by permission of
Academic Press, Inc. Fig. 6-5 reprinted from *Insight vs. Desensitization in Psychotherapy*
by Gordon L. Paul, p. 33, with the permission of the publishers, Stanford University
Press; © 1966 by the Board of Trustees of the Leland Stanford Junior University.
Table 2-1 from L. Postman, P. O. Adams, and A. M. Bohm, Studies in incidental learning: V. Recall for order and associative clustering, *Journal of Experimental Psychology*
(1956), Vol. 51, p. 336; copyright, 1956, by the American Psychological Association;
reproduced by permission. Fig. 2-4 from L. D. DeNike, The temporal relationship
between awareness and performance in verbal conditioning, *Journal of Experimental
Psychology* (1964), Vol. 68, p. 525; copyright, 1964, by the American Psychological Association; reproduced by permission. Table 2-2 data from W. K. Estes, Learning theory
and the new "mental chemistry," *Psychological Review* (1960), Vol. 67, p. 218; copyright, 1960, by the American Psychological Association; reproduced by permission.
Fig. 2-5 from D. O. Hebb, Drives and the C.N.S. (Conceptual nervous system), *Psychological Review* (1955), Vol. 62, p. 250; copyright, 1955, by the American Psychological
Association; reproduced by permission. Figs. 3-1 and 3-2 from O. H. Mowrer, The psychologist looks at language, *American Psychologist* (1954), Vol. 9, pp. 664 and 668;
copyright, 1954, by the American Psychological Association; reproduced by permission.
Fig. 3-3 from C. E. Osgood, On understanding and creating sentences, *American Psychologist* (1963), Vol. 18, p. 740; copyright, 1963, by the American Psychological Association; reproduced by permission. Table 4-1 from D. Ross, Relationship between dependency, intentional learning, and incidental learning in preschool children, *Journal
of Personality and Social Psychology* (1966), Vol. 4, p. 378; copyright, 1966, by the
American Psychological Association; reproduced by permission. Fig. 4-4 from A. Bandura, Influence of models' reinforcement contingencies on the acquisition of imitative

iv

responses, *Journal of Personality and Social Psychology* (1965b), Vol. 1, p. 592; copyright, 1965, by the American Psychological Association; reproduced by permission. Fig. 5-4 from N. Miller and D. T. Campbell, Regency and primacy in persuasion as a function of the timing of speeches and measurements, *Journal of Abnormal and Social Psychology* (1959), Vol. 59, p. 2; copyright, 1959, by the American Psychological Association; reproduced by permission. Fig. 5-5 from J. Carlsmith, B. Collins, and R Helmreich, Studies in forced compliance: I. The effect of pressure for compliance on attitude change produced by face-to-face role playing and anonymous essay writing, *Journal of Personality and Social Psychology* (1966), Vol. 4, p. 9; copyright, 1966, by the American Psychological Association; reproduced by permission. Table 5-1 from W. A. Watts and W. J. McGuire, Persistence of induced opinion change and retention of inducing message content, *Journal of Abnormal and Social Psychology* (1964), Vol. 68, p. 236; copyright, 1964, by the American Psychological Association; reproduced by permission. Fig. 6-2 from J. M. Atthowe and L. Krasner, A preliminary report on the application of contingent reinforcement procedures (token economy) on a "chronic" psychiatric ward, *Journal of Abnormal Psychology* (1968), Vol. 73, p. 39; copyright, 1968, by the American Psychological Association; reproduced by permission. Fig. 6-4 from A. Bandura, E. B. Blanchard, and B. J. Ritter, Relative efficacy of modeling therapeutic changes for inducing behavioral, attitudinal, and affective changes, *Journal of Personality and Social Psychology* (1969), Vol. 13, p. 183; copyright, 1969, by the American Psychological Association; reproduced by permission. Fig. 7-1 from J. L. Gewirtz and D. M. Baer, Deprivation and satiation of social reinforcers as drive conditions, *Journal of Abnormal and Social Psychology* (1958), Vol. 57, p. 169; copyright, 1958, by the American Psychological Association; reproduced by permission. Fig. 7-2 from W. Mischel and J. C. Masters, Effects of probability of reward attainment on responses to frustration, *Journal of Personality and Social Psychology* (1966), Vol. 3, p. 394; copyright, 1966, by the American Psychological Association; reproduced by permission. Fig. 7-3 from A. Bandura and C. J. Kupers, Transmission of patterns of self-reinforcement through modeling, *Journal of Abnormal and Social Psychology* (1964), Vol. 69, p. 5; copyright, 1964, by the American Psychological Association; reprinted by permission. Fig. 7-4 from D. Byrne and D. Nelson, Attraction as a linear function of proportion of positive reinforcements, *Journal of Personality and Social Psychology* (1965), Vol. 1, p. 661; copyright, 1965, by the American Psychological Association; reproduced by permission.

Preface

THE PSYCHOLOGICAL study of human social behavior can be approached from many theoretical points of view. A major theoretical perspective—perhaps the dominant point of view among psychologists in this country—is that of learning theory. This book examines efforts by psychologists with a learning-theory orientation to understand the processes involved in man's social behavior. It summarizes, selectively, a great deal of research representing investigations in many areas of empirical study and attempts to evaluate the success of this enterprise.

Learning theory, as here understood, refers to the tradition of behavioral psychology that has come to characterize American experimental psychology. The defining features of such an approach are discussed at length in Chapter Two, but it suffices here to say that the book is concerned principally with stimulus-response (reinforcement) learning theory and related developments. The author does not review the work of Piaget, Bruner, and others, whose theories of learning are more cognitive and who stress the importance of developmental progressions in learning. To do so would require a work of considerably greater length.

The work of theorists and researchers in the learning tradition is presented sympathetically, but not uncritically. Alternatives to a learning-theory point of view are also discussed, although generally not in as much detail. The reader should be forewarned that learning theory is given more treatment in this book, not necessarily because it is thought to be more valuable as an approach to the phenomena discussed, but because the central theme of the book concerns the uses to which learning theory has been put to understand human social behavior.

An additional note of warning is required—one unfortunately frequently omitted in books of this nature. In reviewing the research of other investigators, the author, no matter how careful he has tried to be, may introduce bias. The reader sees the reported research through the author's eyes. Distortion is hopefully held to a minimum, yet the reader should be aware of the need to check the author's interpretation against the original sources. Indeed, the mere fact that the author had to select a limited number of studies from a vast literature introduces some bias. Numerous studies have been omitted or just mentioned in the text. This does not mean that these studies are necessarily inferior to those discussed, but simply that they did not fit in as well to the overall scheme of this book.

The reader will note that the book is not devoted systematically to theories of social learning. These theories—as well as the general learning theories from which they emanate—are discussed in the first chapter and mentioned throughout the book. Nevertheless, researchers have not, for the most part, been guided by theories of social learning. Instead, research interest has centered on particular substantive areas, and investigators have preferred to use specific, small-scale theories rather than a general, all-encompassing social-learning theory.

For this reason the book is divided into substantive areas. Following the chapter on theory and a chapter devoted to basic issues of an introductory nature, the author reviews research concerned with particular aspects of social behavior: language acquisition, imitative behavior, attitude formation and change, behavior change in psychotherapy, and interpersonal behavior generally. In each of these areas the contribution of learning theory—both theoretical and empirical—is examined and evaluated.

It should be pointed out that a chapter on psychotherapy is included because increasing numbers of psychologists have come to regard therapy as a social-learning process. These psychologists use learning principles to account for the acquisition and maintenance of responses that deviate from social norms and to provide techniques for modifying and eliminating such responses. In no other area in recent years has learning theory been applied with so much energy and enthusiasm.

The book assumes some familiarity with the psychology of learning, although many introductory topics are discussed in Chapter Two, and the book could serve as a self-contained unit for courses in the psychology of human learning. It will most likely be used by advanced undergraduate students and graduate students of psychology and education, although some instructors may find that they can supply enough background material to bring the book within the reach of lower-division students.

The author is indebted to Albert Bandura for a critical reading of earlier versions of parts of the manuscript and for many helpful comments. Carolyn Brown and Monica Bay also assisted in the preparation of the manuscript. In particular, the author wishes to thank his wife, Sigrid, for her encouragement and support throughout the various stages of manuscript preparation. Finally, the author would like to thank The American Psychological Association, McGraw-Hill Book Company, University of Chicago Press, University of California Press, Mouton and Company, John Wiley and Sons, Yale University Press, Stanford University Press, and Academic Press for permission to reprint tables and figures.

Contents

ix

LEARNING AND
SOCIAL BEHAVIOR

I

Learning and Social- Learning Theory

IN 1851 Leo Tolstoy wrote, "In all our memories the middle disappears, and only the first and the last impression, especially the last one, remains" (1935, p. 285). For those familiar with the concepts and findings of contemporary psychologists working in the area of learning and memory, the phenomenon Tolstoy described has another name— the serial position effect. In fact, Tolstoy's statement is empirically quite accurate—in free recall situations the last material presented to a learner is best recalled, and the early material is recalled better than what appeared in the middle.

In many instances the findings of experimental research in the psychology of learning echo traditional wisdom and the insights of great writers and thinkers. To take another example, when an experimental psychologist concludes that more meaningful materials are better recalled than less meaningful materials (e.g., Lindley, 1963), he is simply reiterating what Spinoza had pointed out long before—that "the more intelligible a thing is, the more easily it is retained in memory, and contrariwise, the less intelligible it is, the more easily we forget it" (1677, XI, 81). Many of the "laws" of learning established through experimental techniques in recent decades appear to teach us little more about the nature of man than can be learned from a reading of Aristotle, Descartes, Locke, and other great philosophers. Indeed, the findings of elaborate empirical investigations in the psychology of learning often seem to be restatements of conventional wisdom.

And if the findings of psychological research are not obvious, they frequently appear to be esoteric, with little relevance to human experience. The white rat is a convenient subject for research on learning, but many psychologists have grown skeptical of deriving basic laws of human behavior from the performance of rats in mazes. Increasingly, psychologists have turned to human subjects and have employed sophisticated and complex research designs to study paradigmatic one-person learning situations. A highly specialized and rigorous experimental discipline has evolved that applies to miniature, restricted forms of human learning. Yet the rigor and degree of control achieved in one-person learning situations is not without its disadvantages. In their search for quantitative precision, experimentalists tend to study artificial situations removed from the experiences of man in normal social life.

In recent years some psychologists have become convinced that the best way to obtain information about human social learning is not via the indirect approach of animal research, nor via the study of one-person human learning, but rather by studying human behavior directly in all its complexity. Man, after all, learns in social situations and has needs that require the mediation of other people for their satisfaction. Rather than focusing on simple, one-person situations, these investigators have applied their methodological and conceptual tools directly to social phenomena. They have sought to escape from what they feel to be the artificiality of the one-person learning situation by studying behavior in dyadic or group settings. They have directed their attention to specifically social forms of learning—to how children learn a language, how neurotic behavior is learned and can be unlearned, or how patterns of interpersonal behavior are developed.

The increasing interest of psychologists in social phenomena represents an attempt to work out a science of behavior that will be more meaningful and nontrivial. It is a reaction to the movement toward specialization that exists in experimental psychology and threatens to make the discipline sterile and scholastic. Of course, traditional experimental research in the laboratory setting is needed and must continue. Many psychologists, however, feel that the time has come to apply the principles of behavior derived in tightly-controlled laboratory experiments to complex social situations. Parsimony is a desideratum, and hopefully learning principles derived from one-person situations will be shown to hold for interpersonal situations as well. If these principles apply, so much the better. If not, research must be directed at specifying new principles of learning that do apply to man's social behavior.

Determined effort in this direction is relatively recent, yet attempts to extend the principles of learning to social behavior date back to the beginning of the psychology of learning in this country. The early theorists were concerned with explaining human behavior in its entirety. Behaviorism was not just a way of looking at the activity of a single person in an experimental laboratory; its significance lay in the fact that it was capable, its advocates argued, of explaining the most complicated and intricate aspects of man's social behavior. Watson, for example, felt that all emotional behavior could be explained on the basis of conditioned and unconditioned responses; and Clark Hull, the most eminent of the behavior theorists, planned a major work that would be explicitly concerned with the extension of learning principles to social interactions. Hull died before he could accomplish this project, but a number of his followers have advanced learning-theory explanations of various types of social phenomena. Other theorists, working from different theoretical perspectives, have also proposed social-learning theories. Discussion of these theories will be the concern of this chapter.

Before turning to specifically socially-oriented theories, however, it may be helpful to discuss briefly the various general learning theories from which they developed. Throughout this discussion emphasis will be placed on those aspects of the theory that anticipated and influenced subsequent theory and research on the learning of social behavior. More comprehensive discussions of the general theories of learning are available elsewhere and the interested reader is referred to these sources—especially Hilgard and Bower (1966) and Hill (1963).

LEARNING THEORY

"The most incomprehensible thing about the world," Albert Einstein once said, "is that it is comprehensible." Like all theory, learning theory is directed at making the world more comprehensible. It is intended to clarify, to enrich our understanding of man's nature and his behavior. But theory does more than this. It structures the way we perceive the world. It puts what is known about a domain into systematic form. Theories program information for storage and retrieval. A theory of learning summarizes a mass of data in a way that makes sense to a researcher. It tells him what aspects of learning are most worthy of attention and what language should be used to describe the research findings. Theories of learning are thus intended to make sense of what would otherwise be inscrutable. They tie together and order an otherwise disparate conglomeration of empirical findings.

If a theory is to succeed, it must be falsifiable. It must predict objective events that can be empirically tested. To a certain extent, then, theory leads to testable guesses as to how the variables in a system under study are related to each other. As research progresses and predictions from the theory are investigated, extensive revisions will be necessary. Some theoretical concepts will be found to be redundant, and new concepts will have to be invented to keep pace with empirical findings. A good theory is, in a sense, self-destructive.

The Development of Theories of Learning

The development of theory typically goes hand in hand with the development of a discipline. Since theory exerts a directive influence on research, empirical inquiry is usually guided by theoretical developments and innovations. Empirical advances are rarely made independent of theory. The psychology of learning is no exception to this general rule. Theory has led the way, and research has followed.

Theory, however, has to begin somewhere; there must be data from which the theory can be constructed. For learning theory the basic data derived from two sources in particular: from Pavlov's work on classical conditioning and from Thorndike's work on instrumental (trial-and-error) learning. The empirical work of these two men and the techniques they employed provided the point of departure not just for theory but for much of the research that has been conducted in the psychology of learning during this century.

PAVLOV.   Ivan Pavlov gave psychology the notion of the conditioned reflex, a notion that was to play a central role in all major associationistic theories of learning. But Pavlov's contribution was not just that he discovered the conditioned reflex. What makes his work particularly important for later theoretical developments was that he defined an area of study and gave psychology a terminology with which to deal with the phenomena discovered in that area. Pavlov was the first to explore systematically experimental extinction and spontaneous recovery. He showed that a response conditioned to one stimulus can generalize to other stimuli and that this generalization can be overcome if the stimuli are differentiated from each other. And he conducted this research with a thoroughness and care that stand as models for those who would follow after him.

Pavlov was primarily a physiologist and secondarily a psychologist. As a physiologist, he was very much concerned with internal, neurophysiological events. He hypothesized two processes, excitation and inhibition, as fundamental to the activity of the nervous system. Their interaction accounted for the acquisition of a conditioned response, its extinction, generalization, and differentiation.

American psychologists, however, generally have not shared Pavlov's interest in physiological events. Learning theorists in this country have been much more cautious about making speculations concerning the physiological processes that underlie behavioral phenomena. Some theorists, like Tolman, avoided physiological terms entirely and dealt exclusively with "psychological" concepts. Other theorists, such as Hull, made occasional hypotheses about physiological events, but did so tentatively.

Another of Pavlov's basic orientations that was a point of controversy among subsequent theorists was his belief in the *associationistic* nature of learning. Learning occurs, according to Pavlov, when an association is formed between a conditioned stimulus and a neural center aroused by the unconditioned stimulus. Such an association was thought to be a universal phenomenon, common to both animals and men. What is learned is a specific response connected to a specific stimulus. The stimulus-response, connectionistic, associationistic approach actually dates back to the British empiricists: Locke, Hume, Hartley, and the Mills. But Pavlov showed experimentally how associations are formed.

It was the extension of S-R, associationistic principles to all human me later theorists. These theorists, Gestalt psychology, felt that man's intellectual processes are far too complicated to be reduced to connections between stimuli and responses. Associationistic principles may be sufficient for explaining how animals acquire a conditioned reflex, but they are not very helpful in accounting for behavior in complex problem-solving situations. These theorists argued that problems are solved by testing hypotheses, by seeing relationships, and by various information-processing techniques. What is needed, these theorists maintained, is a cognitive interpretation that allows for the flexibility shown in problem-solving situations, rather than an associationistic interpretation that is far too mechanistic to account for the data.

Regardless of how closely subsequent theorists followed Pavlov in his basic orientations—and most American psychologists were quite willing to accept his S-R, associationistic view of the learning process— all theorists were indebted to him for clarifying basic issues and introducing a terminology and methodology that allowed for scientific investigation. The early American learning theorists were, for the most part, direct descendants of Pavlov. In fact, what distinguishes Russian psychology from American is not so much the basic associationistic interpretation of the learning process—although the cognitive school won many adherents in this country—but the proclivity of Russian psychologists to resort to physiological concepts and processes in explaining behavior. American psychologists, generally speaking, feel more comfortable holding physiological speculation in abeyance and settling for distinctly "psychological" modes of explanation.

THORNDIKE.   Edward L. Thorndike's early work actually preceded Pavlov's. In 1898 Thorndike published his monograph, "Animal intelligence," whereas it was only in 1899 that Pavlov began his research on the conditioned reflex and not until 1927 that Pavlov's book, *Conditioned reflexes,* was published in the United States. Thorndike, like Pavlov, saw learning to be based upon the formation of associations. These associations are established between sensory impressions and impulses to action. Habits are developed or eliminated by strengthening or weakening these associative bonds or, as Thorndike often referred to them, these "connections" between stimuli and responses.

Thorndike experimented with hungry cats confined in a cage from which they could escape and reach a reward by pulling a loop of string. This research convinced him that learning took place slowly, through the gradual "stamping in" of an S-R connection between seeing the string (sensory impression) and pulling it (impulse to action). The cats did not learn the solution to the problem all at once. There was no "intelligent" comprehension of the relationship between the string and the door's opening. Instead, animals went through a long process of wandering around the cage, clawing at the walls, and making a wide variety of responses before they pulled the loop and left the cage. On subsequent trials they continued to make many irrelevant responses, although they took less and less time to pull the string.

Thorndike saw this gradual trial-and-error learning process to be determined by the effects that follow a response. A response is stamped in or strengthened if it is accompanied or followed by a satisfying state of affairs. Similarly, a response is weakened if it is accompanied or followed by an annoying state of affairs. To avoid any imputation of subjectivism in his use of the terms "satisfying" and "annoying," Thorndike defined as a satisfying event that which the animal does nothing to avoid, and as an annoying state of affairs that which the animal does nothing to preserve (1913, p. 2).

The strengthening of the connection through a consequent satisfying event (the *Law of Effect*) was Thorndike's basic law of learning. He was primarily a reinforcement theorist, arguing that the probability of occurrence of a response is a function of the events that follow it. In this he anticipated many of the learning theorists who came after him, particularly Hull and Skinner. Thorndike did not completely reject the alternate non-reinforcement interpretations espoused by Watson and Guthrie, but he did not give much prominence to such learning in his later writings.

Nor did Thorndike agree with Pavlov in viewing the conditioned reflex as the archetype of learning in general. Instead, he argued that the conditioned reflex represented a rather special case of learning. In support of this contention, Thorndike (1932) noted that Pavlov was able to obtain a conditioned reflex in his experimental animals only by carefully restricting both the animals and the stimuli to which they were subjected. In fact, Pavlov was required to remove his experimenters from the laboratory room and even to protect the dogs from extraneous stimuli by surrounding the building with an isolated trench and by employing special structural devices, especially sound-proofing. Only under these conditions were consistent experimental results obtained (Pavlov, 1927).

In contrast, Thorndike argued, the modification of the strength of connections by after-events represents a more general and fundamental form of learning. Both animals and men learn in this fashion in their normal environmental setting. Thorndike (1898) went so far as to argue that this type of associative learning is the basis for human conceptual learning. Thus children learn concepts of "sixness" or "whiteness" by seeing six things and white things and forming definite ideas from vague elementary feelings. Thorndike contended that it is the capacity of the human mind to move, by the process of forming associations, from these vague elementary conceptual feelings to definite ideas that distinguishes human from animal intelligence.

Thorndike's conceptual and methodological contribution, like Pavlov's, was enormous. To a great extent it was his work that determined the form experimental research in the psychology of learning would take over the next half century. His studies of animals in controlled experimental settings, his reliance on quantitative behavioral measurements, his associationistic interpretations, and his emphasis on reinforcement as the determinant of learning became the keynotes of an orthodox S-R position. And it is this position that has dominated the scene in American psychology.

Behaviorism

Another early development of great importance was the influence of the behaviorist school on American psychology. Watson's writings in the 1910s and 1920s won many converts to the cause, and the behaviorists became zealous advocates of a psychology free from all mentalistic and subjective concepts. What they proposed was that psychology concern itself with behavior and its objective study. Consciousness, images, and innate instincts were not objective and therefore could not be scientifically investigated. Instead psychology should deal with what people do. Like any science, psychology must be objective, must be directed toward the prediction and control of phenomena within its realm. If our knowledge of man's psychology was still rudimentary, the behaviorists argued, it was because philosophers had spent so much time trying futilely to study mind instead of behavior. Now that a science of behavior was possible, the days of philosophy were over.

Behaviorism, the study of what people do, had a great appeal in America. It was a doctrine that fitted well with the American proclivity for action and with American pragmatic philosophy as expressed in the writings of William James, Charles S. Peirce, and John Dewey. It coincided with the *Zeitgeist,* since the movement toward objective empiricism and environmentalism had already begun. And it was a boon for psychologists anxious to win their independence from philosophy departments and to establish their discipline as an objective and scientific field.

WATSON.   Watson was the chief spokesman of the behaviorist movement. He wrote more for the educated public than for a specialized professional audience. He was more a propagandist than a major theorist. In time he abandoned the academic world entirely to devote himself to the applied psychology of advertising. Yet during the years between 1910 and 1930 behavioristic psychology had no more vigorous advocate than John B. Watson.

Watson was convinced that all learning could be explained in terms of Pavlovian conditioning and that *the conditioned reflex was the basic unit of all learning*. Each response a person makes has a stimulus. There is no response without a stimulus, and every adequate stimulus must produce a response. The task of psychology is to determine what stimuli call forth what responses. If this enterprise is successful, it will someday be possible to take the worst adult social failure, pull him apart, psychologically speaking, and reconstruct him anew (Watson, 1928). Someday behaviorism will provide man with the "key" to the control of adult human behavior.

This goal may have seemed overly ambitious to some, but Watson was not among them. He felt that a great deal was already known about human learning, and that much of man's behavior, especially in the early years af life, could be shown to have developed through the process of conditioning. Very little of the behavior that the young child engages in consists of untutored (instinctive) acts. Children learn—that is, become conditioned—from the day they are born. By controlling what they learn, we can control what they become. For the behaviorist the human being at birth is a very lowly piece of unformed protoplasm, ready to be shaped by the family in whose care it is first placed. The first two years of infancy are enormously important in shaping the child. What happens then determines the whole course of future events.

Watson turned to the area of *emotional learning* to show specifically why and how this is so. Emotional responses, for the behaviorist, are habits that have to be learned like any other set of habits. Pavlov's research was the first step in this direction, especially studies in which he demonstrated that the glands of the stomach can be conditioned just as salivary glands were. Watson was able to show in his own research (Watson & Rayner, 1920) that fear-arousing stimuli, such as loud sounds or loss of support, could serve as unconditioned stimuli for the formation of conditioned fear responses established to previously neutral stimuli. Thus after a number of pairings of a neutral object like a toy or pet animal (conditioned stimulus) with the striking of a dishpan (unconditioned stimulus), a fear response could be established (conditioned response) that was made to the toy or animal in the absence of the loud sound. The child had been conditioned to react to the neutral object exactly as he had reacted to the noise. In this way the major emotions, fear, love, and rage, become conditioned to stimuli in the individual's environment. In fact, Watson (1914) argued that the simple process of conditioning was quite sufficient to account for the genesis and growth of emotional behavior in all its complexity.

Watson and his associates (Jones, 1924), it should be added, were able to demonstrate that they could eliminate as well as establish emotional responses. A child with a fear of rabbits was seated at a small table where his lunch was covered with a napkin. At the other end of the room was a rabbit in a wire cage concealed from the child's view. The experimenters disclosed the lunch and the rabbit simultaneously to the child. They found that if the rabbit was too close, the child would not eat, but that if the rabbit was far enough away, the child would begin to eat. After some experimentation, a "point of tolerance" was established, and the rabbit was kept at that distance. On subsequent days the rabbit was moved nearer to the child, advancing the point of tolerance. After a few days the rabbit was placed on the table, and eventually in the child's arms. The emotional reaction of fear had been eliminated. Such techniques, Watson argued, held great possibilities, even for the reconditioning of adults.

In fact, Watson felt that the same principles could, in theory, be employed to reshape adult personality. Personality is not a divine gift or some vague, mysterious, and unique power within the individual; instead it is, for the behaviorist, a totality or sum of habit systems, of conditionings. To understand personality it is necessary to observe behavior. No amount of psychological testing can tell us as much about personality as can the careful, prolonged observation of the person's behavior (Watson, 1928). And no amount of persuasion can bring about the changes in behavior that can be effected by reconditioning. Reconditioning, however, is an arduous process. People can change their personalities as long as they can learn, but it is rarely the case that enough control can be exerted on the individual to set the reconditioning processes in motion. Watson felt that if he had absolute control over food, sex, and shelter and had a laboratory where he could recondition and experiment on his subjects for a year at a time, he could undo what home nurture had done for them in 30 years. But since such a behavioristic utopia was practically unrealistic, and other methods, such as psychoanalysis and psychotherapeutic techniques, were futile, Watson grew increasingly skeptical about man's ability to reconstruct personality and to maximize its potentialities.

GUTHRIE. Edwin R. Guthrie, was, like Watson, a behaviorist. His book, *General psychology in terms of behavior* (Smith & Guthrie, 1921), was one of the earliest textbooks on learning written from the behaviorist perspective. Like Watson, Guthrie was quick to dismiss the notion of "mind" from his psychology. His concern was with behavior and specifically with those changes in behavior that provide evidence of learning. Unlike Watson, however, Guthrie had a long career in academic psychology. His writings on the psychology of learning continued until 1959, the year of his death. During this time span he advanced a theory of learning consistently behavioristic and consistently associationistic.

Unlike Watson, who based all learning on the conditioned reflex,

Guthrie proposed as the basis of learning the principle of *condition-ing by contiguity*. Like Thorndike, Guthrie regarded Pavlovian conditioning as too highly artificial a form of learning to serve as the basic unit of habit. His notion of conditioning by contiguity was not dependent strictly on the Pavlovian paradigm. Instead, it represented a more general type of learning, one that required simply the associationistic assumption that once a stimulus is followed by a response, the response will recur whenever the stimulus is subsequently presented. Nothing is said about an unconditioned stimulus, about repetitive pairings of stimulus and response, nor about reinforcement.

Guthrie could avoid these issues because he had a radically distinct notion of stimulus and response. What he meant by a stimulus was not the observable, external stimulus but a pattern or combination of all changes in the physical world that lead to sensory reactions. The totality of stimulation includes not just external but internal stimuli as well. In particular, sensory organs stimulate each other through proprioceptive cues, and these proprioceptive stimuli, or movement-produced stimuli (Guthrie, 1959), integrate and coordinate behavior sequences. What is learned is not a single molar response but small molecular movements conditioned by contiguous association with movement-produced stimuli. Many such movements constitute a behavioral act. Learning is complete once a movement is conditioned to a combination of stimuli. The apparent gradualness of learning is due to the fact that many elements must go together to form a behavioral act, and each of these has to be learned.

Although he agreed with Thorndike in rejecting Pavlovian conditioning as the basic form of learning, Guthrie could not accept Thorndike's law of effect. Guthrie was more like Watson in this respect, preferring not to use the concept of reward in his explanation of how learning occurs. While Watson saw the notion of reward as dangerously subjective and therefore unfit for the science of behavior, Guthrie believed that rewards do influence the outcome of behavior but that they do so only because successful acts, those that lead to rewards, happen to be the last acts that occur in a problem situation and will therefore be more likely to occur if the problem is presented again. There are difficulties with such an interpretation and with the experimental evidence Guthrie and Horton (1946) presented in its support (see Hilgard & Bower, 1966), but even in his last formal theoretical statement, Guthrie (1959) argued for an explanation of learning not tied to reinforcement.

While Guthrie's theory has many interesting aspects to it, one of special importance for our purposes is his account of *how habits are broken*. The simplest rule for breaking a habit, according to Guthrie, is to find the cues that initiate the action and to practice another response to these cues. No matter how well-integrated a habit, if the initial movements of the response can be "sidetracked," the habit can be overcome (Guthrie, 1952). The main feature of such a method is that an incompatible response is associated with the stimuli that elicit the habit. This new response interferes with the old one and prevents its occurrence.

Guthrie specified two other methods for eliminating an undesired habit. The first of these involves the gradual introduction of the stimuli that elicit the response. The stimuli are initially presented in such a slight intensity that the undesired response does not occur. A dog can be trained not to run from the sound of a gun, for example, by habituating him to the sound of a cap pistol at a great distance at first and then nearer and nearer, until he can tolerate the sound of a shotgun close at hand. This "threshold" method is very similar, as we shall see, to methods employed by today's behavior therapists.

Another technique is the satiation or fatigue method, where a response is eliminated by allowing it to be made repeatedly until the person making the response is exhausted and stops responding. According to Guthrie, subsequent presentations of the stimuli should produce the last response (not responding). In this way, for example, a child's temper tantrums can be eliminated. (Punishing the child may have a similar effect, but Guthrie would argue that this is not because of punishment in itself but because punishment leads to the performance of new responses.)

Guthrie believed that the principles derived from a behavioral psychology of learning could be applied to all of man's social behavior. Socialization, for instance, could best be explained in terms of learning. Those responses that meet with the approval of other persons are learned, while those that prove annoying to other people get unlearned (Guthrie & Powers, 1950). The family is the principal agent of socialization because its example directs the child's acquisition of habits. The child learns to take advantage of the habits and ways of responding of those around him. He learns to speak a language that they understand; he learns to use the manners that they expect. The penalty for not conforming to their example is failure to attain a desire or gratify a need. Later the child finds himself in social groups where he must learn specific roles through observation of behavior appropriate to that role. Eventually, when the behavior is well practiced and accepted by the individual, it becomes a part of him and independent of enforcement. In this way, society's standards and demands are implanted within its members.

Personality, according to Guthrie, refers to those habit responses of an individual that are judged to be relatively stable and permanent and that are important determiners of how others respond to the individual. Guthrie was especially interested in the way in which education affects personality, and he hoped that psychologists could give teachers information on how to help pupils in gaining knowledge and furnish them with usable methods for guiding pupils in social adjustment (Guthrie & Powers, 1950). His writings in these areas were more anecdotal than formally theoretical; in general, Guthrie has been influential not so much because of the formal deductions of his theory as because of its informal implications (Hill, 1963). He was at heart a practitioner and perhaps his most important contribution is found in those aspects of his theory that have practical ramifications—especially his views on habit formation and elimination.

The Grand Theories

By any standards the names Clark L. Hull, Edward C. Tolman, and B. F. Skinner are the most important names in the history of the development of learning theory. Their theories are more inclusive, more detailed, more ambitious than any others. Moreover, they have had considerable influence on research and on subsequent theoretical developments. This is true both of subsequent developments in social-learning theory and of research from a learning-theory perspective on interpersonal phenomena.

Hull, Tolman, and Skinner were behaviorists in the tradition of Watson and Guthrie, but they differed widely in their understanding of that tradition. Tolman's "purposive behaviorism" was anathema to Hull and Skinner because of its cognitive orientation, and the formal, deductive, postulational system of Hull was quite at odds with the explicitly a-theoretical approach of Skinner. In fact, Skinner probably would resent being considered a major learning theorist, since he is firmly convinced that theories are not necessary and even constitute an absolute loss in the history of science. Nevertheless, Skinner's approach is, upon rigorous examination, at least covertly theoretical (Scriven, 1956).

The work of these three men spans the "golden age" of theory from the 1930s to the 1950s. During this time most research on learning was conducted to test various predictions of these theories and to compare the predictions of the theories against each other—although the classical controversies in the psychology of learning were, for the most part, controversies between Hullian and Tolmanian schools of thought. The Skinnerians preferred to stand apart from these theoretical disputes and were content to go their own way, doggedly varying schedules of reinforcement and plotting cumulative learning curves.

HULL.   Clark Hull's theory of learning defies brief treatment. Again, the reader is referred to more extended discussions (Hilgard & Bower, 1966; Hill, 1963; Koch, 1954). A few aspects of the theory are, however, of special interest because of the use made of them by theorists and researchers in the Hullian camp who attempted to extend Hull's learning theory to the area of social behavior. This extension was an enterprise to which Hull himself attached a great importance, since he believed that the crowning achievement of behavioral psychology would be the creation of a really quantitative system of social behavior. It was his intention to integrate individual psychology with social psychology, but death kept him from realizing this goal.

For Hull quantitative rigor was a theoretical imperative. To this end he constructed a highly sophisticated system of theoretical postulates and equations. Foremost among these is his performance equation, an equation that purports to tell how the learned component will be influenced by other factors in such a way as to become manifest in overt, observable behavior. Performance, or reaction potential, is defined by Hull in the following terms:

> The reaction potential ($_sE_R$) of a bit of learned behavior at any given stage of learning, where conditions are constant throughout learning and response-evocation, is determined (1) by the drive (D) operating during the learning process multiplied (2) by the dynamism of the signaling stimulus trace (V_1), (3) by the incentive reinforcement (K), and (4) by the habit strength ($_sH_R$), i.e.,

$$_sE_R = D \times V_1 \times K \times {_sH_R}$$
(Hull, 1952, p. 7).

The exact specification of the relationship between these variables has been a matter of considerable dispute (Koch, 1954; Spence, 1956), but there is definite heuristic value in Hull's formulations.

One aspect of the performance equation that is especially important is the notion of *drive*. Drive is an intervening variable and a function of observable independent variables such as deprivation of food, water, and sex. Drives activate and energize behavior: the combination of the strength of drives at a given instant makes up the total energy level of the organism. This activating effect of drives is observable in the general level of bodily activity and in the vigor with which habits are performed. The greater the total drive level, the greater the level of bodily energy and the more vigorous the response.

Each drive produces a characteristic drive stimulus which indicates the particular need of the body. Thus food deprivation produces internal stomach contractions. The reduction of drive or drive stimulus is rewarding and increases the habit strength of responses that serve to bring about this reduction. Learning requires reinforcement, and reinforcement operates by reducing the drive level.

The strength of the bond connecting a stimulus with a response, or *habit strength,* is the basic learning variable in Hull's system. Habit strength never decreases. Each time a response occurs in the presence of a stimulus and reinforcement quickly follows, the habit strength of this S-R connection is increased. Hull's notion of the role of reinforcement in learning (increasing habit strength) is very similar to Thorndike's law of effect (Hull, 1943), although his insistence that all reinforcement involves a reduction in the strength of drive or drive stimulus distinguishes Hull from Thorndike and from other proponents of the law of effect, such as Skinner.

Habit strength develops according to a law of diminishing returns. Each successive reinforcement contributes less to $_sH_R$ than the previous ones. Learning is therefore a gradual, negatively accelerated process. It takes time for habit strength to develop. Eventually the strength of a habit will reach a ceiling, and additional reinforcements will contribute very little, if anything, to its strength.

Several different habits may be learned with respect to a single goal. There may be, for instance, several paths or routes leading to a goal object. These alternate habits constitute a habit family and are arranged in a hierarchy of performance, ranging from the most preferred to the least. Such an arrangement Hull called the *habit-family hierarchy.* The various pathways to objects in space constitute habit-family hierarchies, with the paths involving less work tending to be preferred parts of the hierarchy (Hull, 1952).

The *incentive factor,* or K, was another important element in Hull's performance equation. The value of K is a function of the size of the reward object. Size has no effect on the rate at which habit strength is built up, but it does affect performance. Thus increases in the size of the reinforcement lead to higher levels of K and to subsequent increases in the speed with which a response is made or its vigor. Incentive, however, does not affect learning; it is a nonassociative factor, affecting performance level and not habit strength.

Several other Hullian notions are important for our purposes. The first of these is a construct of considerable theoretical importance for many of the processes of learning we shall be considering in this book. This is Hull's notion of *fractional anticipatory goal response* (r_g). This construct is especially important for accounting for how behavioral events are mediated by processes not directly observable.

Hull asserted that when an animal makes consummatory responses in a learning situation he becomes conditioned to make anticipatory feeding responses to preceding stimulus events that have an appropriate temporal relation. These stimulus events include (1) environmental stimuli associated to those of the goal box through stimulus generalization, (2) proprioceptive stimuli resulting from the responses made by the animal, and (3) drive stimuli arising from the animal's state of deprivation. The responses made to these stimuli are fractional components of the full-blown goal response. These fractional anticipatory goal responses (r_g's) might be chewing movements, salivation, or any response that does not interfere with the animal's ongoing activity. Since the r_g's are conceived to have the properties of responses, they are capable of producing their own proprioceptive stimuli (s_g's) that in turn act as cues for instrumental activity. For Hull, the r_g-s_g mechanism provided the animal with a "directing idea," a means of organizing a sequence of goal-directed activities. The process is represented schematically in Figure 1-1.

Another important concept in Hull's theory is *secondary reinforcement*. When a neutral stimulus is paired with a sudden reduction in drive stimulus, the previously neutral stimulus takes on reinforcing properties. It can be employed, even in the absence of the primary reinforcer, to strengthen responses. When it acts in this manner it becomes a secondary reinforcer. One example of a secondary reinforcer is money which, as Hull puts it, "while usually not capable of *directly* mediating the reduction of any primary need is a dependable indirect *means* to a considerable variety of such need reductions" (1952, p. 335).

Through a similar process, drive characteristics can be attached to a neutral stimulus. In this case, the neutral stimulus is paired with a drive stimulus. Once this learning process has occurred, the *secondary drive* stimulus has the same effects on behavior as the primary drive stimulus. The presentation of such a stimulus heightens the activity level, and its reduction is reinforcing. An example of such a secondary (or learned) drive is fear. In this case a neutral stimulus paired with pain acquires drive properties. The resultant secondary drive is called fear.

Secondary reinforcers and secondary drives greatly increase the

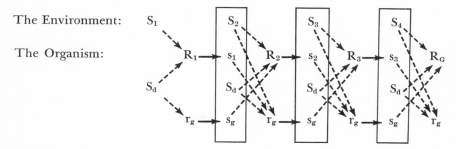

Figure 1-1. Hull's conception of the role of environmental stimuli (S), proprioceptive stimuli (s), drive stimuli (S_d), the anticipatory goal reaction (r_g), and the goal stimulus (s_g) in the organization of a sequence of goal-directed activities. A dashed line indicates that the response becomes conditioned to the stimuli in question. R_G refers to the goal response at the end of the chain of instrumental responses (R's).

ability of the theory to handle complicated phenomena such as human social interactions. Hull, as we have indicated, did not succeed in working out the details of a theory of social behavior, but he did make some suggestions as to how behavioral psychology might approach such phenomena. In fact, the last theorem of *A behavior system* (1952) deals explicitly with social interaction: "Theorem 133. Every voluntary social interaction, in order to be repeated consistently, must result in a substantial reinforcement to the activity of each party to the interaction" (1952, p. 337). This Hull referred to as the Law of Reciprocal Reinforcement. For example, a person who has a supply of meat will induce another person to cook it by promising some of the prepared food as a potential reinforcement or reward. Such social transactions often involve secondary reinforcement and secondary drives as well. Thus Hull gave the example of reacting to coercion by counterattack, thereby causing the offender to take flight. Flight is itself reinforcing because it involves the secession of injury caused by the counterattack. After repeated social interactions, certain signs, such as frowns and threatening movements or words, through their association with attack, acquire the power of evoking incipient flight reactions (fear). Fear then becomes a secondary drive and signs acquire a certain real power to punish. Hull continued:

> And since the statement that a person has transgressed in a certain way is associated with punishment and such a statement is a moral judgment, it comes about that the overt passing of an adverse moral judgment becomes a deterrent to forbidden acts. In a similar manner the passing of a favorable moral judgment becomes a secondary positive reinforcing agent fostering desirable action (Hull, 1952, p. 337).

Through such analyses Hull hoped that behavioral science would ultimately be able to deduce from its principles social phenomena as complicated as the determination of moral judgments.

TOLMAN.   Edward Chace Tolman espoused a behaviorism quite different from Hull's. From the time of his early work, *Purposive behaviorism in animals and men* (1932), until his final theoretical statement (1959), he attempted to work out a behaviorism capable of dealing with cognitive activity. It was Tolman's conviction that animals and men do not react merely to stimuli; they react to their cognitions—to beliefs, attitudes, and goals. What was needed was a theory of learning that would take these cognitive aspects of behavior into account, while at the same time maintaining the rigor and objectivity of behaviorism.

The principal characteristic of behavior for Tolman was its *purposive* nature. Men and animals behave to reach goals. Behavior is not random; it has a meaning, an orientation, and a unity because it is goal-directed. The purpose of behavior is to reach the goal. While such notions as "meaning," "purpose," and "goal" may seem very un-behavioristic and subjective, Tolman attempted to show how such concepts could be incorporated into a behavioristic theory without forfeiting objectivity.

This could be done, he argued, if cognitions, perceptions, and beliefs are regarded as intervening variables. They are not entities, they are merely theoretical abstractions. Conceivably there might be physiological concomitants to cognitive activities, but Tolman was not concerned with physiology. What he was concerned with was tying his theoretical concepts to input and output variables (between which they "intervened"). Certain cognitions resulted from certain experiences with external stimuli. The theorist's task was to specify just how this took place and what outcome could be predicted.

A major intervening variable in the system is Tolman's notion of *beliefs* (or "means-end readinesses"). Beliefs develop directly from training. They are acquired dispositions that produce the expectancy that certain stimuli, when followed by certain responses, will lead to certain goal objects. The organism develops beliefs about different pathways—which one leads most quickly to the goal, which involves the least effort, and so forth. In fact, what is learned, according to Tolman, is a cognitive map, the relationship of each of the pathways (means) to the goal object (end). Learning, then, involves the learning of relationships and not the learning of specific response patterns.

Such an account of learning is quite divergent from the traditional S-R interpretation. It assumes that learning involves the development of cognitions rather than the strengthening of S-R habits. Initially the organism formulates provisional expectancies, or *hypotheses*. Until the situation is structured so that the means-end relationship is obvious, behavior is guided by these hypotheses. In the beginning these hypotheses are based largely on prior experience and on the systematic preferences of the individual subject. As the cognitive field becomes gradually organized and stimuli are differentiated, only those hypotheses survive that are most congruent with reality—that is, those hypotheses or expectations are established that are confirmed by successful goal achievement.

Instead of a reinforcement principle or law of effect, Tolman proposed a principle of confirmation. If a hypothesis is confirmed, its probability value is increased. If it is not confirmed, its probability decreases. Reward, then, has much the same function in his theory as it has in Hull's, but its effects are formulated differently. Rewards, for Tolman, do not affect S-R associations; they affect the learner's knowledge of means-end relationships.

These differences may seem more semantic than real, but Tolman (1948) attempted to show that his theory predicted empirical results quite at variance with those predicted by traditional S-R theory. He placed special emphasis on the results of research on latent learning and place learning. In the *latent learning* experiments, Tolman saw evidence that cognitions acquired in different learning experiences may be coordinated in such a way that the organism can respond adaptively to new situations. Thus, once a cognition has been developed whereby the organism learns to get from place to place, that information can be used to obtain rewards quite different from those obtained while learning. For example, rats that have learned a maze to satisfy exploratory demands when satiated for food can use this information to satisfy hunger demands when they are placed in the maze after food deprivation. In such latent learning situations, the organism apparently learns how the environment is structured and forms cognitions about what paths lead to what places. This type of learning—learning what leads to what—is, according to Tolman, of paramount importance for any theory that hopes to deal successfully with the flexibility and adaptability found in behavior. S-R theories, as they were formulated at the time Tolman did his research on latent learning, were unable to account for the sudden improvement in performance obtained with rats allowed to explore the maze but never reinforced (with food).

In addition, Tolman felt that research on *place learning* favored his interpretation as opposed to one based on S-R associationistic principles. In these studies, Tolman and other researchers found evidence that an organism, once it has learned the location of a reward object, can get to that location by means other than those originally used. For example, rats that have learned to swim through a maze to obtain food will, when the water is removed from the maze, run without error to the goal object. They learn the location of the goal and not discrete S-R movements in space. Similarly animals will show that they have learned the location of the goal object by making appropriate detours when the direct path to a goal is blocked. The evidence, Tolman felt, indicated that learning involves much more than S-R connections. Instead, animals and men learn cognitive maps that enable them to locomote in space and, more generally, to adapt to the environment around them. Tolman argued forcefully against a theory of learning that left the learner a slave to blind habit or automatic habit hierarchies. There was too much evidence, he felt, that learning was flexible, pliant, and even insightful.

Like Hull, Tolman was concerned with the extension of learning theory to social phenomena, although he too did not succeed in working out in systematic detail the implications of his theory for social behavior. He did write a monograph, *Drives towards war* (1946), dealing with the psychological causes of war and the means that could be taken to lessen the probability of wars in the future. This work is a mixture of clinical and experimental material and anticipated in a rudimentary way later attempts to deal with clinical and psycho-analytic phenomena in learning-theory terms. Thus Tolman saw various defense mechanisms as behavioral techniques that have been learned to enable the individual to cope with the frustration of bio-logical drives. When basic drives are frustrated the individual can react through self-assertive techniques or collective techniques. If the individual has "identified" with his parents or with other adults, his self-assertive behavior will be "channeled" into socially approved attacks upon objective problems. This Tolman saw to be a relatively ideal outcome as far as the mental health of the individual and the stability of society are concerned. When identification is weak be-cause of parental punishment, the individual learns that self-abase-ment is a way of avoiding punishment and reproofs, represses his hostility, and resorts to various psychological mechanisms of defense, such as reaction formation, introjection, symbolization, displacement, and projection. The last two are especially harmful to society since they lead to aggression toward others. This is true to an even greater extent if collective-assertive techniques are employed. In this case "identification with the group" leads to an attack on enemies of the group (i.e., war). Tolman suggested various measures that should be taken to avoid such an outcome, including attacks on man's common enemies—disease, corruption, ignorance, and prejudice.

SKINNER. In many of his writings, B. F. Skinner has also shown a deep concern for the future of man and for the development of a psychology of behavior that will make a positive contribution to that future. Skinner's goal has been the prediction and control of man's behavior, although he acknowledged that it will be a long time before behavioral science has advanced to the point where perfect prediction and control are possible. In the meantime, the experimentalist must go his own way in a careful and orderly fashion. It would be a mistake, Skinner has argued (1938), to allow questions of ultimate application to influence the development of a systematic science at an early stage.

In his book, *The behavior of organisms* (1938), Skinner set forth his own system of behavior. A central distinction in this work is between respondent and operant behavior. *Respondent behavior* is elicited by specific stimuli. The response is an automatic consequence of the presentation of the stimulus. Pupillary constriction in response to light or the knee-jerk reflex are examples of respondents. Classical conditioning is also regarded by Skinner as an instance of respondent behavior. In this case the strength of a response is increased because of the approximate simultaneity of stimuli (conditioned stimuli) governing its occurrence with stimuli (unconditioned stimuli) gov-erning the occurrence of a response already existing at some strength.

The unconditioned stimulus was thought to have a reinforcing role in this process, since without it learning will not occur.

In *operant behavior,* as distinguished from respondent behavior, there is no determinable stimulus that elicits the response. Rather than being elicited by a stimulus, operant behavior is emitted by the organism. It is behavior that occurs spontaneously and becomes significant when it acts upon the environment in such a way that a reinforcing stimulus is produced. Thus a rat in a Skinner box will occasionally press the lever, but the rate at which this operant behavior occurs can be greatly increased when reinforcement is contingent upon the response of pressing the lever. The occurrence of the operant, followed by the presentation of a reinforcing stimulus, increases the strength of the operant. Although Skinner appeared to regard all behavior not elicited by specific stimuli as operant behavior, he termed only those responses "operant" that can be brought under experimental control through the operation of reinforcement.

Skinner, in contrast to Hull, made no inferences as to the effect of reinforcement upon drive. In fact, Skinner regarded the notion of "drive" as dangerously animistic and unfit for psychology. For Skinner, a reinforcement has two, purely empirical, effects. First, it increases the strength of a response, where "strength" is defined as proportional to frequency of occurrence. Second, it intensifies resistance to extinction by increasing the "reflex reserve," the store of potential responses that may occur without further reinforcement and that show themselves in extinction (Skinner, 1938). Thus, when reinforcement is no longer presented to the organism, the organism will continue to respond because it can draw on the reflex reserve. If nonreinforced responses continue to be given, resistance to extinction will diminish as the reserve is gradually emptied, finally reaching the point where behavior is at its initial operant strength.

While a great many factors influence the strength of operant behavior and its resistance to extinction, Skinner and his colleagues have concentrated on *schedules of reinforcement* (see Table 1-1). Intermittent reinforcement schedules generally increase the operant level to a much higher rate per reinforcement than do continuous reinforcement schedules. Similarly, when reinforcement is terminated, resistance to extinction is greater under intermittent schedules than under continuous schedules. Apparently, therefore, intermittent schedules contribute more per reinforcement than do continuous schedules to the reflex reserve or, in Skinner's later (1950) terminology, to "the probability of the response."

The probability of occurrence of an operant response, Skinner noted, could be greatly affected by accidental contingencies. In a paper on superstitious behavior in pigeons, Skinner (1953) reported

Table 1-1
Schedules of Reinforcement

SCHEDULE	PROGRAM OF REINFORCEMENT
Intermittent Schedules:	
Fixed-Ratio	Reinforcement administered after a pre-determined number of responses.
Variable-Ratio	Reinforcement administered after a variable number of responses. The ratio lies between certain values and has a fixed mean.
Fixed-Interval	Reinforcement administered after a pre-determined interval of time.
Variable-Interval	Reinforcement administered after a variable interval of time. The series of intervals lies between certain values and has a fixed mean.
Non-Intermittent Schedules:	
Continuous	Every correct response is reinforced.
Extinction	No correct response is reinforced.

For a more comprehensive list see Ferster & Skinner, 1957.

that pigeons were likely to repeat on subsequent trials the behavior they engaged in at the time reinforcement was given. In this way certain conspicuous responses became established, such as hopping from one foot to the other, strutting, raising the head, and turning around. These responses were continuously emitted because they had been accidentally paired with the presentation of reinforcement. Similarly, by controlling the contingencies of reinforcement the experimenter can "shape" the animal's behavior so that animals will perform complex acts that are outside their normal range of activities. Thus by differentiating the component responses and by successively reinforcing only those responses that are to be included in the desired behavior, the experimenter can train animals (as Skinner has demonstrated) to perform complex behavioral sequences not in their original repertoire.

The control of operant behavior in this manner is based entirely on the manipulation of positive reinforcement. Skinner did recognize the possibility of employing punishment to control behavior, but has argued on empirical grounds (mainly Estes, 1944) that the presentation of punishment, such as shock, is not a very reliable way of preventing responses from recurring. The use of an adversive, punishing stimulus may, for example, have emotional side effects engendering hostility in the recipient of the punishment. Moreover, punishment may suppress a response but only temporarily; subsequently the response may reappear in even greater strength. Punishment can be used to hold a response at low strength since, while the response is suppressed, other, incompatible responses can be established. In general, however, Skinner regarded punishment as an inferior method of controlling behavior. An ingenious experimenter should be able to achieve the same results more efficiently and permanently by manipulating the presentation of positive reinforcement.

Skinner has cautioned repeatedly against premature extrapolation from data gathered from rats and pigeons to the realm of human affairs. Nevertheless he has not shown himself to be overly reluctant to engage in the extrapolation enterprise. Like Watson, Skinner has displayed a missionary zeal and an intense dedication to the spread of the behavioristic gospel. This comes across most strongly in his utopian novel, *Walden two* (1948) but is also apparent in many of his more strictly technical works (e.g., 1953, 1957a, 1959). In *Walden two*, one of the characters, Frazier—who as Skinner later admitted, "said many things which I was not yet ready to say myself" (1959, p. 378)—argued that the time had come for the application of learning principles to man's behavior:

> It's a little late to be proving that a behavior technology is well advanced. How can you deny it? Many of its methods and techniques are really as old as the hills. Look at their frightful misuse in the hands of the Nazis! And what about the techniques of the psychological clinic? What about education? Or religion? Or practical politics? Or advertising and salesmanship? Bring them all together and you have a sort of rule-of-thumb technology of vast power . . . but its techniques and methods are in the wrong hands—they are used for personal aggrandizement in a competitive world or, in the case of the psychologist and educator, for futilely corrective purposes. My question is, have you the courage to take up and wield the science of behavior for the good of mankind? (Skinner, 1948, pp. 256–257).

Skinner himself in the course of his career became more and more interested in the application of his techniques, in moving out of the laboratory into the real world. In later chapters of this book we shall examine extensions of Skinnerian principles and techniques to social and interpersonal phenomena. These applications are numerous and have generated a good deal of research. Nevertheless Skinner and his followers have their critics—whom they occasionally acknowledge (Rogers & Skinner, 1956), but more typically ignore. The Skinnerians have established their own journals and tend to work together in various academic and clinical enclaves. Unlike Tolman who left almost no followers, Skinner has succeeded in establishing his own sect, the members of which are devoted and energetic. Like Skinner, their research is rarely dull, frequently imaginative, and always controversial.

SOCIAL-LEARNING THEORY

The preceding summary of various theories of learning is, as has been indicated, by no means exhaustive or comprehensive; it has been intended mainly as introductory to what follows. The theorists concerned with social learning worked out of the framework of general learning theory. Their interest was in the extension of principles derived from research on the individual to the behavior of the individual in society. In doing so they have carried learning theory a step further than the early behaviorists of the 1920s and the major theorists of the 1930s and 1940s were able to do. It seems clear that learning theory was working in this direction, but it was only when Miller and Dollard, Mowrer, Rotter, and others took up the enterprise that the general outlines of a social-learning theory began to emerge.

The Hullian Tradition

The influence of Clark Hull on psychological theory and research has been enormous. His theory has generated more experimental work than any other in the past three decades. His interpretations of acquisition, reinforcement, drive, and extinction must be taken into consideration by anyone discussing the psychology of learning. In fact, learning theory and Hullian theory are often treated as synonomous (although, as we have tried to indicate above, there are considerable differences between his theory and that of Tolman or Skinner). Perhaps the principal reason Hull has played such a prominent role in American psychology is that he had a great influence on students and colleagues at Yale—a group that included such eminent psychologists as Robert R. Sears, Neal E. Miller, Kenneth W. Spence, Clark I. Hovland, and O. Hobart Mowrer.

MILLER AND DOLLARD.   It is not surprising that Miller and Dollard's book, *Social learning and imitation* (1941), was dedicated to Clark L. Hull. Miller and Dollard attempted to apply Hull's theory of learning to human data and to progress by way of such applications toward the development of a theory of social learning. The research reported in the book did not necessarily confirm or fail to confirm the theory. Instead it represented a first approximation of an experimental test of the theory. The concern of the authors, however, was mainly to spell out in some detail Hullian social-learning theory, with particular emphasis given to the concept of imitation.

The necessity of a learning-theory approach was stated at the outset. Learning is fundamental to human behavior. Unless learning occurs the individual cannot possibly take his place as a significant member of human society. Language is learned, good conduct is learned, people even learn how to adjust to each other in the marriage relationship and to grow old gracefully. The analysis of social behavior requires a knowledge of learning principles. This is where the psychology of learning can make a contribution. But learning does not take place in a vacuum. The psychologist needs the help of other social scientists to understand the social and cultural conditions under which human learning occurs. Competitive and aggressive behavioral responses, for example, are in our society familiar learned reactions in the struggle for social advancement. They can be highly effective and rewarding to the individual or they can be ineffective and a source of punishment, depending on the way in which other people react to these learned habits. Social and cultural norms are thus of great importance in predicting how effective learning will be.

The Hullian influence on Miller and Dollard's formulation was most noticeable in their account of the four fundamentals of learning—drive, cue, response, and reward. *Drives* may be innate or acquired. Innate or primary drives are those stimuli that "seem to be the primary basis for the greater proportion of motivation" (1941, p. 18). Pain is an example, as are thirst, hunger, "the bitter sting of cold," and "the insistent goading of sex." The primary drives are obscured and attenuated within modern social organization. It is only during war, famine, or revolution that such drives reach their full strength. Instead, secondary drives are of central significance for modern man protected by an efficient and organized technology. These secondary or acquired drives are learned on the basis of primary drives, represent elaborations of them, and serve as facades behind which the functions of underlying innate drives are hidden. Probably the strongest of the acquired drives is fear or anxiety. Other examples are drives for money and for approval. Any stimulus can become a drive if it is strong enough to impel to action.

Stimuli have both a drive value, depending on their strength, and a *cue* value, depending on their distinctiveness. The more distinctive the stimulus, the more readily different responses can be connected to it. Any given response, however, is not the result of a single stimulus alone; it is a reaction to a pattern of stimuli. This pattern may consist of drive stimuli as well as stimuli that have a cue function. Thus and individual who is hungry is responding both to his hunger and to cues from the environment around him, such as the smell of food, a restaurant sign, and so forth. Cues determine where and when the individual will respond and what responses he will make. The drive stimulus and the cue stimuli act together to elicit an appropriate response.

The *response* can be learned more easily when it is followed by *rewards*. If a response is made often and frequently rewarded, it has a relatively high probability of occurrence and occupies a relatively high position on the "initial hierarchy of responses." The response most likely to occur is the dominant response in this hierarchy. Learning may change the order of the responses in the hierarchy; the new hierarchy produced by learning is called "the resultant hierarchy." Of course, the order of responses in an initial hierarchy is usually the result of previous learning in similar situations. If the order of the responses is primarily the result of hereditary factors and not learning, then the initial hierarchy may be called an "innate hierarchy."

Miller and Dollard felt that the probability that a response will occur or will change its order in a response hierarchy depends upon whether the response is rewarded. If the response is not rewarded it will be extinguished. If it is rewarded, the drive that impelled the person to make the response to cues in the stimulus situation is reduced, and the tendency to make the same response on subsequent exposure to the same cues is increased. Miller and Dollard favored an empirical law of effect—namely, "no assumptions are made concerning the mechanism producing the correlation between reward and strength of connection" (1941, p. 35)—and did not feel that it is necessary to identify the drive that is reduced or the manner of its reduction. In many social-learning situations the acquired drive of anxiety may promote learning and a secondary reward, relief from anxiety, may reduce the drive. At any rate, "without reward, people fail to learn" (1941, p. 32).

Miller and Dollard pointed out that seemingly incidental learning (learning that apparently occurs without drive and reward) probably is a result of faulty analysis of obscure conditions of acquired drive and acquired reward. They give as an example the case of a man who shows almost no incidental learning while driving in the cars of various friends but who shows a good deal of incidental learning while walking through strange forests. This individual has never been punished for failing to note directions when traveling by car (since he left the driving to others), but he has learned that it is to his personal advantage to retain his orientation while walking through the woods. Motivation and reward do, therefore, enter in—even with respect to so-called "incidental" learning.

In their discussion of the learning process Miller and Dollard took a fairly straightforward Hullian orientation. Extinction was viewed as a process of nonreward, and resistance to extinction was held to increase if a strong drive is presented during training and if a relatively large amount of reward is given per training trial. Acquired drives and acquired rewards are as subject to extinction as other learned habits. Delayed rewards are less effective than immediate rewards, although in human social-learning situations symbolic stimuli that have acquired a rewarding value are often employed to bridge the gap between the performance of an act and the reception of the reward. Miller and Dollard again made the point that social and cultural conditions are important; lower-class individuals, for example, may be more influenced by the immediacy of reward.

The Hullian notion of *anticipatory responses* was used by Miller and Dollard to provide a basis for acquired drives and acquired rewards. Miller and Dollard acknowledged that research had not progressed far enough to allow them to be anything but tentative, but because of the importance of these processes for understanding social behavior they felt they should put forth "the best hypotheses that can be ventured at this time" (1941, p. 55). Accordingly, they proposed that stimulus-producing responses (Hull's fractional anticipatory goal responses, r_g) and response-produced stimuli (Hull's goal stimuli, s_g) operate in such a way that response-produced stimuli, like any stimuli, if strong enough, take on drive properties. Thus relatively neutral external stimuli—the sight of a dentist's chair, for example—may create, through learning, an anxiety reaction in the individual. This response then acts as an anticipatory response that produces a strong stimulus (response-produced stimulus) with acquired drive value. The reduction in the strength of acquired drives, when it occurs, is rewarding. Such rewards are acquired, in that they serve to reduce the intensity of response-produced stimuli that have acquired drive value.

Response-produced stimuli can serve not only as drives but also as cues. It is possible, Miller and Dollard argued, to connect to a relatively obscure stimulus a response that produces a distinctive stimulus and thus gives the obscure stimulus an acquired cue value. This has great importance in understanding man's higher mental (symbolic) processes. Learning a language, according to Miller and Dollard, involves the acquisition of an enormous arsenal of cue-producing responses and the development of habits of using these responses in socially valuable ways. A word as such is a weak stimulus, but during the educational process the individual learns to make many fine discriminations among words as cues.

Further aspects of the Miller and Dollard (1941) work—especially their analysis of learning by imitation—will be discussed in subsequent chapters of this book. The next development in their theoretical treatment of social learning that will concern us here is their book, *Personality and psychotherapy* (Dollard & Miller, 1950), a discussion of social behavior from a learning-theory point of view—but in this case a discussion of socially maladaptive behavior, and of its origins and its treatment.

Dollard and Miller retained the Hullian framework of the earlier (1941) book, but they updated the discussion of basic learning concepts by including the findings of more recent research. A drive-reduction theory of reinforcement was espoused but not insisted upon. In fact, reinforcement may operate in such a way that the learner is not aware that he is being rewarded. Dollard and Miller cited the Greenspoon (1950) study in which subjects were conditioned to use plural nouns by an experimenter who rewarded them by saying "Mmm-Hmm" whenever such nouns occurred. Subjects were apparently unaware that they were rewarded for certain responses and that they had increased the percentage of plural nouns. Dollard and Miller concluded:

> This clearly demonstrates that the effects of the reinforcement can be entirely unconscious and automatic. . . . A great deal of human learning seems to be of this direct, unconscious kind. Apparently many attitudes, prejudices, emotions, motor skills, and mannerisms are acquired in this way (1950, p. 44).

Dollard and Miller felt that *unconscious learning* must be accounted for if socially maladaptive behavior is to be understood by psychologists. In general, their approach to neurotic behavior consisted in borrowing structural notions from Freud—such as the notion of the unconscious—and in attempting to relate these notions to principles of learning. Thus responses become "unconscious" because they have not acquired or have lost their cue-producing (labeling) properties. The cue-producing property of a response can be lost because strong aversive drives, such as fear, have become attached to the response and the sudden reduction in drive that occurs when the person stops making the response reinforces a new, maladaptive response. Thus, for example, fear may act as a strong aversive drive whose sudden reduction occurs when a person stops thinking painful thoughts. Fear thereby reinforces the cessation of thought in certain areas ("repression"). If a person has a history of repression, it may become impossible for him to state his problem or take the means necessary to solve it. The cue-producing responses necessary for labeling are no longer available—they are, in Freudian terms, unconscious.

Psychotherapy involves bringing into consciousness what has become unconscious. For Dollard and Miller, this meant labeling formerly unlabeled responses, especially emotional responses, as well as responses that have been repressed, so that these responses can be represented in reasoning. This demands unusual skill on the part of the therapist. He must, by careful administration of reinforcement, assist the patient in labeling (making a cue-producing response to) those situations that have become sources of anxiety or hostility. In addition, patients must be helped in labeling their emotional reactions, although Dollard and Miller were careful to point out that merely labeling is not sufficient and must be linked with other emotional and instrumental responses appropriate to the changing relationship between therapist and patient. Thus labeling is only part of the therapeutic process. A discussion of further aspects of the Dollard and Miller (1950) approach to psychotherapy, however, must be postponed until a later chapter.

The Dollard and Miller (1950) formulations were subsequently revised and updated in a paper by Neal Miller dealing with the "liberalization" of basic S-R concepts (1959). In this paper Miller continued his efforts to extend the boundaries of S-R, Hullian theory to deal with social behavior and personality and thereby to employ basic S-R concepts in a manner that greatly increases their power and range. Miller felt that developments in the 1950s justified such extensions, especially a growing tendency to employ *functional behavioral definitions*.

Critics of the S-R position, such as Tolman, have argued that such a position cannot adequately handle central responses such as images, cognitive responses, and perceptual responses. Traditional S-R theory, the critics contended, was exclusively preoccupied with peripheral events. Stimuli were defined by physical energy measurements and responses by their anatomical location. In liberalizing S-R concepts, Miller (1959) employed a two-step functional definition whereby a stimulus is identified when a specific response can be connected to it by learning and when it can be shown to serve as a stimulus for the acquisition of other responses. Similarly, if a reaction that is associated with one stimulus can be shown to become associated with another stimulus through learning, the reaction can be classified as a response. This "liberalizes" because any specifiable attribute of the environment can be used in the stimulus or the response position of an S-R formulation. Thus S-R theory can include cognitions, perceptions, and other complex higher-order mental processes as stimulus or response events, provided only that it can be shown that they operate functionally as stimuli or responses.

Miller has used such "liberalized" concepts in applying his own research on conflict behavior to social situations. In the experimental laboratory animals can be made to experience conflict by establishing an avoidance response to a goal object that has previously elicited an approach response. Thus a hungry animal that is shocked in the goal end of a straight maze, where he was previously reinforced with food, will show tendencies both to approach and avoid the goal end of the maze. Empirically, it can be shown that when the conflicting (avoidance) response is relatively weak (as in A of Figure 1-2), a greater number of stimuli will elicit approach behavior than when the conflicting (avoidance) response is relatively strong (as in B of Figure 1-2). The displacement curve follows a gradient of stimulus generalization. In fact, spatial distance in an approach-avoidance situation is only a particular case of the general phenomenon of stimulus generalization.

The implication for human social learning is that the resolution of conflict will follow the same basic pattern in man's social interactions that has been obtained in laboratory experiments. The stimuli and responses are much more complex, but the same general principles apply. Miller gave the example of a girl who is prevented from marrying her sweetheart by his death and who has recovered from her grief. In such a case she would be expected to choose a suitor very similar to him, a displaced response occurring to the most similar stimulus present. But if a girl is prevented from marrying her suitor because of a violent quarrel between them, she would be expected to choose someone not completely similar and not completely different, the displaced response occurring to stimuli that have an intermediate degree of similarity to the original one.

In short, Miller argued that conflict theory, based upon laboratory experiments and formulated in terms of S-R, Hullian theory, can be applied in cases of complex human social behavior, provided that a liberalized, functional behavioral definition is made of stimulus and response events. A purist may argue that stimulus and response events in Miller's example have not been given a precise definition, even in Miller's own terms, but the important point here is that behavior not traditionally considered appropriate for S-R analysis can be treated, at least illustratively within the framework of an S-R position.

MOWRER.   O. Hobart Mowrer's work, like that of Miller and Dollard, derived from the Hullian tradition. Like Miller and Dollard, Mowrer was concerned with the extension of learning-theory principles to social behavior and personality. In his book, *Learning theory*

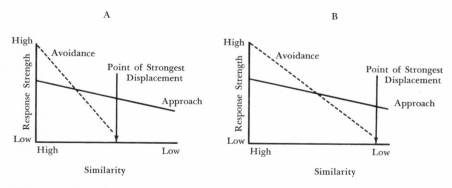

Figure 1-2. Displacement produced by alteration in strength of conflicting (avoidance) response. When the strength of the conflicting response is increased (in the diagram on the right), the point of strongest displacement (greatest approach tendency) shifts to items of decreasing degrees of similarity.

and personality dynamics (1950), he attempted to integrate the concepts and techniques of experimental and clinical psychology. He subsequently revised some of his major theoretical notions and published two books, one of them a systematic conception of the learning process in general (1960a) and the other concerned, in an exploratory manner, with applying learning-theory principles to symbolic operations and communication (1960b).

The key concept in Mowrer's earlier (1950) formulations was the notion of *fear*. Fear is a learned or acquired drive. As such it, like all learned drives, serves to motivate and, when terminated, to reinforce behavior. This process is thought to be the same as is involved in learning motivated by primary ("viscerogenic") drives, on the assumption that there is but one basic learning process. Mowrer came ultimately to reject this assumption and to posit in its place a dual-process theory. This theory identifies two types of learning: *sign learning,* which follows the principles of classical conditioning and accounts for the development of emotional responses to new stimuli, and *solution learning,* which follows the principles of instrumental conditioning and accounts for the development of functional behavior. Solution learning is problem-solving, drive-reducing, and pleasure-giving; whereas sign learning is often problem-making.

Mowrer argued further that the acquisition of appetitive behavior follows the principles of solution learning, but that the acquisition of aversive behavior follows the principles of both sign and solution learning. This is where fear enters in. In aversive learning, a response is inhibited through a dual learning process. In the first stage, fear is conditioned to some (noxious) stimulus by a process of sign learning. This fear response produces stimuli that act as a learned or acquired drive. In the second stage, an instrumental response that reduces the fear response is learned by the process of solution learning. Those instrumental responses that reduce fear by getting the individual away from the fear-arousing conditioned stimulus are reinforcing and therefore learned.

A child, for example, will learn that touching a hot flame is punishing (see Figure 1-3). The unconditioned stimulus of pain from the fire produces emotional responses characteristic of fear. The sight of fire therefore becomes a conditioned stimulus for fear. This process of sign learning takes place through classical conditioning (learning by contiguity, association). On subsequent occasions, the sight of fire produces fear, a secondary or acquired drive. If the child avoids the fire, his avoidance behavior will be reinforced by fear reduction. This process of solution learning involves reinforcement (learning through the law of effect). Thus an adequate understanding of the total learning process demands that both stages be considered.

Mowrer (1950) argued that the two processes of learning that he had identified were roughly similar to Freud's "two principles of mental functioning"—namely, the pleasure principle and the reality principle. Thus solution learning corresponds to Freud's pleasure principle, since solution learning is directed toward a drive-reducing goal object. On the other hand, sign learning involves learning not what is pleasurable and relieving, but what is actual, true, and real. Many of the things Freud had to say in terms of the pleasure and reality principles about repression, resistance, transference, and related clinical phenomena can, Mowrer felt, be meaningfully translated into the language of learning theory, provided that the theory posits the two basic processes of sign and solution learning.

In Mowrer's system *neurosis* does not represent a failure in learning; instead, the socially maladjusted individual is one who has succeeded in his problem-solving learning. He has been so successful in parrying the attempts of his parents and teachers, and later of his conscience, to socialize him that he remains neurotic. His difficulty is that he has satisfied the primitive pleasure principle through solution learning and in so doing has learned how to keep from learning through conditioning—that is, changing through sign learning his emotional and attitudinal responses.

Mowrer (1950) contended that *therapy* must be directed at assisting the individual to achieve better sign learning. He must be helped to unlearn the skills and strategies he has developed to deal with society and conscience. Such strategies must be shown to be ineffective and therefore unnecessary. When this is done, the way is open for the more basic kind of emotional learning against which past solution learning has served as a protection.

Part of this process involves the substitution of what Mowrer calls "normal anxiety" for "neurotic anxiety." Normal anxiety is a response to conflict in which the contending forces are consciously rec-

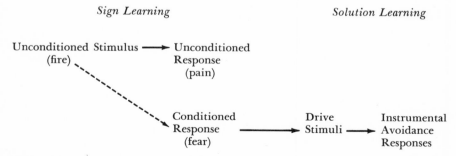

Figure 1-3. A schematic representation of Mowrer's (1950) two-factor theory. In the sign learning stage, fear becomes conditioned to stimuli associated with fire. Fear produces stimuli that act as drives that in turn promote instrumental avoidance behavior and consequent drive reduction.

ognized, whereas neurotic anxiety involves the repression and denial of the contending forces that make for conflict. Normal anxiety is functional and leads to socially acceptable problem-solving (solution) learning. Neurotic anxiety, in contrast, is maladaptive and leads to neurotic modes of problem solving. Consequently in therapy, a great deal of effort must go into emotional (sign) learning whereby neurotic anxiety is replaced by normal anxiety.

Subsequently Mowrer revised his two-factor theory of learning to give a more prominent place to the effect of secondary reinforcement in learning. In his reformulation (1960a) he essentially replaced his two-factor theory with a single-factor theory. All learning, in this version, is sign learning; and the central mechanism for what was previously solution learning is the operation of secondary reinforcement.

Mowrer (1960a) continued to affirm that responses followed by noxious stimulation become associated with *fear* through secondary reinforcement and are consequently inhibited. If this is the case in aversive behavior, he argued, it seems more parsimonious to employ the same logic to the treatment of appetitive behavior. Accordingly, Mowrer suggested that responses followed by reward become associated with *hope* through secondary reinforcement and are consequently facilitated. Thus response strength is increased through the secondary reinforcement mechanism of hope and decreased through the secondary reinforcement mechanism of fear. Although learning is still "two-factored"—namely, with respect to the forms of reinforcement involved—it is reducible simply to sign learning.

Mowrer regarded extinction as a special case of counterconditioning. When a response is no longer followed by a reward, hope is not confirmed and the organism reacts with *disappointment*. This was assumed to be a noxious stimulus that inhibits responding. Similarly, when a previously noxious stimulus is no longer followed by punishment, fear is not confirmed and the organism reacts with *relief,* which Mowrer assumed to be a form of reward. Thus hope is counterconditioned by disappointment (diminishing the strength of the response) and fear is counterconditioned by relief (increasing the strength of the response).

Mowrer's book, *Learning theory and the symbolic processes* (1960b), extended his revised theory to more general areas. He regarded language acquisition, for example, as a special case of sign learning. In the acquisition of language the child initially utters neutral sounds on a random basis. Certain of these sounds become positively conditioned—that is, they become "good sounds." Typically these are sounds that the child has heard its parents and others around him make and that have become associated with reinforcement. In time, these sounds take on secondary reinforcement properties, because hearing them has been associated with more primary reinforcement. When the child himself reproduces the sound, hearing the sound is a source of secondary reinforcement. Hearing himself use a sound somewhat like a word his parents use produces in the child a ready-made, "built-in" reinforcement of that response. The more nearly the sound made by the child approximates (or "imitates") the sound made by his parents, the more the sound is reinforced and repeated. Imitation, as thus interpreted, is a trial-and-error process depending upon reinforcement only in an indirect, derived sense. The secondary reinforcement that has become conditioned to the word stimulus spoken by the parent generalizes to the word stimulus spoken by the child himself.

The details of Mowrer's (1960b) theory of the dynamics of language and his interpretation of such mental processes as attention, memory, thought, and insight need not concern us here. Toward the end of his (1960b) book Mowrer turned explicitly to social learning and human personality, reviewed experimental research on social learning in animals, and concluded that, while this research is suggestive, it does not necessarily tell us a great deal about social behavior in man. In animals, in contrast to man, a large amount of social behavior is unlearned, the product of centuries of evolutionary trial and error. There is, consequently, a static, rigid quality to the social interaction of animals that is not present in human social behavior. Man depends almost entirely on culture, and culture is the product of learning, not of innate mechanisms.

One aspect of human social development that is especially unique is the phenomenon of conscience. Mowrer regarded the training that a child receives during the process of socialization as in many ways similar to the teaching and learning procedures studied in the animal laboratory. Children stay away from certain objects (avoidance learning), are attracted by other objects (approach learning), and in the process develop attitudes of fear and hope and experience relief and disappointment. One learning experience in particular, however, sets them apart from animals, and that is their capacity to experience *guilt*.

Animals appear to experience shame when they are caught doing something that they have been trained not to do. Guilt, on the other hand, involves self-condemnation and self-punishment regardless of the social situation and seems to be absent in lower forms of life. The child is unique in his capacity to internalize parental values and to experience the emotion of guilt when he violates the imperatives of conscience. Mowrer suggested that the development of conscience may require an articulate language, although it may be possible through an investment of a great deal of time and effort to develop in animals the grossest rudiments of conscience. Nevertheless, if conscience is shown to be unique in man, its operation in no way violates the fundamental principles of learning that have been used in discussing the adaptive behavior of lower orgaisms:

> Conscience can "hurt" no less than one's body; and the relief that comes when conscience is "cleared" is equal to, if not greater than, any possible form of organic relief or pleasure. Hence, any account of human motivation and personality that ignores the "moral strivings" of man is grossly incomplete and, by that very fact, misleading and dangerous (1960b, p. 395).

Phenomena such as conscience and guilt are only beginning to receive attention from experimentally oriented psychologists. Mowrer felt that such research is an absolute necessity if psychology is to move beyond the "animal model" to a full understanding of man and human social behavior. The task for the future, as Mowrer saw it, is to show the continuity, if there is a continuity, between those psychological processes that are common to man and beast and those capacities and concerns that we see only at the human level. Until this is done and the unique features of human behavior are specified, an adequate science of human behavior is impossible.

Eclectic Theories

Mowrer's theory provides a point of transition from the Hullian tradition to more eclectic approaches to social-learning theory. Mowrer was initially heavily influenced by the Hullian school, but his theory took on an increasingly cognitive flavor. In several respects he grew closer to Tolman than to Hull. Like Tolman, Mowrer held the view that learning leads to cognitions—which are conceptualized as intervening variables—rather than to specific S-R connections. He also placed a great deal of emphasis upon anticipations and expectancies (through the concepts of fear and hope) in his account of learning. Mowrer (1960a) recognized these similarities, but he stressed the point that his theory was less mentalistic and more mechanistic than was Tolman's. Tolman viewed internal events as "pure cognitions," whereas Mowrer gave them a more dynamic role in his theory. Hopes and fears for Mowrer guide, select, and control behavior and are therefore, at least in part, motivational factors. Moreover, Mowrer did not discuss the complex organization of cognitions that Tolman called cognitive maps nor did he emphasize cognitive patterning to the extent that Tolman did. Nevertheless Mowrer, while less cognitive than Tolman, has in his revised theory moved much closer to a cognitive position.

Several other social-learning theorists share Mowrer's basic orientation. Like him they have attempted to integrate an S-R, Hullian-type approach with one that is more cognitively flavored. S-R theory has the advantage of providing a tight experimental methodology and a body of data based upon carefully controlled laboratory experiments. Cognitive theory, on the other hand, seems less mechanical and more true to human behavior and to the unique centrality of symbolic processes in human learning.

ROTTER.   Julian Rotter's approach to social-learning theory re· flected this dual orientation. In his book, *Social learning and clinical psychology* (1954), Rotter assumed a basically Hullian approach to behavior. Behavior, in Rotter's system, is a function of learning and motivation. Yet the variables involved in learning and motivation are highly cognitive in nature. Reinforcement, for example, was defined by Rotter in cognitive terms, as were other major variables in the system.

Rotter's basic theoretical concepts are behavior potential, expectancy, and reinforcement. *Behavior potential* was defined as "the potentiality of any behavior's occurring in any given situation or situations as calculated in relation to any single reinforcement or set of reinforcements" (1954, p. 105). The term is roughly equivalent to Hull's reaction potential, and the values that define behavior potential serve as the basic performance equation in Rotter's system. In any single situation behavior potential is relative to other behavior potentials, and its value cannot be determined in absolute terms.

Rotter defined *expectancy* as "the probability held by the individual that a particular reinforcement will occur as a function of a specific behavior on his part in a specific situation or situations" (1954, p. 107). Expectancy is independent of the value of the reinforcement and was viewed by Rotter as an internal event. The expectancy that a subject develops with regard to reinforcement is psychological and internal, although not inaccessable to objective measurement. A number of variables, such as the patterning of past experience, generalization, unusualness of an occurrence, and so forth, affect internal probability and can be utilized to estimate its value.

The final term of the performance equation, *reinforcement value,* reflects "the degree of preference for any reinforcement to occur if the possibilities of their occurring were all equal" (1954, p. 107). Rotter gave the example of a man who would consistently choose to be paid $10 an hour for his work instead of $1 an hour if it were a matter of choice on his part, since the reinforcement value of $10 is greater than the reinforcement value of $1. Such preferences can be shown to exist independently of the expectancy of the forthcoming reinforcement. Reinforcement value, like behavior potential, is a relative concept and would have to be calculated in a choice situation with expectancy for the alternatives present held constant.

Rotter's performance equation is, accordingly:

$$B.P. = f(E. \& R.V.)$$

No assumption was made about the mathematical relationship between the values of expectancy (E) and reinforcement value (R.V.) as they determine behavior potential (B.P.). Rotter leaned toward accepting the Hullian multiplicative relationship, although he felt that exact mathematical relationships must wait until techniques have been developed for measuring all reinforcement values along the same scale, so that measurements made on a preference basis in one study or situation can be compared with measurements made in other studies.

Reinforcement, in Rotter's system, is something that changes behavior in some observable way by either increasing or decreasing the potentialities of its occurrence. No assumption was made concerning drive reduction; reinforcements function simply to change expectancies and, consequently, to change behavior potentials. The cognitive flavor of this notion of reinforcement is apparent in Rotter's discussion of internal as opposed to external reinforcement. Internal reinforcement refers to the subject's experience (or perception) that an event has occurred that has some value for him. External reinforcement refers to the occurrence of an event that is known to have predictable reinforcement value for the group or culture to which the subject belongs. The relationship between external and internal reinforcement is not assumed to be identical for all subjects. It varies with the subject and with the conditions of reinforcement.

Thus Rotter's system, while descriptively congruent with Hullian, S-R theory, differs considerably from such an approach. Like the Hullians, Rotter saw performance to be a function of learning and motivation. But in Rotter's system learning refers to the development of expectancies concerning reinforcement, and motivation derives from the value of reinforcement (including "internal" reinforcement) for the subject. Rotter has therefore introduced explicitly cognitive elements that are absent from more rigorous S-R theories. Moreover, while Rotter was keenly aware of the need for quantification and devoted a considerable proportion of his book to problems of measurement of basic independent variables, he admitted that the cognitive and "internal" nature of expectancy and reinforcement required an indirect approach to their assessment. In principle, measurement of these critical variables could be achieved. In practice, however, many problems remained, and Rotter saw the need for prolonged and tedious research.

These difficulties, however, are the concern principally of experimental psychology, which has as its task the experimental testing of theoretical principles of general psychology. In the area of social learning, Rotter argued, progress could be made by using less precisely defined terms. In particular, Rotter maintained that the application of learning principles to personality theory in clinical practice allows for their expression in more molar terms, since the clinician is usually interested in more general and more broadly described behavior patterns. In Rotter's social-learning theory these more molar concepts are need potential, need value, freedom of movement, and the psychological situation.

The first of these concepts, *need potential,* refers to a group of functionally related behaviors that lead to the same or similar reinforcements. Behaviors such as identification with authority figures and sibling rivalry might be grouped together in a category such as need potential for dependence. Yet people employ the same behavior to realize different reinforcements, and the behavior that different people employ to reach the same reinforcement can vary with individual learning experiences. To determine precisely a person's need potential, it would be necessary to have an exhaustive knowledge of the subject's prior learning background, to acquire the subject's own description of his needs and their significance in his behavior, and to gain a broad and general knowledge of all of the subject's behavior and the cues and conditions to which he responds. This information is never available, and the clinician must work with what knowledge he can obtain through an assessment of need potential in the general culture and, in the subject, through observational techniques, pencil and paper tests, and sociometric devices.

The mean preference value for a set of functionally related reinforcements defines *need value.* Functional relatedness can be defined as either a readiness to accept substitutes for the original reinforcement or a generalization of expectancies among functionally related behaviors. Thus two reinforcements are functionally related if they are interchangeable or if the occurrence of either has a generalization effect on the expectancy of reaching other reinforcements. To assess need value accurately an exhaustive study must be undertaken. It is possible, however, to determine the nature of culturally related reinforcements and to use various projective devices, psychological tests, and structured interviews to assess need value in individual subjects.

The concept *freedom of movement* refers to the mean expectancy that a set of related behaviors will lead to functionally related reinforcements. A person's freedom of movement is low if he has a high expectancy of failure or punishment as a result of the behavior with which he tries to obtain the reinforcements that satisfy a particular need. This specific term, "freedom of movement," was chosen by Rotter to convey the relationship of this concept to some frequently used concepts of maladjustment, since freedom of movement expresses the expectancy that a variety of behaviors will provide positive satisfaction. Thus low freedom of movement also implies a constriction in the range of possibilities that will lead to success. Again measurement of freedom of movement can be achieved through various structured and unstructured techniques.

Rotter's concept of the *psychological situation* refers to the meaningful environment of the individual. How the environment looks to a given individual is a function of his past experiences and his reinforcement history. The individual's perception of the world around him and of other persons is of critical importance for a psychologist interested in the prediction and control of behavior. The clinician's problem is to determine what a specific situation means to his patient —what situations the patient is likely to see in the same way as the majority of the culture and what situations he is likely to see in an idiosyncratic way. Rotter suggested that the patient's psychological situation can be assessed by interviews dealing with past experiences and present values, by observing the patient's behavior, and by the use of various psychological tests.

Table 1-2
Summary of the Major Variables in Rotter's System

VARIABLE	DEFINITION
General Behavior System:	
Behavior Potential	Potential for a behavior's occurring in a given situation.
Expectancy	Probability held by individual that a particular behavior in a specific situation will lead to reinforcement.
Reinforcement Value	Degree of preference for any given reinforcement.
Clinical Behavior System:	
Need Potential	Set of functionally related behaviors that lead to same or similar reinforcements.
Need Value	Mean preference value for a set of functionally related reinforcements.
Freedom of Movement	Mean expectancy that a set of functionally related behaviors will lead to functionally related reinforcements.
Psychological Situation	The meaningful environment of the individual defined on the basis of past experience and reinforcement history.

Rotter pointed out that some communality in perception of the psychological situation is necessary if individuals are to learn social roles. Where social situations are relatively clearly identified in a similar manner by members of the same culture, uniformity of categorization and behavior increases. People will learn social roles because there are objective cues enabling them to perform a limited series of behaviors appropriate to the expectations of others.

In discussing social learning, Rotter gave special attention to the significance of language. In social situations language can serve to direct a person's attention to the relevant cues and to help him avoid irrelevant cues. Language can also reinforce behavior, since verbal expressions of love, rejection, shame, and praise can have profound effects on human conduct. Moreover, implicit language can change expectancies and the reinforcement value of objects. By directing a person's attention to new and previously neglected consequences of behavior, verbalizations can substantially modify the individual's expectancies and even create new ones.

Detailed discussion of the application of Rotter's social-learning theory to clinical problems need not concern us here. As a social-learning theory his approach is, as we have noted, markedly eclectic. It attempts to combine the rigor of S-R theory with the flexibility of a cognitive approach. It is, by Rotter's own admission, a first approximation. But even this first approximation yields a relatively complex system. Problems of measurement are enormous, but Rotter has not been intimidated and has gamely tried to mark out the path psychology must follow if it is to develop an adequate theory of social learning.

THIBAUT AND KELLEY. The theory of social interaction proposed by Thibaut and Kelley (1959) was somewhat less ambitious than Rotter's theory. They were concerned primarily with interpersonal relations and group functions and presented no deductive system, nor did they offer any basic postulates or laws. They suggested that their work represented a "point of view" or "framework" rather than a theory. Their interest was "to highlight interconnections and to point out important research areas without necessarily suggesting the answers to be found there" (1959, p. vii).

Their eclecticism was broader than that of Rotter. They made use of learning theory, social psychology, economics, and sociology. By beginning with an analysis of the simplest of social relationships, the two-person dyad, they hoped to formulate as clearly and as explicitly as possible the fundamental conditions of social relationship and the variables that enter into such relationships. Thibaut and Kelley felt that it would then be possible to use the concepts and principles developed through analysis of dyadic interaction in the study of more complex interpersonal processes, such as the behavior of individuals in groups.

Thibaut and Kelley's theory assumes that for a dyadic relationship to be viable it must provide *rewards* (the positive components of the theory) and/or economies in *cost* (the negative components of the theory) that compare favorably with those in other relationships competing for activities available to the two individuals. This notion is reminiscent of Hull's (1952) Theorem 133 and is basically a principle of hedonic gain—that people will behave in a dyad in a way that maximizes their chances to achieve personal goals. If the dyadic relationship does not achieve this end, other relationships will be sought out. The individual has, therefore, many different choices in selecting interpersonal relationships and will tend to choose those friends and workmates who will provide help and aid and with whom he can work with a minimum of tension and restraint. Other people are rejected because they fail to provide help or raise cost by inducing anxiety and discomfort.

Contributing to reduction in cost in dyadic interaction are two variables of particular importance: propinquity and similarity of attitudes and values. *Propinquity* undoubtedly affects the probability that a pair will come in contact at all and is often correlated with similarity in background, values, and social status. If two individuals are physically separated by spatial distance, continuation of the relationship increases costs in effort and expense and therefore lessens the likelihood that the interaction will be maintained successfully. *Similarity of attitudes and values* promotes successful interaction, possibly because expressing agreement with another person's opinions or values constitutes a reward for the individual and also reduces the costs he incurs in the relationship by lessening his concern for expressing opinions that would jeopardize the relationship.

Behavior in dyadic relationships is the consequence of member interaction and may lead to response interference or response facilitation. Interference occurs when one member of the dyad instigates a response that is incompatible with the ongoing response of the other member. For example, when one member teases or criticizes another member or yawns when he is speaking, that activity interferes with the ongoing behavior of the other member. On the other hand, when one member agrees heartily with what is being said by another member, and when that behavior is countered in an appropriate way by the speaker, a facilitative effect occurs. In general, interference increases costs and reduces rewards to the interacting members. For successful interaction, steps must be taken to perform compatible responses through reciprocated role behavior or to eliminate persistent interfering behaviors from the relationship.

Reciprocal role behavior requires the acceptance by both members of behavioral *norms*. Unless both members adhere to these norms, there can be no regularity or predictability to their relationship.

Norms have a functional role, therefore, in a dyadic interaction. They control behavior without entailing the costs involved in the unrestrained and unchecked use of interpersonal power. Their content can be inferred from a consideration of the things about which the group members find it necessary to influence each other. These are not the same for every dyad and depend upon the particular problems the members face. *Roles* consist of clusters of norms providing for a division of labor or specialization of functions among members of a group. During the course of the group interaction a given individual may be required to reconcile the demands of several roles, for example the roles of "work partner" and "friend." Over time the individuals will learn to resolve these role conflicts by establishing an order of preference or eliminating certain roles entirely.

Thibaut and Kelley pointed out that dyadic relationships involve more than the interaction of the two members with each other. Both individuals are also acting on their physical and social environment in various ways. Both are concerned with *tasks*—either with their own personal tasks or with a common task. Success on a task depends upon a number of factors, especially the nature of the task and the person's ability to solve it. When both members are working on the same task in a cooperative setting, the success of one member affects the success of the other. In competitive situations, on the other hand, one member's success is associated with the other member's failure.

An individual's success or failure depends to a considerable extent on whether he has *power* over the other member of the dyad or is controlled by him. One person has power over another to the extent that changes in his behavior, whether they be deliberate or unintentional, can affect the outcome of the other person's task. Thus person A has power over person B to the extent that A's behavior changes the reward value or cost value of B's behavior. In an interdependent dyadic relationship, each person has some power over the other that places limits on the extent to which each person may act with impunity. Social interaction in such a setting was conceptualized by Thibaut and Kelley as a process of reciprocal control.

In considering groups larger than the dyad, Thibaut and Kelley felt that many of the same principles can be shown to apply, although new principles are also required. In larger groups, new ways emerge by which a member's rewards can be raised in relationship to his costs. A member may, for example, reduce his anxieties by sharing them with another member of the group, or he may join with another member in mutual facilitation through appreciative and consummatory responses. Coalitions are likely to form when outcomes are satisfactory to one subset within a group but not between this subset and the remaining members. The joint power of the subset, acting as a coalition, will be directed toward assuring an outcome rewarding to the members of the coalition regardless of the costs to other members of the group.

The achievement of group goals, however, involves a certain degree of *consensus* among the members of the group. This requires that the members of the group conform to its norms. In order that the group control its members' behavior, it must state rules, maintain surveillance, and apply sanctions. Good communication within the group is essential and, in cases where considerable heterogeneity of attitudes exists in a group, more forceful sanctions must be employed to achieve an operating consensus. The more highly organized the group, the more likely it is to accept group norms and goals.

Group organization implies a *status system* in which there is general consensus as to the status of each member. This is determined on the basis of initial differences in power and the contribution each member makes to the group. In addition, organization demands *role differentiation*. As specific activities are performed with regularity by certain individuals within the group, expectations develop that regularize these performances. Where a clearly defined status system exists, there will be a tendency to organize and assign roles that are "fitting," according to common cultural stereotypes, for each status. Decision-making and leadership functions are likely to be sought by high-status persons. Again rewards and costs are factors; efforts to strengthen group organization will depend on the rewards involved in successfully achieving group tasks and on the costs demanded of the individual members.

This discussion should suffice to give the flavor of the Thibaut and Kelley theory. It must be pointed out that the theory has many additional aspects of interest, not all of which, however, are related to learning theory. In their eclecticism Thibaut and Kelley drew heavily on social psychology research, especially work on game theory. Their general view of social interaction as a process of exchange and reciprocal control derives largely from economics. It is the concepts of *rewards and costs* that show most directly the influence of learning theory.

Rewards were defined by Thibaut and Kelley as "the pleasures, satisfactions, and gratifications the person enjoys" (1959, p. 12). Rewards provide the means whereby a drive is reduced or a need fulfilled. Costs, on the other hand, refer to factors that operate to inhibit or deter the performance of a sequence of behavior. The greater the deterrents, the greater the costs of the act. Costs derive from the amount of effort involved in the act, from the embarrassment or anxiety accompanying the action, and from conflicting forces that interfere with performing. The combination of rewards and costs determines *outcome*. Thus the Thibaut and Kelley formulation can be expressed in a performance equation with outcome viewed as a function of rewards and costs.

While certain aspects of this formulation are reminiscent of Hull (especially the notion of reward as drive reduction), Thibaut and Kelley introduced an additional concept that gives their theory a cognitive quality. Rewards and costs are not determined in absolute terms but depend on the individual's *comparison level,* on the standard by which the individual evaluates rewards and costs in terms of what he feels he "deserves." The comparison level is a function of past experience, especially the individual's previous interactions, and acts in Thibaut and Kelley's system in much the same way that expectancy operates in Rotter's theory. Thibaut and Kelley did not attempt to deal with measurement and scaling problems. They were more concerned with the theoretical consequences of their formulation than with its technical properties or even its feasibility.

The emphasis that Thibaut and Kelley placed on norms, roles, and power means that their theory operates at a higher level of analysis than that realized by any of the theories we have discussed so far. They were dealing with sociological problems from within a psychological framework. Basic processes were explained in learning-theory terms, and these processes were employed to discuss more molar psychological and sociological processes.

The Skinnerians

Skinner and his followers have failed to work out the details of a specifically social-learning theory, in part because of their abhorrence of theory and theoretical enterprises and in part because they have been more concerned with specific aspects of social learning—especially verbal behavior and operant techniques of therapy. One exception to this general rule is the work of George Homans who, in the manner of Thibaut and Kelley, has attempted to deal with sociological issues from within a psychological (Skinnerian) framework. His theory merits attention, at least in brief outline.

HOMANS.   Homans, in his book, *Social behavior* (1961), was concerned with explanation. Much of psychological theory, he argued, fails to explain anything. It provides a conceptual scheme, a set of pigeon holes, but has very few general statements from which empirical propositions may be deduced. Homans was of the opinion that two bodies of general statements exist from which empirical propositions regarding social behavior might be derived: these are behavioral psychology and elementary economics.

Homans rejected Durkheim's view that sociology is not a corollary of psychology. Instead, Homans hoped to extrapolate from experimental studies on animals to the behavior of man in social situations;

in addition, he hoped to use a set of statements derived from descriptions of the behavior of men exchanging material goods for money in a so-called perfect market to explain the exchange of intangible social services in a market that is far from perfect. The common denominator in behavior psychology and elementary economics is, he felt, the notion that human behavior is a function of its pay-off—it involves an exchange of activities, more or less rewarding or costly, tangible or intangible, between two persons.

In his use of psychological propositions, Homans was a fairly flexible Skinnerian. He replaced the Skinnerian term "operant behavior" with *activity;* and he spoke of contingencies in the relationship between stimulus, activity, and reinforcement such that the behavior of the organism may be brought under increasingly precise control by its physical and social environment. Punishment is an unsatisfactory means of control because it is costly: unless the activity is punished every time it occurs, it will soon reinstate itself. Superior modes of control are extinction—the withholding of reward—and positive reinforcement—especially praise for correct behavior.

Homans' central variables are value and quantity. *Value* is a function of the degree of reinforcement or punishment that results from a unit of activity. It reflects the preferences of the individual—preferences that are a function of past history:

> Some men find the damnest things valuable—or so it seems to the rest of us. Yet in principle we go about accounting for such values in just the same way as we go about accounting for other ones: we search the past histories of the persons concerned as they affect the present circumstances. The man who is too proud to ask for help may be one whose family thought itself no small pumpkins and taught him to think so too. If there is one thing we have learned from Freud it is that a man's past history, sometimes so long past that he has trouble talking about it, is a powerful determinant of his present behavior (Homans, 1961, p. 45).

Values such as altruism, pride, and competitiveness stay more or less constant over an individual's life span. Other values may vary over time, so that one activity may be valued more at some times than it is at other times.

Homans' second variable, *quantity,* refers to the number of units of activity emitted within a period of time. To study the quantitative aspect of social behavior, Homans argued, any consistent method of defining the unit of activity is appropriate. In studying social interactions, for example, it may be necessary to employ relatively crude measures such as the number of times one person talks to another, although it would obviously be better to have information about the content of their conversation. Nevertheless the propositions about social behavior that Homans proposed are themselves crude, and the development of sophisticated methods of measurement may, he felt, create more problems than enlightenment.

Homans went on to present five propositions about human social behavior. These are:

(1) If in the past the occurrence of a particular stimulus-situation has been the occasion on which a man's activity has been rewarded, then the more similar the present stimulus-situation is to the past one, the more likely he is to emit the activity, or some similar activity, now.

(2) The more often within a given period of time a man's activity rewards the activity of another, the more often the other will emit the activity.

(3) The more valuable to a man a unit of the activity another gives him, the more often he will emit activity rewarded by the activity of the other.

(4) The more often a man has in the recent past received a rewarding activity from another, the less valuable any further unit of that activity becomes to him.

And (5) The more to a man's disadvantage the rule of distributive justice fails of realization, the more likely he is to display the emotional behavior we call anger.

The underlying theme that runs through each of these propositions and the corollaries Homans derived from them is what a learning theorist would call the law of effect. Behavior is engaged in because it is profitable to the individual in some way or another. *Profit* is defined as reward less cost (where cost is defined in terms of the reward from other activities foregone in emitting a particular behavior). Homans argued that no exchange continues unless both parties are making a profit. Thus when a person chooses to engage in one activity (A) as opposed to another activity (B), he foregoes the reward involved in B for that of A and will continue to engage in A as long as it is profitable to him and to his partner.

The notion of distributive justice refers to people's expectations regarding the distribution of rewards and costs between persons. These expectations are a function of past history and other features of the individual and the party he is interacting with. Homans called these features the *investments* of the parties. They include such characteristics as age, race, sex, seniority, or acquired skill. People in exchange relationships will expect that the rewards of each man will be proportional to his cost—the greater the rewards, the greater the cost —and that the net reward or profit of each individual will be proportional to his investment—the greater the investment, the greater the profit. If these expectations are not fulfilled, emotional behavior will be released, especially anger or guilt.

Homans discussed a number of social phenomena in terms of the propositions he had formulated. Like Rotter, he considered the *expectation* of the parties as to the reward value of their activity to be a major factor in its determination. Thus social influence is largely a function of expectations of more or less valuable rewards—expectations that are themselves more or less strong. Where there is a strong expectation of a highly valued reward, the possibilities for social influence are maximal. And like Thibaut and Kelley, Homans took the economic aspect of rewards and costs into account. Thus achieving status in a group was discussed in terms of the reward involved in accurate status perception and the cost involved in maintaining status. Workers with higher status may worry more because of the greater responsibility attached to their jobs, but this cost is accepted if their higher status position is perceived as such and acknowledged by their fellow workers.

In general, then, Homans was broadly eclectic in his approach to social behavior, although the basic psychological orientation was Skinnerian. The topics he discussed range from influence and conformity to justice and innovation. Like most of the theorists we have been discussing, he approached these complex social phenomena tentatively and regarded his theory as a mere first approximation. His basic theme is exchange—the exchange of rewards and costs that men engage in their transactions. The evidence, where there is evidence, seems to support his theory, at least in broad outline. But then, in outline his theory is quite broad indeed. As Homans himself put it: "I am not out to destroy common sense but to make explicit and general the wisdom it embodies" (1961, p. 14).

The Status of Social-Learning Theory

Many criticisms could be made of social-learning theories at the present stage of their development. The most obvious ones are that they have not been adequately tested empirically and that they are so general as to defy empirical verification. To take one example, Rotter's notion that the likelihood of behavior in a particular situation is a function of the subjectively-held probability of the occurrence of a reinforcement and the value of the reinforcement to the individual is quite difficult to specify quantitatively and, lacking that quantification, is general enough to be regarded as a truism. Much the same could be said of the propositions of other theories we have reviewed. Moreover, what research has been generated by Rotter's theory, for instance, has been limited largely to internal concerns of the theory, such as expectancy statements and their modification, and

f the theory as these re-
same criticism can be
s quite limited in scope

l tentatively and with
rt. The study of social
experimental work is
be achieved. Further-
with a learning theory
, frequently animals, to
interaction. The indi-
vidual as an individual may operate in a quite different manner as a
member of a teacher-pupil, a husband-wife, or a leader-follower relationship. The subject matter for research in social learning is social
behavior—behavior learned in interpersonal situations and linked to
needs that require for their satisfaction the mediation of other people.
More research is needed on specifically social behavior before the
value of the proposed theories can be assessed.

Yet in the two decades that social-learning theories have been with
us they have generated relatively little research. There have been a
number of theoretical disputes such as the argument of Miller and
Dollard against Mowrer concerning the nature of learning—whether
it is a single unitary process or dual in nature. There have continued
to be differences of opinion about the need for employing cognitive
concepts, such as expectancy, in learning and social-learning theory.
These controversies, however, have not proven to be empirically
profitable.

In general, the theoretical disputes of yesteryear do not produce
even the heat that they previously did. This applies as much to social-
learning theory as it does to learning theory generally. In recent years
there has been increasing dissatisfaction with large-scale theoretical
enterprises. The potential usefulness of theoretical structures cannot
be denied. Nevertheless the most immediate need of psychology
would seem to be the careful development of a large number of low-
order theories, rather than all-encompassing higher-order theories.

Most contemporary psychologists appear to agree with this argument. There is no Clark Hull on the scene in psychology today. Even
social-learning theorists are more modest in their ambitions, typically
focusing on only one aspect of social behavior and not attempting to
work out in detail a general theory. There is more concern with
empirical facts than with fitting these facts to any theory.

Thus while a great deal of research on social behavior is being
conducted, relatively few studies have been generated by the various
social-learning theories we have reviewed. The phenomena themselves have led to research. People have become interested in how

children learn a language or develop attitudes. Imitation has been studied in detail because of its obvious importance in the process of socialization. The techniques and methods used to control the behavior of animals have been applied to neurotic and psychotic human beings. Low-order theories abound in each of these areas, and higher-order theoretical enterprises, linking together research in different areas, are becoming rare.

For this reason, the chapters that follow are concerned more with various substantive issues than with theoretical derivations. The focus, of course, will be on social learning—that is, on the acquisition of behavior patterns in an interpersonal context. No particular theoretical point of view will be presented. Instead the relative contribution of different learning-theory approaches will be assessed in an effort to determine how well each is able to integrate the empirical evidence that has accumulated and thereby to contribute to our understanding. In addition, we shall attempt to evaluate the adequacy of learning-theory approaches for explaining social behavior by comparing them with other, competing theoretical formulations.

2

Basic Issues: Learning, Awareness, and Reinforcement

IN RECENT YEARS, much of the work in the psychology of learning has taken place within the movements known as *behavior theory* or *radical behaviorism*. Behavior theory is usually associated with the work of Hull and his followers, while radical behaviorism refers to the work of Skinner and his followers. *S-R theory* and *neo-behaviorism* are sometimes used in a generic sense to describe either or both of these movements, as well as other, related developments. *Learning theory* has a wider meaning that can encompass cognitive approaches in the tradition of Tolman and, more recently, neo-cognitive, computer-oriented approaches.

As we have pointed out in Chapter One, two separate developments have occurred. On the one hand, experimenters have confined their attention to increasingly simple forms of one-person learning. Minature, paradigmatic learning situations have been studied in an effort to attain maximal prediction and control of behavior. The trend toward greater precision is epitomized in the work of Ferster and Skinner (1957) and in the development of mathematical models of learning (e.g., Bush & Mosteller, 1955; Restle, 1959) that apply to highly particularized situations. It has resulted in provisional "situational theories" (Estes, 1962), possessing rigorously defined boundary conditions.

On the other hand, there has been a movement toward developing principles and laws that have wide applicability and that extend to a wide range of psychological phenomena—especially to social behavior. While there is less insistence in this case on quantitative rigor and precision, recent developments indicate a similar concern with boundary conditions and a trend away from theory construction on a vast scale.

Before turning to those substantive areas where learning theory has been applied to social phenomena, some attention should be given to conceptual matters. Many of the problems with learning-theory approaches to social behavior stem from a disregard for these issues. As we shall see, much confusion has resulted from a lack of concern for intersubjective consistency in the use of basic terms. What, for example, is meant by learning? How is learning distinguished from performance? What is the role of awareness in learning? Can learning occur without the awareness of the subject? What is reinforcement, and how does it operate?

These are some of the topics that will be treated in this chapter. Admittedly, they involve complex issues that deserve more detailed discussion than will be accorded them here. Nevertheless, it seems better to bring these ghosts out of the attic than to ignore their presence. Too often proponents of a learning-theory approach have attacked other theoretical points of view for conceptual obscurity and imprecision without giving sufficient attention to the deficiencies of their own position.

LEARNING

It is not always an easy matter to determine precisely what a subject in an experimental situation has learned. In most cases the subject probably learns a great deal more than the experimenter measures. In a paired-associate learning task, for example, the subject does not simply learn the S-R association required of him, he also learns an R-S association (Feldman & Underwood, 1957). This backward learning phenomenon is only one example of the "incidental" or latent learning that accounts for a great deal of our learning experience. Before discussing this issue in more detail, however, we shall review briefly the basic experimental paradigms for learning and some points of controversy concerning their relative merits.

The Paradigms

Classical conditioning and instrumental conditioning are usually regarded as the simplest forms of true learning. We shall discuss these paradigms first and then take up operant conditioning as a special form of selective learning. Imitation and vicarious learning will be discussed as processes involving maximal flexibility in behavior. We begin then with simple forms of learning, and work up to more complex forms.

CLASSICAL CONDITIONING.   Pavlov's (1927) research with the conditioned reflex in dogs is of historical significance in psychology, and hence the paradigm he employed is commonly referred to as "classical" conditioning. He taught his dogs to salivate at the sound of a metronome beat by injecting meat powder into their mouths after each presentation of the sound. He thereby demonstrated a form of learning we call conditioning—namely, a modification of behavior in which the capacity to elicit a response is transferred from one stimulus to another.

In this paradigm, the meat powder that produces salivation without training is an *unconditioned stimulus* (UCS) that produces an *unconditioned response* (UCR), salivation to the meat powder. After the conditioning procedure, the metronome sound that produced salivation becomes a *conditioned stimulus* (CS) producing a *condi-*

tioned response (CR), salivation to the sound of the metronome. While the CR appears to be identical with the UCR, most researchers regard the CR as a fractional component of the UCR (Kimble, 1961). The process is represented schematically in Figure 2-1.

Pavlov was committed to the notion that the functions of the nervous system are adaptive; consequently he viewed the process of conditioning as one that allowed the organism to make adjustments to critical situations in the environment. Such reflexes as salivation, blinking, pupillary action, and so forth provide the organism with a set of reactions necessary for survival. Since these reactions in themselves, as unconditioned reflexes, occur in response to a limited set of stimuli, the process of conditioning whereby unconditioned reflexes become conditioned to a broad range of stimuli has obvious adaptive utility. The essence of the conditioned reflex is its anticipatory character: it helps the organism orient itself to critical situations and make necessary emergency reactions.

One reason for the prominence of classical conditioning is that it is supported by common experience. Most people, for example, find that their mouths water at the sight, smell, or even thought of a juicy steak. On the other hand, some involuntary skeletal responses, such as the patellar reflex and the pupillary reflex, have proven to be rather difficult to condition (Kimble, 1961). As we have seen, these difficulties were recognized by Pavlov, who obtained consistent results only by sheltering his animals from extraneous stimuli in a highly artificial setting. Nevertheless, under controlled experimental conditions a wide variety of physiological responses have been conditioned.

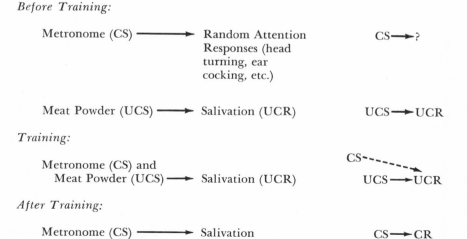

Before Training:

Metronome (CS) ⟶ Random Attention Responses (head turning, ear cocking, etc.)   CS⟶?

Meat Powder (UCS) ⟶ Salivation (UCR)   UCS⟶UCR

Training:

Metronome (CS) and Meat Powder (UCS) ⟶ Salivation (UCR)   CS------⟶ UCS⟶UCR

After Training:

Metronome (CS) ⟶ Salivation Component (CR)   CS⟶CR

Figure 2-1. Schematic representation of the process of classical conditioning.

The fact of conditioning is empirically established; the importance of conditioning for human functioning remains controversial.

INSTRUMENTAL LEARNING.   The essential feature of the instrumental learning paradigm is that the response is instrumental in the achievement of the goal. If a hungry organism is offered a choice of a number of equally attractive responses, only one of which leads to food, the tendency will inevitably be to make the response that leads to food once the consequences of each response are known. The response leading to food will dominate because it is instrumental in goal achievement.

Instrumental learning involves more flexibility in behavior than classical conditioning since a wider range of responses is available. The organism is also more active in instrumental learning than in classical conditioning. In classical conditioning, the organism is relatively passive and has no control over the delivery of the unconditioned stimulus and the conditioned stimulus. In the instrumental learning paradigm, the organism assumes an active role in learning; reward is contingent upon the prior occurrence of the response to be learned.

So far we have discussed the *instrumental reward* situation. In the *instrumental escape* situation, a noxious stimulus is presented and the organism must learn to make a response that terminates it. The similarity between instrumental escape and instrumental reward learning is apparent if the noxious stimulus is thought of as a deprivation state and the removal of the aversive stimulus as reinforcement for instrumental behavior.

Another type of instrumental learning is *instrumental avoidance* learning. This may involve *active* avoidance, in which case the noxious stimulus is preceded by another stimulus event that takes on the properties of a conditioned stimulus. The organism learns to respond to the conditioned stimulus by making an instrumental response that permits it to avoid the noxious stimulus (UCS). If the organism does not respond in the time between the presentation of the conditioned stimulus and the occurrence of the unconditioned stimulus, it receives the noxious stimulation and the situation becomes one of instrumental escape. In the *passive* avoidance situation, the organism is trained to make a response and then given noxious stimulation for continuing to make the response. The organism must learn to avoid the noxious stimulus by not making the response it had learned. This is essentially a punishment situation where the experimenter is concerned with determining the effect of noxious stimulation (punishment) on an established response.

Typically, classical conditioning of the Pavlovian variety is assumed to be based upon stimulus substitution or the contiguity principle of learning. Instrumental learning (also called problem solving or trial-and-error learning) is assumed to follow the law of effect or the principle of reinforcement. Spence (1956), however, turned this around and proposed that classical conditioning depends upon a reinforcement principle, while instrumental learning is based upon contiguity. Other theorists have adopted two-factor positions, according to which learning follows both contiguity and reinforcement principles (e.g., Mowrer, 1950, 1960a).

While most theorists agree that learning involves a number of different processes, some have tried to reduce learning to a single, unitary process. Pavlov (1932), for example, attempted to account for instrumental learning in terms of conditioning principles. He argued that instrumental responses were in essence conditioned reflexes linked to the unconditioned response through proprioceptive stimuli and other forms of stimulation. Thus internal, kinesthetic stimuli are conditioned to the execution of those movements that allow the organism to achieve reward. A similar analysis was presented by Watson (1924) to account for the organization of complex habits (Figure 2-2).

In contrast, Hull (1943) proposed that both classical conditioning and instrumental learning were dependent on the unitary process of reinforcement—specifically, on reinforcement provided by the reduction of drive. According to Hull, the termination of drive strengthens the connection between the stimuli associated with the drive state and the response or responses connected with its termination. This is what happens in instrumental learning. In classical conditioning the reduction of drive strengthens the connection between neutral stimuli, simultaneously presented with those associated with the drive, and the unconditioned response. Thus, according to Hull, differences between the two forms of learning are superficial and involve no fundamentally different principles or laws but only differences in

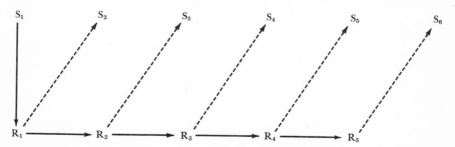

Figure 2-2. Watson's (1924) account of the organization of complex instrumental habits. The initial stimulus (S_1) produces a response (R_1) that becomes a "substitute stimulus" (S_2) for the next response (R_2). The "substitute" stimuli were thought to be kinesthetic in nature.

the conditions under which a single principle of reinforcement operates.

In spite of these efforts to achieve parsimony, most contemporary treatments of learning distinguish between classical conditioning and instrumental learning (Deese & Hulse, 1967; Hall, 1966). A typical approach is represented by Staats (1968) who regarded both processes as essential to an understanding of complex human behavior.

OPERANT CONDITIONING.   Skinner (1938), as we have seen, distinguished operant from respondent behavior because there is no determinable stimulus that elicits an operant response. The behavior is emitted spontaneously and can be controlled by reinforcement contingencies. Operant behavior differs from classical (or respondent) conditioning, therefore, since in the classical conditioning paradigm the responses are all under the immediate control of the experimenter, whereas in the operant conditioning paradigm the responses are under the immediate control of the behaving subject.

Operant conditioning is also distinguished from instrumental learning, since in instrumental learning the alternative responses possible for the organism are usually limited. The animal has only a limited number of possible ways to run a maze or escape from shock. Operant conditioning procedures, in contrast, do not involve these restrictions. The organism is free to do what it wants. It typically makes a great many different responses, some of which are reinforced by the experimenter.

The rate of emission of a response over a period of time prior to reinforcement is called the *operant level* of the response. If each instance of an emission of that bit of behavior is followed by a stimulus and the rate of emission is found to increase, then the reinforcing properties of the stimulus have been established. A *positive reinforcing stimulus* increases the rate of operant responding when applied immediately after the response. A *negative reinforcing stimulus* increases the probability of a response when it is removed immediately after a response. *Punishment* is defined as the removal of a positive reinforcer or the application of a negative reinforcer.

Most operants occur with a high frequency only under certain conditions. People usually do not start talking unless other people are present. A child does not run to meet his father unless he has some reason to think that his father is coming. A man does not kiss every woman he encounters, but only certain women. In each of these cases, operant behavior is under the control of *discriminative stimuli.* The probability of the operant is high only in the presence of certain environmental events, or discriminative stimuli, and is low under other conditions. Discriminative stimuli are said to control the operant response since the operant has been reinforced in the presence of discriminative stimuli and is therefore more likely to occur in their presence.

While the Skinnerian approach to learning nominally relies on two learning processes, respondent conditioning and operant conditioning, respondent or classical conditioning has been underplayed in theory and research. Very little effort has gone into extending the principles of respondent conditioning to complex human behavior, and research has centered almost exclusively on operant behavior. One recent analysis (Reynolds, 1968) has given more attention to respondent behavior, especially in connection with the aversive control of behavior, but the typical approach has been to subordinate respondent conditioning to operant conditioning (Keller & Schoenfeld, 1950) or to ignore it completely.

Most likely the reason for this preoccupation with operant behavior is that the Skinnerians have had a great deal of success in shaping operant behavior through reinforcement. By carefully controlling reinforcement contingencies, they have been able to train animals to make complex responses not originally in their repertoire. Essentially the same procedures are assumed to underlie the child's acquisition of language and other skills. As we shall see in subsequent chapters, operant conditioning procedures have been applied extensively by Skinnerians to account for the learning of almost every aspect of man's social behavior.

IMITATION AND VICARIOUS LEARNING.   Many patterns of social behavior are acquired through the process of imitation and vicarious learning. As we shall see in Chapter Four, a number of different theoretical explanations have been proposed to account for these processes. All authors agree, however, that such learning demands a considerable amount of flexibility and can result in the acquisition of highly complex behavioral patterns.

The distinction between imitation and vicarious learning is typically based on whether the observer is reinforced for patterning his responses on those of the model. In vicarious learning the assumption is that no direct reinforcement accrues to the observer for responding in the same way as the model. As we shall see, there is some disagreement among investigators on this point because of a lack of consistency and precision in the definition of reinforcement. There is considerable evidence, however, that some types of vicarious learning occur. It has been shown, for example, that learning can occur from the mere observation of a model without the observer making a response.

Since two people may have learned to behave the same way in the presence of the same cues, imitation and vicarious learning are not demonstrated merely by showing that the behavior of two people is the same. One must know the conditions under which the behavior was learned to know whether it was truly imitative. In the imitation paradigm, the model typically performs a complex response—of relatively low probability—in the presence of the observer, and the observer matches this response. Both the model and the observer may be reinforced for their response, only the model, or neither.

Once the tendency to imitate is clearly established, the subject can be tested to see if he will continue to imitate other models in situations different from the one where the original training was conducted. A number of theorists have affirmed that imitative behavior will be learned as a generalized response, and that, once acquired, it will occur in a variety of situations. Regardless of the explanation, there is little doubt that imitative learning is a pervasive factor in human social learning—both in the process of the socialization of the child as well as in adult interpersonal behavior.

What Is Learned?

Learning is typically defined as a change in performance that occurs as a result of experience. It is distinguished from maturation since it results from experience and not simply from the development of the organism. It is distinguished from fatigue since the changes in performance involved in learning are relatively permanent and do not simply disappear with rest. It is distinguished from native response tendencies since learning involves changes in performance that result from stimulation from the outside world and not from innate, species-specific propensities (Hilgard & Bower, 1966).

LEARNING AND PERFORMANCE.   Although learning is usually defined as a change in performance, a number of investigators have attempted to distinguish these two constructs. The reason for such a distinction was research by Tolman (1932) and his associates that was interpreted as demonstrating that animals do not necessarily display in performance all that they have learned.

In an early study by Blodgett (1929), for example, a group of rats that did not find food in the goal box was retained there for two minutes a day for seven days. The rats showed no evidence of learning. After the seventh day, however, food was introduced into the goal box and the animals showed a dramatic increase in performance, such that their error score was not significantly different from that of a control group reinforced every day (Figure 2-3).

Since the control group showed gradual and not abrupt changes in performance, Tolman argued that the learning process does not take place rapidly but is a gradual, incremental process. Changes in reward do not affect learning as such. Instead, reward contributes to performance—that is, to the extent to which what has been learned will be revealed in behavior. Abrupt changes in behavior are therefore presumably related to performance variables, whereas continuous changes are related to learning variables.

In spite of the use of the learning-performance dichotomy to account for the results of "latent learning" studies (Blodgett, 1929; Tolman & Honzik, 1930), it may well be that such a distinction is of little importance in the treatment of learning. While the work of Tolman and his associates has demonstrated the empirical validity of such a distinction, the fact remains that the only way one can know that learning has occurred is by an observation of successive performances (McGeoch, 1942). Learning is the relationship between successive performances, and while learning can take place without the experimenter's being able to measure it, no demonstration of learning can be made without measurement of some kind. Thus while the learning-performance distinction is empirically valid, it may prove to have little operational utility (Hall, 1966).

This does, however, leave unresolved the question of what is learned. Is what is learned simply what the experimenter is able to measure in performance? Obviously this is not the case. The experimental evidence for latent learning in animals is too convincing to allow one to argue an exact correspondence between learning and performance. Furthermore, human subjects have repeatedly demonstrated an ability to learn aspects of the task that are irrelevant to its performance. In fact, it may be that a great deal of the learning that

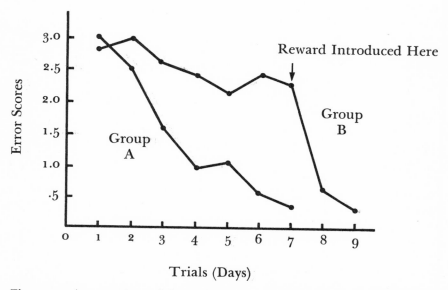

Figure 2-3. A comparison of the performance of two groups in Blodgett's (1929) study. Group A always received reward, whereas Group B received reward from the seventh day on.

occurs in an experimental situation is incidental to the experimenter's purposes.

INCIDENTAL LEARNING.   Incidental learning corresponds on the human level to the latent learning situation in animals. In the latent learning situation the evidence seems to indicate that animals learn without being motivated by deprivation conditions. In the incidental learning situation the evidence indicates that human subjects learn without being motivated by instructions. Consequently, researchers using human subjects have distinguished two types of learning: When formal instructions are given to learn the material, learning is said to be *intentional;* when no formal instructions to learn are given, learning is said to be *incidental.*

A great deal of research has been conducted on the incidental learning phenomenon, much of it pointing to the conclusion that differences between intentional and incidental learning and variations in amount of incidental learning are a function of differences in instructions given to subjects. Mechanic (1962), for example, showed that differences in orienting instructions (number of pronouncing responses required of the subject) produced differential incidental learning. When more pronouncing responses were demanded, subjects learned less incidental material.

Postman (1964) has contended that the difference between intentional and incidental learning can be reduced to zero when learning is either seriously hindered or maximally facilitated by the orienting task. He conceptualized a continuum of orienting tasks ranging from those requiring responses maximally favorable for learning to those requiring responses maximally unfavorable. At either extreme on the continuum the differences between intentional and incidental learning are minimal. At the favorable extreme incidental learning increases through generalization, while at the unfavorable extreme intentional learning decreases because of interference from the orienting activity.

When intentional and incidental learning are viewed in this way, the distinction between them becomes highly tenuous. Data from research show quantitative differences between the intentional and the incidental groups, but all that can be concluded on the basis of such evidence is that learning is more difficult under disadvantageous (incidental) conditions. The incidental procedure does not preclude the possibility of sporadic self-instructions or self-induced motivation, and consequently intergroup differences are attributable only to the functional relations of a number of parameters of efficient and inefficient learning (Postman, 1964).

It therefore becomes difficult to maintain that two qualitatively different types of learning—defined by different operational antecedents—are being investigated in research on intentional and incidental learning. Strictly speaking, "incidental learning," as operationally defined in most research, is a misnomer. There is no experimental evidence demonstrating incidental learning in the traditional sense—namely, a distinct learning process that occurs when there is no motive, self-instruction, or set to learn (McGeoch & Irion, 1952). Whether such learning does occur is an unanswered, and perhaps unanswerable, question (McLaughlin, 1965).

To return to the learning-performance issue, research on the incidental learning phenomenon suggests that instructions to human subjects merely ensure that the material learned corresponds to the performance measure used by the experimenter (Lawrence, 1958). Some support for this comes from a study by Postman, Adams, and Bohm (1956) in which four intentional groups were compared with one incidental learning group. The incidental learning group performed an orienting task that exposed them to the material without requiring that they learn the items. In one intentional condition (intentional task) the subjects performed the same orienting task as the incidental learners and were also required to learn the items. In the other intentional condition (intentional control) subjects did not perform the incidental orienting task. In both intentional conditions half of the subjects were required to learn the items in the list with the implicit understanding that the order was unimportant (items-only), and the other half were instructed to learn the items and the order (items-order). These experimental conditions and the data from the experiment are summarized in Table 2-1.

Postman and his associates found that the items-order intentional groups recalled the *order* better than the items-only intentional groups, but that the performance ranking was the reverse for *recall* of items. The intentional-control groups performed better on all tasks than the intentional-task groups (which in turn were superior to the incidental group). The incidental group was in the disadvantageous condition of having received no instructions to learn what the experimenter was going to measure, yet subjects in this group did learn something about the items and their order, just as subjects in the items-only intentional group learned something about the order. The data suggest that a so-called "intentional" learner may be an "incidental" learner with respect to those features of the task toward which he has not centrally focused.

The intentional-incidental learning distinction underscores the fact that learning of relevant aspects of a task is determined solely on the basis of what the experimenter defines as relevant. A great deal of "irrelevant" (incidental) learning may take place that does not show up in performance because the experimenter is concerned merely with "relevant" (intentional) learning. Since relevant and irrelevant are defined on the basis of instructions, what is measured in perform-

Table 2-1

Groups, Instructions, and Results for Free Recall of Items,
and Rank-Order Correlations between Correct Sequence
and the Subject's Reconstructed Sequence of Items

GROUP	INSTRUCTIONS	FREE RECALL	RANK-ORDER CORRELATION
Incidental	orienting task	4.48	.26
Intentional Task:	orienting task and		
Items-Only	learn items	7.81	.38
Items-Order	learn items and order	5.38	.54
Intentional Control:	no orienting task and		
Items-Only	learn items	12.95	.67
Items-Order	learn items and order	10.14	.86

From Postman, Adams, & Bohn, 1956.

ance may in no way provide an adequate indication of what has been learned.

Experiments in social learning support this contention. As we shall see, young children, in the course of imitative learning, acquire a great deal of incidental information that they learn quite readily. In fact, some children are more likely to learn the expressive ("incidental") behavior of an adult model than they are to learn to perform the model's ("intentional") behavior. Unless care is taken to include "irrelevant" learning as well as "relevant" learning in the determination of what is learned, a great deal of significant information about the learning process may be lost.

AWARENESS

Much attention has been given recently to the question of whether subjects are aware that they are learning. Some investigators contend that learning occurs under conditions where the subject is unaware that he is learning, while others find no evidence for learning without awareness. A lively debate has been generated over this issue and over the way in which an "awareness" construct should be handled theoretically.

The Awareness Controversy

Although the awareness issue dates to Thorndike (1932), the recent controversy over learning without awareness grew out of research on the social reinforcement of verbal responses. Essentially this research involved the extension of operant conditioning procedures to verbal behavior. If a given class of words is reinforced by "good" or other positive responses on the part of the experimenter, that class of words rises above the operant level. The rate with which the class of verbal responses is emitted falls off again when reinforcement is withdrawn. The controversy is over whether subjects are aware of the reinforcement contingencies.

EARLY VERBAL CONDITIONING STUDIES.   The initial studies in this area were by Greenspoon (1950, 1955) and Verplanck (1955). These studies showed that subjects would modify their verbalizations or give more statements of opinion when reinforced in rather subtle ways such as by "mm-hmm" or by nods. Because such findings appeared to have important implications for psychotherapy, a number of researchers became interested in the verbal conditioning phenomenon.

A typical experimental procedure used in studies of verbal conditioning was that worked out by Taffel (1955). Each subject is shown a number of cards on each of which is typed the pronoun "I," "you," "he," "we," and "they," followed by a verb. The subject is instructed to make up a sentence for each card including the verb and beginning with one of the pronouns. Whenever he begins a sentence with "I" or "we," the experimenter says, "good." Usually it is not too long before there is a sharp increase in the number of sentences beginning with "I" or "we."

After the subject has finished constructing sentences for all of the cards, he is asked if he noticed any particular behavior on the part of the experimenter and, if so, what and when did he start to notice it. If he is able to identify the reinforcement contingencies—namely, that the experimenter said "good" every time a sentence included "I" or "we"—he is said to evidence awareness.

In a review of the early studies, Krasner (1956) stated that in over half of the 24 studies covered, none of the subjects evidenced awareness. In all of the studies combined, less than five percent of the subjects were classified as aware. In fact, even when subjects were aware, this did not affect the extent to which they learned. The early studies seemed to indicate, therefore, (1) that learning could occur without awareness and (2) that there was no direct relationship between awareness of the reinforcement contingencies and degree of learning.

EVIDENCE FOR AWARENESS.   It was not long, however, before evidence was obtained in support of just the opposite conclusions. Dulany (1962) and Spielberger (1962) reported experimental data that indicated that learning does not occur in the verbal conditioning situation in the absence of the subject's ability to verbalize mediational steps that occur between the stimulus conditions and changes in his behavior. That is, subjects who learned were aware of the conditions of reinforcement and were able to report this awareness. Moreover, there was a direct relationship between awareness and the extent of conditioning.

Dulany (1962) pointed out that the learning found in the learning-without-awareness paradigm may be attributed to hypotheses that are incorrect but "correlated" with the emission of criterial sentences. For example, in an experiment where subjects are conditioned to use plural nouns by an experimenter who says "mm-hmm" whenever they occur, subjects may form the hypothesis that they are to *associate* to plural nouns when the experimenter says "mm-hmm." The usual procedure would be to regard these subjects as unaware (their hypothesis is formally incorrect), but since plural nouns tend to be associated with other plural nouns, the subjects would show an increase on the criterial measure. When the report of a correct *or* correlated hypothesis was used as the criterion of awareness, subjects who stated such hypotheses were inevitably conspicuous for their dramatic conditioning curves. Dulany concluded that there was no empirical justification for thinking that learning without awareness has the social generality imputed to it by Dollard and Miller (1950) who, as was mentioned in Chapter One, regarded such learning to be the source of many attitudes, prejudices, emotions, motor skills, and mannerisms.

Spielberger (1962) also took exception to the Dollard and Miller notion that "the effects of a reinforcement can be entirely unconscious and automatic" (Dollard & Miller, 1950, p. 44). Spielberger inferred awareness on the basis of subjects' responses to a detailed postconditioning interview conducted immediately following learning trials. In his experiments no evidence was obtained for learning without awareness, and awareness was highly correlated with conditioning.

The evidence from a number of studies (e.g., Cohen, 1964; Dean & Hiesinger, 1964; Lanyon, 1964; Spielberger, Southard, & Hodges, 1966) supports the Dulany and Spielberger contention that there is no learning without awareness. Nevertheless the evidence from other studies appears to indicate the possibility of some forms of learning without awareness (e.g., Davis, 1964; Dixon & Oates, 1965; Hefferline & Keenan, 1963; Manis & Ruppe, 1969; Worthington, 1966). Perhaps these differences are a function of differences in methods used for assessing awareness. If a rigorous definition is employed, relatively few subjects will be classified as aware. If a loose definition is employed, more subjects will be classified as aware. Until consistency is obtained in the use of techniques for assessing awareness, it makes little sense to argue over its presence or absence.

In fact, the search for "real" awareness may be, as Farber (1963) suggested, a search for a chimera. Farber has proposed that the important question is whether by defining awareness in a given way—specifying both the contents of the response and the procedures used to evoke it—it will be possible to give a better account for variations in the subject's behavior. If degrees of awareness can be differentiated on the basis of stimulus and response variables and if these differences can be shown to relate to behavior in lawful ways, then the enterprise will have been worth the effort.

AWARENESS AS A BEHAVIORAL CONCEPT.   Unfortunately, awareness has proven to be a difficult concept to define in operational terms. Spielberger (1962) proposed that awareness be defined as a process that intervenes (mediates) between stimuli and responses and that corresponds to the immediate, direct, phenomenal experience of the subject. Dulany (1962) also thought of awareness as a cognitive mediating process and proposed a theoretical network of mediating entities, such as behavioral hypotheses and behavioral intentions, each of which has empirical meaning through its connection with experimental variables.

As a cognitive mediating process, awareness must be inferred from the verbal reports of subjects. Spielberger, as we have seen, employed a detailed postconditioning interview sheet to assess awareness in his subjects. He contended that previous studies that reported conditioning without awareness employed insensitive interviewing procedures. In his experiment the questions were detailed and specific—so detailed and specific, in fact, that they ran the risk of suggesting the response-reinforcement contingency to the subjects. It is possible therefore that Spielberger's subjects learned the correct hypothesis as they were being questioned.

To show that awareness was not suggested by questioning but was present during conditioning, it is necessary to demonstrate that the acquisition of the reinforced-response class occurs only for aware subjects and only for trials subsequent to their developing correct or correlated hypotheses. DeNike (1964) attempted to determine whether awareness serves such a mediating role in the verbal conditioning paradigm by having his subjects write down their "thoughts about the experiment" after each trial block during learning. He also employed a postconditioning interview to evaluate the comparability of this procedure to customary methods of assessing awareness.

In DeNike's experiment, the subjects were reinforced for "human noun" responses in a word-naming task. Verbal conditioning was demonstrated only for subjects who showed awareness of the response-reinforcement contingencies as assessed through their "thoughts about the experiment." Increments in conditioning were found to occur on the trial block on which aware subjects first recorded their correct hypotheses. These findings supported the contention that the subjects' awareness influences subsequent conditioning (Figure 2-4). Moreover, there was a high correspondence between awareness ratings taken during and after the experiment. This suggests that no large biasing effect was introduced by interviewing subjects after conditioning.

These results, while supporting Spielberger's position, are equally interpretable in other terms. Spielberger and Dulany have opted for a cognitive mediational theory, but more behavioral mediational theories can, in principle, account for the same data. DeNike, citing Farber (1963), has warned against assuming that since some subjects were able to report their awareness of response-reinforcement contingencies, they possessed an autonomous cognitive machinery that guided their every action. Spielberger's conceptualization of awareness lends itself to this mode of thinking, since awareness is not simply defined in operational terms, but refers to the conscious experience of the subject.

An alternative conceptualization has been proposed by Maltzman (1966), who argued that awareness should be defined in terms of antecedent and consequent behavioral events. The antecedents of awareness are the stimulus contingencies—including instructions given the subject—and the consequent conditions are data obtained

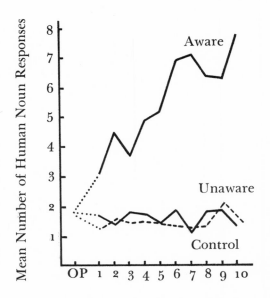

Blocks of 25 Response Words

Figure 2-4. Performance of aware (N = 21), unaware (N = 40), and control (N = 21) subjects (from DeNike, 1964). OP is the operant level of human noun responses.

from interviews and other verbal reports. So defined, awareness has no surplus (phenomenal) meaning.

Whatever the outcome of this definitional controversy, it seems likely that further research with awareness will link it closely with the more general concept of attention. The biological function of the awareness process is to keep the organism attuned to important environmental events (Eriksen, 1962). Since adequate social learning is of critical importance for human organisms, awareness and attentional processes have a fundamental role in social behavior. There may be cases of learning without awareness, but at the present time little is known about the conditions under which such learning occurs (if it occurs at all).

REINFORCEMENT

Perhaps no concept in learning theory has been as controversial as the concept of reinforcement. There are a number of issues involved here, each of which we shall treat separately. First there is the question of definition: What is a reinforcing event, and what logical role should reinforcement play in a particular theory? Second, there is the question of the nature of reinforcement: What are the precise mechanisms assumed to operate when a reinforcer strengthens new learning? Finally, there is the issue of the relationship between reinforcement and learning: Is reinforcement always necessary for learning, or does some learning occur in the absence of reinforcement?

Definitions of Reinforcement

For a number of years there has been a great deal of theoretical confusion among psychologists resulting from their failure to reach agreement over the definition of a reinforcing event. Since agreement on definitional issues is necessary for resolution of theoretical issues, one would hope that discussions about the definition of reinforcement in the psychological literature of the past several decades would have produced some intersubjective consistency in defining the term. Such is not the case, unfortunately, and in spite of prolonged intramural debate a great deal of theoretical and experimental work remains to be done before the concept of reinforcement can be assigned its proper place in the psychology of learning (Deese & Hulse, 1967).

STRONG VERSUS WEAK DEFINITIONS.   A "strong" definition of reinforcement is one in which the theorist commits himself to some precise statement about how reinforcement works. A "weak" definition implies no such commitment. Much of the debate over the concept of reinforcement stems from disagreement over this particular issue—namely, whether the concept of reinforcement should include some explanation of the nature of reinforcement.

Hull's (1943) approach to reinforcement represents the classic example of a theorist who adopts a "strong" definition of the concept. According to Hull, no learning could occur unless practice was reinforced. Furthermore, reinforcement occurred because a need state of the organism was reduced. Hull proposed that food is reinforcing to a hungry animal and water to a thirsty animal because food and water reduce organic needs. Organisms tend to do things that will reduce the intensity of painful stimuli, and a need state such as hunger or thirst involves unpleasant stimulation.

In this respect Hull was in the tradition of Thorndike (1898) and more remotely of Darwin. He was a law-of-effect theorist, in that the responses of the organism were thought to have "good" or "bad" effects that determined whether those responses would survive. Responses followed by "good" effects survived, while those followed by "bad" effects did not. Since Hull committed himself to a particular explanation of reinforcement—namely, a drive-reduction explanation —his position is known as a "strong" law-of-effect position.

Skinner (1938), on the other hand, proposed a "weak" definition; he studiously avoided explanatory statements and restricted himself to the operational definition of reinforcement as a stimulus that increases the probability of a response. He argued that such a definition is not circular since a stimulus identified as a reinforcer in one situation can then be used as a reinforcer in another.

Skinner's definition implies a "weak" or empirical law of effect in that he made no attempt to provide an explanation for how reinforcement operates. Such a descriptive account of the law of effect states merely that responses are fixated and eliminated as functions of their effects. The empirical law of effect has generally been adopted by theorists over the past several decades, even by proponents of the Hullian position such as Miller (1959) and Spence (1956).

BROAD VERSUS NARROW DEFINITIONS.   Another distinction between the kinds of definitions of reinforcement advanced by learning theorists is based on whether the definition is broad or narrow in extension. While most contemporary theorists have come to prefer a "weak" or empirical definition of reinforcement, there is as yet little agreement about what class (or classes) of events qualify as reinforcers.

The broadest definition of reinforcement identifies the process empirically with the operations supplied by the experimenter to produce learning. This corresponds to what Mueller and Schoenfeld called the "distal" view of reinforcement (1954, p. 372). Such a broad use of the concept permits one to speak of the number of reinforcements necessary *before* a conditioned response occurs in classical conditioning. In the paired-associate learning situation, the reinforcing operation is the paired presentation of the stimulus with the response member of an item.

The narrower meaning demands an antecedent response before it is permissible to speak of reinforcement. The conditioned response must be given in the classical conditioning paradigm and only *after* this can one speak of reinforcement increasing the strength of the response. Reinforcement in a paired-associate learning situation occurs only after the subject has made a correct response in anticipation of the paired stimulus-response presentation. According to this narrower usage, therefore, reinforcement involves an increase in some index of response strength following upon the maintenance of a contingency between the response and its consequences. In this case, demonstration that the organism has been reinforced demands that the reinforcing event be defined by what the organism itself does—or"proximally" in Mueller and Schoenfeld's (1954) terms—rather than by what the experimenter does—or "distally."

In a controversial paper, Estes (1960) questioned the assumption that an incremental growth of associative strength results from reinforcement in a learning task. He used a broad or "distal" definition of reinforcement—identifying reinforcement with the presentation of the response member in a paired-associate situation. In a series of "miniature" experiments involving the presentation of a stimulus-response pair (reinforcement) followed by two recall tests, Estes found that if the response of a stimulus-response pair was correctly recalled on an initial recall test, it would most likely be correctly recalled on a second recall test. If the response was not correctly recalled on the first test, it would most likely not be recalled on the second test

Table 2-2
Data from Two Free-Recall Experiments (Estes, 1960),
Showing Percentages of Correct and Incorrect Responses
over Two Tests of Recall

NUMBER OF CASES	FIRST RECALL TEST	SECOND RECALL TEST
280	39% correct	75 % correct
		25% incorrect
	61% incorrect	.5% correct
		99.5% incorrect
816	28% correct	54% correct
		46% incorrect
	72% incorrect	2% correct
		98% incorrect

(Table 2-2). He interpreted these results as running counter to an incremental learning position and supporting an all-or-none, one-trial learning hypothesis. Either the correct response is learned or not; there was no evidence for a gradual incremental growth in associative strength.

Estes' (1960) work has been criticized on a number of grounds (see Underwood & Keppel, 1962), but in the context of the present discussion our main concern is to note that his results are predicated on a particular (broad) definition of reinforcement. Only by defining reinforcement in terms of the paired presentation of the stimulus and response member in the paired-associate situation was he able to argue against the assumption that associative strength increases with reinforcement. It would have been logically impossible for him to do so if he had employed a narrow definition. To define reinforcement—as Skinner (1938) did—as an event that increases the probability of a response, involves the very assumption that Estes called into question.

There is another dimension to the narrow-broad controversy. For Skinner, any stimulus that increases the probability of a response is a reinforcer. Since the notion of a stimulus includes a class of stimulus events (Skinner, 1953), the possibilities for reinforcement are rather large in his system. The verbal community, for example, has a great number of potential resources at its disposal to employ in shaping the language of the child (Skinner, 1957). Thus, while Skinner defined reinforcement in a narrow or proximal sense, the term was given a wide extension. The sole criterion for a reinforcing event in Skinner's system is an increase in the probability of a response.

In social situations a wide variety of events meet this criterion. Information derived from the environment, for example, can serve to increase the probability of responses in the subject's repertoire. Is information therefore to be equated with reinforcement? Or does information have other properties, such as motivational or discriminative functions, over and above its reinforcing consequences? If alterations in motivational variables and discriminative cues can in themselves produce increments in response rate, are these events to be defined as reinforcers?

As we shall see, these questions become especially important when attempts are made to demonstrate that learning occurs through vicarious reinforcement or in the absence of any reinforcement at all. If reinforcement is defined rather narrowly to refer to the actual presentation by the experimenter of rewarding or punishing stimuli, evidence for learning through vicarious reinforcement is easier to come by than if a broader definition is used. Widening the definition to include informational gain, incentive to learn, and discriminative learning (each of which can be thought of as a reinforcing event) makes learning without reinforcement less probable. In fact, Skinner's definition of reinforcement has so wide an extension that it makes learning without reinforcement logically impossible, since learning can only be demonstrated through increases in response probability, which by definition involves reinforcement. Until some agreement is reached concerning the manner in which the reinforcement concept is to be employed in the study of social behavior, theoretical controversies will abound. Criteria must be established for defining stimuli or classes of stimuli as social reinforcers. This may require differentiating between the reinforcing properties of stimuli and their informational, motivational, and discriminative properties. Some agreement will also have to be reached on whether reinforcement should be defined on the basis of what the subject does or on the basis of what the experimenter does. These are fundamental issues, but they have not yet received the theoretical and empirical attention they deserve.

Furthermore, as Rotter (1954) has observed, there is a large element of learning involved in reinforcement when the term is employed to explain social behavior. Care must be taken to determine the value of the reinforcement for the individual subject. While a wide variety of reinforcers may exist for normal subjects, only a very small subset may be reinforcing for a depressive patient or a schizophrenic.

At the present time researchers are aware of these problems but, as we shall see in the course of this book, a great deal of variability still exists in the use of the reinforcement concept in learning-theory approaches to social behavior. Frequently the term is applied in a very loose sense without any effort to achieve operational precision and without attempting to distinguish the term from related concepts. Since reinforcement is such a basic concept in a learning-theory approach, this lack of definitional agreement seriously undermines the theory and leaves it vulnerable to criticism by proponents of opposing points of view.

The Nature of Reinforcement

As one might expect, lack of agreement over the definition of reinforcement is coupled with a lack of agreement over the nature of reinforcement. Theorists have proposed a number of ways of accounting for how reinforcement operates besides the classical Hullian drive-reduction explanation. We shall review these briefly and refer the interested reader to more detailed treatments (Cofer & Appley, 1964; Deese & Hulse, 1967; Hall, 1966).

DRIVE REDUCTION VERSUS DRIVE INDUCTION.   The drive- or tension-reduction interpretation of reinforcement (Hull, 1943) was sharply criticized on empirical grounds by Sheffield, Roby, and Campbell (1954). They reinforced the runway behavior of hungry rats with solutions containing either a nutritive substance, dextrose, or a non-nutritive substance, saccharine, or a combination of both. The consummatory behavior induced by dextrose was weaker than that induced by saccharine, while the combination of the two substances produced the greatest amount of consummatory behavior. Sheffield and his associates found a direct relation between strength of the consummatory response and speed of running. They argued that the *consummatory response per se* was the critical aspect of food reinforcement and not drive reduction, since saccharine, a non-nutritive substance, had a greater effect on running behavior than had dextrose, a nutritive substance.

Sheffield (1966) has argued that the basic mechanism for reinforcement is not drive reduction but rather drive induction. Reinforcing stimuli, he contended, act as incentives that produce a drive state in the organism. Food is a reinforcement because it has certain stimulus properties that set off the sense of taste or smell in a special way, thereby inducing a drive state. Since saccharine is sweet, it stimulates the organism in a certain way, and this tension-inducing process is the basic mechanism of reinforcement.

The results of a study by Miller and Kessen (1952), however, are problematic for a drive-induction notion of reinforcement. In this experiment, Miller and Kessen demonstrated that it was possible for organisms to acquire an instrumental response by having food bypass the mouth and enter the stomach directly, thus eliminating the consummatory response and the incentive (drive-inducing) properties involved in taste or smell. By feeding rats through stomach fistulas, Miller and Kessen were able to train them to run to a goal box at the end of one arm of a T-maze. Rats fed by mouth learned faster, but the stomach-fed rats also learned. These results suggest that the incentive properties of reinforcement are essentially non-learning motivational factors that affect performance, while the drive-reducing properties of reinforcement relate to learning.

Nevertheless, a great variety of stimulus conditions not easily reducible to biological needs and drive states have been shown to be reinforcing. Only by resorting to the concept of secondary reinforcement can a drive-reduction position account for reinforcement effects that involve no obvious connection with hunger, thirst, fear, or sexual needs. Brown's (1953) discussion of acquired drives represents perhaps the most satisfactory attempt to incorporate reinforcement from nonbiological stimuli such as money, praise, prestige, and so forth within a drive-reduction framework. Brown argued that a significant motivational component in behavior reinforced by these nonbiological stimuli is *anxiety in their absence.* Stimulus cues signifying a lack of affection, prestige, money, and so on acquire through learning a potentiality for arousing a state of uneasiness or anxiety having the functional properties of a drive. It is this learned anxiety, according to Brown, that energizes behavior directed toward securing affection, prestige, or money; and the reduction of anxiety realized by achieving these goals is reinforcing.

STIMULUS CHANGE.   A leading alternative to the drive-reduction position is one that stresses the role of stimulus change in reinforcement. According to this position, the basic mechanism of reinforcement is alteration in stimulus conditions. Such a position is related to Sheffield's (1966) drive-induction theory in that Sheffield assumes that stimulus *increase* can operate as a reinforcing state of affairs. But a stimulus-change notion can, in principle, account for all that a drive-reduction theory explains because drive reduction also involves stimulus change—that is, reinforcement is assumed to *decrease* the drive stimuli associated with need states (Hull, 1952).

Evidence in support of a stimulus-change theory dates to Butler's (1953) work on sensory deprivation in which monkeys were found to learn discrimination problems when reinforced by visual exploration. Subsequent research revealed that auditory stimulation was also reinforcing (Butler, 1957) and that these findings applied to human subjects under sensory deprivation conditions as well (Bexton, Heron, & Scott, 1954).

Montgomery (1954) showed that rats would learn to go to one arm of a Y-shaped maze when they were reinforced by having access in that arm to another maze which they could explore for a period of time. When the reinforcing maze was shifted to another arm, the rats reversed their preference, still choosing the arm that allowed them to explore an unfamiliar stimulus situation. Havelka (1956) found that rats would develop a preference for a route leading to a goal box where the location of food was varied from trial to trial rather than to a goal box where the food was always found in the same place. In another study, animals offered a choice between a fixed and a variable delay of reinforcement were found to prefer the variable delay (Pubols, 1952).

Numerous other experiments could be cited in support of the contention that stimulus variation has, at least under certain circumstances, a reinforcing effect on behavior. Harlow's research (Harlow, 1950; Harlow, Harlow, & Meyers, 1950) on manipulatory behavior supports the stimulus variation hypothesis, and Fiske and Maddi (1961) and Berlyne (1960) have advanced theoretical analyses to account for the effects of stimulus variation on motivation and learning.

If stimulus variation refers to stimulus reduction as well as increases in stimulation, the theory would seem to have considerable utility as a way of explaining the effects of reinforcement. The difficulty with such a position, however, is that it is too broad and all-inclusive. More information is needed on the conditions under which increases or decreases in stimulation are reinforcing. Not all increases in stimulation facilitate performance. If the stimulation is shock, increasing amounts lead to response inhibition. Nor do all decreases in stimulation produce learning. As Butler (1953) and others have shown, under certain conditions organisms can be motivated to avoid stimulus reduction. Hebb (1955) has written an interesting discussion of this issue in which he has argued that increases in level of arousal produce increasing alertness, interest, and motivation, up to an optimal point on the performance gradient beyond which further increases lead to emotional disturbances, anxiety, negative affect, and a deterioration in performance (Figure 2-5). Conceivably, increases in stimulation are reinforcing when the organism is operating at a low level of physiological arousal, whereas decreases in stimulation are reinforcing when the level of arousal is high.

More research is needed if this relationship is to be empirically demonstrated. Such an approach, however, does have the advantage of relating physiological events to behavioral measures of reinforcement. Whether a stimulus event is reinforcing may, to a considerable extent, be a function of the physiological state of the organism. It was a concern with the relationship between behavioral and physiological events, presumably, that led Hull to postulate his drive-reduction theory in the first place.

PHYSIOLOGICAL EXPLANATIONS OF REINFORCEMENT. A great deal of research has been carried out in an attempt to determine the

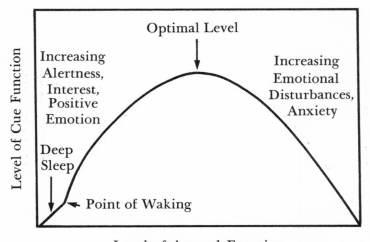

Figure 2-5. Hypothetical "inverted U-shaped" relationship between behavioral efficiency (level of cue functioning) and level of arousal (from Hebb, 1955).

physiological basis of reinforcement. The most dramatic research in this area has been the work of Olds and his associates on intracranial stimulation. In these studies (Olds, 1958, 1962; Olds & Milner, 1954), Olds showed that electrical stimulation of certain parts of the rat's brain would reinforce bar-pressing responses in a Skinner box. Electrodes were implanted in the septal and other areas of the brain and a circuit arranged so that, when the bar was pressed, stimulation would occur in that area of the brain. The rats learned quickly even though they were not deprived in any way and no other rewards were administered.

While there is considerable evidence that intracranial stimulation of the brain produces effects characteristic of reinforcement, there is also evidence that its effects are different from other types of reinforcers (Deese & Hulse, 1967). For example, *the course of experimental extinction* is quite different for responses reinforced by intracranial stimulation than for reinforcements of basic biological drives. A response reinforced by food usually extinguishes slowly under nonreinforcement conditions, whereas responses reinforced by electrical stimulation of the brain typically extinguish extremely rapidly (Olds, 1958). It may take only two or three nonreinforced responses to extinguish a response reinforced by intracranial stimulation even though the response had been given at a very high rate prior to extinction.

Another problem is that very little is known at the present time about how the effects of intracranial stimulation resemble what happens in the same neural structures when biological drives are reinforced. While electrical stimulation may activate "reinforcement centers," there is no evidence that the same mechanisms are involved in food, water, or other biological reinforcers. In fact, the evidence indicates that chemical and humoral factors control the neural centers for eating, satiety, and drinking (Cofer & Appley, 1964). Electrical stimulation may trigger these centers, but the normal process seems to depend more directly on *chemical* deficits or excesses in the blood stream.

Also disturbing is the finding that stimulation of particular points of the brain can have *both* rewarding and punishing effects (Bower & Miller, 1958; Roberts, 1958). Possibly there is some "leakage" of excitation when stimulation is intensified or prolonged (Berlyne, 1964). The demonstration by Brown and Cohen (1959) that stimulation of the same hypothalamic area produces approach learning in one experimental situation and avoidance learning in another is more difficult to explain.

This, of course, does not detract from the value of the research of Olds and others on the physiological bases of reinforcement. It merely suggests that possibly two distinct types of reinforcement are involved, one a consequence of electrical stimulation and the other dependent on drive-reduction or some other mechanism. Continued physiological research of this sort obviously is necessary if progress is to be made in understanding the mechanisms of reinforcement.

Reinforcement and Learning

We have previously discussed the work of Tolman and his associates on latent learning in the context of the learning-performance distinction. Besides making psychologists aware of the necessity—at least in principle—for such a distinction, their research raised the issue of whether learning can occur without reinforcement. Basically, this issue pitted proponents of a contiguity view of learning against those who favored a law-of-effect, reinforcement interpretation.

CONTIGUITY VERSUS REINFORCEMENT THEORY. Contiguity theorists argue that the mere juxtaposition of a stimulus and a response is sufficient for learning. Their model is the classical conditioning paradigm in which the temporal proximity of a conditioned stimulus and the unconditioned response produces the learning of a new response (the conditioned response). The same model is used for instrumental learning, although here the contiguity position must rely on hypothetical stimulus events, such as kinesthetic stimuli, the internal stimuli associated with hunger or thirst—which Guthrie (1959) referred to as maintaining stimuli—and so forth. These stimuli are sources of conditioned stimuli for the particular set of learned responses involved in instrumental behavior.

Reinforcement is not necessary for learning according to the contiguity position. Guthrie, a leading proponent of this position, held that learning is the result of stimulus-response contiguity and that reinforcement merely provides the end to stimulus-response sequences that the experimenter wants the organism to learn. Reinforcement takes the organism out of the situation and thereby prevents it from reacting in other ways to the stimuli (Guthrie, 1952, 1959). Thus food at the end of the maze prevents the rat from continuing to wander through the maze, unlearning what it had learned.

A similar position was advocated by Tolman, who viewed learning as the development of means-ends-readinesses. Strictly speaking, such learning does not require reinforcement and can occur in its absence. All that is required is the learning of "signs" that "signify" the goal. While his theory was more cognitive and less mechanistic, Tolman agreed with Guthrie that reinforcement was not necessary for learning, although it did help to strengthen ("confirm") learned behavior.

Eventually the evidence from latent learning studies and research on conditioning through contiguity were accepted as indicating the empirical validity of learning without reinforcement. Yet most psychologists were inclined to view learning without reinforcement as of little practical importance. Learning may take place through mere contiguity of stimulus and response, but effective learning requires reinforcement.

Recently, however, a strong case for the importance of contiguity learning has been made by Albert Bandura (1969), who, as we shall see in more detail in Chapter Four, argued that much social learning occurs through mere observation. A person need not be reinforced in order to learn—he can experience reinforcement vicariously through the mediation of social models. Bandura's theory has resurrected the reinforcement-contiguity controversy, since in his opinion most human social learning follows contiguity principles and is not controlled by immediate external reinforcement.

REINFORCEMENT AND THE LEARNING OF SOCIAL BEHAVIOR.   One of the problems in determining whether reinforcement operates in social settings is that the conditions of reinforcement may be relatively masked, so that it is difficult to specify precisely what reinforcements, if any, are operating. What often passes for learning without reinforcement may in fact involve reinforcing stimuli or learned discriminative stimuli that control the behaviors that result in learning. For example, a student who works for long hours with no apparent reinforcement contingent upon his behavior may actually receive reinforcement from less apparent sources. His friends and relatives reinforce his behavior, the knowledge he acquires is reinforced in examinations, and the degree that he will eventually receive is a source of future reinforcements. Studious behavior can also be viewed as *a class of responses* initially acquired through direct reinforcement and then generalized to other situations—even situations where no direct reinforcement is administered. The class of responses is maintained on an intermittent schedule of reinforcement, and individual members of the class can be acquired and maintained without reinforcement. As we shall see, reinforcement theorists have applied an analysis of this sort to explain observational imitative learning that occurs in the absence of reinforcement to the observer.

A contiguity theorist, such as Bandura, would explain the same behavior in somewhat different terms. He might argue, for example, that studious behavior is acquired initially through *vicarious reinforcement* rather than through any direct reinforcement to the individual. By observing social models the individual learns that certain consequences follow from studious behavior. Mere sensory contiguity is enough for learning to occur; no direct reinforcement is necessary. In this way people learn that certain outcomes follow certain forms of behavior, and these anticipated, long-term consequences come to guide their own actions. Proponents of such a position do not deny the importance of reinforcement in social behavior; they merely argue that a great deal of human activity is not controlled by immediate external reinforcement. Much behavior is guided by symbolic trial and error and the anticipation of social consequences. Furthermore, people typically set themselves certain standards of performance and respond to their own behavior in self-rewarding or self-punishing ways according to self-imposed demands. Such self-monitored reinforcement mechanisms may serve to alter or maintain behavior in the absence of external reinforcement.

External reinforcements themselves may be quite complex and difficult to specify in naturalistic settings. The possibility of acquired or conditioned reinforcers makes it difficult to determine the source of reinforcement in social behavior. In addition, the research of Berlyne (1960) and others (e.g., Fiske & Maddi, 1962) suggests that the characteristics of stimuli, such as their "novelty," "surprisingness," and "ambiguity" may have intrinsic reward value. It has even been proposed that cognitive consistency is reinforcing for human subjects (Festinger, 1957).

In spite of disagreement as to the role that reinforcement plays in social behavior, most theorists agree that reinforcement is centrally important in the determination of behavior. Even contiguity theorists, who argue for the possibility of response acquisition in the absence of reinforcement, admit its importance as a factor influencing the form that behavior takes. There is general agreement that reinforcement—whether external, vicarious, or self-administered—is a critical motivational determinant of behavior. The task for psychology then becomes one of ascertaining how reinforcement variables interact with other inputs to the motivational system in the control of behavior.

CHARACTERISTICS OF THE LEARNING-THEORY APPROACH

Having discussed some of the more intractable issues involved in a learning-theory approach, we shall conclude this chapter by specifying some of the defining characteristics of such an approach. We shall then turn to particular substantive areas where learning theory, as so specified, has been used as a framework for theory and research on social behavior.

First of all, a learning-theory approach stresses the *learned or acquired aspect of behavior*. This does not imply an a priori exclusion of the possibility of unlearned, species-specific types of behavior, but it does mean that such behaviors should be subjected to systematic study to determine what components, if any, are learned. The concept of instinctive or innate behavior patterns has been counterproductive in the history of psychology because it has not generated research hypotheses and because it has been put forth as an explanatory rather than a heuristic construct. A scientifically useful and valid explanation of so-called innate behaviors will be possible only after more is known about gene-behavior relationships and the way in which these behavior patterns are affected by environmental events. As Beach (1955) has observed, the more that is known about the factors that control such behaviors, the less need there is to talk about instincts.

This does not mean that all behavior is learned. In fact, gene-controlled behavior and species-specific, fixed-action patterns seem to be empirically valid phenomena, especially in subhuman organisms. Research in ethology and behavior genetics strongly indicates the importance of the interaction of hormonal, genetically coded, innate behavior patterns with external stimuli in determining behavior (Thorpe, 1961). On the other hand, it is widely recognized by ethologists that many complex action patterns that had previously been labeled instinctive include important learned components. Like so many of the classical controversies, the acquired-inherited debate now appears meaningless and naive.

A second characteristic of a learning-theory approach is an insistence on *systematic experimental study*. This is in part the result of a tradition of inquiry established by Thorndike and Pavlov and in part the result of the desire of individual investigators to make scientifically valid and meaningful inferences from their data. A sophisticated methodology has developed over the years, and experimental designs have become increasingly refined. The hope of researchers—whether their concern has been the general psychology of learning or the psychology of learning as applied to social behavior—has been to investigate systematically independent and dependent variables in an attempt to specify functional relationships.

The method is experimental because experimental procedures allow for the control of extraneous variables. One could observe the behavior of animals and men in natural settings, but mere observation typically does not permit one to make accurate causal inferences. If we see a child modeling his behavior on his older brother, we can infer that he has learned to imitate his brother, but we know nothing about the conditions that produce such learning. If, on the other hand, the conditions of reinforcement are manipulated, various models are used, and different behaviors are investigated under experimental conditions, more detailed and specific information can be obtained about the nature of imitative learning.

Intrinsic to the experimental method is reliance on *operational definitions*. This requires specification of the operations performed on the environment in defining independent and dependent variables. These operations can be performed by the experimenter or by the subject. In the study of imitative learning in children, for example, the experimenter can manipulate the conditions of reinforcement by giving the subject definite amounts of a certain type of candy upon performance of the appropriate response. The child's responses are defined as imitative when they are judged by observers to match in specific ways those performed by the model. Such defining operations are crucial if experimental results are to be replicated and thereby established as empirically valid and reliable.

Another characteristic of a learning-theory approach is *a commitment to the law of parsimony*. This has reference both to empirical data and theoretical constructs. If empirical data from two areas of research can be shown to involve the same functional relations, it is more parsimonious to incorporate the two phenomena under a single rubric. An example is research on backward learning (R-S learning) and incidental learning. As Underwood (1957) has indicated, both phenomena can be regarded as reflecting fundamentally the same processes if it can be shown that the variables that influence one in specified ways influence the other in comparable ways. Research on this issue (e.g., Cassem & Kausler, 1962) justifies the conclusion that both involve the same processes. Consequently, R-S or backward learning can be viewed as a variant of incidental learning, which in turn, as we have seen, is not intrinsically different from intentional learning (since both are affected in the same way by the same variables). Thus it can be argued that there is only one learning process and that the same principles apply to "backward," "incidental," and "intentional" learning. When this process of "operational identification" (Underwood, 1957, p. 205) is carried out, the number of independent behavioral phenomena can be held to a minimum.

The law of parsimony applies to theoretical concepts as well. Proponents of a learning-theory position have been reluctant to accept conceptual proliferation, especially if such proliferation involves the introduction of untested and untestable concepts. Ideally, the only concepts in the theory should be those linked to observable antecedent and consequent events. Such conceptual parsimony relates to another characteristic of the learning-theory position—namely, its *anti-subjective bias*.

Historically, the behaviorist revolt was directed against a type of psychology that left the door open to vague, unscientific, concepts. The rejection of the instinct concept was one example of this revolt. Instincts were rejected by the behaviorists because they were presented as explanatory concepts, thereby curtailing further investigation. The behaviorists also rejected introspective concepts because the admission of such concepts led to a similar dead end. "Mental" processes could not be measured and therefore should not be included in a scientific psychology.

As Mowrer (1960b) has noted, behaviorism was the antithesis to the original theme, or thesis, in American psychology—namely, subjectivism or introspectionism. Over the years dogmatic behaviorism has given way to methodological behaviorism or neo-behaviorism, which Mowrer saw to be the synthesis of these two extreme positions. The work of contemporary learning theorists on cognitive processes represents a realistic reconciliation of what early psychologists regarded as mutually exclusive concerns (Mowrer, 1960b).

When learning theorists do study cognitive phenomena, however, they are usually careful to define their constructs in behavioral terms. Internal, mediating ("cognitive" or "symbolic") processes are regarded as postulated concepts that are determined by specific antecedent conditions and that can be effectively indexed by behavioral events. They do not explain the data; they are presented as testable processes that have their own controlling conditions. By specifying the determinants of these mediating processes and the direct (or indirect) methods whereby they are to be assessed, learning theorists have attempted to formulate an objective and operational cognitive psychology. The assumption here is that the mediating process is under the control of the same laws as are overt behaviors. Thus mediating processes do not explain behavior; they themselves are explained in terms of the basic laws of classical conditioning or instrumental learning.

Another, related characteristic of a learning-theory approach is a reliance on *S-R terms* in discussing either overt or covert behavior. That is, the basic units of analysis for a learning-theory approach are stimuli and responses. Even when internal, mediating processes are postulated they are expressed in these terms. The mediating events in Osgood's theory of symbolic meaning (Osgood, Suci, & Tannenbaum, 1957), for example, are denoted as r_m–s_m, where the r and s are used to indicate that these concepts are, at least in principle, defined in terms of objective stimulus and response events.

Learning theory, as it is understood in this book, refers therefore to the traditional S-R approach and to the "liberalization" (Miller, 1959) of this approach—especially its treatment of cognitive and other mediating processes (e.g., Aronfreed, 1968; Berlyne, 1960; Kendler & Kendler, 1959; Osgood et al., 1957). Some contemporary theorists, in the tradition of Tolman, have proposed non-S-R theories of learning, where learning is viewed as a process by which information about the environment is acquired, stored, and categorized. The model employed is that of a computer in which information is sifted by means of an autonomous central process. Work by the advocates of this neo-cognitive, computer-oriented learning theory (e.g., Broadbent, 1958; Miller, Galanter, & Pribram, 1960), will not, however, directly concern us here.

A final characteristic of a learning-theory approach as understood in this book is its emphasis upon *the importance of reinforcement*. Although, as we have seen, learning may occur without reinforcement, any analysis of learning in social situations requires consideration of the reinforcement processes involved. Nevertheless learning theorists do not claim to be able to predict behavior solely from the organism's reinforcement history. Skinner (1953), for example, has explicitly called attention to a large number of determining conditions, such as genotype, diurnal cycle, hormonal state, sleep history, developmental level, and so forth—all of which affect the ultimate behavioral outcome.

A large body of experimental evidence, however, indicates that reinforcement plays a central role in determining behavior. This is one reason why learning theory, as here understood, is often called "reinforcement theory." This is not to imply that all learning theorists regard reinforcement as the *sine qua non* of behavior, but simply that a learning-theory position is one in which reinforcement is seen to have important consequences for performance.

One final point should be made. While a learning-theory approach has definite characteristics, some of these are more likely to be ideal than actual attributes. Thus, for example, we shall find that learning-theory attempts to deal with cognitive processes often involve the surreptitious inclusion of explanatory mechanisms not linked to operationally identified input and output variables. In other cases, the principle of parsimony is violated, and processes are introduced that can be shown to be reducible to more fundamental principles. Often operational definitions are not presented for critical concepts. This is especially likely to be true of the use of such concepts as stimulus, response, and reinforcement in explanations of complex social behavior. As we have seen in this chapter and and shall see in more detail in the chapters that follow, there are many empirically unanswered questions, some of which have to do with basic theoretical issues. It is the contention of its advocates, however, that a learning-theory approach provides a framework that will eventually lead to objective analysis of these issues.

3

The
Learning
of
Language

PERHAPS the most controversial application of learning-theory principles to social behavior concerns language acquisition. Psychologists with a learning-theory orientation have argued that language is obviously learned and, consequently, the same principles that apply to learning generally should be capable of explaining this particular form of social behavior. As we shall see in this chapter, a number of theories have been put forth to account for language acquisition in learning-theory terms. These theories, however, have not been without their critics.

On the one hand, criticism has come from within psychology. Many psychologists, most of them sharing the learning theorist's behavioral orientation, feel that too little is known about language acquisition at the present time to permit theoretical analysis. Instead of plunging into theory, psychology should investigate the simpler processes involved in verbal behavior. These psychologists have accordingly concerned themselves with such empirical problems as stimulus and response similarity, serial effects in learning, mediating processes, and the variables that affect storage and retrieval. Such research reflects the conviction of a large number of psychologists that advances will be made only through the time-consuming process of basic research. Careful experimentation, they contend, is necessary if we are to have more than a pseudo-understanding of what is involved in verbal behavior.

A different criticism of learning-theory explanations of language acquisition is advanced by linguists. Here learning theory is attacked not simply on methodological grounds, but on theoretical grounds as well. Many linguists are convinced that the intricacies of language acquisition defy analysis along traditional S-R, learning-theory lines. They contend that an entirely different model is needed to explain the unique aspects of language learning. The controversy between linguists and advocates of a learning-theory position will be treated in this chapter. Elsewhere the interested reader will find further discussions of these topics as well as reviews of research on verbal behavior (e.g., Dixon & Horton, 1968; Goulet, 1968; Kausler, 1966; Keppel, 1968).

LEARNING-THEORY APPROACHES
TO LANGUAGE

Skinner's book, *Verbal behavior* (1957), is the classical theoretical analysis of language in learning-theory terms. The book makes no direct reference to experimental work and is an unabashed extrapolation from laboratory research with nonverbal organisms. Nevertheless Skinner attempted to come to grips with the complexities of linguistic behavior and to provide at least the first approximation of a behavioristic theory of language. Other learning-theory approaches also exist, and we shall discuss several of the more important of these as well.

Skinner

Skinner's thesis is that verbal behavior can be understood in terms of present ongoing external stimulation and the reinforcement history of the organism. Thus the speaker emits a verbal response because of conditions that are objective and determinable, not because of subjective "ideas" or "mental processes." Experimental studies under controlled laboratory conditions have yielded a great deal of objective information about the basic processes of learning, Skinner contended. One may now proceed in the functional analysis of verbal behavior—that is, in the identification of the variables that control verbal responses and in the specification of how these variables interact to determine a particular verbal response.

BASIC CONCEPTS.   For Skinner, the basic concepts involved in the scientific analysis of language were stimulus, response, and reinforcement. It was his view that the general principles uncovered in laboratory experimentation provide the basis for understanding the complexities of verbal behavior. "Understanding" in this context means more than the use of a consistent theoretical vocabulary to describe specific instances of verbal behavior. Skinner hoped to achieve a level of understanding such that he would be able to predict the occurrence of particular verbal responses and eventually control these responses by altering the conditions under which they occurred.

Skinner began with the *response unit,* defined as an emitted operant, a response of identifiable form functionally related to one or more independent variables. For all practical purposes "response" and "operant" are interchangeable, although Skinner regarded the term operant as more general, referring to a kind of behavior rather than an instance of that behavior. The size of the response unit depends upon its functional unity as a verbal operant. A single speech sound may be under independent control of a manipulable variable, as may a rather large segment of verbal behavior, even whole sentences. The verbal repertoire of an individual refers to responses of various forms that appear in his behavior from time to time in relation to identifiable conditions. It describes his potential verbal behavior.

The main concern of the psychologist dealing with language,

Skinner argued, is with the probability of a speaker emitting a particular verbal response. The probability or "strength" of a verbal operant can be indexed by its energy-level, its speed, and its repetitiousness. Energy-level refers to the intensity of response. Skinner's example was the difference between an energetic and prolonged "No!" when compared to a timid, brief "No." In the first case, the intensity of the response suggests a strong tendency to respond that will not easily be overcome by competing forces. In the second case, the operant was assumed to be only weakly connected to the independent variables. The speed of the response refers either to how quickly the successive parts of a sample of verbal behavior follow one another or to how quickly the response itself is emitted after the occasion for it has arisen. Repetition also indicates relative strength; for example, "Yes, yes, yes," can be assumed to be a stronger operant than a single "Yes." Skinner recognized the limitations of these measures of response strength, but he felt that in practice such measures were useful since the speaker's listeners do make inferences about his behavior from the energy, speed, and repetitiveness of his verbal responses.

The emission of a response and its overall frequency can also be taken to indicate the strength of the behavior for the individual. Skinner gave the example of a scientist who continues to talk shop during an exciting football game. Such behavior shows that the verbal response is extremely strong in the speaker's repertoire. Similarly, a speaker who frequently uses first-person-singular pronouns can be assumed to use such pronouns frequently in the future.

The task of the investigator is to specify exhaustively the *stimulus conditions* under which verbal responses are emitted. A stimulus controls a response in the sense that the presence of the stimulus increases the probability of the response. The verbal response "red," for example, is controlled by the property "redness." A single property of the situation or a particular type of situation may control the speaker's response. Stimulus control, however, is never perfect. When the correspondence with a stimulating situation is sharply maintained, the response is said to be "objective," "valid," or "accurate." When, on the other hand, the circumstances are such as to distort the relationship between the stimulus conditions and the verbal response, the response is said to be "subjective," "prejudiced," or "biased." The possibility of such distortion contributes to the problem of determining precisely what stimulus conditions control an emitted verbal response.

Skinner noted that it is difficult, if not impossible, to determine the stimuli that evoke specific verbal responses in a young child. Such responses are spontaneous in the first instance and are not elicited by known stimulus events. Once such responses occur and have been reinforced, however, prior stimuli become important because they may serve as discriminative stimuli. That is, in the presence of a given stimulus, a given response may characteristically be followed by reinforcement. When such a contingency prevails, the organism does not simply learn the response that produces reinforcement, it also learns to emit that response in the presence of the prior stimulus. Thus the prior stimulus becomes a discriminative stimulus that sets the occasion for reinforcement.

Any operant, verbal or otherwise, acquires and maintains its strength when followed by the event called *reinforcement*. The parent teaches the child to talk by reinforcing its verbal behavior. In the initial stages, this may involve a rather laborious process of successive approximations, but subsequently other less tedious procedures for evoking the response become possible. Once the response is established, its strength is maintained by the frequency of reinforcement administered for that behavior by the verbal community. When reinforcement is totally absent, a previously reinforced response will extinguish.

Skinner pointed out that it is possible for changes to occur in the reinforcement practices of the community as a whole. If such changes take place over a long period of time, mutations occur in the language itself. That is, if the verbal community of one generation consistently reinforces a slight deviation from the previously accepted practice, the deviation will become standard. Further deviations may be tolerated by subsequent generations. Eventually the language may be quite different, as a comparison of ancient Greek with modern Greek would indicate.

Much of the reinforcement involved in verbal behavior is technically "generalized" reinforcement. Any stimulus in Skinner's system can become reinforcing by repeated association with an already reinforcing stimulus. In such cases the previously neutral stimulus is called a secondary reinforcer. Those secondary reinforcers that are associated with a variety of different primary reinforcers are called generalized reinforcers. They include such stimuli as money, approval, praise, and so forth.

Verbal stimuli can be reinforcing once they have been associated with reinforcing events. Thus the word "right" can become a secondary reinforcer if it is repeatedly associated with reinforced behavior. In fact, Skinner argued that such verbal stimuli make it possible for self-reinforcement to occur. The young child who has learned that "right" is a secondary reinforcer may use it to reinforce his own behavior, including exploratory verbal behavior.

CONTROLLING VARIABLES.   The emission of verbal responses is controlled discriminatively by various stimuli, and Skinner classified operants in terms of their "functional" relation to these stimuli and other responses. A *mand,* like "Bread, please," was defined as "a verbal operant in which the response is reinforced by a characteristic sequence and is therefore under the functional control of relevant conditions of deprivation or aversive stimulation" (Skinner, 1957, pp. 35–36). To identify the verbal operant as a mand, one must know the kind of variables of which the response is a function. Certain responses, because of their formal properties (imperative, subjunctive, or optative mood; also interrogatives, interjections, vocatives), are very probably mands. Other responses are mands, not so much because of their formal properties, as because of the contingencies of reinforcement maintained by the listener or by the verbal community. A child, for example, may learn to use a long *m* sound as a sign that he wants something. After repeated use, the child learns that adults will, upon hearing the sound, come to find out what he wants and will provide the appropriate reinforcements. Consequently, the sound is learned as a means of obtaining reinforcement.

Although mands are functions of states of deprivation (or aversive stimulation), the specific relation between responses and reinforcement that defines a mand does not involve a specific prior stimulus. In other cases, verbal behavior comes much more under the control of stimuli, some of which are verbal stimuli. In *echoic behavior,* for instance, verbal stimuli generate responses involving a sound-pattern similar to those of the stimuli. Echoic behavior is reinforced when it reinstates the stimulus and permits the speaker to react to it in other ways, as, for example, repeating directions after they are given. In *textual behavior* orthographic stimuli control the verbal operants of the speaker. The stimuli in this case are visual or tactile (as in Braille), while the response is produced through the appropriate vocal behavior. Thus, the child learning to read must respond in one modality to stimuli presented in another. In *intraverbal behavior* antecedent vocalizations become the controlling conditions for subsequent vocalizations. Such is the case when a verbal response (differing from the verbal stimuli) operates sequentially to provide the stimulus for another response in a series. Recitation of the alphabet requires a series of such intraverbal responses, as does counting, multiplying, and reproducing mathematical tables.

In echoic, textual, and intraverbal operants, the prior stimulus is verbal. It is also possible for the controlling stimuli to be nonverbal, to include, in fact, the whole of the physical environment—that is, the world of things and events that verbal behavior is "about." Skinner called a verbal operant concerning this world of things and events a *tact,* which he defined as "a verbal operant in which a response of given form is evoked (or at least strengthened) by a particular object or event or property of an object or event" (1957, pp. 81–82). Tacts are the most important of the verbal operants because of the unique control exerted by the prior stimulus. That is, in the tact the conditions relating to any specific deprivation or aversive stimulation are far less important than the unique relation to a discriminative stimulus. The tact is learned through the consistent reinforcement of a response in the presence of a particular controlling stimulus. The response "specifies" the given stimulus property.

Because, however, stimulus control is not always perfectly precise and because a novel stimulus may contain one feature in common with a stimulus previously reinforced, it becomes possible for *extended tacts* to develop in new situations on the basic of common stimulus elements. In generic extension (e.g., saying "chair" to a new instance), the property on which generalization depends is that upon which reinforcement by the verbal community is contingent. In metaphorical extension (e.g., saying "The child is bright as a dollar"), control is exercised by properties of the stimulus that are present at reinforcement but do not enter into the contingency respected by the verbal community. In fact, when a metaphoric response is consistently reinforced, it ceases to be primarily a metaphor. The response "leg" evoked by the leg of a table probably only rarely represents an instance of metaphorical extension.

Skinner then turned to the process of *abstraction,* which he regarded as a result of consistent reinforcement applied by the verbal community for responses in the presence of the chosen stimulus property, and the failure to reinforce or punishment of responses evoked by unspecified properties. To teach a child the response "red," it is necessary to present a red object as well as a verbal occasion on which color responses are especially reinforced (for example, by saying, "Tell me what color this is"). Subsequently other red objects should be presented and the child rewarded for responding to the property of color.

Skinner also dealt in this context with verbal behavior under the control of private stimuli. These tacts include a large and important class of operants including such responses as "I am hungry," "I am depressed," "It is beautiful," as well as responses referring to past, potential, or future events or behavior. Control in such instances cannot be made in terms of objective stimulus conditions. Instead, such responses are controlled by "events within the speaker himself" (Skinner, 1957, p. 143).

Most verbal responses occur in the presence of an audience. The speaker emits responses that he has learned are appropriate to the audience as well as descriptive of the object. In some instances the speaker may be responding to several audiences—one of which may be the speaker himself. Such *multiple causation* gives some indication of the complexity of verbal behavior and of the problems involved in determining controlling variables with scientific precision.

GRAMMAR AND SYNTAX.   To deal with the question of grammar and syntax, Skinner introduced another class of operants, the *autoclitic*. Some autoclitics describe the state or the strength of a response (e.g., "I guess," "I believe," "I surmise"). Other autoclitics describe the type or manner of a response (e.g., "I recall," "I demand," "I hesitate to say"). Still others are intended to affect the speaker in some way (e.g., "You might say," "I hope you won't think"). Autoclitics are also involved in negation, qualification, quantification, and—of central interest here—in the construction of sentences.

Skinner argued that, when a speaker is composing a sentence, he starts with lexical operants as the raw material and then selects the appropriate autoclitic framework. Skinner gave the example of the "raw" responses: "rent," "boat," "leak," and "Sam." Once the proper autoclitic framework is provided, the gramatically correct sentence "Sam rented a leaky boat" becomes possible. In this way grammar and syntax are applied to latent material.

Until the responses evoked by the situation are dealt with autoclitically, they are essentially nongrammatical. The sentence involves the imposition of a set of responses (nouns, verbs, adjectives) on a skeletal framework. Autoclitics qualify the responses, express re-

Table 3-1

A Summary of Major Verbal Operants in Skinner's System

OPERANT	PRIOR STIMULUS	CHARACTERISTIC
mand	no specific prior stimulus; function of deprivation or aversive stimuli	response to a deprivation condition as means to acquire reinforcement
echoic	vocalizations of other speakers	reproduction of sound pattern
textual	orthographic verbal stimuli	reproduction of visual or tactile verbal stimuli
intraverbal	vocalizations of speaker himself	recitation
tact	nonverbal physical environment	verbal operant concerning world of things and events
autoclitic	no specific prior stimulus; function of reinforcement from verbal community	qualify responses, expresses relations, provide grammatical framework

lations between them, and give words their appropriate grammatical tags. The process whereby large segments of verbal behavior are manipulated and organized into complex arrangements was called *composition*.

Autoclitics are learned like other operants. The verbal community typically reinforces complete, grammatical sentences and punishes broken or incorrect utterances. The child learns that certain sequences of words are acceptable in English while others are not. Skinner gave several examples of weak autoclitic behavior on the part of a two-and-a-half-year-old girl: "When you untry to do it" for "When you try to undo it," "Why did you put milk and coffee to the same gether" for ". . . milk and coffee together," and so forth. Eventually most of these weaknesses are outgrown through interaction with the verbal community.

Skinner noted that once verbal responses are made and feedback is received from the audience, it is possible for the speaker to edit his verbal behavior through the appropriate use of autoclitics. Perhaps even more important, the speaker can edit his utterances before he emits them. That is, Skinner recognized the possibility for subvocal behavior to be revoked before it has been expressed audibly. The speaker, he argued, frequently tests his behavior on himself before offering it to other listeners. "Much of the self-stimulation required in the autoclitic description and composition of verbal behavior seems to occur prior to even subaudible emission" (Skinner, 1957, p. 371). The overt response itself occurs when the autoclitics involved in grammatical tagging and rhetorical ordering have been reinforced to the extent that their probability of occurrence is fairly great. Otherwise, (with adults at least) the response will be suppressed for fear of punishment from the audience.

In the final chapter of his book, Skinner turned to the question of *thinking*. He argued that thinking can be identified with behavior that automatically affects the behaving subject and is reinforced because it does so. That is, thinking is a type of (covert) verbal behavior where the speaker is his own listener. Such behavior may have reinforcing consequences and, if so, becomes strengthened. Daydreams and verbal fantasies, for example, permit the individual to enjoy the covert expression of sentiments that would be punished in their overt form. Other covert verbal behavior may have practical consequences that make it reinforcing. Thus it is often automatically reinforcing to calculate the odds at a poker game rather than to play according to accidental reinforcements. Similarly, covert verbal behavior is a help in complex decision-making processes. The point is that thought is behavior and, like all behavior, is under the control of stimulus variables. As such, Skinner argued, thought is a topic that can be effectively analyzed by a science of behavior.

Other Learning-Theory Approaches to Language

Skinner's approach to language is important, if for no other reason, because of the controversy it has evoked. It is the major learning-theory approach to language because it is the most sweeping and most ambitious. However, other learning theorists have also attempted to work out theories of language. Their formulations, while not so exhaustive, depart in significant respects from the theoretical point of view advocated by Skinner.

MILLER AND DOLLARD.   One of the earliest attempts to deal with language in learning-theory terms was by Miller and Dollard (1941), who took the position that language learning follows the same principles as are involved in the acquisition of any other form of social behavior. That is, language is learned because a response initially performed under conditions of deprivation (drive) is rewarded. They gave the example of a mother who was worried about her child's failure to learn to talk. Since she responded to her child's needs on the basis of his gestures, she was instructed to extinguish this behavior by pretending not to understand the gestures. When the child found that the use of gestures was ineffective, his use of speech was greatly increased.

The first vocal behavior of the child is crying. Crying is an innate response to especially strong stimuli, such as cold, hunger, or pain. At the same time the child is practicing his own crying responses, he is learning to respond to the voices of others. Adults care for him and attend to his needs; when they do so their verbal behavior takes on reward value. Words become *cues,* and the child himself learns to make the response of uttering words (presumably because the rewards for crying generalize to the vocalizations involved in speaking). The process whereby the child learns what vocal sounds are appropriate was seen by Miller and Dollard to involve imitative learning. That is, the child initially learns to imitate simple sound units such as "da" and "dee." Once the component units have been mastered, the teacher can elicit, in specific situations, combinations of responses. The response "daddy" has a low initial probability of occurring in the father's presence, but its probability is increased if the units have been learned separately and then combined imitatively.

The mechanism of reward gradually differentiates language from its original matrix of inappropriate and incorrect overt responses. The child receives meticulous training in prouncing words and in connecting words to other words. Miller and Dollard regarded a *sentence* as a sequence of stimulus-producing responses and *grammar* as habits governing the manner in which learned responses, words, and phrases are combined. The child is corrected thousands of times for his grammatical mistakes and, through trial and error, gradually learns to combine words into larger patterns corresponding to the complex relationships and events he observes in the environment around him.

Miller and Dollard admitted that little was known about the

system of habits involved in combining words into grammatically correct sentences. In this respect, as in others, their analysis was more suggestive than definitive. They merely attempted to sketch the outline of a behavior-theory approach to language. The details of the picture were left for future investigators.

Subsequently, Dollard and Miller (1950) discussed the notion of response generalization and transfer through *labeling*. Verbal labeling allows for considerable economy in behavior. Calling a person an "enemy" is a relatively simple response that can be learned quickly. This label can then be used to control behavior. Certain behavior toward one's enemies is appropriate in formal settings while other behavior is called for in competitive situations. One learns to respond differently when the enemy has the advantage as opposed to when he is at a disadvantage. To learn each of these behavior patterns separately would be extremely laborious (depending on how many enemies one has); it is more economical to learn one verbal response that mediates behavior toward enemies in all contexts.

Dollard and Miller assumed that language and other cue-producing responses play a central role in higher mental processes. Here again their analysis was mainly exploratory. They recognized the difficulty of speaking of the role of language simply in terms of cue-producing responses, since lower organisms are capable of cue-producing responses or "pure stimulus acts." Obviously, "the organism must possess certain capacities the exact nature of which is still unknown" (1950, p. 101) before cue-producing responses can begin to play an essential role in higher mental processes.

MOWRER.   Mowrer's theory of sign learning leads to a somewhat different analysis of language acquisition than that proposed by Miller and Dollard. Mowrer (1960b) placed considerably more emphasis on the role of secondary reinforcement in his system. Words and other human sounds are made by infants in the first instance because they have been associated with relief and other satisfactions. Eventually, however, words take on secondary reinforcement properties and hearing words becomes a source of secondary reinforcement. The child himself utters words and is reinforced in proportion to the extent to which the words correspond to those made by parents and others.

According to Mowrer (1954), words may function either as signals or as symbols. A word is a *signal* (natural sign) when it is followed by its significate, as smoke is a signal of fire. A word is a *symbol* (artificial sign) when it is not followed by its significate. Thus one may say "smoke" and transmit a meaning to another person without smoke (or fire) being physically present. Mowrer (1960b) also noted that the motivation behind the usage is different. When a thirsty child says, "Water, water," he is using a sign. When he is not thirsty but says to another child, "Water is in the pitcher," he is using a symbol; his motive is separated or abstracted from the referent itself.

Words acquire *meaning* in Mowrer's system by being associated with, or occurring within the context of, actual objects. Thus the word "Tom" acquires its meaning by the association of the word with the actual person. Through a process of conditioning the word "Tom" comes to denote or mean the person Tom. In Mowrer's paradigm, the word "Tom" elicits a label R_T of which r_T is a component. As a result of the paired presentation of the word "Tom" with the person Tom, the component response r_T is shifted from Tom-as-a-person to "Tom"-as-a-word (name). The process is viewed as analogous to that whereby a rat, after having received shock, associates a fractional component (fear) of the total response given (involving pain, fear, and physical agitation) to the stimuli that serve as signals or signs of shock. That is, just as fear is "detached" from the total response and is produced in response to conditioned stimuli, so the r_T component is "detached" and produced in response to the conditioned stimulus, "Tom" (Figure 3-1).

Mowrer (1954, 1960b) has argued that language in its true and highest form occurs only when a subject and predicate are present. His analysis, therefore, is largely concerned with *sentences.* A sentence "works" psychologically because signs call up or "arouse" meaning. When John tells Charles that "Tom is a thief," he assumes that the signs "Tom" and "thief" already have meaning for Charles. "Thief" is in Mowrer's terms "a sort of 'unconditioned stimulus' " that calls forth an internal reaction that can be expressed as "a person who cannot be trusted" or "a person who steals things." On the basis of

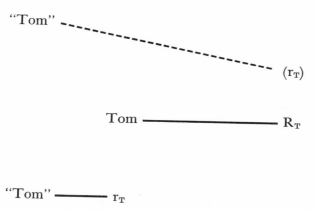

Figure 3-1. Schematic representation of the process whereby the word "Tom" is conditioned to the "detached" component (r_T) of the total response (R_T) to the physical person Tom, thereby coming to mean or denote the person Tom (Mowrer, 1954).

conditioning, some of the reaction involved in the sign "thief" is thus shifted to the sign "Tom" so that Charles, assuming he believed what John said, would be expected to respond to the word "Tom" somewhat as he had previously responded to the word "thief."

In analyzing this process, Mowrer proposed that the word "thief" takes on its meaning through first-order conditioning. Some part of the total reaction elicited by real thieves is shifted to the word "thief." The sentence, "Tom is a thief," is an instance of second-order conditioning. In this case, a part of this same reaction, with some attenuation or weakening, is further shifted to the word "Tom." When Tom-the-person is subsequently encountered by Charles, Tom will elicit in Charles the r_T reaction (to "Tom") which will in turn elicit the r_t reaction (to "thief"). In this process the r_T reaction is viewed as a *representational mediating response* (Figure 3-2).

The notion of a mediating response allowed Mowrer to account for what he called "semantic generalization." By positing a mediating response in the form of a reaction produced by the subject of a sentence and by assuming that the reaction produced by the predicate of a sentence gets conditioned to this mediating response, Mowrer was able to explain how meaning is transferred or generalized from one sign to another. The sentence is simply a device for producing associative shifting or conditioning. The predicate reaction generalizes to the thing, person, or event that the subject sign represents.

According to Mowrer, therefore, the communicative act involves a process whereby a part of the reaction produced by one person, thing, or event gets transferred to or "rubbed off on" some other person, thing, or event. Signs are devices for transferring some of the "reaction potential" (meaning) of one thing to another thing. By using language, people are able to react, without direct experience,

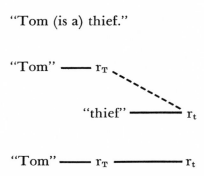

Figure 3-2. Schematic representation of the process whereby the reaction (r_t) to the sign "thief" is shifted to the sign "Tom" through the mediation of the reaction to Tom (r_T) (Mowrer, 1954).

to new realities. This gives language its power but also points to its limitations, because a person's reactions always depend on his previous conditioning experience.

OSGOOD.   Osgood's theory, like Mowrer's, is a representational mediation theory. The basic paradigm is very similar. According to Osgood (Osgood, Suci, & Tannenbaum, 1957; Osgood, 1963), a sign [S], such as a word, when continguous with a significate, S, or stimulus pattern that regularly and reliably produces a total behavioral response, R_T, acquires an increment of association with some portion of that total behavior. This is diagramatically represented in Figure 3-3. The solid arrows represent learned (or possibly reflexive in the case of $S \rightarrow R_T$) eliciting relations. The dashed lines represent dependency relations that are not acquired by experience. Thus the R_T-r_m relation is dependent upon the contiguous association of the significate, S, with the sign, [S], and the $r_m \rightarrow s_m$ dependency follows from automatic sensory-motor feedback. Capitalized symbols refer to overt observables, lower-case to unobservables. R_X represents the mediated response to the sign, which may be either linguistic or nonlinguistic.

The process of mediation takes place in two stages. The first of these is the stage of *decoding* ([S] $\rightarrow r_m$). This involves the association of the sign, [S], with the representational mediator, r_m. The second stage is the stage of *encoding* ($s_m \rightarrow R_X$) during which the mediational self-stimulation, s_m, is associated with the mediated response to the sign, R_X, which presumably is an explicit, physical, and observable event. Both stages are conceptualized as involving fundamental behavior-theory principles. The first stage, whereby the representational mediator, r_m, becomes established, follows the principles of classical conditioning. A fractional component of the total response, R_T, is evoked by pairing the sign, [S], with the significate, S. The second stage, whereby the mediational self-stimulation, s_m, is associated with the mediated response to the sign, R_X, follows the principles of instrumental conditioning. The characteristic stimulus effects, s_m, produced

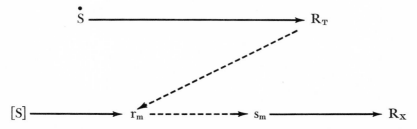

Figure 3-3. Osgood's basic model of the representational mediation process (from Osgood, 1963).

by r_m, act as cues for instrumental behavior—that is, for responding appropriately, linguistically or non-linguistically, to the S, or thing signified.

According to Osgood (1968), such a representational mediation theory is necessary to get around some of the intuitively unsatisfying assumptions of a single-stage theory such as Skinner's (1957). Skinner, for example, held that learning the name of an object (tacting) is a separate operant from learning to ask for it (manding). It follows that a child who has learned to name objects will not be able to ask for them until he has, in an independent single-stage process, learned the appropriate operant response. In Osgood's theory, however, learning the name of objects via classical conditioning and making instrumental responses to them are both part of the same (two-stage) process. Similarly, Skinner held that we must subvocally mimic a speaker in order to comprehend what he says (since thought is covert verbal behavior). In Osgood's theory, comprehension can be part of the second or instrumental stage—some listeners, for example, may be more successful than others in comprehending a complex philosophical argument even though the individual words used by the speaker are equally familiar to all.

It should be noted that the $r_m \rightarrow s_m$ mechanism in Osgood's theory is an unobservable event. Osgood made no assumptions as to the physical nature of these mediators. They might consist of minute but nonobservable reactions of the peripheral system, along with feedback; or they might, as Osgood was inclined to believe, consist of purely central (cortical) representations of what were originally peripheral events. The theory, at any rate, does not depend on the resolution of this issue.

Osgood and his associates (Osgood, Suci, & Tannenbaum, 1957) devised the *semantic differential scale* to index the representational mediation process. This scale will be more fully discussed in Chapter Five in connection with investigations of attitudes, which were conceptualized by Osgood and his associates as part of the semantic structure of the individual. In essence, the semantic differential scale was intended to provide an operational index of the meaning of words to individual subjects. The scale locates concepts in "semantic space" and has been widely used in psychological research to quantify "meaning."

Osgood (1963) criticized Mowrer's simple conditioning model of the sentence for not explaining how we understand a sentence such as "Tom is a thief" without believing it, and for not taking grammatical structure into account—simple conditioning in the sentence, "Tom is a perfect idiot," should lead to a cancellation of the "Tom is perfect" and "Tom is an idiot" effects. Further analysis was required, Osgood felt, to deal satisfactorily with belief and grammar.

Like Mowrer, Osgood assumed that sentences "interpret" their subject. But Osgood did not feel that a conditioning model could adequately account for the cognitive resolution of the sentence as a whole. To deal with the complexities of belief and grammar, understanding the sentence should be seen as involving a series of phrase-resolving *cognitive interactions* terminating in a final resolution. In this way the subject of the sentence is given a uniquely modified meaning.

The first cognitive interaction concerns *belief*. The sentence "Tom is a thief" elicits a different belief response in Tom's mother than it does in the policeman who apprehended him. Osgood discussed the issue of belief in terms of his Congruity Hypothesis (Osgood & Tannenbaum, 1955). In general, the assumption is that whenever two signs are related by an assertion ("Tom" and "thief" by "is"), the mediating reaction characteristic of one shifts toward congruence with that characteristic of the other—the magnitude of the shift being inversely proportional to the intensity of the interacting reactions. Thus the assertion, "Tom is a thief," is congruous for the policeman, but not for Tom's mother. Tom's mother will either attach a new meaning to "Tom" or to "thief" or refuse to believe the assertion altogether.

A second cognitive interaction concerns *grammar*. Osgood proposed a process of cognitive resolution whereby a sentence is broken down into its kernel assertions. Thus the sentence, "The clever young thief was severely sentenced by a rather grim-faced judge," can be broken down into the kernel assertions:

        [The   thief] [was] [clever]
        [The   thief] [was] [young]
        [The judge] [was] [rather grim-faced]
        [The judge] [sentenced severely] [the thief]

The within-bracket phrases (e.g., "rather grim-faced") follow different rules for cognitive interaction than do the between-bracket phrases (e.g., "the thief was clever"). Within-bracket phrases involve quantifying operations weakening or intensifying the meaning of the phrase, whereas between-bracket phrases involve qualifying operations modifying the meaning of the phrase in a manner predictable from the Congruity Hypothesis. Osgood assumed that within-brackets (quantifying) phrases are resolved prior to between-bracket (qualifying) phrases. Thus in the sentence, "Tom is a perfect idiot," the phrase "perfect idiot" is resolved first and then applied to the subject. Such grammatical resolutions allow his system to avoid the pitfalls of Mowrer's simple conditioning model.

Further aspects of the Osgood model need not concern us here. It should be noted, however, that Osgood did not feel that S-R theory is entirely sufficient to deal with the complexities of language. To incorporate the essential characteristics of Gestalt theory of perceptual organization (involved in the development of linguistic perceptual units) and the essential characteristics of motor skills (involved in the development of linguistic response units, like the syllable), Osgood added an *integration stage,* including S-S and R-R learning, to both the decoding and encoding processes. Motivation and reinforcement have nothing to do with the formation of S-S (pairing of stimulus events) or R-R (pairing of response events) integrations. Osgood's theory, then, is actually a three-stage, mediation-integration model, yet he confessed that he was "by no means convinced that even this 'monster' is sufficiently complex to handle language behavior" (1963, p. 741).

STAATS.   Like Mowrer and Osgood, Staats (1961, 1968) has described word meaning as an implicit response. In Staats' theory a word is a conditioned stimulus and a meaning is a conditioned response. The word (CS) comes to elicit this conditioned response by being paired with a stimulus object (UCS) that already elicits the response. The experimental paradigm for this kind of learning involves the conditioning of evaluative meaning to verbal stimuli. Thus in one study (Staats & Crawford, 1962) the word "large" was paired as a conditioned stimulus with aversive stimuli (either shock or loud noise). Subjects were to learn a list of words and received the aversive stimuli nine out of the fourteen times that "large" appeared in the list. After this treatment, it was found that "large" had acquired a negative evaluative meaning. That is, when compared to a control group, the subjects rated the meaning of the CS-word more towards the unpleasant end of a seven-point pleasant-unpleasant scale. At the same time, the subject's galvanic skin response (GSR) to the CS-word was also recorded. It was found that the conditioning of the GSR was positively correlated with the extent of the conditioning of the meaning of the CS-word, supporting Staats' contention that the same processes of conditioning are involved in the establishment of meaning as are involved in the establishment of more objective physiological reactions.

Emotional word meanings, once established, may *generalize* from word to word. That is, Staats argued, a child learns through first-order conditioning to associate "bad" with unpleasant consequences. The child has received a variety of aversive stimuli in contiguity with this word. Subsequently, when the child encounters the word "evil" and is told by his parents that evil means bad, the word "bad" serves as an UCS and the word "evil" as a CS. Through conditioning the new word "evil" comes to elicit the same emotional meaning response as the word "bad." This process is called second-order conditioning—it is not necessary for the word "evil" ever to have been paired with an unlearned aversive stimulus.

A similar process occurs in the sentence. For example, the word "hurt" takes on emotional meaning by being paired with various aversive stimuli. When the child is told, "That is dangerous. You will get hurt," the word "dangerous" takes on the evaluative meaning associated with the word "hurt" by a second-order conditioning process. When the child hears that "Motorcycles are dangerous," the meaning response of "dangerous" becomes attached to "motorcycles" by a similar higher-order conditioning process.

Because much of language learning involves higher-order conditioning of this nature, it is not necessary for humans to have direct contact with environmental situations and problems. This has its disadvantages as well as its advantages. Staats (1968) mentioned the example of the word "Negro" as learned by a child in the southern part of the United States. If "Negro" is systematically paired with words that elicit a negative response such as "poor," "dirty," "stupid," "immoral," Negro people themselves will elicit a negative response even though the child has never had direct contact with them.

In discussing Staats' theory to this point, we have spoken of one aspect of meaning only—namely, the evaluative or emotional aspect. As we shall see in Chapter Five, this aspect of meaning is closely related to the attitudinal dimension. Thus the meaning of "Negro" in the preceding example involves a strong evaluative (attitudinal) component. Staats does, however, concern himself with the denotative aspect of meaning as well.

The basis for *denotative meaning* in Staats' (1968) system is, once again, classical conditioning. Words are paired repeatedly with certain types of stimuli—for example, the word "blue" is systematically paired with blue light, and "squeak" is systematically paired with a certain type of auditory stimulation. Furthermore, Staats suggested that part of the sensory response elicited by a sensory stimulus can be conditioned to a neutral stimulus with which it is paired. When this occurs, the new stimulus comes to elicit the conditioned (implicit) part of the sensory response—namely, an image. Many words are stimuli that in this manner come to elicit conditioned sensory responses (images) in the individual.

To test the image hypothesis for denotative meaning Staats employed the same basic experimental paradigm he had used to study the conditioning of emotional meaning responses. It was expected that when a word eliciting a sensory meaning response is paired with another word, the second word will also come to elicit that sensory meaning response. To test this, Staats, Staats, and Heard (1959) paired a nonsense syllable with a number of different words, each of which elicited the same sensory meaning response. Thus twelve words with angular sensory meaning—"square," "box," "roof," "triangle," "zig-zag," and so forth—were paired with a nonsense syllable for one group of subjects. Twelve words with circular sensory meaning—"coil," "hub," "barrel," "wheel," "marble," and so forth—were paired with another nonsense syllable. When the subjects in these groups rated the nonsense syllables they had learned for their sensory qualities, it was found that the nonsense syllables were rated as having sensory qualities that agreed with those possessed by the words with which they were paired. Staats saw this as evidence that implicit sensory responses (images) mediate denotative meaning.

Staats (1968) argued that the problem of *sentence generation* can be adequately handled by a learning theory that takes into account response hierarchies, word associations, and complex environmental stimulus controls. Initially, the child learns single words such as "ball," "red," "give." Gradually he becomes capable of making the response sequence "red ball" and in time "give red ball." Subsequently, articles and pronouns become habitual, and the child learns to construct the sentence, "Give me the red ball." At the same time, other response tendencies are learned; "give" elicits "throw," "push," "hand," and so forth. "Me" is elicited by these verbs, as are "him" and "her." Staats suggested that at each point in the response sequence there is a hierarchy of responses that tends to be elicited. The possible sentences that can be generated increase enormously as more and more associations are formed.

For the child to generate a novel sentence, such as "Give him that blue car," it is necessary for him to have learned sentences involving the associations that will be employed in the new sentence and to be capable of emitting these associations in the presence of appropriate environmental conditions. Thus the child must know the two-word units (associations): "give-him," "him-that," "that-blue," and "blue-car." If the child has had experience with other sentences containing the required word units, such as "Give him Henry's paper" ("Give-him"), or "That blue ball is mine," ("That-blue"), and if appropriate environmental conditions exist—such as a sibling's aggressively taking another child's blue toy car—it becomes possible for the child to emit the novel response, "Give him that blue car."

Such an analysis of sentence production, Staats has argued, allows one to deal with complicated linguistic phenomena in terms of an "integrated learning theory"—that is, on the basis of a formulation that cuts across theoretical lines. Staats (1968) referred to his theory as a pluralistic learning conception. He relied heavily on the classical conditioning paradigm to account for the learning of word-meaning responses, but he used an instrumental conditioning paradigm to explain the process whereby vocal responses are emitted. His theory has Skinnerian and Hullian elements and in many respects resembles the account Mowrer and Osgood gave of language learning. Such eclecticism is necessary, according to Staats, if human learning is to be adequately explained. No single unitary process is adequate; the complexities of verbal behavior in particular require a "pluralistic" theoretical explanation.

LINGUISTICS AND LEARNING THEORY

Attempts by leading theorists to deal with language have received sharp criticism from linguists. Chomsky's (1959) widely cited review of Skinner's *Verbal behavior* raised serious doubts as to the possibility of integrating behavioral and linguistic approaches to language. Other linguists and psycholinguists have also challenged the adequacy of associationistic S-R theories of language. We shall discuss the linguists' critique of learning-theory approaches first, and then turn to some recent learning-theory analyses of language prompted by this critique. In the final section of this chapter we shall attempt to evaluate in general terms the success of learning-theory approaches to language.

The Linguists' Critique

The critics of learning-theory approaches to language have left few stones unturned. Chomsky (1959) set the pace in his attack on Skinner, a detailed and thorough analysis in which he itemized with devastating logic the deficiencies of Skinner's theory. Other linguists have been equally merciless. This onslaught has not been without its benefits since, as we shall see, the criticisms of the linguists have forced learning-theory oriented psychologists to examine in more detail those aspects of their theories most vulnerable to criticism.

CHOMSKY.   For Chomsky the central problem with Skinner's approach was that, while it had all the trappings of scientific rigor, its claim to scientific objectivity was patently false. At issue here were the fundamental concepts of the theory: stimulus, response, and reinforcement. Chomsky argued that while these terms may be objectively identifiable in laboratory settings their use in connection with ordinary human verbal behavior was far from objective and scientific.

Skinner argued, as we have seen, that verbal behavior is under *stimulus control*—that is, the response that a person makes in a given situation is determined by the controlling stimuli present in that situation. The difficulty, Chomsky argued, comes when an attempt is made to identify the stimuli that control a specific response. If a person looks at a red chair and says "red," the response is under the control of the stimulus "redness"; if the person says "chair," the response is under the control of the stimulus "chairness." Before he responds, however, it is impossible to know the properties of the stimulus object that control the person's response. This is even more true in more complicated cases. What is the stimulus that controls the response "Moscow" or "Eisenhower" for a person who has had no contact with the corresponding object—that is, who has not been stimulated by that object? Chomsky contended that the notion of stimulus control as employed by Skinner was an empty concept that has no meaning since it is simply inferred from the form of the response.

Skinner's notion of *response* was for Chomsky equally vague and unsatisfactory. The unit of verbal behavior in Skinner's system is the verbal operant, a class of responses of identifiable form functionally related to one or more controlling variables. The difficulty with this is that no one method was suggested for determining what the controlling variables are in a particular instance or what amount of similarity in form or "control" is required for two physical events to be considered instances of the same operant. We are left, Chomsky argued, with a system in which the basic dependent variable has not been adequately defined. Nor can it be adequately measured since the notion of "response strength" is based on variables that do not co-vary and that, in fact, do not necessarily provide valid indices of what they are supposed to measure. What is a more effective way to impress the owner of a work of art, Chomsky asked, to shriek "Beautiful" repeatedly in a loud voice with no delay (high response strength) or to pause and murmur "Beautiful" in a low-pitched voice (low response strength)? It is not immediately obvious that one response is "stronger" than the other.

Chomsky then turned to the notion of *reinforcement,* which, as we have seen, plays a central role in Skinner's account of language acquisition. Once again, a crucial concept is judged to be vague, poorly defined, and devoid of objective meaning. For Skinner reinforcement might consist of appropriate behavior on the part of the listener, attention on the part of the listener, speech on the part of the listener, and even self-reinforcement. In addition, a person can be reinforced though he emits no response at all (as in thinking), and even when he does not experience the reinforcing stimulus (as in the case of an artist who is reinforced by the effect his work has on others). Chomsky saw all this to be a type of verbal camouflage whereby a single, scientifically-sounding term was used to describe states of wishing, liking, desiring, and so forth: To say "X" is reinforced by "Y" is merely another way of saying "X likes Y" or "X desires Y."

Even more important, however, is the question of the adequacy of a reinforcement notion in explaining the acquisition of verbal behavior. Does the child, as Skinner claimed, learn a language through careful differential reinforcement by the verbal community around him? The evidence, Chomsky felt, did not support such an interpretation. Young children of immigrant parents, for example, learn a second language in the streets, from other children, with amazing rapidity. A child may pick up a large part of his vocabulary and his "feel" for sentence structure from television, from listening to older children, from reading, and so forth. The child's capacity to generalize, hypothesize, and "process" information in very complex ways may even, Chomsky suggested, be innate or the product of maturation of the nervous system. Certainly there is no solid empirical evidence that reinforcement plays the role in language acquisition that Skinner attributed to it.

Chomsky also found Skinner's discussion of the role of *mands* and *tacts* in verbal behavior to be unsatisfactory. Both concepts were simply reformulations of traditional conceptualizations. Moreover, in Chomsky's view the classification of responses as mands on the basis of the behavior of the listener is nonsensical. A command does not cease to be a command simply because a listener does not comply with it. Similarly, the notion of a tact as under the control of a property (stimulus) of some physical object or event provides no new objectivity and, in fact, obscures the distinction between reference and meaning employed in traditional formulations. When Skinner spoke of tacts that are under the control of private stimuli, he surrendered, in Chomsky's eyes, all claim to objectivity.

Skinner's account of *grammar and syntax* as autoclitic processes, Chomsky argued, conceals a traditional view beneath a spurious scientific terminology. What Skinner proposed is the traditional position that sentences consist of lexical items placed in a grammatical frame. The difficulty with this is that more is involved in sentence construction than insertion of lexical items into grammatical frames:

> "Struggling artists can be a nuisance" has the same frame as "Marking papers can be a nuisance," but is quite different in sentence structure as can be seen if "can be" is replaced by "is" or "are" in both cases (Chomsky, 1959, p. 54).

Chomsky also dismissed as implausible Skinner's speculation that in the internal process of composition, the nouns, verbs, and adjectives are chosen first and then are arranged, qualified, and so forth by autoclitic responses to these activities.

Skinner's analysis, Chomsky concluded, is superficial, pseudo-scientific, and grossly inadequate. The child who learns a language has in some sense constructed the grammar for himself on the basis of his observation of sentences and non-sentences. He has succeeded in doing this in a remarkably short period of time. The task is so complex as to suggest the presence of built-in biological structures resulting from genetically programmed maturational processes. Any theory of language acquisition that ignores these structural aspects is, in Chomsky's view, doomed to failure.

We have discussed Chomsky's analysis at some length because it is widely regarded as the classic linguistic critique of learning-theory approaches to language. Other critics have made similar points, both with respect to the application of learning theory to language acquisition and to its application to social phenomena generally. As we have seen in Chapter Two, failure to provide rigorous definitions of such basic concepts as stimulus, response, and reinforcement leaves the theory open to precisely the sort of criticism that Chomsky brought against Skinner.

A word should be said about Chomsky's own concept of language acquisition since his basic approach is shared by many who have been critical of those working from a learning-theory orientation. As we have just seen, Chomsky assumed that children have a capacity for language that is biologically based. In the process of learning a language children are exposed to a corpus of speech and generate sentences on the basis of this language. That is, they develop and test a theory about regularities that appear in the corpus. The child's theory is concerned with the detection of essential aspects of utterances, with the structure of sentences, with the prediction of future sentences, and so forth. Children do this because they possess an *internal structure* that converts the corpus of speech into a theory of grammar.

The task of linguistic analysis, for Chomsky, is to account for this ability to produce and understand an indefinite number of new sentences, to distinguish between sentences and non-sentences, and to interpret certain kinds of ill-formed sentences. According to Chomsky (1957), the grammar of a language can be hierarchized into an elementary part called the "kernel" of the language and a second part consisting of a set of transformational rules for deriving complex sentences from the kernel. The *kernel grammar* contains a definition of the main parts of speech and describes rules for constructing simple declarative statements without complex nouns or verb phrases. The *transformational rules* make it possible for the speaker to generate complex sentences, or phrase or clause segments of sentences, that cannot be derived from the kernel grammar. From the kernel grammar the speaker could, for example, generate a sentence such as "The boy hit the ball." Transformational rules would then show how this sentence could be converted into a passive or negative construction, how it could be phrased as a question ("Did the boy hit the ball?") or a relative clause (". . . who hit the ball"), and so forth. All languages have transformational grammars, but the particular transformations that appear in each language are unique. Children must acquire the particular transformations of their own language.

It is the contention of Chomsky and other linguists that the type of learning involved in generative sentence construction and in the acquisition of transformational grammars cannot be accommodated by the S-R approaches advocated by learning theorists. In fact, it may be that most of the rules involved in language are the result of genetically determined biological structures and innate species-specific mechanisms (Lenneberg, 1964). At any rate, the S-R, associationistic position advocated by learning theorists such as Skinner simply cannot account for the development of a transformational grammar whereby the child generates sentences he has not heard and understands new sentences (Chomsky, 1959).

OTHER CRITICS OF A LEARNING-THEORY APPROACH. The criticisms advanced by Chomsky have been echoed and elaborated by other linguists and psycholinguists. Generally speaking, these critics have been disdainful of learning-theory models of language, which they considered to be vastly inferior to the more powerful models proposed by linguists. Their criticisms have concentrated on a number of topics—in particular, linguistic meaning, language acquisition, and the development of grammar and syntax.

Fodor (1965), in a paper criticizing Osgood's notion of *meaning*, argued that since r_m (the representational mediation concept) is a proper part of R_T (the total behavioral response), each r_m that unambiguously mediates the meaning of a sign must bear a one-to-one unique relation to its R_T. If such a one-to-one relationship exists, Fodor argued, the formal differences between single-stage (e.g., Skinnerian) and mediation (e.g., Mowrer, Osgood) theories disappear, and the only real difference between the two types of theories is that a mediation theory makes reference to unobservables while a single-stage theory does not. The two are logically identical and so suffer from the same infirmities.

Fodor (1965) also noted that all behaviorist theories of meaning derive meaning from thing-naming—that is, a sign (word) is conditioned to a significate (thing). The problem with such an approach is that not all words name things—what is the significate of "meaning," of "significate," of "mediational"? Furthermore, the nature of "things" is often not immediately given in experience. Nor is the meaning of a word independent of speech contexts. In addition, thing-naming words usually have varied referents. Each of these points poses problems for the typical behaviorist approach to meaning. In the face of these difficulties, Fodor contended, the adequacy of such approaches to meaning must be seriously questioned.

Other S-R attempts to deal with meaning have also been criticized. Weinreich (1958), for example, noted that the typical experiment conducted by Staats (e.g., Staats & Staats, 1958) cannot be said to be concerned with linguistic meaning, but only with an affective response. Staats presented a strong case for the conditionability of certain behaviors associated with words, such as affective ratings and GSR responses, but "meaning" in this sense is not linguistic meaning. Glucksberg (1968) has criticized Staats' (1968) attempt to deal with denotative meaning for involving the classical difficulties of an image theory of meaning—such as, what could an image of "loud" look like?

The theories of *language acquisition* proposed by learning theorists have also been subjected to strong criticism. Basically, such formulations are based on a word-to-word associative-chain model. That is, S-R, associationistic theories of language acquisition typically assume that the successive elements of a linguistic series are dependent upon the stimulus consequences of their predecessors. Skinner (1957), for example, seemed to regard the composition and production of an utterance as a matter of stringing together a sequence of responses under the control of outside stimulation and intraverbal associations. Staats (1968) suggested that children produce new sentences that they have never heard because they have previously learned specific sequences of words (two-word pairs or associations) that can then be combined in novel ways. Other learning-theory accounts of language acquisition assume that each response element produces a stimulus that emits the next element in the sequence. All of the responses are integrated in an associative chain in which response-produced stimuli are part of a stimulus complex that exists at the time the next element in the sequence is produced.

The first serious attack on the chaining model was presented by Lashley (1951), who argued that language responses occur at such a high rate that it is not plausible to assume that successive elements are dependent upon the stimulus consequences of their predecessors. The time between elements is too short. Moreover Lashley contended that the central characteristic of serially ordered behavior is the programming of response sequences into "schema of action." In language we do not simply generate consequences according to the associative bond between words. Instead, there is some central determining event that not only selects the response elements that will occur but determines, at least in part, the order in which the elements occur within the response sequence. The structure of the sentence indicates a multiplicity of integrative processes that can be inferred only from the final results of their activity (Lashley, 1951).

The chaining model has been criticized on other grounds as well.

Recent work on intra-sentence word association patterns indicates that these associations are not, as the chaining model assumes, linear from left to right (Glucksberg, 1968). Nor does the model provide any mechanism for predicting the particular words that a speaker utters. It is not enough to say that external (or internal) stimuli elicit and control verbal responses; some account must be given of the way in which they do so.

Garrett and his associates (Garrett & Fodor, 1968; Garrett, Bever, & Fodor, 1966) have criticized the S-R, associationistic model of language acquisition in general terms. It was their contention that the associationistic model assumes that the organism possesses a finite repertoire of behaviors, any one of which may, on occasion, be selected by specific stimulus parameters. The probability of such a selection presumably depends upon the organism's history of reinforcement and may be represented by a construct such as habit strength or associative connection. The difficulty with such a theory, they argued, is that a model that assumes that the behavioral repertoire of the organism is finite simply cannot account for the facts of language acquisition.

An adequate model demands that the organism's behavioral repertoire be inherently infinite. According to Garrett and Fodor (1968) a speaker internalizes a finite set of linguistic rules that are, in principle, sufficient to provide him with a repertoire of infinitely many distinct linguistic responses. The S-R, associationistic theory is insufficient because it requires the speaker to select from a pre-existing response repertoire on the basis of some previously established association. Such a model is incapable, in principle, of accounting for indefinitely diversified response repertoires.

In the eyes of its critics, then, an S-R, associationistic theory of language acquisition is found wanting because it places too many restraints on the speaker. The model proposed fails to take account of the "selective mechanisms" (Lashley, 1951) involved in the actual construction of a particular linguistic utterance. The speaker does more than generate response sequences according to associative bonds that exist between words. He does more than merely look up words from a finite response library. Instead, the speaker somehow manages to compute the novel response sequence appropriate to a novel input. An adequate theory of language requires computing machinery that S-R models fail to make available (Garrett & Fodor, 1968).

A related line of criticism concerns the adequacy of S-R, associationistic theories of *grammar* and *syntax*. Jenkins and Palermo (1964), for instance, proposed a learning-theory formulation of the acquisition of grammatical structures that has been sharply criticized by linguists. In the Jenkins and Palermo conceptualization, words belonging to the same grammatical class are associated together when they occur in the same or equivalent contexts. Thus random en-counters with "John is jolly" and "John is pleasant" lead the child to place "jolly" and "pleasant" in the same class because both words appeared after "John is." This represents an instance of the response-equivalence paradigm. In the stimulus-equivalence paradigm, "John is jolly" and "Christmas is jolly" provide the condition for the estab-lishment of "John" and "Christmas" as a class. More complex para-digms are employed to establish more complex grammatical classes. The organization of classes into sentences depends on mediated S-R chains. Consequently, "Christmas is pleasant" can arise from sequen-tial association between the two classes established in the examples above, even though "Christmas" and "pleasant" were not actually compared in any of the sentences presented. The Jenkins and Palermo model was advanced to resolve some of the inadequacies of the earlier learning-theory approaches to grammar and sentence generation.

Their model, however, does not satisfy the critics of a learning-theory approach. McNeill (1968) characterized such a theory of the acquisition of grammar as a finite-state grammar (Chomsky, 1957). Such grammars, McNeill argued, employ a Markovian model of language structure in which a speaker begins in an initial state, pro-duces the first word of a sentence, thereby switching into a second state that limits the choice of the second word, and so forth. A proba-bility can be assigned for each transition from state to state, and each state through which the speaker passes restricts subsequent choices. In the Jenkins and Palermo model the states are grammatical classes, the transitions are the associations among grammatical classes, and a single word from the preceding grammatical class is produced at each transition.

Linguists see several problems with such finite-state models of grammar. The first of these is arithmetical. The number of gram-matically permissible English sentences of twenty words or less in length is equal to many times the number of seconds in human child-hood (Miller, Galanter, & Pribram, 1960). It is obviously impossible to learn the set of transitions covering all possible sentences. Second, as Chomsky (1957) has argued, a Markovian model of language does not adequately characterize human language in any case. Such a model fails to account for relatively simple grammatical constructions and certainly cannot handle such matters as self-imbedding and more complex constructions.

Thus the traditional probability model of grammar, espoused by proponents of an S-R, associationistic theory of language, is regarded by linguists as utterly inadequate. What is required, they contend, is a phrase-structure model of the type proposed by Chomsky (1957). Such a grammar employs symbols representing phonemes and phrase classes, and rules of the form Z → Y, which reads "Z may be rewritten as Y," where Z and Y represent strings of symbols. There is a privileged symbol, S, or Sentence, and the first rewriting rule applied in generating a sentence is of the form $S \to$ . . . . Each subsequent rewriting rule permits one symbol to be rewritten, and the rewriting rules are successively applied until all symbols have been rewritten. This leaves a string of morphemes ("terminal string"), which is the sentence generated.

Chomsky (1957) listed the following rules as a simple example of a phrase-structure grammar:

(i)   Sentence → Noun Phrase + Verb Phrase
(ii) Noun Phrase → determiner + Noun
(iii) Verb Phrase → Verb + Noun Phrase
(iv) determiner → *the*
(v)   Noun → *man, ball,* etc.
(vi) Verb → *hit, took,* etc.

These rules were then employed to derive the sentence "The man hit the ball." The number at the right of each line of the derivation refers to the rule of the "grammar" used in constructing that line from the preceding line:

Sentence	
Noun Phrase + Verb Phrase	(i)
determiner + Noun + Verb Phrase	(ii)
determiner + Noun + Verb + Noun Phrase	(iii)
the + Noun + Verb + Noun Phrase	(iv)
the + *man* + Verb + Noun Phrase	(v)
the + *man* + *hit* + Noun Phrase	(vi)
the + *man* + *hit* + determiner + Noun	(ii)
the + *man* + *hit* + *the* + Noun	(iv)
the + *man* + *hit* + *the* + *ball*	(v)

Grammars defined in this manner comprise a large family of possible models, each of which is specified by defining kinds of rewriting rules that are permitted (Chomsky, 1963).

Linguists prefer a phrase-structure grammar to a finite-state grammar because it allows recursion, a property essential to account for grammatical dependencies that extend across constituents (McNeill, 1968). That is, if the generation of a sentence is diagrammed as a tree structure (Figure 3-4), a recursion refers to the filling out of each sub-branch attached to a particular branch before passing on to the next branch. A phrase-structure grammar can therefore account for a "language" containing the following sentences: *ab, aabb, aaabbb,* . . . , in which each *a* is paired with a *b* and the initial *a*'s are linked with the terminal *b*'s. For example, in the sentence, "The car which the man drove was red," there is a dependency between "The car" and "was red" that extends across the imbedded portion, "which the man drove." This sentence is an example of the form *aabb*. A single phrase-structure rule generates all such sentences:

$$Z \rightarrow a(Z)b$$

where Z in an abstract recursive element never included in the final form of any sentence. In the string *aaabbb*, for example, *ab* is a Z, *aabb* is a Z, and *aaabbb* is itself a Z (Chomsky, 1957).

For Chomsky (1957) the grammar of a language L should ideally be regarded as a mechanism that provides an enumeration of the sentences of L in something like the way in which a deductive theory gives an enumeration of a set of theorems. It should be possible to derive from a properly formulated grammar rules for determining the integrative processes and "selective mechanisms" that control the generation of sentences. Phrase-structure grammars are attempts in this direction. They provide a model that does not rely on similarity or identity of grammatical frames. A person accepts and understands sentences not because they are related to those with which he is already familiar, but because they are generated by a grammar that the person has somehow and in some form internalized. What matters is not the association of elements that have occurred in the same or equivalent contexts, but the fact that the individual possesses a built-in structure for information processing that enables him to

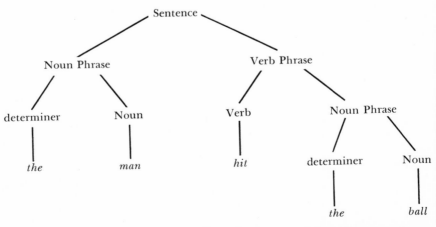

Figure 3-4. Chomsky's (1957) example of sentence generation diagrammed as a tree structure.

arrive at the grammar of a language from the available data in the available time (Chomsky, 1959).

Developments in the
Application of Learning Principles to Language

The linguists' critique of learning-theory approaches to language has not gone unanswered. In fact, the attack by linguists of early S-R approaches to language learning has greatly contributed to recent learning-theory formulations and to research efforts by investigators favoring an associationistic approach to language. It may be too early to predict how successfully S-R theory will respond to the challenge of developments in linguistics, but some initial efforts in this direction can be discussed.

THE SKINNERIANS.   For the most part the Skinnerians have reacted to their critics by ignoring them. Skinner did not reply to Chomsky and seems to have regarded Chomsky's critique as beside the point. In one oblique reference to Chomsky, Skinner (1966) compared the behavior of a poker player to that of a child learning grammar. The behavior of a poker player who evaluates his chances before making a play merely resembles that of a player whose behavior is shaped by prolonged exposure to the game. The efficiency may be the same, but the controlling variables are different and the behaviors therefore are different. Similarly, the behavior of one who speaks correctly by applying the rules of grammar merely resembles the behavior of one who speaks correctly by long experience in a verbal community. To argue, as Chomsky (1959) did, that the child who learns a language has in some sense constructed the grammar for himself is "as misleading as to say a dog which has learned to catch a ball has in some sense constructed the relevant part of the science of mechanics" (Skinner, 1966, p. 29). Rules can be extracted from the reinforcement contingencies in both cases, but the direct effect of the contingencies is considerably different.

Weist (1967) has argued from the radical behaviorist position that a theory, such as Chomsky's, which refers to internalizing complex sets of rules or "selective mechanisms" is not needed to explain the regularity of verbal behavior. To argue that the child has internalized grammatical rules involves a theoretical inference that may have heuristic value but is not logically required. To demonstrate empirically that a child has learned the rules of grammar would require that he exhibit the performance called "uttering the rules of grammar." Weist pointed out that the experience of many grammar school teachers would seem to indicate that such performance requires special training.

For the Skinnerian, Chomsky's criticism of Skinner's notion of stimulus control was seriously mistaken. Chomsky concluded that stimulus control was an empty concept, devoid of meaning because the controlling property was simply inferred from the form of the response. Such an interpretation, Skinnerians argue, is not consistent with the typical experimental procedure in which particular stimulus properties are identified as controlling behavior only after it is demonstrated that the behavior varies with but *one* of the many manipulated properties of the stimulus array (e.g., Ferster & Skinner, 1957; Holland & Skinner, 1961).

Weist (1967) also took exception to Chomsky's statement that the concepts stimulus, response, and reinforcement were used by Skinner in a way that did not preserve the rigor of the experimental laboratory. Skinner, Weist felt, would certainly admit that his theory of language involved extrapolation beyond the well-controlled conditions of the laboratory. This is why the theory is a theory. Whether the theory will be shown to be "true" depends on the extent to which it can provide good research. Certainly Skinner's theory is one of the more interesting interpretations of language acquisition. How productive it will be is up to Skinner and his followers. Weist, at least, thought that some progress was being made.

OSGOOD AND THE THEORY OF MEANING.   As we have seen, linguists—especially Fodor (1965)—have been critical of Osgood's representational mediation theory of meaning. Fodor, it will be recalled, argued that the two-stage mediation model does not differ, in any non-trivial sense, from a single-stage model and consequently shares the defects of such a model. In fact, the recourse by mediation theories to unobservable events makes them all the more objectionable.

Fodor's argument was based on the necessity of a one-to-one relationship between r_m, the representational mediation response, and R_T, the total behavior to the significate. To deny a one-to-one correspondence is to assume that the same r_m could be part of many R_T's produced by many different significates. Signs would then refer ambiguously to many different significates. Once a one-to-one relationship between r_m and R_T is accepted, however, representational mediation responses can be shown to lack the status of theoretical entities since they are devoid of "surplus meaning." Mediational theories would then be no different from single-stage theories.

Osgood (1966, 1968) replied to this criticism by pointing out that while he accepted the one-to-one relationship between r_m and R_T, he did not accept the implication that such a relationship nullified the formal difference between single-stage and mediation theories. He argued that the difference in observability that exists between the two types of theories is not a trivial one. The principal difficulty with Fodor's critique, according to Osgood, is that Fodor presumed r_m to be a single reaction, whereas it is a multicomponent reaction system. The total momentary pattern of components of r_m can be thought of as a kind of code that represents for the organism those differences among R_T's that are necessary for it to respond adaptively to persons and things. One cannot simply substitute the corresponding R_T for any r_m, because r_m's do not reflect *all* of the ways in which R_T's differ from each other. It is sufficient for the r_m's to represent those features of R_T's that make a difference in meaning to the organism (Osgood, 1968).

Osgood's formulation concerning the multicomponent properties of r_m represents an important clarification of his mediation model. Such a model was seen to be necessary to avoid the dangers of a single-stage theory. The only way a single-stage theory can deal with meaning is by reducing it (as Skinner did) to subvocal responses (Osgood, 1968). For Osgood, in contrast, meaning is conveyed by means of a hypothetical construct, r_m, a nonobservable mediating response. Osgood's r_m's are mediating reactions to signs derived from R_T's or the total overt reactions to things signified. The r_m's are representational, since they are part of the decoding ($[S]—r_m$) process involved in meaning. In addition, r_m is a mediating response, since it gives rise to the encoding ($s_m—R_x$) process involved in instrumental behavior. As hypothetical constructs, r_m's stand in a part-to-whole relationship to R_T's in the sense of being distinctively representative of their R_T's. Each r_m is componential in character and is related to its R_T uniquely.

CONTEXTUAL GENERALIZATION.   One of the most elaborate and detailed applications of learning-theory principles to language acquisition is Braine's (1963) theory of the way in which grammatical structures are acquired. As we have seen, linguists have been critical of learning-theory approaches because, for the most part, such approaches employ a Markovian, finite-state grammar in which it is assumed that sentences consist of nothing more than left-to-right, associative transitions. Braine attempted to avoid these difficulties in his theory of the process of "contextual generalization."

Essentially, Braine argued that, as the child hears a sentence from his parents, he notices from time to time the position that particular words or phrases occupy. He learns in such cases the proper location of words in sentences. For example, when the child hears the sentence, "John's ball struck Michael's foot," he may notice that "John's ball" occupies a position in the beginning of the sentence. Through contextual generalization "John's ball" may be employed by the child in the beginning of other sentences. Similarly, "Michael's foot" may be employed at the conclusion of other sentences. Contextual generalization in this sense is a special case of the more general process of stimulus (or response) generalization. In stimulus and response generalization certain intrinsic properties of the stimuli or responses are thought to mediate generalization. In contextual generalization the mediating property is an external one—namely, temporal location in an utterance.

In addition, when the child learns that the phrase "John's ball" is in the beginning of the sentence, "John's ball struck Michael's foot," he may also learn that the word "ball" is in the last half of the phrase. If he notices the relative position of the words in the phrases and the phrases in the sentence, he can learn how to construct a noun phrase. The position of the word is defined in terms of the phrase, and the position of the phrase is defined in terms of the sentence.

What is learned, then, are the *temporal positions* of units in verbal arrays. The position learned is the position of a unit within the next-larger containing unit of a hierarchy of units. Position within a unit may be defined absolutely (e.g., first, second) or relatively (e.g., before f, first after f, second after f—where f is some frequently occurring morpheme). All such positional relationships assumed to be learned could be represented by rewriting rules of the type discussed by Chomsky (1957). The system is therefore a phrase-structure grammar, since it has the capacity for representing hierarchically organized positional relationships (Braine, 1965).

Location determines the syntactic properties of sentence segments. A noun is a word that characteristically appears in the first position in simple sentences. A verb is defined as a word that characteristically appears in the second position in simple sentences. If a person hears the sentence, "People stime every day," he would probably deduce the existence of a verb "to stime" and accept sentences like "George stimes" as grammatical. Given the position a word occupies in one sentence, it becomes possible to predict the position it will occupy in new sentences. It is this generalization process that enables one to use a given word in a given position in a new sentence.

So understood, language acquisition is not limited by the restrictions of associative learning. Braine's theory is an advance over previous learning-theory analyses because it provides a basis for *productivity* in language. The theory offers an explanation for how the child can produce and comprehend an almost limitless number of novel grammatical utterances. Words learned in one context generalize to other contexts, even though no association may have previously formed between the word and its new context.

One of the difficulties with such a theory, however, is that there are many different kinds of sentences allowing nearly all possible orders of words and phrases. To take account of all the types of sentences in which the linguistic unit can occur would require indefinitely many permissible locations. Consequently Braine restricted the scope of his theory to the assimilation of the grammatical properties of *simple declarative sentences*. This constitutes a necessary first step in the development of an adequate theory of the structure of language as a whole. Once the grammatical structure of simple declarative sentences is understood it may then be possible to deal with "sublanguages"—that is, with complex sentences produced by transformations. One sublanguage exists for each type of sentence (passive, question, and so on) as well as for certain clauses or phrases (relative, extended noun phrases, and the like). The sublanguages differ in that the sequential arrangement of morphemes in each sublanguage is peculiar to that sublanguage. Nevertheless any class of words that constitutes a part of speech in one sublanguage constitutes a part of speech in all others. Since the sublanguages have a great deal in common (the same vocabulary and parts of speech, as well as many of the same word arrangements), it may prove possible to treat the learning of sublanguages as a problem in transfer of training. At any rate, Braine felt this to be a task for the future; it was enough for the present merely to deal with learning the structure of simple declarative English sentences.

Braine (1963) then turned to the question of contingencies between positions. Certain linguistic sequences follow positional regularities and behave as units. A given location in a sentence can be occupied by one word or a unit of words. Thus the verb position can be held by a single word, "throw," or a phrase, "has been throwing." In order to explain how units are learned and retain their integrity, Braine drew a distinction between *primary phrases* and *components of phrases*. Primary phrases are sequences such as "is throwing," "the book," "accurately," each of which consists of component morphemes (e.g., "is," "throw," "-ing," "accurate," "-ly").

Braine assumed that the "psychological cement" that binds the morphemes of the primary phrase more closely to each other than to other components of a sentence is the formation of associations between morphemes. He postulated *associative bonds* between "closed-class" morphemes (i.e., articles, prepositions, plurals "-s," pronouns, auxiliary verbs, verb endings "-ing," "-ed," and so on, adverbial "-ly," noun and verb suffixes "-ment," "-ence," "-ize," and so on) and "open-class" morphemes (i.e., nouns, verbs). On the basis of the law of exercise (i.e., the assumption that the strength of an associative link is proportional to the frequency of occurrence of the pair), it can be expected that, since the most frequently occurring morphemes are members of closed-classes, these morphemes should become the foci of associational links. The strongest associative bonds therefore are formed between closed-class morphemes such as prepositions and articles ("near the," "of a") or auxiliaries and verb endings ("is -ing," "has -ed"). Weaker associative bonds are formed between closed- and open-class morphemes such as articles and nouns or the auxiliary and verb endings and the verb stems. The weakest associative bond exists between open-class morphemes, except for certain pairs which have a high frequency of joint occurrence ("drink-coffee," "drive-car," and the like).

The notion of associations formed between morphemes (components of phrases) is intended to explain how it is that the morphemes of a primary phrase go together as a unit. If the strength of an associative link between morphemes is a function of the frequency of the joint occurrence of morphemes in sentences and if it is also assumed that the proximity of the morphemes affects the associational link, it follows that each morpheme in a sentence is more strongly associated with other morphemes of the primary phase in which it occurs than with morphemes outside the phrase. Furthermore, because of the associative bonds that have been formed, the morphemes of the primary phrase follow definite positional regularities: "has been throwing accurately" is acceptable, whereas "has accurately throwing been" is not.

To summarize, Braine's (1963) theory of contextual generalization assumes that what is learned in the process of the acquisition of grammatical structure is the location of units within a sentence. By the process of contextual generalization, the individual who learns the position of a word or phrase in a sentence is able to place this segment in the same position in other contexts. The location learned is that of the primary phrase within the sentence and that of the morpheme within the primary phrase. While the ability to construct and comprehend novel sentences is regarded as a special case of stimulus and response generalization, the learning of positional regularities and the manner in which morphemes combine to constitute the primary phrase are based on the formation of associational links. To avoid the complications involved in more complex utterances, Braine restricted this theory to the assimilation of the grammatical properties of simple declarative sentences.

BERLYNE'S STRUCTURAL ANALYSIS.   Berlyne's (1965) work on the structure and process of thinking represents an important development in the learning-theory analysis of language, even though Berlyne did not direct his attention specifically to language but was concerned with intellectual processes generally. Linguists have long been critical of psychological theory for ignoring the structural properties of language. S-R principles, it has been argued (e.g., Bever, 1968), cannot account for the linguistic structure of language as expressed in the formalisms of transformational grammar. In the light of these criticisms Berlyne's work on the structural properties of S-R—or "Neo-associationistic"—behavior theory becomes relevant (Berger & Lambert, 1968).

According to Berlyne one of the prime requisites for an adequate

S-R psychology is that the concepts of stimulus and response be defined not in terms of single stimuli and single responses but in terms of classes of stimulus situations and classes of behavior. In fact, he preferred to define a stimulus situation as a collection of items of information, any single one of which, or any combination of which, may be associated with a particular type of behavior. This approach is reminiscent of Miller's (1959) "liberalization" of S-R concepts.

Berlyne placed heavy emphasis upon the notion of *equivalence*. Stimulus equivalence is said to exist whenever two stimulus situations possess a common most probable response. Response equivalence exists whenever two response patterns are associated with a common class of stimulus situations. In a situation involving response equivalence only one of the two possible response patterns will be evoked. Both patterns will, however, be more probable when such a situation exists than they would have been otherwise.

One instance of response equivalence is the *habit-family hierarchy* (Hull, 1943). Here equivalence exists between sequences of responses (behavior chains) rather than between single responses. Each chain of responses is associated with and can be set off by the same stimulus situation, S_O, and every chain ends with the same goal situation, S_G. Not every chain has the same probability of occurrence, however. Instead, they may be listed in decreasing order of probability of occurrence—that is, hierarchically. Berlyne used the Hullian (1943) notion of the r_g—s_g mechanism as the "lynch-pin" or "cement" that binds the habit-family hierarchy structure together. The internal, fractional anticipatory goal response (r_g) gives rise to distinctive feedback stimulation (s_g), and an association grows up between s_g (Hull's "goal stimulus") and the various response chains that lead to the goal situation (S_G). The notion of the habit-family hierarchy (Figure 3-5) constitutes the basic structural element in Berlyne's system.

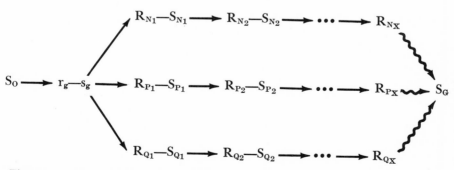

Figure 3-5. The habit-family hierarchy of behavior chains (from Berlyne, 1965). Each response (R_N, R_P, and R_Q) is bound to the original situation (S_O) through the r_g—s_g process and initiates a sequence of responses (behavior chain) that terminates in the goal situation (S_G).

Berlyne added another structural element to his system with the concept of *compound habit-family hierarchies* (Maltzman, 1955). In this case, the components of the habit-family hierarchy are themselves habit-family hierarchies. Each hierarchy corresponds to a condition of the organism—that is, to a class of states in which that particular hierarchy is dominant (more probable). Each hierarchy also has its own mediating r_g–s_g mechanism, a "switching mediator" whose response-produced stimulus puts the organism into a state in which that hierarchy is dominant (Figure 3-6). Physiologically, the switching mediator presumably corresponds to the activation of a neural center whose excitation brings a certain kind of behavior to the fore.

As we have seen, Chomsky (1957) has argued that grammatical speech is constructed by a speaker who uses rules (rewriting rules) to carry out a series of substitutions that gradually delineate the major portions of the sentence together with their mutual relations. Essentially this involves a tree structure in which the human programmer must make decisions at nodal points between alternative ways of continuing until the contents of the sentence are filled out. Thus a noun phrase is broken down into the article and the noun, which in turn are broken down into the words "the" and "man." The verb phrase is broken down into the verb ("hit") and a noun phrase, which is further reduced to an article ("the") and a noun ("ball"). Each of these substitutions follows the rewriting rules of the grammar.

Berlyne (1965) would account for the structures involved in the generation of such a grammar on the basis of compound habit-family hierarchies. The switching mediator corresponds to the nodal points

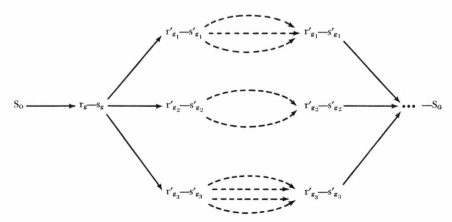

Figure 3-6. The compound habit-family hierarchy (adapted from Berlyne, 1965). Subhierarchies are themselves habit-families of behavior chains with their own switching mediators (r'_{g_1}–s'_{g_1}, r'_{g_2}–s'_{g_2}, etc.). Each subhierarchy is regarded as a subgoal whose attainment contributes to the final goal situation (S_G) which is common to the entire compound hierarchy.

in a tree-structure analysis. A sub-hierarchy is selected, then a sub-hierarchy of a sub-hierarchy, and so forth until a particular behavior chain is embarked on. The sub-hierarchies correspond to the branches of a tree and are selected, via the r_g-s_g "switching" mechanism, in accordance with their dominance in the hierarchy. In the case of grammatical speech, the child presumably learns, over a period of time, that certain forms are correct and appropriate, whereas other forms are incorrect and inappropriate. Correct and appropriate grammatical forms are thereby rendered more dominant—that is, their probability is raised. It is therefore possible for the child to generate new, grammatical sentences on the basis of these acquired structures of behavior.

Admittedly, such an analysis is only a first step toward the development of a satisfactory learning-theory account of linguistic structures. Berlyne does not go into detail, nor does he devote more than cursory attention to the question of language acquisition. What his analysis does suggest, however, is that it is possible for S-R theory to describe in its own terms structures corresponding to the "schemata," "programs," and "selective mechanisms" favored by more cognitively-oriented psychologists. How successful this enterprise will be depends on the outcome of future research and on subsequent theoretical developments.

EVALUATION

In this chapter we have restricted our attention to the more important learning-theory approaches to language, to the linguists' critiques of such approaches, and to some recent attempts by behaviorally-oriented psychologists to deal with these criticisms and thereby construct a more adequate theory of language. We have not discussed the work of other psychologists, less committed to a learning-theory approach, in the field of the psychology of language. To do so would take us too far afield from the central concern of this book. It should be noted, however, that a split has developed within psychology between those who approach linguistic phenomena from a learning-theory, behavioristic point of view and those who approach language in more cognitive terms. The second group has been strongly influenced by the work of Chomsky and other linguists, and their research has been concerned largely with laboratory applications of linguistic theory (for a review, see Miller & McNeill, 1969).

How successful has a learning-theory approach to language proven to be, and what promise does such an approach hold for the future? It is not easy to answer these questions at the present time. To a considerable extent, as is perhaps evident from the previous discussion, learning theorists have been put on the defensive by their critics. They have been forced to concern themselves with theoretical clarification and elaboration. Perhaps the reason for this is that in the initial phases, it is easier to deal with theoretical issues than to carry out meaningful research. Yet it seems evident that more empirical information is needed before an adequate theory can be developed.

Meaning

Linguistic meaning allows the speaker to paraphrase verbal behavior, to interpret a person's actions, or to express a judgment about the truth value of an utterance. Because words have meaning an audience will understand ambiguities, laugh at anomalies, or fail to agree with a speaker's statements. Two major learning-theory models are used to explain linguistic meaning: the single-stage model and the representational mediation model. The first of these models is based either on Pavlovian classical conditioning or Skinnerian operant conditioning. In the classical conditioning paradigm, it is assumed that reactions to significates are transferred to signs through the contiguous occurrence of the significate (unconditioned stimulus) and the sign (conditioned stimulus). In the operant conditioning paradigm, it is assumed that the emission of a response, followed by reinforcement, serves to strengthen the dependency of this response upon its antecedent conditions.

It now appears to be widely accepted that such a single-stage model is inadequate. The chief difficulty is that such a model makes no provision for symbolic processes. If the Pavlovian paradigm is employed, one would expect the response to the sign to be, in many respects at least, highly similar to the response to the significate. Yet it seems evident that people do not respond to words in the same way that they respond to the things signified. On the other hand, if the Skinnerian operant-conditioning paradigm is used, the response to the sign is some subvocal replication of the overt verbal response (Skinner, 1957). To understand a speaker it would be necessary to subvocally mimic his words. Since this contradicts our experience, it would seem that a single-stage model cannot satisfactorily explain the process of linguistic meaning.

Osgood's representational mediation model, critics have argued, suffers from essentially the same defects since it is not formally different from single-stage models (Fodor, 1965). Fodor contended that the representational mediation response (r_m) differs from the response to the significate (R_T) only in terms of observability. There is a one-to-one relationship between the two, and hence a representational theory of this sort suffers from the same limitations as a single-stage theory.

Osgood's (1968) argument in defense of his theory was, as we have seen, based chiefly on his contention that while a one-to-one relationship exists between r_m and R_T, the representational mediation response is not a single reaction but a multicomponential reaction system possessing combinatorial properties. The components of r_m constitute a code that corresponds to significant differences in R_T's of adaptive importance to the organism.

The work of Osgood and his colleagues using the semantic differential scale (Osgood, Suci, & Tannenbaum, 1957) represents a major attempt to measure meaning. The generality of the dimensions found in earlier studies—evaluation, potency, and activity—has been repeatedly demonstrated. Research has indicated, however, that the semantic differential scale measures principally qualitative meaning in a metaphorical or affective domain, and not denotative meaning (Miron & Osgood, 1965).

Thus the correspondence between the representational mediation reaction, r_m, and specific operational procedures for measuring meaning remains problematic. The difficulty here is one recognized by Osgood (1968)—namely, that mediational theory, with its reliance on unobservable concepts, may be able to explain too much and hence may become untestable. How is one, for example, to determine the distinctive combinatorial properties of a given r_m? How, in other words, will it be possible to crack the code of a given representational mediation reaction?

One final word on Osgood's theory: As we have noted earlier in discussing his theory, Osgood (1963) recognized that a strict S-R approach could not account fully for symbolic processes. He therefore added an integration level to both the encoding and decoding stages in order to account for the development of linguistic perceptual and response units. The integration level incorporates the essential characteristics of a Gestalt theory of perceptual organization as well as the essential characteristics of motor skills (Lashley, 1951). It includes learning in which stimulus elements (S-S) and response elements (R-R) are paired through frequency, redundancy, and contiguity—but not reinforcement—principles. It allows the psychology of language to make what Osgood saw to be a crucial distinction—between words as meaningless forms (sensory and motor integrations) and words as psychological units of meaning (by virtue of their semantic and grammatical coding). Finally, it brings within a behavioristic, associationistic theory a body of well-documented Gestalt phenomena (closure, good figure, "thing perception," and so on).

It appears then, at least with respect to meaning, that a straightforward, heavy-handed application of traditional learning principles is insufficient. What is required is a more liberalized, "neo-behavioristic" approach, broadly eclectic in its principles and concepts. This is still a learning-theory approach, since the assumption remains that an adequate theory of language behavior must be a learning theory (Osgood, 1963).

If this assumption is to prove viable in practice, however, a number of additional objections raised by Fodor (1965) and other linguists must be answered. How, for example, does a learning-theory explanation account for the fact that some words do not name things? And even when words have objective referents, the nature of the "thing" signified is not always apparent in experience. What is one to make of the fact that the meaning of a word is not independent of speech context or that thing-naming words usually have varied referents? If an adequate learning-theory analysis of linguistic meaning is possible, it will be an analysis that can successfully cope with these problems.

Language Acquisition

As we have seen, the word-to-word associative-chain model of the structure of language, long favored by learning theorists, has been sharply criticized by linguists. Such a conceptualization assumes that the organism possesses a finite repertoire of responses, any one of which may be selected as a function of stimulus parameters and previously established associations. Words selected from the finite, preexistent repertoire are then linked into the chain.

The difficulty with this position, linguists argue, is that it fails to account for the productivity of syntactic and semantic habits. In practice, people are able to generate indefinitely diversified response repertoires. The problem with the learning-theory model, its critics argue, is that it presents an impoverished view of the organism's behavior. It leaves the organism capable of mastering a mere finite number of distinct responses. Similarly, the position that behavior is a function of associative connections formed between stimuli and responses leads to an impoverished view of the organism's perceptual capacities. It assumes that although the individual is continuously confronted with novel stimulus configurations, he can respond appropriately to only a finite number because his response repertoire is limited. This is at odds with the facts, since the speaker's perceptual repertoire, like his response repertoire, includes the capacity to analyze indefinitely many distinct linguistic objects (Garrett & Fodor, 1968).

Osgood (1968) countered this criticism of learning-theory approaches by pointing out that, while it was true that the organism operates with a finite number of response components—in exactly the same sense that any language operates with a finite number of phonemes—the laws by which these components are combined into larger units are such that the number and variety of compound responses is potentially infinite. That is, the manner in which the phonemes combine into words and the words into phrases and clauses is such that it allows for the indefinitely diversified responses obtained in behavior.

Osgood argued further that the fact that the individual's response repertoire is limited (in its basic components) does not necessarily place limitations on his capacity to respond appropriately to novel stimuli. In fact, it is a principle of learning that two or more arbitrarily different physical stimuli can be associated with the same response through replicative conditioning. Moreover, the concept of a representational mediation response precludes the need for external stimuli to be similar in any physical respect. Thus the word "joy" can be associated with the word "glee" through generalization based on semantics or with "boy" through generalization based on physical similarity. In any case, there is no restriction placed on the individual's capacity to respond appropriately to impinging stimuli.

When a psychologist begins to deal with the acquisition of language in children, he is confronted with the problem posed by Chomsky (1959) in his critique of Skinner—namely, how is one to account for the remarkable fact that children in a relatively short period of time are able to generate sentences that are extremely complex and grammatically correct. Some psychologists have proposed that the learning of language is basically an instance of imitative learning. Lenneberg (1962), however, has presented evidence that indicates that comprehension of language can be acquired with no overt practice at all. Moreover, the presence of idiosyncratic regularities, such as the correct use of plural endings when a noun is not preceded by a numeral but an incorrect use when it is (as, "four horsie"), truncated sentences ("that mommie spoon"), and novel utterances indicate that the child's acquisition of language cannot be explained on the basis of imitation alone.

Consequently, an adequate learning-theory model must be able to explain how it is that children generate sentences they have never heard. Perhaps the most successful attempt in this direction has been Braine's (1963, 1965) work on the process of contextual generalization. As we have seen, Braine's theory is an advance over other theories because it provides a basis for productivity in language. Word order does not depend on associative connections between items. Instead, the child learns through contextual generalization the position of a phrase in a sentence and is subsequently able to employ that phrase in the same position in other sentences. Furthermore, the child learns the position of the elements (morphemes) in the phrase unit and can therefore construct phrases in accord with the positional regularities of the language.

Nevertheless, Braine's work has been attacked by linguists on a number of grounds. Because his theory was especially concerned with the way in which grammatical structures are acquired and because the controversy has tended to revolve mainly around the grammatical aspect of language acquisition, we shall turn now to this specific question—how it is that a child learns to follow the rules in his linguistic behavior.

Grammar and Verbal Behavior

Braine (1965) regarded his system as a phrase-structure grammar, since it had the capacity for representing hierarchically organized positional relationships. It was not, therefore, a finite-state grammar in which a finite number of states was connected by transitions with words produced on transition from one state to another. Although Osgood (1968) has made a case for the existence of such Markov-type transitional dependencies, most linguists and psycholinguists (e.g., Bever, 1968; McNeill, 1968) have followed Chomsky (1957) and rejected such models. In Braine's (1963) system, the word is defined in terms of the phrase and the phrase in terms of the sentence. What is learned is an inclusion relation—the inclusion of the smaller unit within the larger—and this is carried by contextual generalization to analogous contexts.

Linguists have criticized Braine's theory for (1) denying the possibility of transformations and (2) essentially reducing the power of a phrase-structure grammar to the level of a finite-state grammar (Bever, Fodor, & Weksel, 1965; McNeill, 1968). The first criticism stems from Braine's identification of the simple declarative sentence as the base form from which all syntactically related sentences are directly or indirectly derived. Such an identification ignores what linguists regard as essential—the distinction between "base structure" and "surface structure." The simple declarative sentence cannot be identified with the base structure. In fact, the base structure is not a sentence of any sort but is rather an abstract structure that is transformed into a variety of sentence types, of which the simple declarative is one (Chomsky, 1957). To identify the simple declarative with the base structure is to disallow the possibility of a transformational grammar (Bever *et al.*, 1965).

Braine attempted to avoid this difficulty by redefining the notion of transformation. According to his definition, some sentence types are transformed into other types via various "sub-languages." The linguists were critical of such a procedure, however, since the sub-language must operate on the surface structure of one sentence to yield the surface structure of another sentence (McNeill, 1968). Moreover, the number of separate sub-languages needed for each variant of the declarative sentence is enormous (Bever *et al.*, 1965).

Thus the system loses the economy of a true transformational grammar.

Braine's (1965) reply to this criticism was based essentially on methodological considerations. He denied that a system that eliminates the distinction between base (underlying) and surface (manifest) structure would be unnecessarily complex. What matters is whether the validity of the generative grammar can be assessed. If the base structure is an underlying abstract structure that corresponds to nothing in reality, then there are no independent data against which phrase structure and transformational rules can be separately tested. The grammarian can write a base structure on the basis of convenience, free to correct any poor fit with the surface of the language by using transformations to reshuffle the elements. Indeed, transformational grammars, as defined by Chomsky and other linguists, have not proven to be susceptible to experimental test. It is difficult, if not impossible, to structure a verbal learning experiment to ensure that a subject is faced with the task of learning a transformation. On the other hand, Braine's system has the initial advantage of making the underlying structure overt. The component parts of the grammar are then separately responsive to data. Braine would admit that his system is limited in its scope, but he would prefer a grammar susceptible to experimental confirmation to one that cannot be validated and may in fact be an artifact of the type of linguistic description employed.

The second criticism that linguists have raised against Braine's system is that it is not powerful enough to account for natural language. In the natural language there is an indefinite number of possible imbedded structures that can occur in a sentence ("The lady who bought the hat which she saw in the store which is located . . ."). A system based on the learning of an inclusion relation (the smaller unit within the larger) cannot account for such recursive situations (where larger units are imbedded in smaller units). That is, while Braine's system allows for expansion rules of the type:

Sentence   → Noun Phrase, Verb Phrase
Verb Phrase   → Verb, Noun Phrase
Noun Phrase → determiner, Noun

it does not allow a rule of the type:

Noun Phrase → Sentence

It is therefore a grammar without recursion and cannot account for a language in which an arbitrary number of dependent clauses are permitted in a sentence (Bever, 1968; McNeill, 1968). It follows that Braine's phrase-structure grammar suffers from a critical deficiency of finite-state grammars and is therefore not a phrase-structure grammar in any real sense.

Braine conceded that his theory was only a partial one. What he proposed was a limited phrase-structure grammar. It remains to be seen whether his approach can be extended to the whole of a natural language. His critics among the linguists say that in principle it cannot, since it does not allow for abstract terms such as are required to explain recursion. It may be, however, that a learning-theory approach such as Braine's can incorporate some of the S-R structural notions suggested by Berlyne (1965). The concept of compound habit-family hierarchies, for example, could conceivably be employed in a manner analogous to the way in which tree-structures are employed by linguists to generate sentences. Berlyne, at least, argued that this was the case, although he did not specify how a recursive process could occur in behavioral chains based on compound habit-family hierarchies. In a recursive tree-structure every sub-branch of a particular branch is worked out before the next sub-branch is taken up. In Berlyne's description of compound habit-family hierarchies, however, the process is sequential, from higher to lower levels, until the organism is committed to a specific behavior chain. There is no provision for working back from lower to higher levels as recursion would demand. Here again, therefore, considerable modifications seem to be required before the system is capable of handling the complex linguistic structure of language as expressed in the formalisms of a transformational grammar such as Chomsky's.

General Considerations

The revolution in linguistics initiated by Chomsky (1957) has only gradually been appreciated by psychologists. As Jenkins (1968) has pointed out, psychologists worked hard to build a bridge to linguistics, only to find out that the terrain on the other side was entirely different from what they had expected. Chomsky's "generative grammar" was not merely an improvement over the older "descriptive grammar," it was a radically new approach. Descriptive linguistics defined language as speech sounds that people utter under particular stimuli. Such a definition was a comfortable one for psychologists; learning principles seemed to fit well. Chomsky, however, viewed language as a creative instrument for the free expression of thought. The traditional learning models do not work as well here. In fact, some linguists have argued that they do not work at all—and that no amount of revision, patching, or adding *neo-* to the name will make them work.

The new developments in linguistics grew out of Chomsky's insight that the individual's normal, everyday use of language is creative. The individual is constantly uttering sentences he has never spoken before and understanding sentences he has never heard before. Various learning-theory explanations have been advanced to explain how such verbal behavior can occur. Some of these theories stressed the relationship between certain stimuli (Skinner's "controlling stimuli") and verbal behavior. Other theories explained verbal behavior on the basis of complex habits of language use. Still other theories proposed that new sentences are learned by analogy from old ones. For the linguist, however, none of these explanations is adequate.

The reason for this extends beyond mere technical considerations. Chomsky's work was revolutionary because it challenged the entire modern empiricist tradition. In his *Cartesian linguistics* (1966) Chomsky came to grips with this issue directly. To the empiricist, language could be understood only in terms of training, habit, or insight from experience. Chomsky, on the other hand, was convinced that the creative aspect of language lies in the innate capacities of the human mind. While the empiricists started with a *tabula rasa* and worked from there following the principles of association and habit, Chomsky, like the rationalists before him, assumed that there was a fixed schematic structure within which man's linguistic capacities develop. Experience will affect this development, but its ultimate form will be a function of those language universals that exist in the mind.

This explicit nativism does not sit well with most psychologists. In spite of their theoretical differences, most contemporary psychologists would subscribe to the behavioristic paradigm and to the belief in empiricism and environmentalism that is the philosophical cornerstone of the behavioristic paradigm. This is true especially of those psychologists committed to a learning-theory approach to behavior. It is not surprising, therefore, that a psychologist like Braine (1965) should object to what he sees to be the arbitrary, non-empirical character of transformational grammars.

In addition to these basic philosophical differences, contemporary linguists and psychologists differ in their methodology. One of the classical distinctions in linguistic literature is that of de Saussure (1916) between *la langue* and *la parole*. *La langue* refers to language as an abstract system. *La parole* refers to language as actualized speech events. The linguist is characteristically interested in *la langue,* while the psychologist is chiefly interested in *la parole*. It follows that the linguist and the psychologist are often talking at cross purposes.

Nevertheless psychologists cannot ignore the success that contemporary linguistics has achieved by working from the base structure and employing abstract elements in its grammatical rules. Since philosophical assumptions and methodology are fundamentally different there can be little hope for a reconciliation between contemporary linguistics and behavioral psychology. If learning theorists are to come to grips with the challenge proposed by developments in linguistics, they will have to demonstrate that their models are as powerful and successful as those proposed by linguists.

At the present time the issue is unresolved. Some valiant attempts have been made to generate appropriate theories of language based on learning-theory principles, but these have not been entirely successful. Moreover, the theories themselves have generated relatively little research on language. Since psychologists with a learning-theory orientation are committed to the principles of empiricism, they must demonstrate empirically that language acquisition is part of the lawfulness of human behavior generally and that the same models apply to both.

4

Imitation and Vicarious Learning

MUCH of a child's early learning is accomplished through the process of imitation. In fact, imitative learning occurs throughout the life cycle: The child imitates his parents, the youngster imitates his peers, adults imitate one another. Indeed, imitative behavior is so pervasive a part of our experience that we are often unaware that we are actually imitating those around us.

Early social scientists were impressed by this tendency to imitate and used the concept of imitation to explain social conformity generally. Imitation, according to this viewpoint, was a conserving agency in society and provided the motive and means for the preservation of a culture (Allport, 1968). Thus Tarde could assert that "Society is imitation" (1903, p. 74), and other early theorists saw imitative behavior as an innate tendency of the human organism. Children, according to Walter Bagehot, are "born mimics" (1873, p. 101). William James (1890) subscribed to this innatist position, as did McDougall, although McDougall (1908) regarded imitation as an innate tendency that was nonspecific, serving merely as a means whereby other specific motives reach their goal.

Subsequent theorists gave equal importance to the role of imitation in the process of socialization and in social behavior generally but, under the influence of the behaviorist movement in this country, began to view the process of imitation in more specifically behavioral terms. Rather than resorting to imitation as an explanatory concept that was itself innate (and therefore beyond explanation), psychologists in the 1920s and 1930s concerned themselves with accounting for the mechanisms that underlie imitative behavior. In doing so, they inevitably relied upon the models of learning that were then available, since they viewed imitation as simply one other instance of learned behavior.

THEORIES OF IMITATION

For the most part, psychological theories of imitation have in this country been behavioral—that is, learning theories. Of course, the Freudian alternative exists, although Freud's theory of identification has been criticized for internal inconsistencies (Brown, 1965; White, 1963) and for not yielding unequivocal empirical predictions (Bandura, 1969; Flanders, 1968). This is not to imply that learning-theory approaches are never deficient in these respects, but since our concern in this book is with learning theory, we shall restrict our attention to theory and research in this tradition and shall not consider Freudian and neo-Freudian theories of identification.

Learning theories of imitative behavior have usually been patterned on general learning theory. Thus early theories of imitative behavior were modeled upon Pavlovian or Thorndikian theories. Subsequently, in the heyday of Hullian theory, Miller and Dollard (1941) propounded a Hullian interpretation of imitative learning. More recently, however, theories of imitative behavior have moved beyond general learning theory and, at least in some cases, have uncovered phenomena that require the modification and extension of learning principles.

Early Theories

THE PAVLOVIAN MODEL.   As behaviorism developed in this country, psychologists began to apply its principles to a wide range of phenomena including imitative behavior. Many of these early theorists felt they had found an explanation for imitative behavior in the principles of classical conditioning. George Humphrey (1921), for example, took the position that imitative acts are merely a special case of ordinary conditioned reflex activity. Imitation ceases when "the reflex has disappeared by 'lack of support' from the primary stimulus" (1921, p. 4).

F. H. Allport (1924) espoused a similar associationistic viewpoint. He denied the existence of a general instinctive drive to imitate and argued that the capacity for imitative behavior is the result of a general capacity for responses to become conditioned to stimuli. Watson (1925) also regarded imitative responses as learned through the process of conditioning (although he was somewhat vague about the precise mechanisms).

Perhaps the most detailed early attempt to account for imitative behavior in these terms was E. B. Holt's (1931) theory. According to Holt, a child spontaneously engages in vocal behavior, and eventually a conditioned reflex is established such that the specific impulses that a sound elicits acquire a synaptic connection with the motor nerves going out to the same muscles used in producing that sound. This he called a reflex-circle. Once it is established, the child begins persistently to repeat sounds that he hears himself make. After the process is well learned, the child begins to articulate sounds that other people make. Self-stimulation Holt called *iteration;* stimulation from others he called *imitation.*

This same conditioning process was used to explain non-verbal imitative behavior as well. Initially random responses become conditioned to the motor nerves that are connected to the muscles used in producing the action. This accounts for the iterative nature of the child's behavior and also provides a base in time for imitative conditioning to occur. If another person's performance of an act stimulates the child's sense organs at a time when the child is engaging in the same act randomly, the child will be conditioned to imitate the behavior (Holt, 1931).

Such an explanation requires, however, that the child initially performs by chance the behavior to be imitated. The random behavior of the child serves as the unconditioned response in the classical conditioning paradigm. Yet it seems apparent that children can learn to imitate behavior sequences not in their repertoire. Thus Holt's model seems unduly restrictive. Moreover, although Holt is better than most authors in this respect, early proponents of a classical conditioning approach to imitation were vague when it came to describing precisely how imitation fits the Pavlovian paradigm. For the most part, these early theorists used the principles of conditioning uncritically and did not concern themselves with details. When, as in Holt's writings, an attempt was made to obtain greater precision, the results were not entirely satisfactory—perhaps because there was not enough concern with relating the hypothesized processes to specific behavioral examples.

THE THORNDIKIAN MODEL.   In F. H. Allport's (1924) discussion of imitation there was some recognition of the instrumental role imitation plays in behavior. Imitative responses are learned in the course of goal-seeking activity. Other writers put even more stress on this aspect of imitation, taking the Thorndikian position that if the imitative behavior does in fact lead to the achievement of some goal, it will be more likely to occur subsequently; if not, it will be less likely to occur in the future.

Thorndike (1898) himself had little patience with the argument that imitation occurs simply because individuals do what they see done. From his research with animals he became convinced that mere observation of a successful solution to a problem does not help the observing animal solve the problem. On the other hand, once a response has been learned, the sight of others performing the response may lead to the response being made.

Thorndike felt that imitation comes about because its consequence is reward. Animals and humans imitate because they derive satisfaction from such behavior. On the human level certain behavior is approved by the society within which the individual finds himself, and other behavior is not. When imitative behavior leads to approval, it is strengthened; when it leads to ridicule, it is weakened.

Thorndike did not go into much more detail than this. A number of other writers espoused similar views. Cooley (1902), for example, maintained that imitative behavior was learned through trial-and-error processes. But here as elsewhere, no attempt was made to analyze the process of imitation in detail. The matter received very little attention for a number of years until the work of Miller and Dollard (1941) on social learning and imitation.

THE HULLIAN MODEL.   Miller and Dollard (1941) argued that imitation should not be viewed as a unitary process. Instead they proposed that at least three different paradigms are involved in imitative behavior. The *matched-dependent paradigm* involves a situation where a young, stupid, subordinate, or unskilled individual must depend upon an older, brighter, superordinate, or skilled person to read cues that he himself cannot discriminate. In the *same-behavior paradigm*, two people can perform the same act in response to independent stimulation by the same cue, each having learned independently to make the response. In the *copying paradigm*, there is specific guidance by the model of the observer's behavior; the model tells the observer what are the relevant cues and responses and trains him through continuous correction to make the appropriate responses.

Of the three paradigms, matched-dependent behavior has received most attention in Miller and Dollard's treatment. In accord with their social-learning theory, Miller and Dollard spoke of four major parameters of matched-dependent behavior: *cue, response, reward,* and *drive.* These parameters apply both to the behavior of the model and to the behavior of the observer. The example they discussed involved two siblings who wanted candy. One child (the older) had previously learned to run to the door whenever he heard his father coming because his father gave him candy when he met him at the door. If the younger child happened to be running behind his brother when he ran to the door, he also received candy from his father. Eventually the younger boy would learn to run whenever he saw his brother doing so. In this example, the two boys are assumed to be in a state of hunger, a drive state, and candy is assumed to reward their hunger. The model's behavior is assumed to be a discriminative cue for the observer's response of running.

The behavior of the model in this paradigm has primarily a directive function. It directs or guides the behavior of the observer because the observer is reinforced for matching the model's response. The initial occurrence of this response on the part of the observer was assumed to happen randomly—that is, initially the younger boy happens by chance to be running behind his older brother. Once this response is reinforced by candy, it becomes more likely to occur in the future. Henceforth the younger child runs when the older child runs, not only on the father's arrival, but in many other situations where time and place stimuli are different. The relationship between the acts of the model and observer is shown in Figure 4-1.

Miller and Dollard (1941) reported a number of laboratory experiments with animals and with children that indicated that imitative behavior generalizes from one situation to another. In the experiments on children, an independent subject, or model, was given a cue enabling him to determine in which of two boxes candy was to be found. This cue was given by the experimenter before the dependent subject, or observer, was brought into the room. The dependent subject watched the leader make his choice and then made a choice himself. Half of the dependent subjects were rewarded only if they chose the box that the leader chose, and the other half were rewarded only if they chose the box that the leader did not choose. After the dependent subjects had reached a criterion of learning (two successive correct trials), they were given a set of test trials in the same situation to measure the direct effects of learning and a set of test trials in a different situation to measure generalization.

The learning trials clearly demonstrated that the imitative response had been learned by those subjects who had been rewarded for imitating. Similarly, in a slightly different situation (where there were four boxes rather than one), it was found that those subjects who had been rewarded for imitation chose the same box that the leader chose, while those subjects who had not been rewarded for imitation chose boxes other than the one chosen by the leader. Miller and Dollard concluded that "imitation of a given response will be learned if rewarded and that, when learned in one situation, it will generalize to new, somewhat similar situations" (1941, p. 131). The less similar the new situation to the old one, the less generalization occurs.

Miller and Dollard pointed out that the generalized response is initially weaker than the original imitative response. With practice, however, the generalized tendencies will become strong enough for the correct response to occur in the absence of the model. In this way, a socially appropriate response will occur independently. Rather than relying on imitative cues, the child can now make the correct response on the basis of environmental cues. Furthermore, Miller and Dollard suggested that imitation itself can be established as a means of secur-

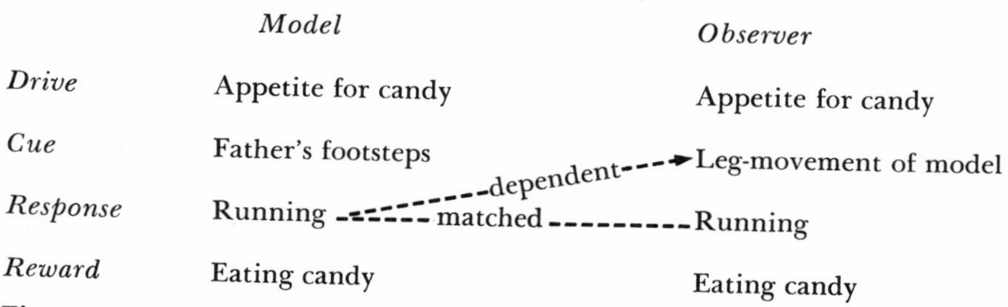

	Model	*Observer*
Drive	Appetite for candy	Appetite for candy
Cue	Father's footsteps	Leg-movement of model
Response	Running — matched —	Running
Reward	Eating candy	Eating candy

(with "dependent" arrow from Response—Cue linking Model to Observer, and "matched" linking the Running responses)

Figure 4-1. The matched-dependent paradigm for imitative learning (from Miller and Dollard, 1941).

ing various rewards. The child will learn to imitate (regardless of the specific activity involved) because he has learned that imitative behavior is rewarding.

They noted, however, that not all imitative behavior is necessarily functional. If the observer, in watching the model, does not notice the relevant environmental cues, imitation will delay the process of learning to respond independently. The observer will not be able to perform the correct response when the model is not present. If, on the other hand, watching the model directs the observer's attention to the relevant environmental cues, the observer will more readily perform the response in the absence of the model.

To recapitulate, Miller and Dollard (1941) regarded imitative learning as a special case of instrumental conditioning in which social cues serve as discriminative stimuli and the observer's responses are differentially rewarded or not rewarded according to whether they match or fail to match those made by the model. Imitative behavior will generalize to other situations; eventually the observer, by identifying the relevant discriminative cues, will learn to perform the response independently in the absence of the model. Should matching behavior not lead to a reward, the imitative response will not be learned. In the Miller and Dollard theory, therefore, imitation (like any learned response in an essentially Hullian behavior-theory approach) is contingent upon reinforcement.

Recent Developments

For two decades the Miller and Dollard, Hullian model was the standard behavioristic explanation of imitation. During that time, however, psychologists showed little interest in imitation phenomena. Possibly the notion of "imitation" retained too much of the innatist flavor it had acquired by entering psychology as an instinct. Possibly imitation carried pejorative connotations, implying rigid, stereotyped mimicry. The "matched-dependent" paradigm lends itself to such an interpretation, especially since the generalization effects about which Miller and Dollard had speculated remained unexplored. At any rate, it was not until the 1960s that imitation became the object of serious theoretical and empirical concern.

SECONDARY REINFORCEMENT THEORIES.   One of the most important recent developments in learning theory generally is an increasing concern about the role of mediating processes. This actually dates to Hull and his discussion of the fractional anticipatory goal-response and the r_g—s_g mechanism that was thought to mediate responses in a behavior chain. As we have seen, similar concepts have been used by Osgood (Osgood, Suci, & Tannenbaum, 1957) and Mowrer (1960b) in their discussions of the development of verbal responses.

The work of Mowrer (1960b) is of special interest at this point; he proposed what was essentially a theory of imitation to account for verbal learning in the child. According to the theory, the child-observer is dependent upon the parent-model for his welfare and nurturance. In the course of gratifying the child's needs, the parent utters various sounds that occur contiguously with gratification. These sounds therefore acquire secondary reinforcement properties, and subsequently the child will himself utter these sounds apart from his parents to experience their secondary reinforcement effects. Thus, in Mowrer's theory, a response is made by the observer at a time when it is not being made by the model. This describes a situation different from the matched-dependent behavior described by Miller and Dollard.

Mowrer's explanation was also different since he saw the observer's behavior to be performed *for its own sake* rather than as a means of reaching some other source of reinforcement as in the Miller and Dollard paradigm. Response strength is increased through a mediating secondary reinforcement (affective) mechanism, and learning is based on the principle of contiguity (Mowrer's sign learning).

Mowrer also described another form of imitation which he called "empathetic learning." In this case the model alone experiences the reinforcement. The observer simply sees the model being reinforced and "intuits" the model's satisfaction. On subsequent occasions, the observer makes the imitative response because he has been able to empathize with the model—that is, to experience the reinforcement *vicariously*. The essential feature of such learning is not so much the ability to imitate behavior as the ability to imitate affect. This seems to be clearly possible for humans, and some evidence has been found (Church, 1959) that empathetic learning occurs in the behavior of animals as well.

The central point of disagreement between Mowrer's approach and that of Miller and Dollard is that for Mowrer the observer does not have to perform the response and then be rewarded for his behavior; the secondary reinforcement provided by the behavior is alone sufficient to bring it into existence. The inadequacies of the Miller and Dollard formulation were especially apparent, Mowrer felt, in the area of language learning. A child does not imitate speech as a means of solving the problem of getting food. Instead he speaks because speaking has acquired secondary reinforcement value and therefore can be used instrumentally, as a means of indicating some desire or need. But the essential first step, according to Mowrer, is one in which words and other human sounds are imitated not because of their utility, but because they have been associated with relief and other satisfactions and, as a result, have themselves come to sound good. Only secondarily does the child discover that words can be used to satisfy needs and control others in the environment. Initially, the process is "autistic," aimed at subjective comfort. Because of their temporal contiguity with primary reinforcements, words gradually take on secondary reinforcement (affective) properties. Later, through the mediation of these affective responses, words are used instrumentally for their objective utility.

A theory of imitative behavior similar to Mowrer's has been proposed by Sheffield (1961) in a discussion of how an observer is able to elicit, some time after an instructional demonstration, those complex response patterns that correspond to the ones demonstrated. Sheffield assumed that mediating perceptual and symbolic responses possess cue properties and thus enable the observer to span the time gap between the demonstration and his own performance of the responses in question. Sheffield thought that this type of learning is based on the principle of contiguity and is mediated by cue-producing cognitive or imaginal responses. He did not, however, see affective mediating responses to play the central role they did in Mowrer's theory.

In contrast, Aronfreed (1968, 1969) has recently proposed a mediational theory of imitation in which mediating affective responses are given as much, if not more, importance than they receive in Mowrer's theory. Aronfreed assumed that children form a cognitive template of the model's behavior that serves for storage and retrieval of performance. This template derives from the child's observation of the model and acts as a *mediating representation* of the model's behavior. It is an internal model for the subsequent replicative behavior of the child. Attached to this cognitive representation is an affective value that controls imitative behavior.

Aronfreed (1968) argued that this value derives ultimately from the intrinsic value of the behavior on the occasion of its first occurrence. Like Mowrer, he saw this as essentially a secondary reinforcement process whereby stimuli obtain acquired value for control over behavior. The support of external reinforcement for the behavior strengthens it further, and some of the behavioral products of imitative learning will be extinguished if they are not reinforced. On the other hand, certain kinds of imitative behavior may have their affective control taken over by self-produced cues that are directly inherent in their very performance.

Aronfreed's theory is one of the more elaborate mediational positions on the scene at the present time. Nevertheless, the central role given to affective value must be justified empirically, and so far the data are meager and indirect. Also, as Flanders (1968) has pointed out, definite criteria are needed for determining the presence or absence of affect in a given case. More precisely, since Aronfreed's theory assumes that affective value is always attached to the child's cognitive representation of the observed behavior, some way of indexing the value of affect should be specified. These and related issues, however, will be discussed later in this chapter.

CLASSICAL CONDITIONING APPROACHES.   One consequence of the development of mediational theories has been the resurrection of the Pavlovian classical conditioning approach to imitation. Such an approach has been used in various ways by recent authors, but the most typical use is to view classical conditioning as a significant part of the process of imitation, rather than as descriptive of the total process. Thus, for example, classical conditioning can be regarded as essential to a mediational theory, since such theories are basically two-factor theories. The emotional or cognitive mediating response can be thought of as a conditioned response that is learned by the observer as a reaction to the model's behavior. This response then mediates instrumental activity.

Such a viewpoint corresponds in part to the paradigm used by the older classical conditioning theorists (Allport, 1924; Holt, 1931). As we have seen, early theorists proposed that the model's behavior serves as a conditioned stimulus and the random behavior of the observer serves as an unconditioned response. After a number of pairings, the conditioned response (formerly random behavior) becomes attached to the stimuli of the model's behavior. In a mediational interpretation, however, the conditioned response is not overt behavior but some emotional or cognitive response that is attached to the stimuli of the model's behavior through conditioning and acts in turn to mediate subsequent instrumental behavior.

Another classical conditioning approach involves the use of a somewhat different paradigm. In this case, the model's behavior acts as an unconditioned stimulus that elicits an unconditioned response in the observer. Thus Berger (1962) found that the sight of a model supposedly being shocked could elicit a spontaneous emotional reaction in an observer. Subsequently, neutral stimuli associated with the shock to the model (conditioned stimuli) were found to produce an emotional response (conditioned response) in the observer (who had never been shocked himself). The observer's reactions were therefore conditioned to neutral stimuli contiguous to the model's behavior.

Such a classical conditioning paradigm emphasizes the cue aspects of the imitative situation, whereas earlier classical conditioning models emphasized the response aspect. That is, in the theories of Allport (1924) and Holt (1931) the focus was upon the imitative response that becomes conditioned to random behavior. The same was true of Miller and Dollard's (1941) theory—the younger boy happened to be running behind his brother and therefore received the reward. The observer's matching behavior was regarded as a chance event. In view of the rapidity with which imitative behavior develops, it seems unrealistic to rely on chance matching (Berger & Lambert, 1968). If, however, one assumes the possibility of prior conditioning whereby neutral stimuli associated with the model's behavior take on the properties of conditioned stimuli, then the acquisition of matched-dependent behavior can be speeded up and greatly facilitated.

This approach does not represent a fully articulated theory of imitative learning. Nevertheless, the role of classical conditioning in the process of imitation has been noted by a number of authors (e.g., Berger, 1962; Mowrer, 1960b; Staats, 1968). Most likely, as Staats (1968) suggested, an adequate theory will require integration of both classical conditioning and instrumental learning principles.

BANDURA'S THEORY OF OBSERVATIONAL LEARNING.   Perhaps the most important recent explanation of imitation is that proposed by Albert Bandura. Bandura's work represents a particularly good example of the tendency of psychologists working in the area of social learning to focus systematically upon limited phenomena and to study these phenomena directly in complex settings. Bandura felt that formulations derived from animal studies or from one-person human learning situations are unlikely to provide a sufficient explanation of social learning (Bandura & Walters, 1963). The old principles simply do not go far enough.

Imitative behavior, Bandura argued (1965a), provides a case in point. Most theories that have been advanced to explain imitation can account satisfactorily for the control of previously learned matching responses but fail to explain how new response patterns are learned observationally. Human subjects in social settings learn new responses by merely seeing a model make them. These responses can be learned even though the observer does not overtly perform the model's responses during the acquisition phase ("no-trial" learning) and in cases where neither the model nor the observer are reinforced. Such phenomena, Bandura contended, indicate the importance of perceptual and other symbolic processes in imitative learning. Through observation of the modeling stimuli the observer acquires *internal representational responses* that mediate subsequent behavioral reproduction. Bandura's theory is therefore a mediation theory of imitative learning, yet one that differs in important respects from other mediation theories.

The acquisition of imitative responses involves two representational systems—an imaginal and a verbal one (Bandura, 1969). *Imagery formation* was assumed to occur via a process of sensory conditioning. Stimuli from the model's behavior elicit perceptual responses in the observer that become sequentially associated and centrally integrated through temporal contiguity. After repeated contiguous stimulation, these perceptual responses come to form imaginal representations of the stimuli involved. Thus through observation transitory perceptual phenomena produce relatively long lasting, retrievable images of modeled sequences of behavior.

Since human subjects are able to reproduce observed behavior with remarkable speed and to retain the contents of that behavior for long periods of time, Bandura argued that the observed events are *coded verbally* and that the dominant cognitive processes that govern imitative behavior in human subjects are verbal rather than visual. These verbal responses greatly facilitate the processes of retrieval and reproduction of imitative behavior.

The manner in which mediating responses are acquired distinguishes Bandura's system from previously discussed S-R mediational approaches. Theorists such as Mowrer and Aronfreed stressed the importance of affective feedback whereby pleasurable or aversive states become conditioned to internal mediating processes. Bandura regarded such theories as insufficient in that they fail to explain the acquisition of imitative behavior when reinforcers are dispensed neither to the model nor to the observer. In the absence of reinforcers, affective feedback theories provide no mechanisms for learning. Bandura, on the other hand, did not regard reinforcement as necessary for learning—imitative behavior is acquired simply through stimulus contiguity (S-S learning) and symbolic mediation.

It should be noted, however, that Bandura did not maintain that the mere contiguity of sensory stimulation produces imitative behavior. Sensory stimulation is not independent of motivation, reinforcement, and other factors. A group of people in an automobile, for example, are exposed to the behavior of the driver, but this does not mean that they can reproduce his behavior perfectly (Bandura, 1962). Exposure to a complex set of stimuli does not necessarily guarantee that the observer will select and learn relevant cues while disregarding irrelevant ones, or even that he will perceive the cues accurately. Imitation is not a passive observational process, but an active process in which a number of variables operate in conjunction with sensory stimulation to determine performance.

Bandura (1969) has recently attempted to specify the variables that determine imitative behavior. According to this formulation observational learning involves four interrelated subprocesses, each with its own controlling variables. The first of these processes concerns *attention*. If the observer fails to attend to the model or fails to discriminate the distinctive features of the model's behavior, little imitative learning will occur. A great deal of research is needed to determine the effects on attention of such variables as the frequency, duration, rate, saliency, and complexity of visual cues. In addition, motivational conditions, prior training in discriminative observation, and the presence of incentive-oriented sets may strongly determine those features of the environment and those models to which a person attends. Model characteristics and the interaction of model and observer characteristics may also prove to be important factors in the attentional process.

A second process involves the *retention* of modeled events. In order to reproduce social behavior without the continued presence of external modeling cues, a person must be able to retain the original observational input in some symbolic form. Rehearsal operations—whether overt or covert—have been shown to play an important role in the process of retention (Bandura, Ross, & Ross, 1963b), as have symbolic imaginal and verbal coding operations (Gerst, 1968).

The next process concerns *motoric reproduction*. At issue here is the manner in which symbolic representations guide and determine overt performance. Bandura (1969) argued that the process of representational guidance is essentially the same as the process whereby behavior is controlled by external stimuli; the only difference is that in representational guidance the controlling stimuli are not external, but symbolic counterparts of absent stimuli. Consequently the same variables operate in each form of behavior. The complexity of behavior, for example, affects its motoric reproduction whether performance is determined by symbolic representation or is dependent upon external stimuli. More complex behavior sequences are learned gradually in stepwise fashion; less complex sequences are learned more quickly.

The final process in Bandura's scheme involves *incentive and motivation*. A person may acquire, retain, and possess the capacity to reproduce a modeled behavior, but the learning may not be activated into overt performance because of negative sanctions or the absence of incentive conditions. Once reinforcement is introduced, however, observational learning is likely to be translated into action. Bandura therefore distinguished between the acquisition of imitative responses and their performance. He and his associates have demonstrated that verbal (Bandura & Harris, 1966) and non-verbal (Bandura, Grusec, & Menlove, 1966) responses can be acquired observationally, without the responses actually occurring. Overt performance of the response depends on incentive and motivational factors.

In Bandura's system behavior may be maintained by reinforcement that is externally administered or by *vicarious reinforcement*, in which case the model receives reinforcement but the observer does not. Bandura (1965a) saw vicarious reinforcement to produce diverse psychological effects such that various operations could be responsible for consequent behavioral changes. Thus vicarious reinforcement could serve a discriminative or informational role for an observer. The outcome of the model's behavior might confirm or fail to confirm the observer's hypotheses as to the outcome of his own behavior. The consequences of the model's behavior may also serve to enhance the relative distinctiveness of stimuli to which the observer attends and may provide incentives for certain forms of behavior. In addition, Bandura pointed out that vicarious emotional effects are often produced in the observer as a consequence of what happens to a model (Berger, 1962). Finally, the model's behavior and its outcome can increase or decrease the prestige of the model in the observer's eyes, thereby affecting subsequent modeling attempts.

In addition to externally administered reinforcement and vicarious reinforcement, behavior may be determined by *self-reinforcement*. In this case control in achieved over one's own actions through self-generated stimuli (Bandura, 1969). Thus the individual judges his behavior according to certain standards of self-evaluation and administers self-reward or self-punishment depending on whether performance exceeds, matches, or falls short of self-prescribed demands. Self-reinforcement is of considerable importance in human social behavior and will be discussed in greater detail in Chapter Seven.

A final aspect of Bandura's theory of observational learning relates to the generality of modeling effects. Bandura and his coworkers (Bandura & McDonald, 1963; Bandura & Mischel, 1965) found that observers were able to respond to new stimulus situations in a manner consistent with the model's dispositions, although the observer had never witnessed the model respond to the same stimuli. In these studies models and observers responded to entirely different stimuli, and tests for generalized imitative effects were conducted by different experimenters in the model's absence. Bandura (1969) argued that such findings indicate the possibility of a *higher-order form of modeling* in which the observer abstracts relevant attributes and formulates response-guiding rules on the basis of the model's behavior. Subsequent responses that embody the observationally derived rule are likely to resemble the behavior that the model would be inclined to exhibit in similar circumstances. The process by which rules are abstracted involves vicarious discrimination training (Bandura & Harris, 1966) in which responses containing the relevant attribute are reinforced while those that lack the relevant attribute are consistently nonrewarded.

Bandura (1969) argued that such higher-order modeling indicates that observational learning is not limited to mere mimicry but also explains innovative and generative behavior. This allows for a social-learning explanation of language development and production, since the rules of grammar may be viewed as the result of abstraction from verbal modeling cues. The child does not simply imitate specific verbal responses, he acquires rules about grammatical relations between words.

Bandura's theory of observational learning has been highly productive of research, as we shall see when we turn to empirical issues. In these terms the theory has been a successful one. It has, however, been mildly criticized for certain inconsistencies (Staats, 1968) and for failing to specify the conditions under which acquisition and performance of imitative behavior are manifested (Flanders, 1968). A more serious and detailed critique has recently been presented by Gewirtz and Stingle (1968), who proposed an alternative explanation of observational learning.

GENERALIZED-IMITATION LEARNING.   Gewirtz and Stingle (1968) took exception in particular to the tendency of Bandura and other mediation theorists (e.g., Aronfreed, 1968) to regard imitation as learning that could occur without specific instrumental training. In their discussion Gewirtz and Stingle distinguished between *imitation,* defined as behavior matched to cues provide by the model's response; *generalized imitation,* or behavior that involves copying many different responses of the model in diverse situations often without apparent reinforcement; and *identification,* or the process of taking on abstract psychological characteristics of a model such as motives, values, and ideals, rather than specific behavior patterns.

According to Gewirtz and Stingle, imitative responses occur initially by chance (or direct training). When such responses occur, they are strengthened by direct reinforcement from environmental agents. After several imitative responses become established in this manner, a set of diverse but functionally equivalent behaviors is acquired and maintained by reinforcement on an intermittent schedule. This *set of behaviors* is what Gewirtz and Stingle referred to as generalized imitation. Thus if accurate reproduction (imitation) of modeling stimuli is rewarded, the behavior class of imitative responses takes on reinforcement properties (generalized imitation). Individual behaviors of the class may be performed even though they themselves are not reinforced; it is the response class that has acquired reward value.

To clarify the mechanisms involved in the acquisition and maintenance of generalized imitation, Gewirtz and Stingle presented as an analogy the matching-to-sample discrimination-learning paradigm. In this paradigm, each subject chooses from a number of comparison stimuli one that shares a common property with a sample stimulus. After performing a number of matching responses under the control of reinforcement, the subject acquires the relevant matching-response class—a "concept" or, as Gewirtz and Stingle preferred to call it, a "conditional discrimination"—that then governs the subject's responses to a wide range of stimuli differing in content. This process Gewirtz and Stingle saw as analogous to an observer's selecting from a set of alternatives (the responses in his own repertoire) those responses that match the cues provided by the model's response. Once a number of matched responses are made, the subject acquires the relevant matching-response class—in this case the functional imitative class—that then governs the subject's behavior to a wide range of social stimuli differing in content. A similar analysis of imitative learning was presented by Baer and Sherman (1964) and Staats (1968).

According to Gewirtz and Stingle, such an analysis provides an alternative to Bandura's "no-trial" observational learning (in which the observer has no apparent opportunity to practice the observed response prior to testing) since it can be argued that observational learning of this sort represents a specific instance of generalized-imitation learning. Gewirtz and Stingle were uncomfortable with Bandura's analysis because it implied that learning could occur without prior instrumental training. Lacking precise knowledge of the learning experience of the individual, they felt, there was no practical way to exclude the possibility of prior instrumental learning. They therefore proposed that instrumental learning is a *necessary* ingredient of all imitative behavior, but that a given instance of behavior could be performed not because that specific response has been previously learned but because a response class of functional matching responses has been learned. The individual has not simply learned a given response, he has by instrumental training *learned to learn* when exposed to a model's responses. Since intermittently reinforced imitative behavior is likely to have characterized a child's experience in life settings prior to exposure to the model, generalized imitation of varied responses with a wide range of models can account for the child's observational learning.

Gewirtz and Stingle viewed vicarious reinforcement in essentially the same terms. When a child sees a model reinforced for a specific behavior, he will tend to imitate that behavior because the responses for which the model was reinforced are likely to be reinforced in the same settings. The response itself usually is one that is already in the child's repertoire due to its having been reinforced earlier (especially if the response is one that is likely to occur in the context or if reinforcement is likely to occur there). Reinforcement administered to the model functions as a *generalized cue* for a high probability of reinforcement to the observer when he engages in that behavior. In this way reinforcing stimuli contingent upon the model's behavior come to provide discriminative cues that facilitate or inhibit imitative behavior.

One of the criticisms frequently brought against an instrumental conditioning analysis of imitative behavior is that it does not account for the rapid acquisition of imitative responses (Bandura & Walters, 1963). Gewirtz and Stingle answered this criticism by arguing that imitative behavior, conceptualized as a response class, is learned very early in the child's development because parents and others deliberately set out to teach the child to imitate. Since an abundance of reinforcements are administered by a wide variety of reinforcing agents on an intermittent schedule and for diverse imitative responses, generalized imitation is learned quickly, maintained at high strength, and kept relatively resistant to extinction. It serves as an important mechanism for social learning and acts as a means whereby the verbal responses of a child are acquired and maintained (Gewirtz, 1969).

Gewirtz and Stingle also extended their generalized-imitation paradigm to imitation in the model's absence, to imitation of the model in play, and to generalized imitation of the model's values. In each of these cases, imitative behavior occurs because the child has learned to discriminate the common elements of responses exhibited by the model in a set of related stimulus contexts. That is, the child has learned a *functional class* of imitative responses that it can apply to situations where the model is absent and even where the child has never seen the model perform. Thus the generalized-imitation paradigm can be employed to explain imitative behavior in situations where some of the relevant discriminative and reinforcing stimuli for imitation are absent. This brings Gewirtz and Stingle to the question of identification.

By identification, it will be recalled, Gewirtz and Stingle referred to the process of adopting abstract psychological characteristics of the model rather than specific behavior sequences. These characteristics include motives, values, ideals, roles, and conscience. The model is assumed to be the child's parents and especially the same-sex parent. The classic analysis of the identification process is Freud's (1920), but other more recent analyses exist as well (e.g., Kagan, 1958; Kohlberg, 1966; Whiting, 1960). All of these are deficient, Gewirtz and Stingle argued, because they employed "cognitive-flavored abstractions or intrapsychic euphemisms as mechanisms to account for identification phenomena" (1968, p. 393). Instead, Gewirtz and Stingle proposed a functional approach according to which the phenomena usually grouped under identification were assumed to be consequences of generalized-imitation training.

Essentially, such an approach regards the development of identification as the result of *reinforcement* of the child's imitation of his parents' behavior. The child imitates diverse responses performed by his parent-models because he is consistently reinforced for that class of behaviors, perhaps even more consistently than for behaviors he initiates on his own. Moreover, such imitative responses are likely to be reinforced in a variety of social settings. After the response class has been established through reinforcement, many imitative responses will occur without reinforcement and in the model's absence. These responses will include some that were reinforced, as well as some that were never reinforced but which do belong to the class of behaviors that is (intermittently) reinforced. In addition, they will include responses that the child has never seen the model perform but that are under the control of *discriminative stimuli* similar to those that control the model's behavior.

The relevant independent variables for the study of identification are therefore variations in discriminative and reinforcement parameters, while the critical dependent variable is the similarity between the child's responses and those of the model in structured stimulus settings. The Gewirtz and Stingle approach suggests that the similarity of the child's responses to his parents' will be a function of the value to the child of the reinforcement contingent upon imitation of that particular behavior. In addition, it will depend upon his exposure to other models and the reinforcement received from imitating them, the frequency of reinforcement for original, non-imitative responses, and the value of reinforcers provided for each of these behavior classes.

The Gewirtz and Stingle theory is more Thorndikian and behavioristic than is that of Bandura. The child learns instrumentally, by doing rather than merely by observing. Where Bandura and others resorted to mediational processes to span the gap between observation and behavior, Gewirtz and Stingle relied simply on the child's history of instrumental learning. There was no need for representational or cognitive processes. Once the child has learned to imitate varied responses to a wide range of models, it does not matter whether the model is reinforced or even present.

In eschewing mediational concepts Gewirtz and Stingle allied themselves with hardcore behavioristic tradition. Like Skinner, they focused on the reinforcement history of the individual and on the stimuli that controlled his behavior. They did not deal simply with discrete responses but, like Skinner (1938), their analysis assumes that responses may be generic in nature and that an operant may be defined as a class of responses. By doing so, they attempted to avoid the pitfall of explaining the how and why of this particular response by viewing it as an instance of a set of (generalized) imitative responses.

Nevertheless, the theory is convincing only if it survives empirical scrutiny. To test its adequacy fully will most likely require the use of animals, since it is necessary for the subjects' reinforcement history to be strictly regulated. When children are used as subjects, it will be necessary to specify the discriminative cues that control their behavior, as well as the value of the reinforcements available to them. Similarly, the relation between the child's behavior and that of the model must be carefully specified, especially when the behaviors of the child are termed identification and relate to values, ideals, or roles. The problems in such specification are considerable, and it remains to be seen whether the theory will be successful in indexing operationally its independent and dependent variables.

RESEARCH ON IMITATION AND VICARIOUS LEARNING

Now that we have discussed the major learning-theory explanations of imitation, we can turn our attention to research in this area. In doing so, it will hopefully be possible to evaluate how well the various theories account for the empirical data. Consequently, our intent here is not to provide a comprehensive review of the research literature on imitative behavior (see Bandura, 1969; Flanders, 1968), but rather to deal with studies from that literature that have particular theoretical relevance and can thereby be presumed to contribute to our understanding of the processes involved.

In discussing this literature we shall use Mowrer's (1960b) distinction between *imitation*—that is, behavior in which the observer is directly reinforced for imitating the model's behavior—and *vicarious learning*—that is, imitative behavior for which the observer is not directly reinforced. Such a distinction is not entirely satisfactory because, as Berger and Lambert (1968) pointed out, it involves the determination of an absence of a condition (reinforcement)—which is difficult to specify with full confidence operationally. Nevertheless, the distinction is a useful one.

Imitation

Typically, experiments on imitation involve the observation by a subject of the behavior of a model and the comparison of the subject's subsequent behavior with that of subjects who had no exposure to the model. Imitative behavior is assessed by judges' ratings of the degree of similarity between the observer's behavior and that of the model. In another design, the tendency of the subjects to engage in the behavior in question is first assessed and then the experimental subjects are exposed to the model while control subjects have no exposure to the model. In this case, the dependent variable is the increase in frequency or amplitude of response.

MECHANISMS OF IMITATION.   According to the Miller and Dollard (1941) conception of imitation as "matched-dependent behavior," imitative responses are attached to cues transmitted by the model to the observer through repeated trials and external reinforcement. The experimental evidence in support of this theoretical position came from experiments with both rats and children. In these studies subjects were trained to make either the same or an opposite choice in response to cues that they had observed. Essentially the same paradigm has been used to induce adults to engage in imitative responses (O'Connell, 1965; Schein, 1954). The nature of these experiments is such, however, as to support the theoretical position from which they originated. The task is basically a discrimination training task in which the relevant cues happen to be socially transmitted. The criticism has therefore been made that Miller and Dollard were not studying imitation at all, but simply behavior in response to *specific cues* (Bandura, 1962). The theory fails to explain imitative behavior that occurs in the absence of these cues—for example, when the observer has no opportunity to perform the behavior after seeing the model and only subsequently makes imitative responses. The Miller and Dollard theory provides no way of bridging the gap between observation and behavior lacking necessary discriminative cues.

There is a second difficulty with the Miller and Dollard paradigm. In their research a model performed a specific set of responses and observers were subsequently tested for precise matching behavior in similar or identical situations. Under these limited conditions the only possible response was *mimicry* of specific modeled responses. Yet later studies (e.g., Bandura & McDonald, 1963; Bandura & Mischel, 1965) have demonstrated that imitative behavior is a broad phenomenon—that subjects will respond to new stimulus situations in a manner consistent with the model's disposition without ever having seen the model respond to particular stimuli. Imitation is therefore not reducible to simple mimicry or "matching" of behavior but includes "higher-order" forms of modeling as well (Bandura, 1969).

In short, it appears that the Miller and Dollard theory works best when there is a close relationship between the occurrence of cues and the imitative behavior and when imitation involves precise matching of the model's behavior. The theory is less satisfactory as an explanation of more complex imitative behaviors. To account for more complicated phenomena theorists have resorted to mediational theories. Rather than depending on the relationship between external cues and behavior, such theories assume that external stimuli elicit internal responses in the observer that control overt behavior.

As we have seen, there are two major mediational approaches to imitative behavior. The first of these stresses the importance of *conditioned affectivity* (Aronfreed, 1968; Mowrer, 1960b). Pleasurable or unpleasant consequences of behavior become attached to mediating internal responses, giving these responses an affective tonality. It is this reinforcement-derived affective value that controls imitative behavior. In contrast, Bandura (1969) has argued that the mediation involved in imitative learning does not depend on reinforcement but derives simply from *contiguity* between the stimuli involved in the model's behavior and the observer's perceptual responses that come to form imaginal or verbal representations of the stimuli involved.

Bandura's position was supported by research in which subjects learned imitative responses from demonstrations that did not involve the positive or aversive stimuli essential for the classical conditioning of affective responses. In these studies (e.g., Bandura, Grusec, & Menlove, 1966; Bandura, Ross, & Ross, 1961) subjects who merely observed the model, under conditions in which neither the model nor the subject experienced reinforcement, displayed the behavior in question to a greater extent than did control subjects who had no exposure to the model. It would seem, therefore, that affective mediational theories apply most directly to situations in which the modeled responses produce reinforcing outcomes that endow stimuli associated with the responses with motivational or secondary reinforcement properties. It is possible nevertheless for imitative behavior to occur in the absence of such conditions.

In the Bandura, Grusec, and Menlove (1966) study some subjects who observed the model verbalized the behavior of the model while other subjects did not. A third group was instructed to engage in competing symbolization (counting) while watching the model's behavior. Incentive set was also manipulated by offering children attractive incentives for reproducing the model's behavior. A test for imitative learning revealed that those subjects who verbally coded the model's behavior performed more matching responses than subjects in the passive observation condition, while subjects who engaged in competing symbolization showed the least amount of imitative behavior (Figure 4-2). Bandura and his coworkers interpreted these findings as indicating that implicit symbolic coding responses (verbal rehearsal) mediate subsequent task performance.

The importance of *rehearsal* has also been demonstrated by Berger (1966) in a study in which observers were exposed to a model learning items from a manual alphabet for the deaf. In this case, subjects did not rehearse the task verbally but engaged in behavioral motor rehearsal. The subjects, supposedly out of sight of the experimenter, tended to practice the hand signals overtly and distinctly. Thus it was possible to record the amount of rehearsal the subjects engaged in and its effect on their learning.

Berger found that the model's behavior determined to a large extent what was practiced by the subjects (81 percent practiced one or more of the hand signals), and that this in turn determined what was learned. He concluded that there is an ongoing tendency to imitate the model during the exposure period. This is reflected in the tendency of observers to make behavior motor responses, as well as fragmentary movements, vocalizations, and mouth movements—all of which can conceivably be regarded as cue-producing responses that mediate imitative behavior. As Berger recognized, however, more intensive research is needed to determine precisely how overt responses affect imitative behavior.

Since children are capable of very rapid and accurate modifications of behavior on the basis of brief observation of a model's actions, it seems likely that rehearsal is not simply representational but, as Berger suggested, often involves overt practice. Moreover, since the capacity to imitate increases with age, it can be assumed to reflect general *developmental changes*. Thus research has shown developmental increments in the child's ability to observe and copy verbal and motor behaviors (e.g., Bühler, 1935; Terman & Merrill, 1937). Aronfreed (1968) regarded these developmental findings as indicating that the child's capacity to store and reproduce the behavior of others is a function of more general changes in his cognitive capacities. As the child grows older he becomes capable of storing programs of increasing complexity and of rapidly forming a cognitive representation of the model's behavior.

Analysis of the mediating processes involved in imitative learning has only begun. At the present time, little is known empirically

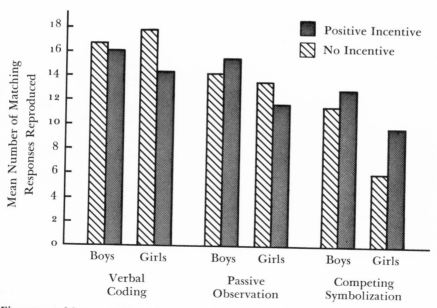

Figure 4-2. Mean number of matching responses reproduced by children as a function of symbolization and incentive set (data from Bandura, Grusec, & Menlove, 1966).

of the relative importance of overt and covert responses in mediating imitative behavior. Theoretical formulations have been elaborated with increasing sophistication but without much experimental support. In part, this is a function of the form the theory has taken. If mediational approaches are to prove to be experimentally testable, they must be linked to operational manipulations. This has been the problem to date—to specify immediate behavioral measures that can be related directly to the postulated mediating processes. It may be that increasing attention will be given to the role of implicit verbal responses, as Berger and Lambert (1968) have suggested. In this case, verbal behavior paradigms will become important theoretically for the analysis of imitative behavior.

It should be noted, however, that the theoretical approach taken by Gewirtz and Stingle (1968) represents an alternative to mediational theories. Here again, however, supportive research, while suggestive, has not been definitive. Since this research tends to be concerned mainly with the effect of reinforcement (or its absence) on imitative behavior, we shall turn now to this topic.

THE EFFECTS OF REINFORCEMENT.   The Miller and Dollard (1941) formulation gave central importance to the role of reinforcement. It was assumed that the more reinforcement the observer receives for imitating the behavior of the model, the more he will tend to imitate. There is considerable empirical support for this proposition (e.g., Bandura, 1965b; Miller & Dollard, 1941; Wilson, 1958). If reinforcement does not always follow the imitative response, there will be a corresponding decrease in imitation, although such a partial reinforcement schedule will be more resistant to extinction than is the case when imitative responses are continuously reinforced (Lewis & Duncan, 1958).

If punishment follows imitative behavior, it leads to a suppression of imitation, especially if the observer has been punished at the start of the prohibited act rather than at its termination (Walters, Parke, & Cane, 1965). In general, research has indicated that rewarding desired responses *and* punishing undesired ones is a highly efficient way to produce the desired imitative behavior (Miller & Dollard, 1941; Mischel & Liebert, 1967).

As we have seen, Mowrer (1960b) and Bandura and Walters (1963) regarded vicarious reinforcement as an empirically demonstrated phenomenon. In this case, imitative responses are made, although no reinforcement is given to the subject for his imitative behavior. We shall discuss empirical evidence for vicarious learning later in this chapter. The point we wish to make here is that imitative behavior learned in the absence of direct reinforcement to the subject poses problems for a straightforward application of reinforcement principles to imitative learning such as was proposed by Miller

and Dollard (1941). According to Miller and Dollard, vicarious reinforcement should have no effect on imitation, nor should non-reinforcement training (when neither the model nor the observer are
reinforced). The evidence, however, suggests that in both cases imitative learning occurs. Thus mere exposure to a model produces more
imitative behavior than no exposure, even when the model is not
reinforced (Bandura, Ross, & Ross, 1961; Berger, 1966).

If the observer is rewarded for his imitative behavior, it may be
hypothesized that one determinant of the degree to which he will
make imitative responses is the *value* of the reinforcement. The
greater the value, the more imitation might be expected. Some evidence exists in support of this hypothesis (Liebert & Ora, 1968;
Mischel & Grusec, 1966), but the topic has not been thoroughly re-
searched.

Baer and Sherman (1964) reported that reinforcement to the observer could increase imitative behavior for reinforced responses as
well as for responses that were not reinforced. In their study, young
children were reinforced for matching three responses of an animated
talking puppet but not for imitating a fourth response. As a result
of reinforcement to the three responses, the fourth response was spontaneously imitated by some of the children. In a similar study Baer,
Peterson, and Sherman (1967) physically assisted three retarded children in making imitative responses that were immediately reinforced.
After being trained to make a few such responses, the subjects were
able to imitate new modeled behavior and eventually response chains
without assistance. They did this although previously they had shown
no signs of being capable of imitative behavior. Thus through initial
physical assistance and reinforcement the children had learned to
imitate or, as Baer and his associates put it, had developed an "imitative repertoire" (1967, p. 407).

Baer and his associates accounted for their results on the basis of
conditioned reinforcement. They argued that the subjects had been
taught a series of responses, each of which was topographically similar
to the demonstration given by the model. Initially each response was
established as matched-dependent behavior. Eventually the child was
able to discriminate the topographical similarity between the model
and himself. This was possible because there existed a correspondence
of some sort between the stimulus output of the child himself and
that of the model. That is, the child learned "to discriminate a correspondence between the appearance of his hand and the model's
hand, his arm and the model's arm, his leg and the model's leg, his
voice and the model's voice, etc." (Baer *et al.*, 1967, p. 416.) In this
manner the stimulus class of behavioral similarity was, through repeated trials, made discriminative for the reinforcement of various
directly imitative responses. It therefore acquired conditioned-rein-

forcement value, strengthening responses that produced it—even responses that occurred in the absence of reinforcement.

The work of Baer and his associates provided the point of departure for the conceptualization of imitative learning proposed by Gewirtz and Stingle (1968). As we have seen, according to this approach the reinforcement that children receive for imitative behavior gradually induces a *generalized disposition* to imitate the behavior of others. Imitative behavior resulting from such a generalized disposition might be attached not only to precise imitative replication of the behavior of the model but to any acts that roughly correspond to the acts of others. Since generalized imitation is acquired and maintained on an intermittent schedule, the child need not be reinforced for every imitative act. It is therefore possible for him to display imitative responses when neither he nor the model is reinforced and when the model is no longer present.

An alternate explanation for generalized imitation has been proposed by Bandura (1969). Rather than ascribing this phenomenon to reinforcement processes as Baer and his associates (1967) and Gewirtz and Stingle (1968) did, Bandura stressed the importance of *discrimination processes*. The experimental evidence for generalized reinforcement (Baer *et al.*, 1967; Lovaas *et al.*, 1966) derives from studies in which nonrewarded modeled responses were randomly embedded among a large number of responses that were consistently reinforced. It was therefore extremely difficult for subjects to distinguish the two sets of modeled responses and consequently both sets were performed with equal frequency. If, however, the nonrewarded responses are highly distinguishable, Bandura predicted that they would eventually extinguish. A discrimination hypothesis therefore predicts that the longer differential reinforcement practices are continued, the more likely the observer is to distinguish between rewarded and nonrewarded imitative behavior. In contrast, the reinforcement hypothesis predicts that continued differential reinforcement increases the strength of the generalized imitative disposition, thereby increasing the resistance to extinction of nonrewarded matching responses.

To test the discrimination hypothesis, Bandura and Barab (1969) reinforced matching responses in children until a high level of imitative responding was attained. The children were then exposed to two models and consistently reinforced for reproducing the behavior of the first but never reinforced for reproducing the small subset of motor responses modeled by the second experimenter. In the final phase of the experiment the rewarding experimenter modeled three sets of responses: (1) twenty of the original rewarded responses that continued to be rewarded, (2) five nonrewarded motor responses interspersed among rewarded motor responses (and therefore difficult to discriminate from rewarded responses), and (3) a second subset of five nonrewarded verbal responses modeled one after another rather than interspersed among the rewarded responses (therefore highly discriminable). Bandura and Barab found that over blocks of trials children continued to imitate rewarded matching responses and nonrewarded motor responses but that they decreased their imitations of the discriminable nonrewarded verbal responses.

The findings of the Bandura and Barab (1969) study suggest that generalized imitation is not the product of conditioned reinforcement but merely of a failure to discriminate. Rather than employing an explanation based largely on reinforcement mechanisms, Bandura would interpret generalization in imitative responding on the basis of discriminability of stimuli signifying probable consequences, prior history of selective reinforcement, and subjective reinforcement contingencies derived by individuals from other informative cues. Such an interpretation does not deny the role of reinforcement; it merely gives it less central emphasis.

EFFECTS OF MODEL CHARACTERISTICS.   In his review of research on imitative behavior, Flanders (1968) itemized a number of variables relating to antecedent characteristics of the model. For example, if the model controls resources, he is more likely to be imitated than if he exerts no such control (e.g., Bandura, Ross, & Ross, 1963a; Mischel & Grusec, 1966). Models who are older, more skillful, and higher in social status than observers are more readily imitated (Bandura & Walters, 1963). Studies of the effect of the sex variable have not yielded consistent results (e.g., Bandura & Kupers, 1964 vs. Bandura, Ross, & Ross, 1963a).

One area that has received extended treatment in the research literature relates to the role of *nurturance* in imitative learning. Generally, the outcome of these studies has indicated that nurturant models of either sex are imitated more by observers of either sex (Bandura & Huston, 1961; Hetherington & Frankie, 1967). Mussen and Parker (1965) found that girls who had highly nurturant mothers reproduced more of the mother's behavior than did girls whose mothers were less nurturant. Not all experiments supported these findings, however. In some studies nurturant and rewarding characteristics of the model have had no effect, or even a disruptive effect on imitative behavior (Aronfreed, 1964; Rosenhan & White, 1967).

In the Bandura and Huston (1961) study, children who had a nurturant relationship with the model were found to be more inclined to imitate the model's stylistic or expressive, task-irrelevant behavior than were children whose model had assumed a non-nurturant role. Similarly, in the Mussen and Parker (1965) study, the girls more readily adopted the expressive ("incidental") behavior of highly nurturant mothers than they did the behavior of less nurturant mothers.

These findings may serve to reconcile some of the inconsistencies obtained in research on the relationship between nurturance and imitative behavior. If a distinction is made between the expressive (incidental) and instrumental (intentional) features of the model's behavior, it may be that nurturance is peculiarly effective in focusing the attention of the child on the expressive aspects of the model's behavior. Because young children generally give more attention to the expressive aspects of behavior and because they have only a limited capacity to separate relevant and irrelevant information in the course of instrumental learning (Siegel & Stevenson, 1966), it may be, as Aronfreed (1968) suggested, that imitative learning of expressive behavior is controlled by the affective value of the behavior itself, whereas imitative learning of instrumental behavior is controlled by the value of external outcomes or criteria of performance.

Table 4-1
Comparison of Intentional and Incidental Learning Scores for Low- and High-Dependent Subjects.

GROUP	N	INTENTIONAL BEHAVIOR	INCIDENTAL BEHAVIOR
Low-Dependent Boys	10	37.6	12.7
High-Dependent Boys	10	31.0	29.5
Low-Dependent Girls	10	41.8	12.1
High-Dependent Girls	10	34.4	23.5
All Low-Dependent Children	20	39.7	12.4
All High-Dependent Children	20	32.7	26.5

From Ross, 1966. Scores are mean scores for each group; all differences between dependent groups attained statistical significance.

A number of studies lend support to this argument. For example, Ross (1966) found that high-dependent children learned less of the intentional behaviors and more of the incidental behaviors of an adult model than did low-dependent children in a situation in which nursery-school children were taught to play a game through imitation of a model (Table 4-1). Since highly dependent children can be expected to be more oriented toward nurturance and attention of adults than low-dependent children, Ross' findings are consistent with the view that the salience of the nurturant attributes of the model facilitates learning of the model's expressive behavior.

Grusec and Mischel (1966) also found a facilitative effect of nurturance on the learning of expressive behavior. In their study, children were asked to recall and reproduce the actions of the model. Those children who had received nurturance from their models were found to be better able to recall subsequent expressive behavior than were children whose models did not assume a nurturant role. Moreover, the effect of nurturance extended to recall for the expressive behavior involved in criticizing and delaying the child's play activity. It appears therefore that nurturance may produce a generalized facilitative effect (on recall and on learning) for both positively and negatively toned expressive behavior.

Research on model characteristics will in all likelihood continue in view of the importance of this variable for understanding how and under what conditions imitation occurs in daily life. Model characteristics and the interaction of model and observer characteristics appear to play a central role in what Bandura (1969) called the attentional processes involved in imitative learning. The child does not attend in the same way to all people around him in the environment. In fact, he chooses selectively from the models he encounters and even from behavior of individual models. Future research should lead to a better understanding of the variables governing this selectivity.

Vicarious Learning

In the vicarious learning paradigm the observer is not directly reinforced for imitative behavior. In one experimental procedure (non-reinforcement) neither the model nor the observer is reinforced. In a second procedure (vicarious reinforcement) the model is reinforced but the observer is not. In this section we shall first discuss vicarious responding in general, then turn to empirical studies of non-reinforcement training and of vicarious reinforcement training.

VICARIOUS RESPONDING. As we have seen, Mowrer (1960b) described a situation in which the observer merely sees the model being reinforced and subsequently imitates the model's behavior—not because it provides him with reinforcement but because he is able to *empathize* with the model and thereby experience reinforcement vicariously. According to Mowrer, such behavior is possible because the observer imitates both the behavior and the affect of the model. People can respond vicariously because they can imaginatively (or empathetically) put themselves in someone else's position.

According to a somewhat different explanation, the model's behavior acts as a cue for emotional arousal in the observer. Thus, in an experiment mentioned earlier in this chapter, Berger (1962) was able to show that the sight of a model supposedly being shocked elicited a spontaneous emotional reaction in an observer. In a similar study (DiLollo & Berger, 1965), the sight of another person's pain cues was found to have a generalized arousal effect on the observer's responses in a simple reaction-time task.

According to Berger's position, vicarious responses are initially attached to a perceptual experience of another person through *classical conditioning*. Developmentally, vicarious responses are learned by close and repeated association of the cues that convey the experience of other people and stimulus events that have affective consequences to the child. For example, events that have positive affective consequences may be experienced simultaneously by the child and another person. When this happens external cues of positive affect are emitted by the other person in close contiguity with the child's own experience of positive affect. In this way the child's own affective response is conditioned to the cues of other persons. Subsequently the individual can draw on this backlog of conditioning experience so that observation of a model's emotional response will trigger a corresponding emotional reaction.

Another approach to vicarious responding emphasizes the role of mediational processes (Aronfreed, 1968; Bandura, 1962; Lewis & Duncan, 1958). In the Lewis and Duncan analysis, for example, a distinction was made between *representational* and *emotional mediating responses*. The representational mediators have an associative or directive function, and the emotional mediators have an arousal or motivating function. When a subject is rewarded for a correct response, he presumably makes a subvocal response, such as "I pulled this lever," that becomes associated with definite responses or response sequences. This is the associative or representational mediating response in the theory. When he is rewarded, an emotional response also occurs that results from the pleasurable aspects of reward. If he is not rewarded, a different emotional response occurs—one of displeasure or frustration resulting from the failure to obtain reward. These emotional responses constitute motivational mediating responses and become associated with such subvocalizations as "good" or "not good." The observer presumably goes through a similar process. If he observes someone pulling a lever and receiving a reward, he may subvocalize: "He pulled that lever" (an associative mediating response) and "Good, he won" (a motivational mediating response). The first of these responses helps the observer decide which response to make to receive the reward; the second mediating response motivates him to engage in imitative behavior.

In an experimental test of this theory, Lewis and Duncan (1958) had observers watch a model pull a lever on a machine that paid off either 100 percent of the time or 25 percent of the time. Half of the subjects in each of these groups were paid whenever the model won, and half were not paid when the model was. Lewis and Duncan were interested in seeing whether a partial reinforcement effect (increased resistance to extinction) could be produced in the observers regardless of whether they received the reward themselves. Lewis and Duncan found, however, that the partial reinforcement effect was obtained only for subjects who actually received the reward. They attributed the absence of a partial reinforcement effect in the vicarious reinforcement condition to an absence of emotional arousal in this group as compared to the group that watched and actually received the reward. That is, subjects who merely watched the model and received no reward themselves were apparently less involved in the situation emotionally (motivationally) and hence did not persist in responding during extinction to the same extent that subjects who were reinforced (and were therefore more emotionally involved) did.

This interpretation, however, runs counter to evidence from a number of studies by Bandura and his coworkers (e.g., Bandura, 1965b; Bandura, Ross, & Ross, 1961, 1963c; Walters & Parke, 1964) which indicates that observation of the model's behavior in itself produces vicarious responding. Bandura (1969) has therefore opted for a single-process explanation: Mere *sensory contiguity*—even in the absence of a mediating emotional response—is enough for learning to occur. Reinforcement may affect performance—the overt manifestation of behavior—but the only mechanism necessary to explain the acquisition of a response is an associative one connecting sensory events with symbolic coding processes that possess cue properties capable of eliciting overt responses corresponding to those that had been modeled.

Finally it should be pointed out that the *generalized imitation* theory proposed by Gewirtz and Stingle (1968) is even more parsimonious. Their explanation of vicarious responding involves neither associative nor emotional mediating events. Like all radical behaviorists these theorists eschewed mediating concepts and preferred an explanation based on the acquisition of a set of functionally similar responses that is maintained on an intermittent schedule of reinforcement. Since each response emitted need not be reinforced, it is possible for responses to occur in the absence of reinforcement, so-called "vicarious responding."

NON-REINFORCEMENT TRAINING.   The most dramatic form of vicarious responding occurs in a situation in which neither the model nor the observer are reinforced. In such cases, mere observation of another person's behavior produces imitative behavior, although no explicit outcome is observed. In one study (Bandura, Ross & Ross, 1961), for example, children were assigned to three experimental conditions: One group observed an aggressive adult model, a second group observed a model who displayed inhibited and nonaggressive behavior, while a third group had no prior exposure to the model. The children who observed aggressive models were found to display the greatest number of precisely aggressive responses, while such responses rarely occurred in the nonaggressive-model or control groups.

Subjects in the aggressive condition also exhibited more partially imitative and non-imitative aggressive behavior than subjects in the other two groups (Figure 4-3).

Bandura, Grusec, and Menlove (1967) found that children who had phobic reactions to dogs could be induced to approach and engage in physical contact with a dog after having observed another child's progressively more intimate contacts with the dog. This effect was obtained even when the model was not physically present (although he had been present on earlier occasions). A similar effect was obtained by Bandura, Blanchard, and Ritter (1969).

While such studies are presented as evidence that observers will imitate aggressive or approach behavior without knowledge of the outcome of this behavior for the model, it should be noted that the observed behavior itself might well provide information as to the outcome of the observer's own behavior. That is, mere observation of a model who engages in aggressive behavior without being punished or who approaches a feared object without suffering pain may provide the observer with social cues that furnish information about the permissibility or appropriateness of his own behavior (Aronfreed, 1968). Some may argue that such training involves reinforcement, at least in a broad sense of the term: If reinforcement is defined operationally as an event that increases the probability of a response, information provided by social cues constitutes reinforcement. As was noted earlier, it is rather difficult methodologically to demonstrate the absence of a condition.

In a study concerned with the effect of reinforcement contingencies on the acquisition of imitative responses, Bandura (1965b) tested the hypothesis that reinforcement affects the *performance* of imitatively learned responses, whereas *acquisition* of imitative responses in a function of mere contiguous association of sensory events and symbolic coding processes. In this study children observed a film-mediated model who exhibited novel physical and verbal aggressive responses. In one treatment condition, the model was severely punished for this behavior; in a second, the model was rewarded; and in the third condition, there were no response consequences to the model. After a post-exposure test of the imitative behavior, children in all three groups were offered attractive incentives for reproducing the model's behavior. The theory predicts that reinforcement contingencies would produce differential performance of the imitative behavior but that these differences would be eliminated by the introduction of positive incentives.

The results of the study were generally confirmatory of the theory (Figure 4-4). Reinforcement was found to influence performance in the post-exposure test. The group that saw a model rewarded for aggressive behavior displayed the greatest amount of imitative be-

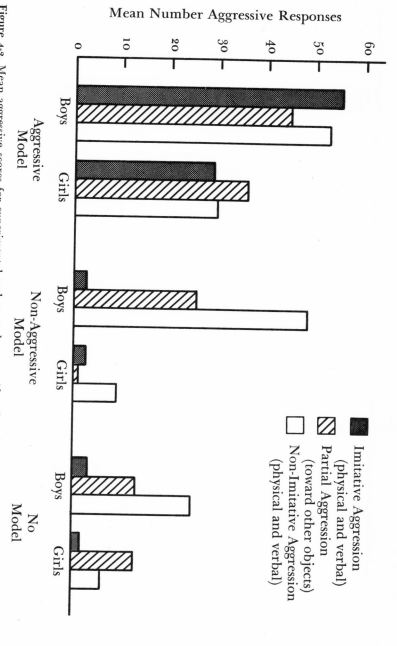

Mean Number Aggressive Responses

Imitative Aggression
(physical and verbal)

Partial Aggression
(toward other objects)

Non-Imitative Aggression
(physical and verbal)

Aggressive
Model

Non-Aggressive
Model

No
Model

Boys

Girls

Boys

Girls

Boys

Girls

0 10 20 30 40 50 60

Figure 4-3. Mean aggressive scores for experimental and control groups (data based on Bandura, Ross & Ross, 1961).

havior, whereas the group that saw the model punished showed the fewest imitative responses. The non-reinforcement group was intermediate. When positive incentive was introduced, these differences were wiped out, revealing an equivalent amount of imitative learning among children in the model-rewarded, model-punished, and non-reinforcement conditions. Acquisition was therefore equivalent, whereas performance was a function of reinforcement contingencies. Since the subjects in the non-reinforcement condition showed imitative behavior in excess of what would be expected by chance, Bandura concluded that imitative responses can be learned when neither the model nor the observer receives reinforcement.

Additional evidence for this phenomenon comes from studies in which the imitative responses of observers trained under non-reinforcement conditions were compared to those of control subjects exposed to no model (Angermeier, Schaul, & James, 1959; Berger, 1966). Such research provided evidence that training under non-reinforcement conditions does transmit the modeled behavior into the response repertoire of the observer. Even in this research, however, complete elimination of sources of reinforcement is extremely difficult if not

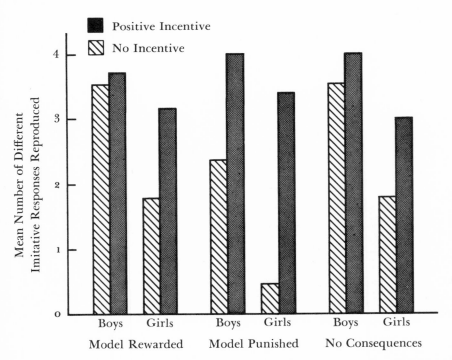

Figure 4-4. Mean number of different matching responses reproduced by children as a function of positive incentives and model's reinforcement contingencies (from Bandura, 1965b).

impossible. The Bandura (1965b) study is open to the criticism mentioned earlier—that observation of a model displaying aggressive behavior without being punished provides information as to the permissibility of the observer's displaying similar behavior. In the other studies, discriminative cues may have a reinforcement function for observers.

VICARIOUS REINFORCEMENT TRAINING.   Many of the same problems exist in studies of vicarious reinforcement. In this paradigm the model is reinforced, but no reinforcement is administered to the observer. Usually reinforcement is defined narrowly—as actually administering reward or punishment to the model, but not to the observer. If reinforcement is defined more broadly, it becomes necessary to include control groups in the design to assess the impact of less obvious forms of reinforcement. This was the case, for example, in Berger's (1961, 1962) studies where reinforcement was defined broadly to include the anticipation of reinforcement.

In fact, Berger (1961) argued that situations where the model's response serves as a discriminative stimulus signifying subsequent reward for the observer or where the act of observing the model's behavior is in itself reinforcing do not qualify as vicarious training procedures but should be thought of as involving direct reinforcement to the observer. This can easily degenerate into a semantic issue and, at present, the decision as to whether to include or exclude the informational value of vicarious reinforcement seems to be left entirely to the whim of the investigator (Flanders, 1968).

Nevertheless it seems clear that the transmission of information resulting from observation of the outcome of another person's behavior is an important determinant of performance. This effect has been obtained in studies with children (e.g., Rosenkrans, 1967) and with adults (Kanfer & Marston, 1963; Lewis & Duncan, 1958). Walters and his associates (Walters & Parke, 1964; Walters, Parke, & Cane, 1965) have reported research in which a child's violation of a prohibition was suppressed by the child's previous observation of the punitive outcomes of another child's violation. Similar suppressive effects have been reported on the aggressive behavior of children who witnessed the punishment of corresponding aggressive behavior in adult models (Bandura, 1965a; Bandura & Walters, 1963).

In a different research design, observation of the behavior of adults or peers was found to influence self-imposed criteria of reward (Bandura & Kupers, 1964; Bandura & Mischel, 1965; Mischel & Liebert, 1966). In these studies a child typically watched a model playing a bowling game with varying quality of performance. For each discrete performance the model either took or did not take some candies or tokens of reward in accordance with criteria that were made explicit (verbalized aloud) for the child. Ordinarily, the child-observer assumed the same reward criteria as his model had assumed in playing the game. Such behavior was seen to indicate vicarious learning because the child had not been reinforced for adopting the same reward criteria as his model.

In another study, Bandura and McDonald (1963) reported evidence that observation of the behavior of others can influence the child's verbal expression of moral judgments. They identified two groups of children whose verbalized judgments of the magnitude of various transgressions were dominated by their orientation either toward the intentions or toward the consequences of the act (Piaget, 1948). By having the child make judgments after hearing an adult make a judgment discrepant with the child's own orientation, it was possible to produce sharp changes in the direction of the child's judgments. These studies on self-reinforcement and the formation of moral judgments have important consequences for understanding the process of socialization, and we shall discuss them in more detail in Chapter Seven.

A number of studies have been conducted to determine the relative efficacy of vicarious and direct reinforcement procedures (e.g., Berger, 1961; Kanfer & Marston, 1963; Marston & Kanfer, 1963), but this research has not yielded unambiguous results. Since both direct and vicarious reinforcement occur together in the course of normal social behavior, the interactive effects of these two sources of control are of greater interest than their independent controlling power. In fact, Kanfer and Marston (1963) found that the combination of vicarious and direct reinforcement produced greater resistance to extinction than either method alone.

In general, the evidence from research on vicarious reinforcement warrants the conclusion that behavior can be enhanced or reduced by observation of its outcome for another. The mechanism whereby this effect is produced remains subject to debate. The role of reinforcement cannot be assessed until some agreement is reached concerning the definition of a reinforcing event. It seems clear, however, that more is involved than mere social facilitation resulting from observation of another's behavior. The effects produced in vicarious reinforcement studies are a function of consequences to the model. Most likely, observation of another person's behavior and its outcome transmits information to the observer, and subsequent performance is largely controlled by the informational properties of the model's stimuli.

EVALUATION

The major contemporary theories of imitative behavior are of two kinds: mediational and non-mediational. A number of different mediational theories exist, including those that rely heavily upon cognitive representational mediating processes (e.g., Kohlberg, 1966; Piaget, 1951). Since these cognitive theories do not derive from learning-theory tradition, however, we have not discussed them in this chapter. Those we have discussed make explicit use of learning principles, such as secondary reinforcement or conditioning through contiguity.

The theories of Mowrer (1960b) and Aronfreed (1968) are of this first type in that they employ the mechanism of *conditioned (secondary) reinforcement*. In both theories the assumption is made that the reinforcement properties of external behavior become conditioned to internal mediating responses. These internal responses are therefore affectively valenced and exert a determining influence on the form that behavior takes.

There are several problems with such theories. On the one hand, the theory is open to criticism in that it is not empirically testable. What is the precise nature of the internal mediating events assumed by the theory? How are overt responses translated into internal mediating responses and how are the mediating responses converted back to overt behavior? How does such a theory differ from other theories in the predictions it makes as to the form behavior will take? Lewis and Duncan (1958), whose theory of emotional and representational mediating processes is quite similar to Aronfreed's, admitted that the results of their research might be explained equally well on the basis of other theoretical formulations. Unless the theory can be more precisely specified in operational terms, there is no way of determining its relative worth.

Another criticism of theories that explain imitation through secondary reinforcement mechanisms is that they give reinforcement an importance that might not be justified. According to such theories, imitative responses are acquired because they have become affectively valenced as a consequence of reinforcement. Yet it seems that much imitative behavior is acquired even though no direct reinforcement is dispensed to the observer or the model. Conceivably, subtle forms of reinforcement are involved in imitative behavior acquired under conditions of non-reinforcement or vicarious reinforcement, but it remains to be demonstrated how such subtle reinforcement mechanisms supply internal mediating processes with the affective value required by the theory.

Reinforcement does not occupy as central a position in Bandura's (1962, 1969) *contiguity mediation theory* of imitative learning; instead, it is seen as one of a number of determinants of performance. As a mediational theory, however, Bandura's approach is open to the first criticism mentioned above—namely, that it fails to link mediating concepts to operational manipulations. Such a charge was made by

Gewirtz and Stingle (1968), who argued that the representational mediating processes invoked by Bandura were inferred from the behavior they were designed to explain and therefore have no independent empirical status.

To justify the empirical status of representational mediating processes it must be shown that the symbolic events presumed to operate can be independently manipulated and are not merely hypothetical cognitive processes. In some recent research Bandura and his coworkers (Gerst, 1968) have had some success along these lines, demonstrating, for example, that observers who were instructed to transform a complex motor response into a verbal code reproduced and retained the modeled response, whereas the imitative performances of subjects who did not code the modeling stimuli into symbolic forms were limited and impoverished. While this research does not demonstrate conclusively that verbal responses covertly mediate imitative learning, it does indicate that they facilitate such learning.

Bandura's emphasis on the importance of symbolic coding processes is reminiscent in some respects of Osgood's work on linguistic meaning (Chapter Three). Both theorists have attempted to treat symbolic, "cognitive" processes in the framework of learning theory and have employed representational mediating mechanisms for this purpose. Osgood, however, was closer to the Hullian tradition in that he utilized the r_g—s_g mediating mechanism, while Bandura employed a Guthrian S-S contiguity principle as a necessary, but not sufficient, condition for imitative learning.

Yet Bandura moved beyond the older tradition because of his conviction that human social behavior involves different principles of learning than those described in the classic theories. It is possible, for example, for an observer to show better retention of the model's behavior than the model who actually performed the behavior (Craig, 1967; Rosenbaum, 1967). Subjects often go beyond mere mimicry and display innovative behavior based on imitation of general behavioral orientations. Such phenomena indicate to Bandura the importance of symbolic coding operations in human imitative behavior. The observer recalls the behavior of the model better than the model himself because he has coded it better; the observer displays innovative patterns of behavior that represent general behavioral orientations because he has abstracted rules from modeled cues through vicarious discrimination learning. An adequate social-learning theory of imitation must explain such symbolic operations.

Some psychologists, however, regard Bandura's explanation as unsatisfactory. Rather than postulating a unique type of learning—Bandura's "observational" learning—and resorting to symbolic coding processes, these psychologists argue that a sufficient explanation can be given in terms of instrumental-learning principles. Gewirtz and

Stingle (1968), as we have seen, attempted to show how this could be done via the process of *generalized imitation*. To some extent their work was an elaboration on the argument of Miller and Dollard (1941) that, since imitative behavior has been utilized to secure various rewards, the child may learn to imitate (even in situations where no direct reinforcement accrues to him personally) because he has learned that imitative behavior is, generally speaking, rewarding.

Such a theory, however, may explain too much. If imitative behavior acquires reward value, the intrinsic reinforcing effects of imitation should result in widespread reproduction of all types of behavior. Yet this is not what typically happens. People do not reproduce the behavior of milkmen, traffic police, and bus drivers indiscriminately. Instead, people tend to be highly *selective* in their imitative behavior. The theory, as stated, provides no explanation for this selectivity.

In general, little attention has been given to the question of selectivity in imitative behavior. A boy of six will not imitate those aspects of his mother's behavior that a boy of three will imitate. The older the child, the more capable he is of discriminating among social stimuli, conceivably because different social stimuli acquire different reinforcement value. If his peers begin to possess more reinforcement value for the child than his parents, the child will tend to imitate his peers' behavior rather than his parents'.

Another aspect of the selectivity issue concerns the actual *performance* of imitative behavior. It has been shown, for example, that some observers know what the model does but do not display that knowledge in behavior (Hicks, 1965). Bandura (1969) has suggested that variables such as motivation, information conveyed as to the appropriateness of the modeled act, assessment of the efficacy of the behavior, and so forth, operate to determine what aspects of learned behavior actually show up in performance. Obviously more research is needed to determine the relationship between those aspects of the model's behavior that are learned (are attended to, retained, and comprehended by the observer) and those aspects that show up in behavior. We know very little at the present time about the variables that control attention, retention, comprehension, and behavioral manifestation.

Some investigators have questioned whether imitative learning occurs at all in many of the studies Bandura used in support of his theory of observational learning. Aronfreed (1968) and Gewirtz and Stingle (1968) have argued that for learning to be demonstrated the learner must acquire a new behavioral response. In many of the Bandura studies, especially those dealing with imitation of aggressive responses (e.g., Bandura, 1965b; Bandura, Ross, & Ross, 1961, 1963a), children made aggressive responses similar to those made by models, but the mere presence of a target of aggression (a large inflated doll) provided an intrinsically pleasurable outlet for the children's aggressive tendencies. Consequently, the argument runs, the aggressive behavior observed in such experiments is already *prepotent* in the child's repertoire, and its performance does not depend on imitative learning. The behavior is not learned but simply released by appropriate situational cues (Aronfreed, 1968).

One problem with such a line of criticism is that the Bandura studies typically employed control groups of children who did not display the aggressive behavior. If the responses were simply released by situational cues and were prepotent in the children's repertoires, it is difficult to explain why the doll did not release the responses in the control group. In fact, the aggressive responses employed in the Bandura studies were idiosyncratic ones with a low initial probability of occurrence. While it is true that the components of the responses made by the children already existed in their repertoires, this does not mean that the responses were not learned. The components of any new response are usually present in the individual's repertoire. New verbal expressions, for example, are learned by combining existing sound elements.

Nevertheless it is possible that in certain situations the observer's behavior is not the result of imitation but rather a consequence of informational cues and motivational stimuli derived from the observation of another person. In such cases the observer's behavior may show only a gross correspondence to that of the model. The behavior may be, strictly speaking, the observer's own, although the source of the cues that release it may be the model's behavior. In fact, in such a case, the observer does not actually use the other person as a model. Cues are transmitted through the other person, but the behavior is not imitative since it is not faithful in any but the crudest way to the behavior of the model.

Obviously, there is a continuum between imitative and nonimitative behavior of this sort. At one end are behaviors that have almost no correspondence to the behavior performed by the model; at the other end are behaviors that are precise copies of the model's behavior. Somewhere in between are behaviors such as those obtained by Miller and Dollard (1941) in studies in which subjects were found to make relatively gross matchings of simple behavioral choices. Indeed, in a given study it may be that different aspects of the modeled behavior are reproduced by the observer with differing degrees of fidelity. Bandura (1965b) found that children reproduced the verbal components of observed aggression with a much lower frequency than they did the physical components. It becomes imperative therefore for investigators to distinguish among the discrete components of the observer's behavior and to determine the frequency and fidelity of each to the behavior of the model. There can be little doubt, however, that imitation involving a high degree of correspondence between the behavior of the model and that of the observer occurs.

As research in imitative learning proliferates, many of the issues we have raised will, hopefully, be resolved. More knowledge will be gained about the specific psychological processes involved in imitation, about how information provided by a model is absorbed, retained, and utilized, and about the role of representational and motivational cues in imitation. It seems likely that the future will see elaboration of representational mediation models and clarification of the psychological processes thought to underlie such models. Whether learning-theory principles and concepts will suffice to explain these increasingly sophisticated processes remains to be seen.

5

Attitude Development and Change

IF ANY single topic can be regarded as the dominant concern of social psychologists, it is that of attitudes. More research has been carried out on attitude development and attitude change than has been conducted in any other area of social psychology. An enormous literature now exists on the topic, and it should not be surprising that one way of conceptualizing attitude development and change derives from learning theory.

Since learning theorists differ among themselves considerably, even on basic issues, they tend to have different, though related, notions of what is meant by "attitude." One of the earliest approaches to this question was Doob's (1947) discussion of attitudes as implicit, drive-producing responses of social significance to the individual. For Doob attitudes had both anticipatory and mediating functions. They had a temporal or anticipatory function in that they help the individual anticipate a reward or punishment, and a mediating role in that they lead to instrumental behavior that increases the likelihood or reward rather than punishment in connection with a goal object. The anticipatory function is essentially *cognitive* in nature and the mediating function relates to overt *behavior*. In effect, then, Doob's formulation was an attempt to tie together cognitive and behavioral aspects of attitudes within a single, learning-theory conceptualization.

A more rigorous behavioral approach was adopted by the Skinnerians, who regard attitudes as simply overt verbal behavior related to social objects. No reference is made to cognitive states, and attitude change is considered to be one other instance by behavior modification. In this system attitude change is achieved by varying reinforcement contingencies in such a way as to shape verbal behavior.

While the Skinnerian "radical behaviorism" approach has its adherents, the typical learning-theory approach has been one in which attitudes are viewed as implicit, covert responses that mediate overt behavior. In the tradition of Doob, most psychologists with a learning-theory orientation attempt to integrate the cognitive and behavioral aspects of attitudes. A particularly sophisticated effort in this direction was made by Campbell (1963) in his discussion of attitudes as "acquired behavioral dispositions." Further discussion of definitional issues will not concern us here, however; the interested reader should consult McGuire's (1969) review.

DEVELOPMENT OF ATTITUDES

Experimental research on attitudes from within the learning-theory tradition has been concerned either with the formation of attitudes or with their modification. The second topic has received greater attention, although a number of studies on attitude formation have been carried out. Two somewhat different approaches have been taken, the first viewing attitude acquisition as an instance of classical conditioning or instrumental learning or both, and the second regarding it as an example of operant learning.

The Conditioning of Attitudes

Some investigators have focused on the evaluative component of attitude and have attempted, through conditioning procedures, to form evaluational meanings. Typically such an approach involves classical conditioning. Other approaches to the acquisition of attitudes employ the instrumental conditioning paradigm. A third approach is based upon a dual theory that involves both Pavlovian and Thorndikian processes.

THE CLASSICAL CONDITIONING OF ATTITUDES.   Staats and Staats (1958, 1963) restricted their definition of attitude to the evaluative dimension. In one study (1958) they attempted to condition attitudes (evaluative meanings) to socially significant verbal stimuli through classical conditioning procedures. They used national names (Swedish, Dutch) and familiar masculine names (Tom, Bill) as socially significant verbal stimuli. The unconditioned stimulus was either a positively evaluated word (sacred, happy), a negative evaluative word (ugly, failure), or words that had no meaning on the evaluative dimension (chair). Their model is schematically represented in Figure 5-1.

Through classical conditioning procedures Staats and Staats (1958) were able to produce different evaluative judgments about the conditioned stimulus words. Thus the subject's attitude towards the national names could be conditioned in either a positive or negative direction. The same was true for the masculine names. Moreover, subjects showed no awareness of the conditioning experience to which they had been subjected.

In this study, the dependent variable was the subject's score on the Osgood semantic differential scale (Osgood, Suci, & Tannenbaum, 1957). Staats and Staats contended that what was conditioned by the classical conditioning procedure was not the rating response on this scale but rather an implicit attitudinal response that mediated the

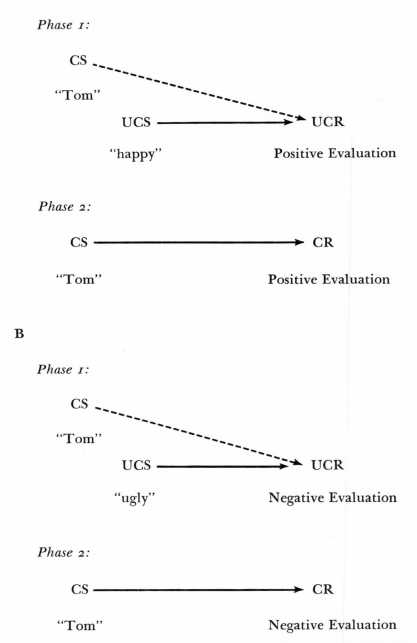

Figure 5-1. Diagram of the manner in which positive (A) or negative (B) evaluative responses are conditioned to verbal stimuli (Staats & Staats, 1958). Through repeated pairings with the unconditioned stimuli that elicit positive or negative evaluations (Phase 1), the conditioned stimuli become capable of eliciting corresponding evaluative responses (Phase 2).

behavior of scoring the semantic differential scale. The rating scale, they argued, could be considered as analogous to an item on an attitude testing device. The effect of conditioning was to modify an implicit evaluative response to the conditioned stimuli (the names) by means of unconditioned stimulus words (happy, ugly, and so on).

Such an explanation, Staats and Staats felt, could be applied to the interpretation of two earlier studies in the literature. In these studies (Razran, 1938, 1940), ratings of ethnically labeled pictures of girls and sociopolitical slogans were modified by showing these stimuli while subjects were eating a free lunch or while the subjects were presented with unpleasant olfactory stimulation. Attitudes (evaluative meanings) were conditioned in these studies because the response elicited by the food or the smell became the mediational process that in turn elicited the favorable or unfavorable rating. Thus the ratings could be considered the result of the conditioning of an implicit evaluative response to the conditioned stimuli by means of the lunch or the unpleasant odors.

Once attitudes (evaluative meanings) are established through classical conditioning, they may take on an instrumental function as reinforcing stimuli (Staats, 1967). Thus it was hypothesized that words with positive evaluative meanings would serve as positive reinforcers, words with negative evaluative meanings would act as negative reinforcers, and neutral stimuli would have an intermediate effect upon behavior. In a test of this hypothesis (Finley & Staats, 1967), children were given either a positive evaluative word (fun, sunshine), a negative evaluative word (ugly, poison), or a neutral word (dip, bridge) when they made one of two motor responses. The words had been previously rated by other subjects in the same age group. The results supported the hypothesized relationship between the evaluative meaning of the word and their reinforcement value. Words with positive evaluative meanings functioned as positive reinforcers or rewards, words with negative evaluative meanings served as negative reinforcers or punishment, and neutral words were found to have no reinforcing function.

Such findings were interpreted by Staats (1968) as indicating that evaluative meanings (attitudes) established through classical conditioning as conditioned responses will in certain cases also act as reinforcers. According to this conceptualization, an attitude is more than a response—it may also have an instrumental function serving to *reinforce* overt behavior. It should be noted, however, that this definition of attitude is quite specific to Staats' approach and refers solely to the affective, evaluative, emotional dimension.

Weiss (1962) has proposed a somewhat different use of the classical conditioning paradigm to account for the acquisition of attitudes. In some cases people form opinions through *implication*. Thus a person may hear an argument that clearly implies an opinion. Acceptance of the argument will lead, through a process analogous to classical conditioning, to acceptance of the implied opinion. To test this model, Weiss (1962) gave subjects a cue statement (neutral material) concerning the makeup and manner of selection of the British House of Lords. They then heard the argument, "It is possible that where heredity is one of the factors taken into account in selection, there may be some limitation of ability." Under such conditions subjects were found to draw the conclusion implicit in the argument—namely, "The British House of Lords should be reorganized."

Weiss (1962) saw such a process to be analogous to classical conditioning (Figure 5-2). The sequence is: conditioned stimulus (cue statement), unconditioned stimulus (the argument), and unconditioned response (implied opinion). Through repetition of the sequence, the implied opinion becomes conditioned to the cue statement and thus becomes a conditioned opinion (conditioned response). Such an analysis, Weiss argued, involves what Miller (1959) referred to as "the liberalization of S-R concepts" and has considerable heuristic value as an approach to attitude formation.

ATTITUDES AS INSTRUMENTAL LEARNING.   Weiss (1962) has also suggested that attitudes may be acquired by a process analogous to instrumental learning. In this case, the situation is such that a subject is required to read a communication aloud, state an opinion, read

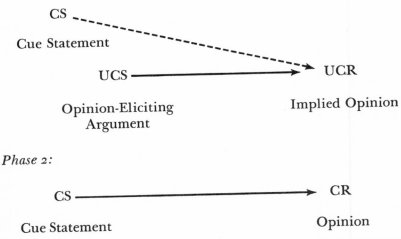

Phase 1:

CS
Cue Statement

UCS
Opinion-Eliciting Argument

UCR
Implied Opinion

Phase 2:

CS
Cue Statement

CR
Opinion

Figure 5-2. Weiss' (1962) classical conditioning model in which the implied opinion associated with an argument is conditioned to a cue statement (Phase 1). Subsequently, hearing the cue statement leads to acceptance of the opinion contained in the argument (Phase 2).

some neutral material, and finally state an argument supporting the opinion. This sequence of events is regarded as analogous to the sequence involved in instrumental conditioning: stimulus, response, delay, reinforcement. The sight of the written communication is the *stimulus,* the opinion is the *response* to be learned, and the interval between the opinion and the argument (when the subject reads some neutral material) corresponds to the *delay of reinforcement.* The argument is a *reinforcer* because it increases the probability of a response (stating the opinion).

Weiss argued that such a conceptualization is of value if it can be shown that the principles that apply to instrumental learning apply analogously to attitude formation. He and his coworkers have had some success along these lines, demonstrating that empirical relations found to obtain for instrumental learning apply to their attitude formation paradigm. Thus Weiss, Rawson, and Pasamanick (1963) have shown that the speed with which the response (opinion agreement) is made is a function of delay of reinforcement (time between opinion and argument). In another study, Weiss (1967) demonstrated that the probability of agreement with an attitude was a negatively accelerated decreasing function of delay of argument (just as instrumental learning is a negatively accelerated decreasing function of delay of reward). Similarly, research on number of exposures (Weiss & Pasamanick, 1964) has been shown to lead to faster agreement with the attitude (the same relation that is found for instrumental learning generally).

In these studies the reinforcing event is an argument in support of the opinion to be persuaded. As Weiss noted, other analogies between instrumental learning and attitude formation are possible. Scott, for example, conducted a series of studies (Scott, 1957, 1959a, 1959b) in which the reinforcing event consisted of group approval or disapproval for the subjects' expression of attitudes opposed to their initial opinion. Scott found that reward prompted subjects to make the appropriate response—attitude conformity. Other researchers (e.g., McGuire, 1957; Rosnow, 1966) have used similar paradigms.

OSGOOD'S DUAL-PROCESS THEORY.   So far we have discussed learning-theory approaches to the acquisition of attitudes that involve analogies either to classical conditioning or to instrumental learning. Osgood and his associates (Osgood, Suci, and Tannenbaum, 1957) in their discussion of the semantic differential scale have, in effect, proposed a dual-process theory of attitude formation. This theory is based upon Osgood's notion of "meaning" (r_m) and how meaning can be understood in behavioral terms. This theory was discussed in Chapter Three, but it will perhaps be helpful to review it briefly at this point.

Meaning, according to this formulation, is a representational mediation process. Certain stimulus patterns (unconditioned stimuli) have a "wired-in" connection with certain behavior patterns (unconditioned responses) and additional stimuli acquire this capacity (conditioned stimuli). Osgood defined those stimuli that regularly and reliably produce a predictable pattern of behavior as *significates*. Thus shock is a significate for an (unconditioned) aversive reaction and meat powder is a significate for an (unconditioned) appetitive reaction in a hungry organism. In contrast, other stimuli must acquire the capacity to produce the behavior pattern. For the naive organism a buzzer does not reliably produce the escape behavior that shock does, nor does a metronome reliably produce food-taking reactions in the same way that presentation of meat powder does. How then do these initially meaningless stimuli become meaningful *signs* for the organism affected by them?

To account for this process Osgood proposed that: "Whenever some stimulus other than the significate is contiguous with the significate, it will acquire an increment of association with some portion of the total behavior elicited by the significate as a representational mediation process" (Osgood, *et al.*, 1957, p. 6). Thus the buzzer becomes a sign of shock because it evokes in the organism a mediational process that is a fractional part of the total behavior elicited by shock (the significate). The more frequent the contiguous presentation of sign and significate, the greater the associative strength of the sign. The mediational process ($r_m \rightarrow s_m$) is part of the behavior produced by the significate itself and is learned by association through contiguity according to the principles of classical conditioning.

The theory is a dual-process theory because it divides the usual S-R paradigm into two stages. The first stage, which Osgood called *decoding*, involves the association of signs (buzzer, metronome, or words used in reference to objects) with representational mediators, or "meanings." The second stage, which was called *encoding*, involved the association of mediational self-stimulation with overt instrumental sequences. Thus a classical conditioning process occurs by which meanings (r_m) become established—that is, the sign of an object evokes a fractional component of the responses evoked in the past by the actual object or by words used in reference to that object. The characteristic stimulus effects (s_m) of these meanings can then act as cues for instrumental learning.

Since meanings are established through a learning process, the meanings that different words have will vary to the extent that experiences toward the things signified have varied. Within a given culture there is an essential stability of learning experiences and meanings for most common verbal signs tend to be highly similar. The adjective "sweet" will be understood in much the same way by the members of a common culture. On the other hand, the meanings of many signs may reflect the idiosyncrasies of individual experience. "Father," "mother," and "me" are examples that Osgood listed of words that allow for considerable variation in meaning.

To assess this variation in meaning, Osgood and his associates developed the *semantic differential* scale. This scale was intended to serve specifically as an index for measuring the representational mediation process ($r_m \rightarrow s_m$) that the theory identified with meaning. Subjects are provided with a series of concepts (e.g., "my mother," "Republican," and "modern art") that are to be differentiated along seven-point scales defined by verbal opposites (good-bad, hot-cold, fair-unfair, fast-slow, and the like). Subjects judge the set of concepts along these adjectival scales. For example:

MY MOTHER

active: ____:____:____:____:____:____:____: passive
happy: ____:____:____:____:____:____:____: sad
hard: ____:____:____:____:____:____:____: soft
and so on.

By postulating a multidimensional *semantic space* defined by the set of bipolar adjectives that constitute the semantic differential scale and by employing factor analysis procedures, Osgood and his associates attempted to uncover the orthogonal dimensions that exhaust the dimensionality of this space. Their analysis revealed three dominant factors along which meaningful judgments were differentiated. These were the evaluative factor (represented by ratings such as "good-bad," "pleasant-unpleasant," and "positive-negative"), the potency factor (represented by ratings such as "strong-weak," "heavy-light," and "hard-soft") and the activity factor (represented by ratings such as "fast-slow," "active-passive," and "excitable-calm"). Each of these factors were thought to represent independently variable (but not exhaustive) dimensions of meaning. The *evaluative* factor is especially important in Osgood's theory of attitude.

Osgood, like Doob (1947), regarded attitudes as internal, anticipatory mediating responses, but he attempted to be more precise and to localize attitudes within the general system of mediational activity. Within his theoretical model, an attitude is part of the semantic structure of the individual and may be defined as the projection from a point in multidimensional space onto the evaluative dimension. To index attitude it is necessary to use sets of scales that have high loadings on the evaluative factor across concepts generally and negligible loadings on other factors.

Osgood and his associates (1957) have employed the semantic differential with some success to predict voting behavior by assessing attitudes toward Presidential candidates. Another typical use of the instrument in research on attitudes was the work of Staats and Staats (1958) mentioned earlier, where the semantic differential scale provided information concerning the evaluative meaning of social stimuli.

Osgood was careful to point out that an attitude is only one component of meaning. The meaning of a concept to an individual is far richer than what is revealed in his attitude score. Two people may have identical attitudes toward a concept (as determined by allocation to the evaluative dimension alone) but quite different meanings (as determined by the scale as a whole). To predict behavior, knowledge of the meaning of the concept to a subject is more helpful than knowledge of his attitude toward the concept: It is not necessarily true that the same attitude implies the same behavior. In this connection, the semantic differential scale provides valuable predictive information since it allows for the assessment of emotional and expressive, as well as evaluative, meaning.

Expressed in terms of Osgood's two-factor theory, the question of the relationship between attitude and behavior is essentially a question of the relationship between the decoding and the encoding processes. Attitudes, as components of meaning, are established through classical conditioning and may in turn serve as cues for instrumental (overt behavioral) learning. The precise effect on overt behavior is not, however, determinable solely in terms of attitude. Other components of meaning affect instrumental behavior, as does the situation within which the behavior is to take place. Thus overt behavior can seldom be predicted from knowledge of attitude alone.

Attitude as Operant Learning

The operant learning approach to attitude acquisition is based on the notion that attitudes consist simply of overt verbal behavior. An attitude, like any other verbal behavior, can be taught by varying reinforcement contingencies so as to shape behavior in the desired direction. Just as grammatical forms of speech (the use of plural nouns, first person pronouns, and the like) can be conditioned through operant procedures, so complex evaluative expressions can be learned given the appropriate reinforcement contingencies.

VERBAL CONDITIONING EXPERIMENTS.   In an early study, Verplanck (1955) reported that subjects showed an increase in statement of opinion when reinforced by experimenters who either agreed with the subject ("Yes, you're right," nodding or smiling affirmation) or paraphrased the speaker's statements. The rate with which the speaker stated an opinion varied with the administration of reinforcement, and the effect was found in a wide variety of settings (in restaurants or private homes, over telephones) and on a wide variety of topics. Ekman (1958) and Centers (1963) also found attitude expression to be conditionable by operant procedures.

In a study more specifically concerned with the effect of reinforcement of the *directionality* of attitudes, Hildum and Brown (1956) found that if an interviewer biased his answers in a favorable direction by saying "good" whenever the subject (interviewed by telephone) expressed a favorable statement on an issue, subjects tended to assume a favorable opinion when compared to subjects reinforced by "good" for unfavorable statements or by "mm-hmm" for favorable statements. Thus "good" served as an effective reinforcer for favorable statements, whereas "mm-hmm" had little or no effect.

Singer (1961) reported that reinforcing pro-democratic responses on the F scale (Adorno *et al.*, 1950) with either "good" or "right" significantly increased the number of such responses over blocks of twenty trials. Moreover, a *generalization effect* was demonstrated in that more democratic responses were obtained on the E scale (Adorno, *et al.*, 1950) even though reinforcement was not given for responses on this instrument. It is interesting to note that Singer felt that the generalization response is difficult to explain in strictly Skinnerian terms since the scale items on the F and E scales bear such little resemblance to each other. He suggested that the findings might be better explained in terms of a theory such as Osgood's (Osgood *et al.*, 1957) which employs representational mediating processes.

Krasner and his associates (Krasner, Knowles, & Ullmann, 1965; Krasner, Ullmann, & Fisher, 1964) also reported generalization effects as a result of operant conditioning through verbal reinforcement. In their studies, however, generalization affected performance on a motor skill task. They found that favorable attitudes toward an examiner could be modified by reinforcement and that this change in attitude was related to the individual's performance on a motor task (dynamometer performance) requiring a great deal of physical effort. The implication of these findings, according to Krasner and his coworkers (1965), is that simple reinforcement cues ("yes," "good," "that's fine"), by affecting the subject's attitude toward the examiner, can lead to compliance in behavioral tasks. They felt that further research along these lines would lead to an improved understanding of the nature of the doctor-patient relationship and of factors that increase the patient's receptiveness to treatment.

Insko and Butzine (1968) pointed out that, although operant procedures have used various issues in various contexts, verbal reinforcement is not equally effective in all situations. In their study *rapport* was manipulated by having the experimenter, speaking with his subject over the phone, mildly ingratiate or insult the subject for his responses to an initial series of two questions. Subsequently they found that the reinforcement effect was greater with positive than with negative rapport, even though the reinforcement effect was still significant within the negative rapport condition. Insko and Butzine concluded that rapport makes a difference in the effectiveness of operant verbal conditioning procedures, but that reinforcement itself was generally a robust phenomenon.

In a further study of the role of rapport in the verbal conditioning of attitudes, Insko and Cialdini (1969) gave some subjects both an approving reinforcement ("good") for responses in the appropriate attitude direction and a mildly disapproving reinforcement ("huh") for responses in the inappropriate direction. Under these conditions no more conditioning occurred than when only the approving reinforcement ("good") was given. Insko and Cialdini interpreted these findings as indicating that the gain in information that occurs when approving *and* disapproving reinforcements are given is offset by the loss of rapport incurred by the use of disapproving reinforcement. They suggested that reinforcement affects attitudinal statements by conveying information as to the appropriate attitude and by strengthening rapport between experimenter and subject.

To summarize, research on the operant conditioning of attitudes indicates that the incidence of attitude statements can be increased by the use of verbal reinforcement, that the directionality of the attitude can be altered, that the effects of verbal reinforcement generalize to other attitudes and tasks, and that rapport plays an important role in determining the effectiveness of verbal reinforcement techniques. While other interpretations are possible, these findings lend support to the radical behaviorist argument that attitudes are responses governed, like other responses, by reinforcement contingencies.

So far in this chapter we have discussed various learning-theory explanations for how individuals acquire attitudes. These explanations derive from the basic paradigms of learning described in Chapter Two. Some theorists regard attitudes as responses conditioned to previously neutral verbal stimuli, while others conceptualize attitude formation as instrumental learning designed to help the individual cope with the demands of the social environment. Osgood's dual-process theory attempts to capitalize on features of both approaches. The Skinnerians employ different principles and view attitude acquisition as a process in which the operant rate of verbal responses is increased through reinforcement contingencies. Research on verbal conditioning is cited as evidence for such an interpretation, although the data need not be explained in Skinnerian terms. In fact, many psychologists share Singer's skepticism concerning the adequacy of Skinnerian notions.

In spite of the variety of approaches to attitude acquisition adopted by psychologists with a learning-theory orientation, relatively little attention has been given to the possibility of attitude acquisition through imitation and observational learning. There is some evidence from research by Bandura and his coworkers (e.g., Bandura & McDonald, 1963) that attitudes can be affected by imitative learning, but further research is needed. Since many attitudes are formed in the early years of life and since imitation plays so prominent a role in the socialization process, it would not be surprising to find that imitation and observational learning are important processes affecting attitude acquisition.

ATTITUDE CHANGE

We have seen how learning theorists would explain attitude formation according to learning principles. This does not in itself, however, demonstrate that learning theory represents a major theoretical approach to the study of attitudes. The real battles are fought in the area of persuasive communication and attitude change. Psychologists today are interested in the dynamics of attitudes, and the processes underlying attitude change have become the subject of active experimental inquiry and intense theoretical debate. If learning theory is to represent a serious theoretical alternative, it must be capable of generating hypotheses and of integrating in a coherent way the results of research on attitude change.

Very few systematic endeavors of this sort have been undertaken by advocates of a learning-theory position. Instead, a number of investigators have assumed the relevance of learning theory, worked within a learning-theory framework, and applied the principles of learning to their research on attitude change. This has been true in particular of the Yale studies on attitude change conducted under the leadership of Carl Hovland.

The Yale Studies

While Hovland and his associates were eclectic in their theoretical approach, they relied heavily on learning theory in accounting for their findings. Their research was carefully conducted in an effort to identify the main and interactive effects of characteristics of a communication's source and its content on the attitudes of various audiences. They established attitude change as a field of active investigation, and it was their work that led to the major theoretical positions regarding attitude change that exist in psychology today. A few examples of this research and of studies it generated should clarify the manner in which learning theory was employed by the Yale group as a theoretical orientation for understanding attitude change.

THREATENING APPEALS.   In a classic study Janis and Feshbach (1953) investigated the effect of fear-arousing appeals on persuasive communication. They found that the *higher* the level of fear aroused by the persuasive methods, the *less* compliance it produced. That is, Janis and Feshbach demonstrated that minimal fear arousal in connection with the communication was more effective than high fear arousal in producing attitude change.

To interpret these paradoxical findings, Hovland, Janis, and Kelley (1953) proposed that fear-arousing communications generated an emotional reaction in subjects through a process of conditioning. Thus threatening communications elicit an emotional response of anxiety. The greater the threat, the greater the emotional reaction. Since this emotional reaction is unpleasant, the subject is motivated to try out spontaneous responses until he hits upon one that succeeds in reducing the emotional tension. Subjects may cease to pay attention to the communication, may display aggression toward the communicator, or may engage in defensive avoidance reactions. Evidence from the Janis and Feshbach study indicated that the last response was the one most frequently employed.

What Hovland and his associates suggested therefore was essentially a *two-factor theory,* according to which two separate habits are acquired when a threat appeal succeeds in producing a defensive avoidance reaction in the subject. The threatening communication, through a process of conditioning, elicits an emotional response of anxiety. This in turn acts as a drive that motivates the subject to learn (instrumentally) interfering responses that will successfully enable him to avoid the source of the threat. The greater the drive, the greater the tendency to learn interfering responses. Consequently, more threatening appeals are less effective in producing attitude change.

As a learning-theory interpretation, the process postulated by the Hovland group most closely resembles Mowrer's early (1947, 1950) two-factor theory. It should be noted, however, that empirical support for the Janis and Feshbach effect is relatively weak (McGuire, 1966). The results of other studies using threatening appeals have required consideration of additional variables that mitigate the effect; these variables frequently produce not the classic negative relationship but a positive relationship between intensity of threat and attitude change.

COMMUNICATOR CREDIBILITY.   Another interesting use of a learning-theory framework by the Hovland group is found in their discussion of communicator credibility (Hovland, Janis, & Kelley, 1953). In this case learning theory was not employed *post factum* to provide a theoretical interpretation of empirical data, but instead principles of learning were used to generate hypotheses. Conceptualizing the reception of a persuasive communication as a problem situation for the subject, Hovland and his associates argued that the individual's responses to various communications depend, in part, on the degree to which he *generalizes* from earlier experiences in which he had acquired expectations about expertness, trustworthiness, and so forth. The subject's behavior in a particular problem situation could therefore be examined in terms of the process of generalization.

Research on stimulus generalization has shown that the learned response to a given stimulus can be elicited by other, similar cues, but that the response tends to appear less frequently and less strongly the more different the other cues are from the original stimulus. This phenomenon gives rise to what is known as the generalization gradient. The Hovland group (1953) suggested that such a gradient could be applied to studies in communicator expertness. This is represented by the solid line in Figure 5-3. On the ordinate is the strength of the tendency to accept communications given by any specific source, and on the abscissa are the cues as to the various sources' expertness. At the left end of the abscissa would be a source identical with or very similar to one the subject had learned to regard as extremely expert. Moving to the right, the cues become increasingly different from those associated with expertness and consequently, as indicated by the gradient, there would be a decreasing tendency to accept communications from such sources.

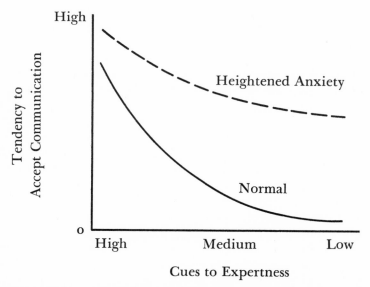

Figure 5-3. Hypothetical generalization gradients for communicator expertness (from Hovland *et al.*, 1953).

Any factor that affects the shape or height of the gradient will affect the individual's responsiveness to various communications. A specific example is heightened anxiety. The dotted line in Figure 5-3 represents the gradient of generalization that would be expected if the subject found himself in a situation where he became highly anxious. In such situations he would be expected to show a greater tendency to accept communications from sources differing in expertness—that is, he would discriminate less sharply between sources of different degree of expertness. He would also be expected to accept all communications more readily, and this tendency would be most noticeable for communications from experts at the low end of the scale for expertness. Finally, the prediction could be made that certain sources at the lower end of the scale for expertness who normally elicit no acceptance would, under conditions of heightened anxiety, come to exert some influence.

Hovland and his coworkers (1953) offered no systematic empirical data bearing directly on these predictions. They did, however, cite studies from the literature on social influence that seemed to lend them support. Thus there is evidence that in times of stress and uncertainty rumors are more readily accepted (Allport & Postman, 1947) and new leaders come to power (Cantril, 1941). Similarly, in emergency situations there is less tendency to question the credentials of a mechanic or a doctor. Finally, Hovland and his associates noted that such an interpretation may apply to the behavior of subjects in the Asch conformity situation (Asch, 1952). Ordinarily a person seeks evidence that his judgments are accurate and valid. He checks his judgment against evidence he obtains directly from the physical world. When the evidence of the physical world is ambiguous and unstructured he resorts to the opinions of other people. In certain circumstances he may make less fine discriminations as to the credibility of other people and may, under social pressure of the sort applied in the Asch situation, become responsive to the opinion of people who had previously carried little weight for him.

In short, Hovland and the Yale group used learning theory either to provide a framework for explaining research findings or to generate empirically testable hypotheses. Yet the success of their research was in no way contingent upon the success of a learning-theory explanation. They used the theory as a tool, flexibly and without commitment to any particular viewpoint. Principles of learning seemed to offer a reasonable explanation of the phenomena in question, but other theoretical approaches were possible. In fact, some of Hovland's followers later rejected the learning-theory approach, although others have continued working in this tradition. To trace these developments, however, would require a comprehensive review of attitude-change research during the past two decades (which fortunately can be found in McGuire, 1969).

Learning Theory and Order Effects

It may be helpful, nevertheless, to examine the use to which learning theory has been put in one particular area of empirical concern. Investigators studying attitude change have long been interested in the question of order effects. Does a communication advocating attitude change have a greater persuasive impact when it precedes or when it follows a message arguing for the other side? What effect does acceptance of an initial argument have on acceptance of subsequent arguments? Is it better to present the strongest argument early or later in the course of a communication? Is the audience more affected by the first arguments it hears (primacy) or by the last arguments it hears (recency)? A number of investigators have attempted to study these issues from within a learning-theory framework. In fact, learning theory has probably been employed more frequently in this substantive area than in any other in attitude-change research. We shall first discuss some early work by William McGuire, one of Hovland's coworkers, then examine how other investigators, outside the Yale group, used learning principles to study order effects.

MC GUIRE.   The particular issue to which McGuire (1957) directed his attention was the effect upon attitude change of *variations in the order* in which material is presented *within* a communication. He postulated that the reception of each message in a series of messages is a separate conditioning trial on which the source constitutes a stimulus to which the response of agreement is being conditioned (or extinguished). The response of agreement with the position advocated by a source comes only as a final response in a chain of stimulus-producing responses initiated by the message. To be influenced, the subject must make the preliminary response of paying attention to the message, must comprehend its contents, accept the conclusions advocated, and rehearse this acceptance sufficiently to permit later expression of the induced change on the attitude questionnaire. Unless all of these intervening responses occur, the ultimate response in the chain—the index of attitude change—will not be given.

McGuire saw *reward for agreement* to be a critical factor in the process of attitude change. If reward is given the response is strengthened, if not (or if it is punished) it will extinguish. Accordingly, earlier messages from a source will augment or reduce the subject's acceptance of later ones, depending upon whether his agreement with the earlier messages was rewarded or not. Moreover, if agreement with the earlier messages was actually punished, acceptance may have constituted "avoidance training," so that on subsequent trials the subject's tendency to agree will be weaker than if agreement with the earlier messages had simply not been rewarded.

To test these predictions—which derived from a straightforward application of learning principles—McGuire had a single source transmit a series of messages that had either pleasant or unpleasant contingencies. It was predicted that when those messages supporting the likelihood of pleasant contingencies were presented first and those supporting the likelihood of unpleasant contingencies offered later, a greater total amount of agreement with the message contents would be evoked than when the messages were presented in the reverse order.

McGuire further hypothesized that this effect of sequence on opinion change would be *mediated* by the effects of earlier messages on the intervening responses of attending to and comprehending the message contents. These intervening responses should lead to greater learning and therefore greater acceptance of the positions advocated. If the earlier messages argued for the further occurrence of a desirable event, an acceptance response would be rewarding to the individual. If, on the other hand, the earlier messages were undesirable ones, their acceptance would be unrewarding or even punishing. Acceptance of these earlier unpleasant messages would then serve as avoidance training in which the subject would learn to withhold attention and comprehension. Thus the theory would predict that on subsequent trials, even though the messages argue for pleasant positions, there would be less persuasion because the pleasant contents would not be so readily recognized and learned.

McGuire administered a questionnaire to his subjects one week before and immediately after the persuasive communication. The questionnaire contained statements regarding college life, such as using federal aid to pay for textbooks and scheduling classes at 7 A.M. to relieve classroom shortage. A statement was rated for its desirability, and on the basis of these ratings four high desirability and four low desirability items were selected. The subjects received a communication about the items that consisted of a series of replies written by a fictitious university president. All of these replies were plausible, factual arguments that the events in question were likely to occur. Each subject received only four of the eight replies. One half of the subjects received the high desirability items first, followed by the low desirability items; the other half received the items in reverse order.

As predicted, the effects of the source's earlier communications on the persuasiveness of his later messages was found to depend in large measure on the extent to which agreement with those earlier messages was rewarding to the subject. Specifically, for seven of eight items, ratings were higher if the pleasant arguments came first than if the reverse order was followed. Moreover, it was demonstrated that the effectiveness of the persuasive communication depended not only on its capacity to evoke agreement responses, but also on its capacity for evoking those other responses that were thought to intervene between the presentation of the communication and the ultimate response of agreeing with its content—that is, such responses as paying attention, studying the content of the message, and so forth. This was investigated by having subjects answer questions on the content of communications immediately after they had been presented. Those subjects who received the more desirable messages first showed better recall than those who received the undesirable information first.

McGuire's work represents a particularly good example of the research of the Yale group. McGuire subsequently changed his theoretical orientation considerably and has come to regard the learning-theory approach as "a fertile error" (1969, p. 266). Yet McGuire's early work shows how Hovland and his students used learning principles heuristically to set the terms of an empirical problem and to provide a frame of analysis. This approach, however, was not limited to members of the Yale group.

MILLER AND CAMPBELL.   In a particularly sophisticated application of learning principles Miller and Campbell (1959) used research on the *curve of forgetting* (Ebbinghaus, 1913) to predict circumstances in which primacy and recency order effects might be expected. These investigators assumed that attitude is a direct function of retention of message content. If the time interval between the presentation of two communications is varied, retention (and therefore attitude) will be affected. Miller and Campbell hypothesized forgetting curves applying to the relative weighting of two communications presented and measured at varying intervals. These curves are shown in Figure 5-4, where the solid line (A) represents the contribution of a communication presented first, its strength decaying as time elapses. The two dashed lines (B and B′) represent the contribution of a second opposing communication. In one instance (B), the second communication is presented immediately after the first; in the second case (B′), the second communication is presented one week later.

As show in Figure 5-4, there are four separate conditions: (1) the successive presentation of two communications with a measure of opinion directly following the second communication, (2) successive presentation with the measure of opinion a week after the second communication, (3) the presentation of two communications a week apart with the measure of opinion directly following the second communication, and (4) the presentation of two communications a week apart with the measure of opinion a week after the second communication. Miller and Campbell made five predictions. Stated in terms of the relative magnitude of the recency effect—that is, the dominance of the second communication in determining attitude—they expected: $(3) > (4)$, $(3) > (1)$, $(3) > (2)$, $(1) > (2)$, and $(4) > (2)$. Each of these predictions followed from the general assumption of similar negatively accelerated decrements for the curves involved.

In their experiment, Miller and Campbell used a tape recording of an edited transcript of a lawsuit concerning an automobile accident as the communication source. The testimony of witnesses for the plaintiff, the cross examination by the plaintiff's lawyer of the witnesses for the defense, and the opening and closing speeches of the plaintiff's lawyers were called the "pro" communication. The testimony of the witnesses for the defense and so forth were called the "con" communication. The two communications were approximately equal in length and number of points to their arguments. A nine-point rating scale was used to enable the subjects to express the degree to which they thought either the plaintiff or the defense was responsible for the accident. Communications were administered to

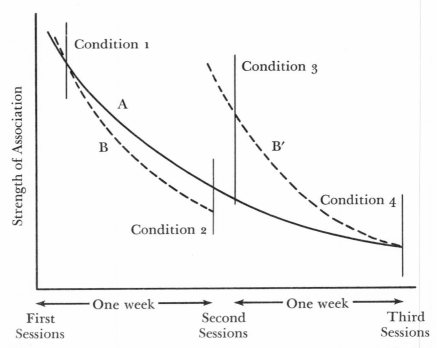

Figure 5-4. Hypothetical forgetting curves for two competing communications. The initial communication is represented by Curve A, and the second by either B or B'. The primacy effect is represented by the higher initial starting point and final asymptote of Curve A compared with Curve B or B' (from Miller and Campbell, 1959).

groups of subjects in each of four conditions, and all five predictions were confirmed.

It should be noted, however, that the data for *recall* of information were not entirely consistent with the data for *attitude*. That is, while measures of attitude as affected by each of the four treatment conditions supported all five predictions, measures of recall failed to support the theory in one case [(1) was not greater than (2)] and, for the most part, failed to show primacy or recency effects that corresponded to those obtained for attitude scores. In addition, the average within-group correlation between attitude scores and recall scores was not significant ($-.10$).

Nevertheless, Miller and Campbell's approach was, as McGuire put it, "an esthetically pleasing learning-theory approach to the primacy-recency question" (1966, p. 487). It received support from a study by Insko (1964) in which he used a similar experimental procedure and found that the longer the time interval between the two communications the greater the recency effect. Furthermore, Insko reported that delayed measurement in all of the conditions with a time interval between communications decreased the recency effect. Insko, however, took exception to Miller and Campbell's assumption that attitude is a direct function of retention of message content. The average within-group correlation between attitude scores and recall scores in Insko's study was .10—somewhat greater than that obtained by Miller and Campbell but still not statistically significant. Insko argued that retention does not mediate the effect of time upon opinion, but that time independently affects both opinion and retention. This is a complicated issue to which we shall return shortly.

The adequacy of the Miller and Campbell forgetting theory was also called into question by Schultz (1963) who failed to find an increase in recency as a result of a two-week interval interpolated between opposing communications dealing with the amount of time and money that should be devoted to cancer research. On the other hand, some studies (e.g., Anderson & Hubert, 1963; Watts & McGuire, 1964) lend at least partial support to the theory. The evidence pro and con has been reviewed by Lana (1964) and McGuire (1966).

ROSNOW.   To gain some appreciation for the diversity of learning-theory approaches to the problem of order effects in persuasive communication we shall conclude this section by discussing briefly Rosnow's reinforcement theory. Rosnow (1962, 1966) argued that reinforcement occurring *before* the presentation of opposed arguments would yield a *primacy* effect, whereas reinforcement occurring *after* the presentation of opposed arguments would yield a *recency* effect. These predictions were made on the supposition that contiguity between the reinforcement and either first- or second-presented argument would strengthen the tendency to respond in that direction.

Rosnow and his associates have reported findings generally consistent with the model (Rosnow, 1965, 1966; Rosnow & Lana, 1965; Corrozi & Rosnow, 1968). The results of these studies indicated that subjects' opinions tended to change in the direction of whichever arguments were closer in time to a positive reinforcement or farther from a negative reinforcement. Presumably contiguity between a positive reinforcement and an argument serves to strengthen the tendency to respond in the direction of the argument, while negative reinforcement weakens any such tendency. Thus primacy effects have been found to predominate if a two-sided communication follows a positive reinforcement or precedes a negative reinforcement. Recency effects predominate if the two-sided communication either precedes a positive reinforcement or follows a negative reinforcement.

For example, Corrozi and Rosnow (1968) found that by manipulating reinforcement by presenting subjects with statements with which they strongly agreed (positive reinforcement) or with statements with which they strongly disagreed (negative reinforcement), they were able to produce primacy-recency effects generally consistent with Rosnow's theory. They argued that statements with which the subject agrees constitute a reward in that they provide the recipient with social evidence of the correctness of his opinion. Statements with which he disagrees constitute punishing events. Contiguity between a reward and an argument was found to strengthen the tendency to respond in the direction of the argument, while punishment weakens this tendency.

In Rosnow's model central emphasis was placed upon the importance of reinforcement. Reinforcement was manipulated by reducing subjects' anxiety (Rosnow, 1962) or by presenting subjects with statements with which they agreed (Corrozi & Rosnow, 1968). Other investigators have employed quite different definitions of reinforcement in attitude-change research. Scott (1957, 1959b), for example, defined reinforcement in terms of group approval for subjects' performance in advocating a position; Weiss (1962) defined reinforcement as an argument in support of a certain position; McGuire (1957) limited reinforcement to messages with pleasant contingencies for the subject. Yet, however defined, reinforcement was a critical factor for each of these investigators. In fact, because of the centrality of reinforcement in various learning-theory approaches, such approaches are often referred to simply as "reinforcement theories" of attitude change.

We have discussed research on the problem of order effects in some detail because a number of different learning-theory approaches have been taken in this area. This does not mean that researchers with a learning-theory orientation have neglected other areas. Hovland's students especially have applied learning principles to a wide range of attitude-change phenomena (Insko, 1967). Recently, however, certain particular issues have attracted the interest of advocates of a learning-theory explanation. The reason for this is the challenge of a major alternative theoretical explanation, dissonance theory.

Learning Theory and Dissonance Phenomena

It need hardly be pointed out that on the basis of criteria such as the amount of research and controversy it has generated, dissonance theory represents a major theoretical framework in present-day psychology. Festinger's (1957) initial conceptualization and the subsequent formulation of Brehm and Cohen (1962) have had an enormous impact on research in social psychology. The controversy over dissonance theory still rages, but rather than discussing all aspects of this provocative theoretical approach, we shall focus on a number of specific research topics. In doing so, our main interest will be on points of disagreement between the dissonance theory interpretation and an interpretation based on learning (reinforcement) theory.

COUNTERATTITUDINAL ADVOCACY.   A classical study in the dissonance literature, one cited repeatedly as evidence of the power of the theory to predict counterintuitive results, is the Festinger and Carlsmith (1959) study of "the cognitive consequences of forced compliance." They induced participants in a very boring task to tell another person that the task was quite interesting in order to help the experimenter entice the other person into participating in the study. Subjects were given one dollar or twenty dollars for engaging in the deception. Subsequently, those subjects given one dollar were found to change their ratings of the experiment in a favorable direction more than those subjects given twenty dollars.

To explain these findings Festinger and Carlsmith (1959) invoked dissonance theory. They argued that the cognitions "I said the task was interesting" and "I think the task was dull" are logically incompatible and therefore dissonant. Since the payment of twenty dollars added a significant consonant cognition, subjects in this condition were *less likely* to change their attitude about the worth of the experiment than subjects in the one-dollar condition. That is, when a person is forced to advocate a position contrary to his own internal belief, the amount of attitude change toward the position overtly advocated will increase as the justification for the overt compliance decreases. In this study low reward (low justification) does not offset the dissonance produced by lying to another person, whereas high reward (high justification) does. Consequently, greater attitude change occurs in the low-reward condition. These "counterintuitive" findings have been obtained in other studies, even when amounts as low as fifty cents versus one dollar (Brehm & Cohen, 1962) or five cents versus fifty cents (Lependorf, 1964) were used. The smaller the reward employed, the greater the amount of attitude change.

In contrast, Janis and Gilmore (1965) failed to support the dissonance predictions concerning the effect of reward in the counterattitudinal situation. In their study subjects who wrote counterattitudinal essays showed greater subsequent attitude change when reinforced by high (twenty-dollar) rather than low (one-dollar) rewards. Similar findings were obtained in a study by Elms and Janis (1965). Instead of the negative relationship predicted by dissonance theory, Janis and his associates found a *positive* relationship: the greater the justification the greater the attitude change.

Janis and his associates interpreted their findings on the basis of reinforcement theory, or as they preferred to call it, "incentive" theory. According to this interpretation, when a person accepts the task of improvising an argument in favor of a point of view at variance with his own personal convictions, he becomes temporarily motivated to think up all the good positive arguments he can and at the same time to suppress all negative arguments that might interfere with the assigned task. This "biased scanning" increases the salience of the positive arguments and therefore increases the chances of accepting and internalizing the new attitude position. Different results would be predicted, however, if resentment or other interfering affective reactions are aroused by *negative incentives.*

Thus in the Festinger and Carlsmith (1959) study subjects were informed by the experimenter that he regularly deceived subjects and were asked to perpetrate this type of deceit themselves by lying to a fellow student. Janis and his associates argued that under such circumstances the positive incentive effects accruing from the twenty-dollar reward were offset by the negative incentive effects involved in deceiving a fellow student, as well as by suspiciousness, guilt, and other negative incentive factors. Consequently, the smaller reward, because it involved less negative incentive (created less suspicion, made the subject less guilty, and so on), led to greater attitude change.

In their research, however, Janis and his associates (Elms & Janis, 1965; Janis & Gilmore, 1965) had subjects write counterattitudinal essays on behalf of public service agencies or governmental agencies. Under these conditions large amounts of money produce little suspiciousness or guilt (presumably because such agencies spend a great deal of money on all sorts of strange activities). Consequently, their research designs involved very little negative incentive for the subjects, and Janis and his associates found a direct relationship between amount of monetary reward and attitude change.

Nevertheless there were a number of procedural differences in the research designs employed in the Janis studies and in studies supporting dissonance theory. In the dissonance studies subjects engaged in counterattitudinal behavior involving a *face-to-face encounter* with another person; in the Janis studies subjects merely *wrote essays* favoring a counterattitudinal position. These differences may explain why it is that the studies produced different results.

To test this possibility Carlsmith, Collins, and Helmreich (1966) conducted a study in which half of the subjects were enticed into telling the next subject that the experimental task was interesting (when in fact it was quite dull), and the other half wrote an anonymous essay to the same effect. Subjects were paid from fifty cents to five dollars for their counterattitudinal behavior. Carlsmith and his associates found that the face-to-face encounter with another person led to results that essentially replicated the negative trend between reward and attitude change obtained by Festinger and Carlsmith (1959). On the other hand, in the essay-writing condition a positive trend was obtained between reward and attitude change (Figure 5-5). Thus the dissonance-theory interpretation appeared to work best for the face-to-face situation, but not for the essay-writing situation. Incentive theory seemed supported by the findings in the essay-writing condition.

Carlsmith and his associates, however, argued that such findings in no way contradict dissonance theory. The inverse relationship between monetary reward and attitude change predicted by dissonance theory did not occur in the essay-writing condition because no dissonance was created in this condition. When a subject writes a counterattitudinal essay, he looks on the task as an opportunity to prove his intellectual ability to think up arguments opposed to the position he holds on an issue. Consequently, since the experimenter knows that the person does not believe what he has written, there

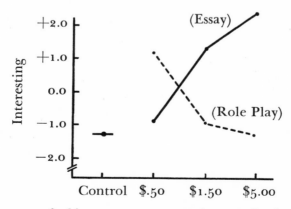

Figure 5-5. Responses of subjects on a post-test question regarding how interesting the subject found the experiment. Counterattitudinal advocacy is assumed to be indicated by variations from the opinion level of control-group subjects (from Carlsmith, Collins, & Helmreich, 1966).

should be little dissonance produced by the existing cognition and the cognition that a counterattitudinal essay was written for the experimenter. Carlsmith and his associates hedged on this a bit by admitting that some dissonance may be created by these manipulations but argued that such dissonance was not "dissonance *of the particular kind* studied by Festinger and Carlsmith" (1966, p. 5). At any rate, not enough dissonance was created to produce the inverse effect; instead the findings can be explained by invoking common-sense hedonic principles.

An incentive interpretation is also possible. Janis and his associates could conceivably account for the negative relationship obtained in the face-to-face situation by arguing that more suspicion is aroused under these conditions than in the essays-writing situation. If the subject adopts a duplicity set, as he must to attempt to mislead the next subject, negative incentive effects are involved that interfere with acceptance of the conclusions advocated. These would be magnified if the monetary reward is thought to be excessive and thus a negative relationship is obtained. In contrast, there is little or no duplicity involved in the essay-writing condition; the subject is merely doing what the experimenter asks him to do without harm to anyone. Consequently no negative incentive effects are created, and a straightforward positive relationship between monetary reward and attitude change is obtained.

A somewhat different interpretation has been proposed by Linder, Cooper, and Jones (1967). These investigators replicated a study by Rosenberg (1965) in which subjects wrote counterattitudinal essays and found, as Rosenberg had, that attitude change increased with larger inducements to comply. In contrast, when extra care was taken to ensure that subjects had a high degree of *choice* in their decision to write or not to write the counterattitudinal essay, the negative relationship predicted by dissonance theory was obtained. Linder and his associates concluded that the crucial factor in determining the experimental outcome is the extent to which the subject feels himself forced to comply. According to this interpretation, the negative relationship predicted by dissonance theory is obtained only when subjects feel they have a considerable degree of freedom of choice.

Another factor appears to be the amount of *commitment* to the counterattitudinal position required of the subject. Helmreich and Collins (1968), for example, found that when subjects were highly committed to a counterattitudinal position (public espousal with no opportunity to recant), the negative relationship between amount of reward and attitude change was obtained. When subjects were less committed (anonymous espousal with opportunity to recant), the positive relationship was obtained.

Dissonance theorists interpret the results of these last two studies as supporting their position. When dissonance is aroused (in the high choice or high commitment situations), the negative relationship between magnitude of reward and attitude change applies. When dissonance is not present (low choice or low commitment), the counterintuitive effect is not predicted and does not occur. Incentive theory, however, could explain the findings equally well. The high choice and the high commitment conditions involve negative incentives and therefore a large reward interferes with acceptance of the conclusions advocated. Thus when a person voluntarily or publicly advances an opinion opposed to what he actually believes, guilt and anxiety (negative incentives) are created. When financial rewards are added to this, negative incentive effects increase proportionately, and the likelihood of attitude change diminishes. In the low choice or low commitment situations, there are no negative incentives and hence a position relationship between monetary rewards and attitude change is obtained.

It appears, therefore, that both theories have considerable resilience. It is extremely difficult to specify experimental conditions that lead to different theoretical predictions. Thus, even though Helmreich and Collins (1968) ruled out suspiciousness as a possible factor influencing their results, the advocate of incentive theory could simply argue that a negative relationship between monetary reward and attitude change was found because more guilt and anxiety (negative incentives) were aroused in the high commitment condition. The concept of dissonance is equally elastic—so much so that it is frequently difficult to determine beforehand just what the theory predicts (Chapanis & Chapanis, 1964). In fact, it would seem that wherever a dissonance theorist can find "dissonance," an incentive theorist can discover "negative incentive." Since the presence of each leads to the same predictions in the counterattitudinal advocacy situation, little progress will be made in evaluating the claims of the competing theories until better operational precision is achieved.

EFFORT. A second area of controversy between dissonance theory and reinforcement theory concerns the effect of effort expenditure on attitude change. Here, it would seem, the theories predict different empirical results. This was the contention of dissonance theorists who argued that the logic of reinforcement theory leads to the prediction that high effort, because it is less rewarding, results in *less* attitude change than low effort. In contrast, dissonance theory predicts that overt compliance entailing high effort produces *more* attitude change than does compliance entailing low effort. This paradoxical prediction follows from the assumption that more dissonance is created in the condition where more effort is required. Experimental research on this topic (e.g., Cohen, 1959; Ostrom, 1966; Zimbardo, 1965) supports the dissonance interpretation, although not unambiguously

(Insko, 1967). Thus in Zimbardo's (1965) study increased effort (manipulated by delayed auditory feedback) led to more attitude change, although the difference between experimental conditions did not attain conventional levels of statistical significance. In other studies cited in support of dissonance theory the effect was slight or confounded by uncontrolled variables (see Chapanis & Chapanis, 1964).

In a variation of this general approach Aronson (1961) argued that if a person exerts a great deal of effort to reach a goal but fails to do so, dissonance will be created. If conditions are such that the person cannot convince himself that the goal was worth the effort (the sour grapes alternative), the most convenient form of dissonance reduction is through *increased valuation* of the task or the stimuli associated with the task. Thus dissonance theory predicts that if a person continuously expends effort to reach a goal and fails, the stimuli associated with this task become more attractive to him.

Aronson saw this prediction to run counter to the prediction of reinforcement theory. The findings of research on secondary reinforcement (e.g., Skinner, 1938; Wolfe, 1936), would lead one to expect that only stimuli associated with reward gain in attractiveness. According to dissonance theory, the stimuli associated with "nonreward" gain in attractiveness, provided that effort is expended to reach the goal. The greater the effort, the greater the gain in attractiveness.

To test these predictions, Aronson had subjects fish for cans, two thirds of which were empty and one third of which contained two, three, or four dimes. Subjects in the low-effort condition could pull the cans out with a horseshoe magnet. Subjects in the high-effort condition had to catch a hook in a metal ring attached to each can. The rewarding cans (containing money) were colored differently from the nonrewarding cans. Subjects rated the two colors before and after carrying out the task. Aronson found that after the task the rewarding color was rated significantly more attractive than the nonrewarding color in the low-effort condition, but that in the high-effort condition the colors were rated approximately equal in attractiveness. Aronson interpreted these results as indicating that secondary reinforcement operates in the low-effort condition, but is neutralized in the high-effort condition because of dissonance reduction.

The Aronson study has been criticized (Chapanis & Chapanis, 1964) because high- and low-effort conditions differed in reinforcement rates. Because their task is more difficult and took more time, subjects in the high-effort condition received reinforcement at a much slower rate than subjects in the low-effort condition. Consequently if secondary reinforcement is a function of reinforcement rate, significantly greater attractiveness of the rewarding colors in the low-effort condition could be explained as the result of a higher reinforcement rate. Some indirect evidence (Ferster & Skinner, 1957) argues against this, but the matter has not yet been empirically resolved.

Theoretical objections to the Aronson study were raised by Lott (1963a), who contended that Hullian theory can provide an alternative explanation for Aronson's results. Specifically, Lott disagreed with Aronson's assumption that "any effects due to secondary reinforcement should remain constant regardless of effort" (Aronson, 1961, p. 376) and attempted to show that Hullian theory would predict that the development of secondary reinforcement is *negatively* affected by effort. Thus in Hull's system increased effort leads to increased inhibition of instrumental activity ("reactive inhibition"), and stimuli associated with instrumental activity become conditioned to inhibit behavior ("conditioned inhibition"). Since these stimuli (color in Aronson's study) are the same stimuli that lead to the goal response (thereby acquiring secondary reinforcement value), Lott argued that the same variables affect both processes. When greater amounts of effort are required in the instrumental activity, more inhibition develops and learning is slower (the stimuli acquire less secondary reinforcement potential). If the task requires less effort, the effects of secondary reinforcement are increased. Such an explanation, Lott contended, accounts for Aronson's data and makes it unnecessary to postulate the existence of cognitive dissonance. Aronson (1963) did not agree, but Lott (1963b) refused to concede. Both authors did agree, however, that further research was needed.

The controversy between proponents of a learning-theory interpretation and those who favor a dissonance-theory interpretation has even spread to animal research. In their book, *Deterrents and reinforcement,* Lawrence and Festinger (1962) argued that data from a number of areas conflict with some basic assumptions of learning theory. One type of experimental evidence they cited has to do with the relation between effort expenditure and habit strength. They saw evidence in a study by Aiken (1957) that habits acquired during conditions requiring considerable effort are more resistant to extinction than habits acquired under less effortful conditions. Such evidence is not consistent with conventional learning theory since it should be less enjoyable (rewarding) to the animal to expend a great deal of effort than it is to expend a small amount of effort. Consequently increasing the amount of effort required should weaken habit strength rather than strengthen it.

Lawrence and Festinger proposed a dissonance-theory explanation of such findings. They argued that when the animal voluntarily engages in an action that is unpleasant (e.g., requires a great deal of effort), dissonance is aroused. Dissonance can be reduced by changing the behavior and refusing to repeat the action. But if the animal continues to engage in the unpleasant activity, it reduces its dissonance by finding "extra attractions" (Lawrence & Festinger, 1962, p. 35) in the situation. Thus when a basic source of reinforcement, such as food, is withheld, the animal will continue to respond because it is held to the task by these extra attractions. In this way increased effortfulness of a task during acquisition will produce increased resistance to extinction.

Mowrer (1963), in his review of the work of Lawrence and Festinger, concluded that the experimental evidence that they cited can readily be explained in terms of learning theory and does not at all require the special assumptions postulated by these authors. Thus, to take the example of the effort variable, it need only be assumed that increased effort during acquisition constitutes a kind of frustration for the animal. If this is true, then it is not unreasonable to infer that the animal has learned to tolerate frustration occasioned by effort during acquisition. This adaptation effect will then generalize to the frustration involved in the absence of reward during extinction. Conventional learning theory can deal with such a finding without recourse to dissonance interpretations. It should be added that Mowrer went on to argue that, in any case, the empirical evidence that Lawrence and Festinger cited that increased effort produces increased resistance to extinction (Aiken, 1957) is not above suspicion.

In short, research on the relationship between effort expenditure and attitude change, like research on counterattitudinal advocacy and attitude change, has produced no clearcut victory for either dissonance or reinforcement theory. Dissonance theorists contended that their research findings contradicted the predictions of reinforcement theory, only to have reinforcement theorists argue that their theory leads to no such predictions and that, in any case, the dissonance research is empirically suspect. Nevertheless, while the empirical support of dissonance theory is not unequivocal, there is enough evidence to embarrass advocates of a learning-theory point of view. As McGuire (1966) noted, dissonance theory provides a single explanation for a wide variety of empirical phenomena. If learning theory is to be used as an alternative to dissonance theory, it must, at least, be capable of dealing with the whole range of data that dissonance theory, more or less successfully, attempts to explain.

BEM'S THEORY OF SELF-PERCEPTION.   Recently, Daryl Bem (1967a) has proposed a major learning-theory interpretation of cognitive dissonance phenomena. In fact, Bem has attempted to go one step further than dissonance theory and to provide a theoretical explanation both for the major dissonance phenomena *and* for the secondary pattern of results that have appeared in supporting experiments but that were not predicted by the theory.

Bem's framework was essentially Skinnerian. He found objectionable the dissonance theory emphasis on the individual's current phenomenology; he put forth in its place a theory intended to account for observed functional relations between current stimuli and responses in terms of the individual's past training history. Applied to dissonance phenomena, such an approach begins by analyzing the variables that control the particular form of behavior in question—namely, the subject's self-descriptive statements of attitude or belief.

At this point Bem introduced his concept of "self-perception," which he regarded as a special case of interpersonal perception characterized by the individual's ability to respond differentially to his own behavior and to the variables that control that behavior. Like other forms of interpersonal perception, self-perception is learned through interaction with the socializing community. Since, however, self-descriptive verbal statements (the most common responses comprising self-perception) describe internal events to which only the individual himself has direct access, it becomes necessary for the members of the verbal community to teach the individual the correct response to impinging private stimuli. This is done by various means (Skinner, 1957), but most often it is possible because observers are able to identify the moment when certain private stimuli are impinging on the individual (e.g., the stimuli accompanying pain) on the basis of observable stimuli and responses. Thus an observer can infer from external stimulus conditions and from the overt behavior of the individual that certain private stimuli are accompanying these public events (Bem, 1965).

What this analysis suggests is that many self-descriptive statements that appear to be exclusively under the control of private stimuli are, in fact, at least partially controlled by those public events used by the training community to infer the individual's inner states. Many subtle discriminations that individuals make in describing inner events are based on cues *potentially available to an outside observer*. Bem argued that this is often true of self-descriptive attitude statements. Such statements can be based on the individual's observations of his own overt behavior and the external stimulus conditions that control it.

Consequently, it is often possible to view an individual's attitude statements as inferences from his own overt behavior and accompanying stimulus variables. If this is the case, it would follow that an individual's attitude statements and those that an outside observer would attribute to him are often *functionally similar*, because both sets of statements are "partial inferences" from the same evidence—namely, "the public behaviors and accompanying stimulus cues upon which the socializing community has relied on in training him to make such self-descriptive statements in the first place" (Bem, 1967a, p. 186).

Bem's principal aim, however, was not simply to work out a theoretical account of how attitudes develop and are controlled by stimulus variables but rather to present his interpretation as an alternative to dissonance theory. Consequently, he discussed the three major categories of dissonance experiments: (1) forced-compliance studies, (2) free-choice studies, and (3) exposure-to-information studies (Brehm & Cohen, 1962). In each case he presented as an alternative to the dissonance explanation an interpretation based on self-perception theory.

The example of a *forced-compliance study* discussed by Bem was the research of Festinger and Carlsmith (1959) on the effects of twenty-dollar versus one-dollar rewards. As we have seen, according to dissonance theory a twenty-dollar reward will offset dissonance because it acts as a compensation for engaging in deceptive behavior, whereas a one-dollar reward is not sufficient compensation and hence will not offset dissonance. As a result, subjects in the one-dollar condition are predicted to (and in fact do) display more attitude change. Bem's analysis predicts the same results but for different reasons.

According to Bem, to understand what is happening it is necessary to consider the viewpoint of an outside observer who hears the subject making favorable statements about the task to a fellow student and who knows, in addition, that the subject was paid twenty dollars (or one dollar) to do so. If asked to state the attitude of the subject, the observer would most likely conclude that the subject given twenty dollars is not credible and that his statements could not be used as a guide for inferring his attitude. This is because, in Skinnerian terms, the subject in the twenty-dollar condition would be thought to be under the control of the reinforcement contingencies of the money and not at all under the discriminative control of the task he appears to be describing. In contrast, subjects in the one-dollar condition would be judged as being more likely to express their actual attitude to the fellow student. Consequently, the observer would most likely come to the conclusion that the subjects in the one-dollar condition held more favorable attitudes to the task than did subjects in the twenty-dollar condition—a conclusion that would be consistent with the results obtained by Festinger and Carlsmith.

In fact, Bem (1967a) found that subjects acting as observers were able to infer the attitudes of subjects in the original study. That is, he conducted a replication of the Festinger and Carlsmith study but separated the observer and the observed. Rather than having subjects who observed their own behavior, he had subjects act as observers who were to estimate the attitudes of the original subjects. The observers' judgments replicated the inverse functional relationship reported by Festinger and Carlsmith. Thus Bem concluded that the self-judgments of the original subjects could be viewed as based upon the same kinds of public evidence that the community originally employed in training them to infer the attitudes of any communicator, themselves included.

The second major category of data on dissonance theory comes from *free-choice studies* where subjects are permitted to make a selection from a set of objects or courses of action. According to dissonance theory, unfavorable aspects of the chosen alternative and favorable aspects of the rejected alternative are dissonant with the subject's having chosen as he did. Therefore, to reduce dissonance, the subject will exaggerate favorable features and play down what is unfavorable. This leads to an enhanced rating of the chosen alternative and a lower rating of the rejected alternative. A number of studies have confirmed these predictions (Brehm & Cohen, 1962).

One example is the study by Brehm and Cohen (1959), in which school children could select toys from either two or four alternatives. Some children chose from qualitatively similar toys, while others chose from qualitatively dissimilar alternatives. The results of the study were interpreted as supporting dissonance theory because (1) ratings of chosen toys were displaced in the more favorable direction and ratings of the rejected toys were displaced in the unfavorable direction, (2) the displacement effect was larger when there were more alternatives and hence more to give up (greater dissonance), and (3) the displacement effect was larger when the choice was made from dissimilar rather than similar alternatives, a situation which increases the disparity between what is given up and what is gained (greater dissonance).

Again, Bem's interpretation of these findings is based upon the judgments of an observer trying to estimate the child's ratings of the toys. If the observer has not seen the child engage in any behavior with the toys, his estimate of the child's ratings would be expected to be different than it would be if he had seen the child choose one of them. In the latter case, he would be predicted to displace the estimated ratings of the chosen and rejected alternatives further from each other simply because he has some behavioral evidence upon which to base his judgments. Similarly, if the observer has seen the selected toy chosen over more competing alternatives he might be expected to increase the estimated displacement between the chosen toy and the rejected alternatives. Finally, stimulus generalization effects could be employed to account for the increased displacement that occurred when the alternatives were dissimilar. To the extent that the chosen and rejected alternatives are similar to each other, they will be rated closer together on the scale.

Bem (1967a) reported an interpersonal replication of the toy study in which these predictions were confirmed. By having college students estimate how an eleven-year-old boy would rate different toys under the various conditions, Bem was able to reproduce the findings of the Brehm and Cohen (1959) study. The ratings of the observer-subjects showed the same displacement effects under the various conditions as had been obtained in the original study.

The third category of dissonance studies relates to *exposure to information*. In these studies subjects are either involuntarily exposed to discrepant (i.e., dissonant) information or are asked to expose themselves to such information. Dissonance theory predicts that a person will avoid exposure to sources of dissonant information or, if involuntarily exposed, will seek to reduce dissonance by attitude change. Unfortunately for the theory, the data are not entirely consistent (McGuire, 1966; Freedman & Sears, 1965). Even if the effects could be shown to hold up empirically, Bem reasoned that it would not be implausible to suppose that punishment is often contingent upon being inconsistent and illogical. Such an interpretation is, he felt, considerably more parsimonious than postulating an internal aversive motivational state such as a drive for consistency or a drive to reduce dissonance.

Bem, it will be recalled, argued that the value of self-perception theory is not simply that it can explain what dissonance theory explains but that it is able to explicate functional relations *not predicted* by the original theory. One example cited relates to the observed relationship between the amount of behavior evoked by the subject in a forced-compliance situation and his final attitude change. Festinger and Carlsmith (1959) found that with subjects given one dollar to deceive a fellow student, the greater the number and variety of arguments stated by the subject about the task, the more favorable his final evaluation about it. The reverse was true for subjects in the twenty-dollar condition.

In terms of self-perception theory this might be explained by arguing that an outside observer who considers a communicator credible might be more likely to view his statements as expressing his actual attitude the more arguments he put forth. If on the other hand, the observer has some reason to question the credibility of the communicator, he might become skeptical as to the correspondence between the communicator's statements and his actual attitude if it appears to the observer that the communicator, by bringing forth more arguments, "doth protest too much." In a test of these hypotheses, Bem found that by attributing to the original subjects in the Festinger and Carlsmith study long and imaginative or short and unimaginative arguments, the ratings of the observer-subjects replicated the positive correlation between number of arguments and attitude change in the one-dollar condition and the negative correlation between these two variables found in the twenty-dollar condition. He was thereby able to obtain a result not predicted by dissonance theory but consistent with his own formulations.

Bem's theory represents a significant attempt to interpret from a learning-theory (in this case, Skinnerian) point of view data previously thought to be explicable only in terms of dissonance theory. Specifically, it represents a way of accounting for the results of attitude change studies that avoids any appeal to a hypothetical internal state of the organism. Nevertheless there is a cognitive flavor to Bem's theory that is strangely un-Skinnerian. Observer-subjects "make judgments" on the basis of a person's behavior; they "infer" inner states; they "duplicate the phenomenology of the subject in the experiment" (Bem, 1967b). What Bem has attempted to do, however, is to show that the behavior of the subject in the experiment is under the control of stimuli that can be observed objectively by another person and by the subject himself and that the inferences as to the subject's attitude that both can make on the basis of overt behavior and controlling stimuli are functionally similar. The data of the theory, therefore, are not internal, private, cognitive events, but external, public behavior.

Bem's approach, it should be noted, is not the only one that a learning theorist can take to explain dissonance phenomena. If one assumes that there is a learned drive to be logical and consistent and to interpret the environment accurately, consonant and dissonant communications can be seen as rewarding (drive-reducing) or punishing (drive-increasing) events. A number of investigators with learning-theory orientations have made such suppositions (Corrozi & Rosnow, 1968; Dollard & Miller, 1950; Golightly & Byrne, 1964). No detailed program of experimental research, however, has been conducted in pursuit of the implications of such a point of view.

Learning and Persuasion

One assumption that underlies a learning-theory approach to persuasive communication is that the effectiveness of the communication in producing attitude change is a function, at least in part, of the extent to which the contents of the communication are *learned and retained* by its recipient. This is what Hovland, Janis, and Kelley (1953) referred to as the "learning" factor—the assumption "that the degree to which a communication produces opinion change depends in part on learning the contents of the communication" (Hovland *et al.,* 1953, p. 123). They saw two variables in particular to affect the extent to which the contents of the communication are learned and retained: (1) the individual's motivation to learn the communication and (2) the "associative" factors intrinsic to the contents of the communication. Little data, however, were presented by the Hovland group bearing on the learning factor in persuasive communication.

RETENTION OF CONTENTS.   Subsequent research on the correlation between learning and retention of contents and attitude change has not produced unambiguous results. As we have seen, Miller and Campbell (1959) and Insko (1964) failed to find significant correlations (average within-group correlations) between attitude scores and recall scores in their studies. A systematic investigation of this question has been conducted by Watts and McGuire (1964). They had subjects read four different communications spaced over a six-week interval. There were four time intervals during this period, and the communications dealing with each of the four topics were rotated among these time intervals. Immediately after the last communication exposure, opinion and retention measures were taken. The measure of opinion was a 15-point agree-disagree scale, and retention was assessed by a series of tests. The first retention test required the subject to recall the topics of each of the four communications. The second test reinstated the topics and required the subject to state whether a "pro" or "con" stand was taken on each. The third test reinstated both the topics and the stands and required the subject to select the sources from a list of four for each communication. The final test was a multiple-choice assessment of retention for the three specific arguments contained in each communication.

Watts and McGuire combined the data for all four communications and found that the overall decay rate for opinion was linear. The decay rates for the four retention curves, on the other hand, were all negatively accelerated functions, similar to the characteristic curves for forgetting of verbal material (Table 5-1). By analyzing their data further, Watts and McGuire were able to show that opinion was directly related to retention of the side taken and the arguments used over all time intervals, but that it was negatively related to recall of the communication topic after an interval of six weeks. In addition, the credibility of the source appeared to be a factor. They found that opinion was positively related to recall if the communicator was high in credibility, but negatively related to recall if the communicator was low in credibility. It seems, therefore, that a number of variables enter into the opinion-recall relationship and that persistence of attitude change is only partially dependent on communication retention.

Additional evidence for the complexity of the relationship between attitude change and recall comes from a study by Watts (1967) in which a comparison was made of the relative persistence of opinion change induced by improvising and writing an argument advocating a counterattitudinal position (active participation) with that induced by reading a persuasive message in favor of the same position (pas-

Table 5-1 Temporal Decay of Induced Opinion Change and
of Recall for Aspects of the Communication

VARIABLES MEASURED	INTERVAL BETWEEN MESSAGE RECEIPT AND OPINION CHANGE			
	Immediately after	*One week*	*Two weeks*	*Six weeks*
Opinion Change:				
Change in the induced direction from 5.95-point, no-message, control level	2.53	2.12	2.09	0.78
Retention:				
Percentage of subjects recalling message topic (Test 1).	94	60	63	61
Percentage of subjects recalling the side taken in the message (Test 2).	93	65	65	60
Percentage of subjects recognizing message source (Test 3).	85	44	50	34
Percentage of subjects recognizing all three arguments in the message (Test 4).	72	29	24	11

From Watts & McGuire, 1964.

sive participation). Both the method of induction and the temporal persistence of the induced opinion change were further related to the subjects' memory of the topic and of the side taken in the induction session.

Watts found that, over time, the active participation conditions led to superior temporal persistence of attitude change. Active participation also produced greater recall of the topic and side supported. The relationship between recall and persistence of attitude change was negative, however, in the passive participation condition. That is, those subjects in this condition who were unable to recall the topic and side taken maintained more of the initial induced opinion change than subjects who showed good recall. This finding was in general agreement with the Watts and McGuire (1964) finding that, for subjects who had read persuasive messages, memory of the topic (but not the side taken) was inversely related to opinion change over a six-week interval. Apparently, therefore, the relationship between the persistence of attitude change and retention of the topic and side supported depends, in part, on the mode of induction of opinion change.

Further evidence against the assumption of a single functional relationship between opinion and memory was reported by Cook and Insko (1968), who, like Watts and McGuire (1964), found that the persuasive impact of a communication decreased rectilinearly over time, while recall was a negatively accelerated decreasing function of time. Taken together, these data suggest that induced attitude change is to some extent *autonomous of recall of the contents of the inducing communication.* Further evidence for this autonomy has been mentioned by McGuire (1966). He cited as an example the delayed-action effect that is commonly found in opinion change studies but is a rare phenomenon (long-term reminiscence) in studies of recall for verbal material. Thus there is little similarity between the "sleeper effect" obtained in attitude change studies (Hovland & Weiss, 1951; Kelman & Hovland, 1953) and effects obtained in the study of long-term memory.

AN AMENDED LEARNING MODEL.   The discrepancy between the assumptions of a learning-theory model and the data from research investigating the relationship between the persistence of attitude change and retention has led Greenwald (1967) to offer what he referred to as "an amended learning model of persuasion." On the basis of research conducted in his laboratory, Greenwald concluded that the learning model, as traditionally understood, is inadequate as an explanation of persuasion. Instead, he proposed that persuasion be viewed as involving modification through learning of the *cognitive component* of an attitude. According to this approach the critical element in determining the effectiveness of a persuasive communication is the cognitive reaction of the recipient of the communication.

When a person receives a persuasive message and must accept or reject it, he can be expected to relate this new information to his existing attitudes, knowledge, feelings, and so forth. Greenwald argued that in the course of doing so he is likely to generate substantial cognitive content beyond that of the original communication and may also review issue-related thoughts already stored in his memory. Thus the recipient's rehearsal and learning of *his own cognitive reactions* to persuasion may provide a basis for explaining in learning terms the persisting effects of communication. Learning this internal content may be more fundamental than learning the communication content as such.

Greenwald distinguished between the recipient's cognitive reactions to persuasion ("recipient-generated cognitions") and the contents of the communication itself ("externally-oriented cognitions"). In an experimental investigation of this distinction, Greenwald and his associates found that subjects who had heard a communication advocating specialization in education and who were asked to spend ten minutes listing their thoughts pertinent to this issue, listed more recipient-generated cognitions—that is, thoughts not traceable to the contents of the communication—than externally-oriented cognitions, although their thoughts were tapped immediately after hearing a communication containing a dozen or more distinctly relevant thoughts that could have been listed. Moreover, attitude change in favor of the position advocated in the communication tended to be more highly correlated with an index of the extent to which the subject judged his recipient-generated cognitions favorable to the communication than with an index of the extent to which externally-oriented cognition were judged to favor the communication. Greenwald interpreted these findings as providing evidence of the relative importance of the recipient-generated cognitions in the individual's attitude structure.

The relationship between attitude change and retention was explored explicitly in another study in which subjects received a communication consisting of ten statements supporting the United States foreign policy, either immediately, one week, or three weeks before being tested for their opinion on that policy and for retention of the ten statements. After hearing the statements, subjects were allowed a short period of time to write down any issue-relevant thoughts that occurred to them. It was thus possible to obtain a sample, for each subject, of the recipient-generated content rehearsed at the time of the communication. Subsequently, in addition to recalling communication content, subjects were asked to recall the reactions they had written down at the time of the communication.

Greenwald and his associates found that the correlations obtained between posttest opinion and retention of communication contents differed considerably from those obtained between opinion and retention of recipient-generated statements (Table 5-2). On the basis of these data, Greenwald concluded that it is not so much learning the contents of the communication that affects subsequent attitude change as the learning of self-generated cognitive reactions. The effectiveness of the communication appears to be significantly related to the retention of issue-related cognitions not contained in the communication itself but aroused and rehearsed by the recipient at the time of the communication.

Table 5-2 Correlations between Retention and Posttest Opinion

	TIME INTERVAL		
CORRELATION	*Immediately after*	*One week*	*Three weeks*
Opinion and Communication Contents	−.19	−.21	−.07
Opinion and Recipient-Generated Pro Statements	.66	.52	.46

From Greenwald, 1967. Correlations contain a correction by partial correlation for opinion level and intelligence.

Greenwald (1967), like Bem (1967a), was concerned with extending the range of learning-theory interpretations of attitude-change phenomena. Learning the contents of an attitude is in some way related to accepting the attitude, but Greenwald felt that the nature of this relationship is clarified only when the subject's cognitions are taken into account. His procedure represents an attempt to make objective the subject's self-generated cognitive reactions to communication messages. Bem took a somewhat different approach to the same problem. He recognized that the individual's cognitions affect acceptance of a communication, but preferred to have his subject-observers infer cognitive states from descriptions of overt behavior and controlling stimuli. Nevertheless both Greenwald and Bem agreed that an adequate learning-theory explanation of attitude-change phenomena must come to grips with the cognitive aspect of attitudes.

EVALUATION

An accurate assessment of learning-theory approaches to attitude development and change is fairly difficult at the present time. Certainly the emergence of dissonance theory and the increasing amount of research in the attitude-change area has created strain for an all-encompassing learning interpretation. In fact, however, systematic application of learning principles to all areas of attitude research has not been undertaken. Even in areas where learning theory has been widely applied, its success is difficult to evaluate. In investigations of order effects in persuasive communication, for example, the theory has produced remarkably good results in predicting the relative effectiveness of communications presented at different time intervals (Miller & Campbell, 1959), but it has faltered when increasing quantitative precision was demanded (Anderson & Hubert, 1963; Insko, 1964). Recent theoretical developments (e.g., Bem, 1967a; Greenwald, 1967) are promising and have received empirical support (Bem & McConnell, 1970; Greenwald, 1969, in press). Nevertheless, it would be premature to evaluate these theories before they have been subjected to further empirical scrutiny.

Nor is older work easily assessed. The research of Hovland and the Yale group on persuasive communication was one of the most important research enterprises in American social psychology. Empirically, it was highly successful in its demarcation of the parameters that affect attitude change. Theoretically, it was less successful. As a learning-theory approach to attitude change, the work of the Yale group lacked the discipline and theoretical rigor that characterized, for example, Spence's (1956) application of Hullian theory to animal behavior. Learning theory was not a controlling and consistent point of view for Hovland and his followers. They did not typically devise their experiments to test deductions from learning theory. Instead, learning theory was used in an *ad hoc* manner as a source of interpretive analogies or as a heuristic to suggest lines of future research.

Weiss' (1962) theory also exemplifies this tendency. In his research attitude development and change were conceptualized in terms of both classical conditioning and instrumental learning. Weiss took Miller's (1959) appeal for the liberalization of S-R concepts to heart. His use of concepts such as stimulus, response, and reinforcement is so liberalized that it would send shivers up the spine of a traditional S-R behaviorist. For this reason, presumably, Weiss did not insist upon a literal interpretation of these terms but emphasized instead that he was using them by analogy only.

Other investigators, however, are not as careful as Weiss was in this respect. This becomes especially problematic if one considers the status of reinforcement in learning-theory accounts of attitude development and change. A researcher can opt for a merely operational use of the concept of reinforcement. According to this definition, anything that increases the probability of a response is reinforcing. Oranges, pussy cats, and polar bears may all, under certain circumstances, be reinforcing in these terms. Razran (1938) used free lunch, Golightly and Byrne (1964) used consonant arguments, Scott (1957) used winning a debate. Should we think of these various procedures as actually reinforcing behavior or simply as operating in a manner analogous to reinforcement? If they are to be thought of as reinforcers, by what criteria is this justified? A Skinnerian's reply to this question is simply a restatement of the operational procedures used to define reinforcement. But for many psychologists this is not enough. What is missing is a theoretical statement of the nature of reinforcement. This, of course, is no simple matter and has for years been a major point of controversy among learning theorists. Lacking agreement on this point, it seems likely that researchers with a learning-theory orientation will continue to use what works, leaving larger theoretical concerns in abeyance.

To do so, however, muddies the theoretical waters. If, for example, one assumes that there is a learned drive for consistency and that consonant communications are rewarding to the subject and dissonant communications are punishing (Corrozi & Rosnow, 1968; Golightly & Byrne, 1964), learning theory begins to merge with dissonance theory. This, of course, is not cause for alarm and, on the face of it, supports Campbell's (1963) argument that there is a trend toward the unification of theory in psychology. Conceivably, in the not too distant future an integration will be achieved between cognitively-oriented, phenomenological approaches to attitude change and behavioristic, learning-theory approaches.

It would be nice to end this chapter on this rather cheerful and optimistic note. But here, as elsewhere, another interpretation of theoretical and empirical developments is possible. According to this interpretation, the widespread resistance to dissonance theory and the elaboration of competing learning-theory interpretations indicate that proponents of the two positions are rather sharply, perhaps hopelessly, divided. On the other hand, dissonance theorists focus primarily on the internal, phenomenological state of the individual. In contrast, a learning-theory approach emphasizes objective descriptions of environmental events.

Thus, it can be argued, as Katahn and Koplin (1968) have done in another context, that proponents of these two theoretical approaches are working in different paradigms. The controversy between them represents a particular instance of a "paradigm clash" (Kuhn, 1962). In such controversies, each of the antagonists criticizes the other for inadequately understanding the opposing theory and for a lack of knowledge concerning relevant supporting data. At the same time each describes the other's position in the most extreme form in order to demolish it effectively. Basically, such differences are irresolvable since each works from a set of metatheoretical assumptions that dictate the methods of investigation to be employed, the data that are relevant, and the manner of relating the data to theoretical concepts. There are no logical grounds for deciding that one paradigm is to be accepted and the other rejected. Indeed any attempt to choose one over the other will inevitably fail because the proponents of each paradigm view the domain so differently that their arguments pass by each other without making meaningful contact.

To a certain extent this is what has happened in the debate between learning theory and dissonance theory. As we have tried to indicate, both theories are flexible enough (or imprecise enough) to interpret the major research findings. On the other hand, neither theory successfully integrates all the empirical data in attitude research (McGuire, 1969). According to the paradigm-clash interpretation, however, this does not mean that both theories will be discarded. Instead, one will come to dominate because it is more productive. The issue will not be resolved in a few years or even a few decades, but eventually the superiority of one paradigm will be apparent to all. According to this view there will be no integration; it will simply become obvious that one approach works and the other does not.

If a learning-theory, behavioristic approach is in fact to become the dominant paradigm for psychological research on attitudes, it will

of necessity have to provide some account of the cognitive and phenomenological aspects of attitudes. At the present time only rudimentary efforts have been made in this direction. But there are signs
that investigators working from a learning-theory orientation are
concerned with this question. The work of Bem (1967a) and Greenwald (1967), in particular, attests to this. Whether such approaches
will succeed in incorporating cognitive data within the learning-
theory paradigm, or whether, as Campbell (1959) hoped, some higher-
level integration of behavioristic and cognitive theories will be
achieved is presently a moot question.

6

Learning and Psychotherapy

ONE OF the most important recent developments in psychology is a growing dissatisfaction with traditional methods of psychotherapy. Increasingly, psychologists are coming to regard "mental illness" as a problem in social behavior. The psychologically disturbed individual, according to this position, is one whose behavior does not correspond to what is socially permissible or acceptable. The psychologically "sick" are persons whose capacity to deal effectively with others in social situations has been impaired. What appears to be "pathology" is actually a defect in social learning. "Treatment" is essentially a question of new learning.

Accordingly many psychologists have become interested in the application of learning principles to psychotherapy. Recent developments in this direction—especially in "behavior therapy" (Eysenck, 1960)—have produced a new and radically different conception of the psychotherapeutic process. Therapy is seen as a technique to help the individual unlearn maladaptive social behavior and learn more appropriate responses. In addition, the therapeutic interaction itself is regarded as a social-learning situation in which both the behavior of the therapist and that of the patient are forms of social behavior.

In this chapter we shall discuss early attempts to understand neurotic behavior and the psychotherapeutic process in terms of the principles of learning, and then turn to recent work in behavior therapy. We shall also discuss criticisms of learning-theory approaches to psychotherapy and relevant theoretical and empirical issues. Once again coverage will of necessity be selective. Developments in this field cannot be adequately treated in a single chapter. Some excellent reviews and general discussions now exist in the literature (e.g., Ban, 1964; Bandura, 1961, 1969a; Franks, 1964, 1969; Kalish, 1965; Ullmann & Krasner, 1965, 1969). Our intention here is simply to survey the field briefly, to discuss controversial issues, and to evaluate in general terms the success that has been achieved in the therapeutic modification of man's social behavior through the application of learning principles.

THERAPY AS A LEARNING PROCESS

The first psychologists to view therapy as a learning process were the early behaviorists of the 1920s and 1930s. They were convinced that the principles of conditioning that applied to normal behavior could be applied equally well to abnormal behavior. They argued that therapeutic methods based on psychoanalysis were inadequate and misdirected and that learning methods should be employed in their place. In the next two decades, however, psychologists with a learning-theory orientation showed a willingness to accept the traditional psychoanalytic model, but attempted to interpret what took place during psychotherapy on the basis of learning principles. This approach dominated until the 1960s, when the behavior therapists, in the tradition of the early behaviorists, rejected the traditional model in its entirety and substituted a learning model.

The Conditioning and Extinction
of Neurotic Behavior

Many of the early behaviorists were interested in the relationship between conditioning and the acquisition of pathological behavior. They regarded psychoanalytic interpretations as grossly inadequate since such interpretations rested on unproven and unprovable assumptions about "mental" processes. To attempt to explain pathological behavior in such mentalistic terms, the behaviorists argued, leads one into a semantic quagmire. No true scientific understanding is possible because the explanatory concepts used are not objective. Behavioristic concepts, on the other hand, are objective and offer the possibility of genuine scientific explanation.

THE CONDITIONING OF PSYCHOPATHOLOGY.   In Chapter One we discussed the research by Watson (Watson & Rayner, 1920) that demonstrated that fear-arousing stimuli can serve as unconditional stimuli for the formation of a conditioned fear response established to a previously neutral stimulus. In the Watson and Rayner (1920) study a neutral object like a toy or pet animal was paired with the striking of a dishpan until a conditioned fear response was established such that the toy or animal was feared in the absence of the loud sound. Watson (1914) was convinced that all emotional responses, adaptive or maladaptive, were established through such conditioning processes.

Similar views were expressed by other early psychologists as well. In an interesting discussion of the etiology of phobias, Bagby (1922) argued that the Freudian notion of the sexual origins of phobia was incorrect and that phobias could be explained as disturbances that date from a traumatic episode to which the person reacted with intense fear. Since the episode was one involving some forbidden action such that the experience could not be discussed with the individual's parents, guilt was associated with the experience and the anxiety deriving from guilt was subsequently associated with certain stimulus features of the environment.

Smith and Guthrie (1922) argued against the Freudian interpretation of the origins of exhibitionism. They contended that Freud was incorrect in asserting that exhibitionism involved instinctual behavior of sexual origin. Instead, Smith and Guthrie felt that exhibitionism is acquired like other habits, through conditioning, and is intended to secure attention from other people. If a child receives favorable attention for exhibiting himself, that behavior will develop as a habit and will tend to occur at other times when attention is desired.

The early behaviorists were convinced that, in principle, all behavior was learned through conditioning. Aside from these few attempts, however, little serious attention was given to the analysis of behavioral disorders; eventually, interest in the origins of psychopathology seems to have died out. The behaviorists retreated to the laboratory and left the clinical arena to psychiatrists and psychoanalysts.

THE EXTINCTION OF PSYCHOPATHOLOGY.   As we have seen, Watson and his associates were not simply concerned with demonstrating that emotional responses could be established through conditioning; they also wanted to demonstrate that emotional responses could be eliminated by extinction. That is, the interests of these early behaviorists was not simply to show that there was a relationship between conditioning and the acquisition of pathological behavior, they also wanted to demonstrate that behavior principles could be applied to the treatment of psychopathology.

Jones (1924) was able to eliminate a child's phobic responses by feeding him in the presence of initially small but gradually increasing anxiety-arousing stimuli. As we have seen in Chapter One, this method involved establishing a "point of tolerance" and gradually bringing the phobic object (a rabbit) nearer to the child, thereby advancing the point of tolerance.

Other methods were proposed by various behaviorists such as Dunlap (1932), who suggested that behavior deviations could be eliminated through the method of "negative practice," in which the subject reproduced the negative behavior voluntarily without reinforcement. This method was applied by Fishman (1937) to the treatment of speech disorders. More direct methods of extinction were employed by Max (1935), who used a strong electric shock as an aversive stimulus in treating a patient who displayed homosexual behavior following exposure to a fetishistic stimulus object. By administering shock in the presence of the fetishistic object, Max was able to eliminate both the fetish and the homosexual behavior.

A variation of this technique was employed by Mowrer and Mowrer (1938) to treat enuretic patients. They devised an apparatus consisting of a sensitive electric circuit arranged so that a small amount of urine activated a buzzer that aroused the subject. It was assumed that bladder tension would become, through conditioning, a cue for waking up which in turn would be followed by sphincter contraction. Once bladder pressure became a cue for the sphincter-control response, the child should be able to remain dry without wakening from sleep. Mowrer and Mowrer (1938) reported complete success with this method in treating thirty enuretic patients.

In spite of research of this sort, the dominant concern of most behaviorists during this period was to establish through carefully controlled laboratory experiments basic principles of learning, rather than to apply what was known to the treatment of behavioral disorders. Until the 1960s there was no systematic attempt to use a behavioral model in the practice of psychotherapy. In part, this was due to a feeling that more basic research was needed before progress could be made in the clinical area. In part, as Kalish (1965) noted, the application of behavioral techniques was delayed because of attempts to translate the traditional psychotherapeutic model into the language of learning theory.

Learning-Theory Approaches to Psychotherapy

Essentially, what Dollard and Miller (1950) and others (e.g., Shaw, 1946; Shoben, 1949) attempted to do was to describe in the terms of learning theory those events that occurred during psychotherapy. The traditional psychoanalytic model was accepted in its entirety, but the explanatory machinery was lifted from learning theory and fit to the model. Such a learning-theory approach contrasts sharply with that of contemporary behavior therapists who regard the translation enterprise as futile.

THERAPY AS DISCRIMINATION AND GENERALIZATION.   In Chapter One and elsewhere in this book we have spoken of the drive-cue-response-reinforcement paradigm of the learning process employed by Dollard and Miller (1950). In this paradigm the concepts of drive, cue, and reinforcement are subclasses of the general concept of stimulus. Every event (stimulus) has a certain intensity (drive value) and certain distinctiveness (cue value). The attribute of intensity (drive) initiates activity, but the attribute of distinctiveness (cue) determines what the person will do. A reinforcement is an event that follows the occurrence of a response and has the effect of reducing the drive.

Dollard and Miller employed this basic paradigm to account for the development of neurosis. To do so, however, they had to include in their theory two additional concepts: conflict and repression. *Conflict* typically stems from the incompatibility of response sequences of biological origin, such as hunger or sex, with those of emotional origin, such as fear, anger, or guilt. To avoid the conflict produced by opposing drives the individual resorts to the *repression* of verbal and other cue-producing responses. By not thinking of situations that produce conflict, the individual reduces his drive state. When repression becomes habitual, however, it impairs the individual's capacity to adjust to his environment. Fear and guilt then become increasingly unrealistic and repression is resorted to even more frequently.

Eventually the combination of conflict and repression leads to the development of neurotic *symptoms*. This process is outlined schematically in Figure 6-1. All neurotic symptoms derive from an underlying conflict that is inaccessible to verbal awareness because of the habitual and automatic inhibition of thought (repression). Symptoms are learned because of their effectiveness in reducing fear (guilt is thought to be a type of fear), and the removal of symptoms only intensifies the fear and motivates the individual to learn new—and perhaps more serious—maladaptive responses.

As an example of this process we might consider the case of an adult who is neurotically dependent upon his mother. This behavior is maladaptive because the individual is prevented from following the career he wishes to pursue, cannot make his own decisions, is unwilling to marry, and so forth. The origins of such a disorder would be seen by Dollard and Miller to lie in unresolved conflict—perhaps between hostility toward the mother and guilt. This conflict is in turn repressed and denied. Fear and anxiety build up and symptoms develop—for example, psychosomatic illnesses that increase the individual's dependence and enable him to postpone major life decisions such as career and marriage. These symptoms would be viewed by Dollard and Miller as ways of coping with fear.

The goal of therapy, for Dollard and Miller (1950), is to resolve the underlying conflict, to unlearn the automatic responses of repression and inhibition, and to substitute in their place more discriminative responses under conscious control. Because one of the consequences of the patient's disorder is that he has repressed certain thoughts and is therefore not aware that they are creating fear and causing conflict, he must be helped to verbalize what has been repressed. This is accomplished through the technique of *free association*. In therapy a social situation should exist such that the patient is urged to say whatever comes to his mind, especially what he feels himself ashamed, afraid, or reluctant to say. The therapist does not punish him or show any sign of disapproval; he remains warm and accepting. Under these permissive social conditions the fear, shame, and guilt attached to talking about tabooed topics can be extinguished. The patient in our example would be encouraged to discuss his attitude toward his mother, until he is able to verbalize his negative feelings toward her. When he finds that talking in this manner is not punished by the therapist, the guilt and anxiety associated with expressions of hostility toward the mother can extinguish. Once the

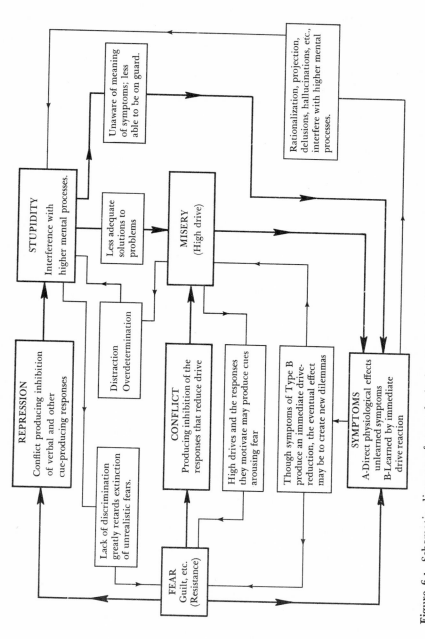

Figure 6-1. Schematic diagram of some basic factors involved in neurosis according to Dollard and Miller (1950). Arrows indicate "produces" or "tends to contribute to." Heavy arrows indicate major causal sequences; lighter arrows, subsidiary ones.

The following text appears within the diagram:

REPRESSION
Conflict producing inhibition of verbal and other cue-producing responses

STUPIDITY
Interference with higher mental processes.

Less adequate solutions to problems

Distraction
Overdetermination

Unaware of meaning of symptoms; less able to be on guard.

Rationalization, projection, delusions, hallucinations, etc., interfere with higher mental processes.

MISERY
(High drive)

Lack of discrimination greatly retards extinction of unrealistic fears.

CONFLICT
Producing inhibition of the responses that reduce drive

High drives and the responses they motivate may produce cues arousing fear

Though symptoms of Type B produce an immediate drive-reduction, the eventual effect may be to create new dilemmas

SYMPTOMS
A-Direct physiological effects unlearned symptoms
B-Learned by immediate drive reaction

FEAR
Guilt, etc.
(Resistance)

negative emotions connected with words is extinguished, Dollard and Miller felt that the negative emotions associated with thoughts would also extinguish through generalization.

The permissive environment of the therapeutic situation has as its intended effect to teach the patient to *discriminate* between therapy and other social situations. The conditions that follow the utterance of fearful thoughts in the therapeutic situation are entirely different from those in the original learning situation. Instead of meeting with anger, criticism, rejection, and punishment, the patient receives calm acceptance and sympathetic understanding. Since the ordinary conditions of social life favor the learning of repression and the generalization of fears learned in the past, the therapeutic situation is established to provide the patient with new conditions that permit new learning. Once the patient has learned to discriminate between therapy and other social situations, learned fears will not transfer from previous interpersonal situations to the therapeutic one. This is the necessary first step on the road to cure.

During this period the therapist's objective is to assist the patient to verbalize appropriately those aspects of situations and behaviors that the patient has been in the habit of avoiding. He does this by providing the patient with the appropriate *labels* (cue-producing responses). These labels make events verbally explicit and thereby permit the patient to become aware of them and acquire control over his responses to them. The assumption here is that if a patient is aware of the cues producing his behavior, of the responses he is making, and of the reasons he responds as he does, his behavior will be better controlled and more in accord with objective reality. Labelling provides the means for verbally-mediated awareness. Once the patient has the necessary labels (for example, to describe feelings of hostility), voluntarily guided discriminative behavior will replace automatic, overgeneralized reactions.

Dollard and Miller distinguished between two phases of therapy. The first of these is the phase of "talking." It consists of everything we have discussed to this point: free association during which anxiety reactions are unlearned in the permissive atmosphere of the therapeutic situation, and therapeutic interpretation during which new labels are attached to previously repressed words and thoughts. The second phase of therapy is the "outside" or "real world" aspect. In this second phase the patient must directly confront the distortions of his current life produced by neurotic behavior. The patient must *generalize* the positive effects of the therapeutic situation over into the real world. The discrimination that the patient has learned between the therapeutic situation and the outside world must now be broken down. Habits of feeling and thinking learned in the safe and permissive atmosphere of the therapeutic situation must be transferred to real life. The therapist's concern at this point is to facilitate such transfer by directing the patient's attention to potential rewards that await him in his life situations if he tries out new responses. In the case of the individual suffering from neurotic dependence, for example, the therapist may point out how important it is for him to overcome his dependence so that he can follow the career he wishes to pursue—which the patient may have hesitated to do because it would involve travelling or living in a city distant from his mother. The therapist would emphasize the positive consequences of such behavior and the benefits the patient would derive.

According to Dollard and Miller this stage of therapy involves approximation and correction. The therapist asks the patient to make certain responses in his normal social environment. In our example, the patient may be encouraged to express his feelings more openly at home, even to the point of admitting and expressing hostility when he feels it. It is likely, however, that these initial attempts outside the therapeutic situation will be only partially effective. The patient must discuss their effectiveness periodically with the therapist and then plan modified behaviors that hopefully prove more effective. In time the patient should be able to make responses of increasing difficulty. Eventually, as the patient's anxiety-avoiding behaviors are reduced and his capacity to think, discriminate, and generalize effectively is increased, there is less need for the therapist. When the patient is reasonably sure that he can handle his life without assistance, therapy can be terminated.

BEHAVIOR THERAPY.   Behavior therapy represents an approach to therapy radically different from that taken by Dollard and Miller (1950). It is true that both approaches emanate from the learning-theory tradition; however, where Dollard and Miller started with the traditional psychoanalytic model of therapy, behavior therapy rejects that model. Dollard and Miller conceptualized psychotherapy in learning-theory terms, but the effect was to leave the practice of therapy essentially unchanged. Behavior therapy analyzes the therapeutic process in learning-theory terms and uses techniques derived from learning theory in therapeutic practice. The effect has been a revolutionary change in the practice of therapy. In essence, behavior therapy represents a return to the thinking of the early behaviorists and to their somewhat abortive attempt to relate behavior principles to treatment.

Various methods of behavior therapy have been developed, but despite differences in emphasis and technique there are certain themes that bind behavior therapists together and distinguish them from other major schools of psychotherapy. For one thing, a behavior therapist views behavior disorders as the product of persistent maladaptive habits that have been learned and are maintained because they are reinforcing (especially in their reduction of anxiety). The task of the therapist is to develop more adaptive reactions by patients to situations in which they have previously responded inappropriately. This is accomplished by *direct manipulation of behavior* rather than by indirect methods, which the behavior therapists regard as based on the invalid assumption of an underlying cause that must be treated prior to effecting any change in overt behavior. For behavior therapists the symptom is the disease. Removing the symptom removes the disease; in fact, the behavior therapist is not concerned with "disease" at all, but rather with overt behavior.

Behavior therapists prefer to *do* something about behavior rather than talk about it—or even "label" it. The behavior therapist's clinic is a laboratory for relearning. The methods employed are based on principles derived from the various sources of learning studied in the experimental laboratory. Emphasis is on the behavioral response in question and, consequently, the behavior therapist attempts to provide precise definitions of the behaviors to be examined. Analysis is systematic and detailed. Measurement operations are specified in an effort to yield consistent and reproducible results. Attention is given to environmental variables and to the use of controls. All behavior therapists give at least lip service to such methodological concerns.

In the section that follows emphasis will be placed on the differences between behavior therapists. These differences are based chiefly on disagreement as to the technique to be employed in given situations. The selection of therapeutic procedures will depend largely on the particular notion of learning (e.g., Skinnerian or Hullian) with which the therapist operates.

TECHNIQUES OF BEHAVIOR MODIFICATION

Since a considerable variety of techniques have been employed by behavior therapists, we shall classify the various procedures according to the paradigm of learning that they follow. We argued in Chapter Two that at least four basic paradigms can be distinguished: classical conditioning, instrumental learning, operant conditioning, and imitation and vicarious learning. We shall use the same classification here.

Classical Conditioning Procedures

In the classical conditioning paradigm the conditioned stimulus acquires the capacity to elicit a conditioned response resembling the unconditioned response. The conditioned response may be adaptive or maladaptive. If the response is maladaptive, one technique to eliminate it is counterconditioning. That is, if strong responses that are incompatible with the conditioned maladaptive response can be made to occur in the presence of the cues associated with the maladaptive response (conditioned stimuli), then the incompatible responses will be attached to these cues and thereby weaken or eliminate the maladaptive response. This essentially was the technique employed by Jones (1924) to cure a child's phobic responses to furry objects: The pleasure responses associated with eating were incompatible with the maladaptive anxiety reactions associated with the presence of a rabbit. Contemporary behavior therapists employ similar methods in reciprocal inhibition therapy and desensitization therapy.

RECIPROCAL INHIBITION. Wolpe's (1958) method of treating neurotic behavior is based on an elaborate theoretical structure consisting of Hullian learning theory, Sherrington's description of reciprocal inhibition on the neurological level, Jacobson's methods of relaxation training, and the work of Watson and Jones on the conditioning and elimination of fear. Neurosis, for Wolpe, consists in persistent habits that are learned in anxiety-generating situations. The core of neurosis is anxiety—that is, a specific response of the autonomic nervous system. It is always part of the original neurotic learning situation and usually a part of the eventual symptom pattern.

The task of therapy, according to this view, is to alter the learned connection between previously neutral stimuli and anxiety responses or the maladaptive responses that follow upon anxiety responses. This is to be accomplished by presenting anxiety-eliciting events, or a symbolic representation of them, in temporal contiguity with responses that are innately *antagonistic* to anxiety reactions. Wolpe (1962) assumed that a response inhibitory or antagonistic to anxiety and occurring in the presence of anxiety-evoking stimuli will weaken the connection between the stimuli and the anxiety responses. The justification for this assumption came from Sherrington's (1906) description of the reciprocal inhibition that takes place in one set of muscles (flexors) when another set (extensors) is activated. To determine which responses are antagonistic to anxiety Wolpe has experimented with any that seemed to hold some prospect of utility. Among those that have been found effective are: (1) assertive responses such as anger or resentment, (2) respiratory responses using carbon dioxide, (3) competitively conditioned motor responses, and (4) "anxiety-relief" responses.

Wolpe placed no limitations on the type of patients who might be helped by his therapy beyond specifying that the disorder must be learned ("neurotic"). Some patients may not be able to learn the antagonistic responses, but they are rare exceptions. Other patients may not honestly report the anxiety-eliciting behavior (which is the first step of therapy), but they are also regarded as exceptions.

The therapist first obtains a detailed history of the patient's difficulties and symptoms. Special attention is given to identifying the original learning conditions and to determining the patient's habitual responses to major situational contexts: family, occupation, school, sexual relationships, religious training, and so forth. The therapist has the duty of accepting the patient's statements without criticism or questioning. He is to maintain a non-moralizing, objective attitude and to convey to the patient that he is sympathetic to him and to his needs. Once he has obtained all the information necessary, the therapist explains to the patient that his difficulties may be traced back to inappropriate fear responses. He uses concrete examples to illustrate how such responses are learned—including examples from the patient's own behavior. Finally, the therapist explains the rationale for treatment, especially the notion that inappropriate emotional responses can be eliminated by techniques that increase the probability of responses antagonistic to anxiety.

The technique of *inhibition through assertive responses* is used by Wolpe to extinguish anxiety produced by interpersonal situations. It is limited to those situations where the therapist is reasonably sure that the patient's anxiety is inappropriate and that no unpleasant repercussions will follow from the patient's assertiveness. The therapist prescribes specific assertive responses that the patient is to make in concrete, real-life situations. For example, an overly meek person may be encouraged to express his opinion at social gatherings. The supposition is that constant encouragement from the therapist will gradually change the patient's attitude toward evoking the desired response.

Wolpe (1958) reported that *inhibition through respiratory responses* with carbon dioxide therapy has been dramatically effective in the treatment of "free-floating" anxiety. The patient lies down, completely exhausts the air from his lungs, and then takes a deep inhalation of a mixture of approximately 70 percent carbon dioxide and 30 percent oxygen. The course of treatment is from one to four inhalations spread over a period of time. The results are quite immediate—presumably because the intense stimulation of the respiratory system and the complete muscle relaxation produced by carbon dioxide are antagonistic to anxiety.

Wolpe attempted to use the method of *competitive motor responses* with a girl whose hands trembled when eating in company. This technique requires that the patient be given a mild electric shock in the presence of a situation or image that elicits neurotic anxiety. The therapist attempts to condition the patient to produce a well-defined motor response to the situation or image. If this process is repeated several times, the occurrence of the anxiety response will supposedly decrease. This was in fact what happened with the girl, although Wolpe admitted that he has had only limited success with this method.

Occasionally Wolpe has used the technique of *"anxiety-relief" responses* to alleviate symptoms. In this case a stimulus is made to acquire secondary reinforcement properties by being paired with shock reduction. For example, the patient may be required to say "calm" to switch off a shock—the word thereby serving as an "anxiety-relief" response. If this procedure is repeated ten to twenty times a session, the word may acquire secondary reinforcement properties and generalize to real-life situations. Wolpe reported that this procedure was very effective with about 15 percent of his patients, while a few reported no effect at all. He hypothesized that it is most effective with patients in whom the shock elicits strong emotional responses as distinct from sensory discomfort.

SYSTEMATIC DESENSITIZATION.   Wolpe's most widely used technique is that of systematic desensitization. It is a special case of his general therapeutic method of reciprocal inhibition in which inhibition of anxiety is achieved through the establishment of a *relaxation response* antagonistic to anxiety. As a form of treatment it requires the gradual introduction of stimuli that are anxiety-arousing to the patient, while the patient is relaxing.

Relaxation is typically induced through the methods of progressive relaxation described by Jacobson (1938). The patient may, for example, be instructed to focus on particular muscle reactions—perhaps those in the neck. He is told to tense these muscles and then relax them, to see how it feels. Presumably, after several trials, he will have learned to control these muscles so they can be relaxed at will. After this he is taught how to relax other muscle groups. The training continues until the patient can relax most of his body.

After this training period the patient is asked to relax his whole body as completely as possible. He is then asked to imagine life situations based upon a *hierarchy of stimuli* that are anxiety-arousing for him. This hierarchy is constructed on the basis of interviews with the patient and may be one of several developed, each dealing with different themes (hostility, sexuality, rejection, and so on). The patient begins by imagining the scene for a given theme that is least anxiety-arousing, and progresses to those that create greater anxiety. Once the anxiety to a particular theme is reduced, the patient moves on to other themes. Wolpe assumed that reducing the anxiety to imagined stimuli reduces anxiety felt when confronted by the same stimuli in real life.

For example, a patient who suffers from acrophobia (fear of heights) would be asked in the interview sessions with the therapist to describe those situations that create greatest amounts of anxiety in daily life (e.g., looking from a tenth-floor window, being in air-planes or elevators) and those that involve less anxiety (e.g., looking from second-floor windows, climbing stairs, sitting in balcony of a theater). He would be required to list these different situations in the order in which they arouse anxiety in him. The therapist then instructs the patient how to achieve deep relaxation, until the patient can relax at will. Next the hierarchy of anxiety-arousing stimuli are introduced and the patient imagines each scene, beginning with the least anxiety-arousing and progressing to those that arouse the greatest anxiety. If a scene creates anxiety, the patient deliberately relaxes until he can imagine it without feeling anxious. This procedure is followed until the patient can imagine all the scenes without feeling anxious.

Using this technique Wolpe (1958) reported that 90 percent of 210 patients were very much improved after a mean of about 30 sessions. Approximately 60 percent of his cases required five or fewer interviews. Improvement rates were based upon therapists' judgments and the criterion used was symptom-free behavior, where the symptoms included inferiority feelings, depression, hysterical paresthesias, paranoid obsessions, impotence, and various phobias.

A number of other investigators have reported successful treatment using Wolpe's systematic desensitization procedure. Lang and Lazovik (1963), for example, treated 24 snake-phobic subjects using desensitization techniques. Subjects were trained in deep muscle re-laxation and, at the beginning of the first session, were hypnotized and instructed to relax. They were then instructed to imagine an item that induced a small amount of anxiety. If relaxation was un-disturbed by this item, the subsequent item on the hierarchy was presented. Successive items were presented from session to session until the subject could visualize the most frightening stimuli without an impairment of his calm state. When subjects who went through such desensitization training were compared with control subjects who did not, the subjects who experienced desensitization showed greater reduction of phobic behavior and tended to hold their therapy gain six months later. There was no evidence of symptom substitution.

Lazarus (1961) compared desensitization therapy with interpreta-tive therapy in a group setting. The groups included subjects suffering from various phobic disorders, all of which were severe enough to interfere with social relationships. Patients were assigned to the groups at random and matched for sex, age, severity of disorder, and so forth. Desensitization procedures consisted of instructions in deep relaxation prior to the introduction of the anxiety hierarchy lists. The interpretative groups were treated by a form of insight therapy with reeducative goals (Wolberg, 1954). Of 17 patients treated by interpretative methods only two recovered, and these two had received relaxation training after interpretation. Of the 18 patients treated by desensitization techniques 13 recovered and 10 of these 13 maintained their freedom from phobic symptoms 15 months later (one of the two patients in the interpretative relaxation group relapsed).

These examples give some indication of the claims of success put forth by proponents of desensitization techniques. In recent years there have been numerous converts and successful treatment through desensitization has been reported in a large number of studies with various types of disorders (e.g., Davison, 1968; Lang, Lazovik, & Reynolds, 1965; Moore, 1965; Paul & Shannon, 1965). Not all investigators, however, agree with the theoretical rationale proposed by Wolpe. Many reject the notion of reciprocally inhibitory processes occurring at the level of the autonomic system and prefer an explanation based simply on the counterconditioning of behavioral responses.

Instrumental Learning and Operant Conditioning

So far we have been discussing techniques of behavior therapy based on the classical conditioning paradigm. We shall now turn to those techniques that are based on instrumental learning and operant conditioning paradigms. In Chapter Two a distinction was made between instrumental learning and operant conditioning on the basis of the number of options possible in the two situations. Thus in instrumental learning the possible responses are limited to those appropriate to the problem situation. In operant conditioning, on the other hand, the number of possible responses is unlimited and includes all responses in the organism's repertoire. This distinction is somewhat artificial and may cause problems in some instances (e.g., in the case of organisms with extremely limited repertoires). In fact, many researchers use the two terms interchangeably, and we shall not insist on the distinction here. Instead, we shall distinguish between those situations in which the use of positive reinforcements predominates and those in which punishment is the principal means of inducing behavior change.

POSITIVE REINFORCEMENT TECHNIQUES.   The majority of situations in which instrumental learning or operant procedures are employed involve the manipulation of positive reinforcements. In an early study with chronic schizophrenics, for example, King, Armitage, and Tilton (1960) administered food reinforcement and cigarettes to patients for learning to operate a series of levers on a multiple-operant problem-solving apparatus. The problems were solved individually and in cooperation with another patient. The patients were reinforced for every response that involved a verbalization. Ultimately, through successive approximation procedures, the patients were required to verbalize the solution to the problems and to work together cooperatively with one another in mutual solution of the problems. King and his associates reported considerable improvement for eight of 12 patients given such treatment. The criteria for improvement included level of verbalization, motivation to leave the ward, and decreased enuresis. Six months later the patients retained the gains acquired during treatment.

In other research with psychotics (Lindsley, 1956, 1959; Skinner, 1956) and with autistic children (Ferster, 1961; Wolf, Risley, & Mees, 1964) operant procedures have proven effective in producing simple impersonal reactions. In these studies schedules of reinforcement were varied, and patients were required to respond in specific ways to receive reinforcement. For example, Ferster and DeMeyer (1961) trained autistic children to learn to manipulate simple devices for which food, candy, and music were given as reinforcement. Subsequently more complex devices were introduced and coins established as generalized reinforcers. The children learned to use the coins and to make complex responses. In spite of the gain shown in the laboratory, however, there was little transfer to activities outside the laboratory.

Risley and Wolf (1966) were able to demonstrate generalization outside the laboratory in the case of a withdrawn, six-year-old autistic child who initially exhibited bizarre mannerisms and echolalia. Using operant conditioning procedures, Risley and Wolf reinforced the child's independent verbal behavior and picture-naming behavior in the laboratory and then transferred the child to his parents, who employed identical procedures in the home. Under these conditions the child showed rapid learning both in the original tasks and in the new tasks required of him by his parents.

One of the most ambitious studies involving positive reinforcement techniques was that of Ayllon and Azrin (1965) in which they established a *token economy* in a hospital ward containing long-term female patients. The hospital staff was instructed that specific behaviors (e.g., serving meals, sorting laundry, washing dishes, and the like) were to be reinforced. Reinforcement took the form of tokens exchangeable for activities that had a high level of occurrence when freely allowed (e.g., eating, watching television, being allowed to talk to the ward physician or psychologist, and so on).

Ayllon and Azrin reported a series of experiments in which they were able systematically to vary patients' behavior by token reinforcement. For example, when reinforcements were discontinued for certain off-ward job assignments, patients inevitably switched their jobs and selected other jobs that were reinforcing. In general, performance on the tasks involved in each experiment fell to near-zero when a response-reinforcement relationship was disturbed. When reinforcement was reintroduced, performance almost immediately achieved its prior level.

In a similar study Atthowe and Krasner (1968) established a token economy in a ward containing male "chronic" schizophrenic patients. The patients had been hospitalized a median of 22 years and were extremely apathetic and socially withdrawn. Tokens were administered for appropriate social behavior, such as grooming, keeping living facilities clean, dressing neatly, interacting with other people. Dramatic changes were observed in these behaviors, as well as in other reinforced behaviors, such as attendance at group activities (Figure 6-2). In addition, staff morale improved and marked changes occurred in staff expectations of what the patients were capable of achieving.

Systematic manipulation of positive reinforcement has also proven effective in the treatment of juvenile delinquents. Slack (1960) and Schwitzgebel (1961, 1964) used successive approximation techniques

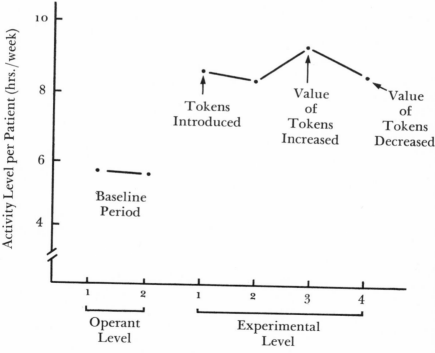

Figure 6-2. Group activity level before (operant level) and after (experimental level) tokens were introduced as reinforcements (from Atthowe and Krasner, 1968). When more tokens were given for group attendance, an increase in attendance occurred.

with delinquent boys to induce them to attend therapy sessions. Initially these sessions were represented as part of an experimental project, and no attempt was made to schedule appointments. The boys were reinforced with food whenever they came. Eventually attempts were made to promote prompt arrival at scheduled times (by giving unexpected monetary bonuses). In the final stage the attempt was made to rely solely on the reinforcement inherent in the relationship between the experimenter-therapist and the subject.

Schwitzgebel and Kolb (1964) reinforced prosocial behavior in delinquent boys through the administration of positive reinforcement, such as small change and cigarettes, on a variable-interval schedule. The boys received reinforcement for keeping appointments, appropriately discussing and analyzing their feelings, and performing job-training tasks. Three years after treatment these subjects showed a significant reduction in frequency and severity of criminal offenses as compared to a control group with which they had been matched on relevant variables.

An even more rigorous application of behavior principles in the treatment of delinquents is illustrated by the work of Cohen and his associates (Cohen *et al.*, 1966) at the National Training School for Boys. In this study the environment was specially designed to allow systematic contingent application of reinforcement. The goal of the study was to shape academic work in the form of programmed instruction. The boys had to achieve a score of at least 90 percent on a unit of program to be eligible to take an examination on which they could earn reinforcements in the form of points worth one cent. These points could be used to gain entrance to a lounge where friends were, to buy food, to make telephone calls, and so forth. In time more relevant reinforcements were employed, such as renting books, getting time in the library, and registering for new programs.

The results of the study were dramatic. The 16 students in the project were highly successful in their educational activities. There were no discipline problems over a four-and-a-half-month period. The boys did no damage to the special facilities and, in fact, the social behavior of the delinquents matched that of a nondelinquent control group.

The experiments discussed above are only a small sampling of the uses made of reinforcement procedures. More detailed coverage can be found in Ullmann and Krasner (1969) and Bandura (1969a). The studies we have cited suggest, however, that many forms of behavior disorder that have proven resistant to traditional treatment procedures—such as childhood autism, psychosis, and delinquency—can be treated by behavioral methods.

DIFFERENTIAL REINFORCEMENT AND PUNISHMENT.   Often both positive reinforcements and punishments are used to modify maladaptive behavior. Tate and Baroff (1966), for example, punished self-destructive responses while at the same time using verbal reward to strengthen prosocial behavior in a psychotic boy. Boardman (1962) also used both rewards and punishments to control the generalized negativism of a five-year-old child. Marshall (1966) used food reinforcement and mild punishment to toilet train an eight-year-old autistic child. In these studies reinforcement was used differentially, to induce appropriate behavior (through positive reinforcement) and to reduce inappropriate behavior (through negative reinforcement).

The power of differential reinforcement was demonstrated in a study by Brawley and his associates (1969) in which they selectively reinforced the behavior of an autistic child in order to show that bizarre and inappropriate behavior was largely a function of the attention given to that behavior by the clinical staff. Reinforcement in the form of food and verbal approval was given for appropriate behaviors such as compliance with requests, comprehensible verbalizations, the use of play material, and the learning of academic material. Punishment through withdrawal of attention and approval followed self-hitting, "junk" verbalizations, and tantrums. Under these conditions the appropriate behaviors increased considerably and the inappropriate behavior disappeared. When the reinforcement contingencies were reversed, some appropriate responses dropped 50 percent and inappropriate responses increased. By reinstating the original contingencies, the experimenters were able to bring the behaviors to their previous treatment levels.

In some cases behavior is especially resistant to change, and therapists have had to rely almost entirely on punishment procedures. Liversedge and Sylvester (1955), for instance, used electric shock to treat patients suffering from writer's cramp. The patients were required to trace various line patterns (similar to those involved in writing) on a metal plate with a stylus; any deviation from the path produced a shock. After this training subjects wrote with an electrified pen and received a shock whenever their thumb pressure was excessive. All of the seven patients who received this training were able to resume work, and a follow-up study several months later showed that improvement was maintained. Sylvester and Liversedge (1960) reported complete recovery for 24 of 39 patients when the follow-up period extended to four years.

Beech (1960) employed similar methods for treating patients suffering from writer's cramp but did not obtain as good a recovery rate. His sample apparently suffered from more anxiety than did that of Sylvester and Liversedge. Beech concluded that punishment achieved results in cases with low initial anxiety. When the patient's anxiety level is greater, as it was in Beech's sample, desensitization procedures proved more effective.

Lovaas and his associates (Lovaas, Berberich, Perloff, & Schaeffer, 1966; Lovaas, Schaeffer, & Simmons, 1965) have treated self-destructive behaviors in autistic children through the administration of punishment via electric shock, critical comments, and slapping. Once the child's attention had been focused by these means on relevant social stimuli, appropriate social behaviors could be effectively rewarded.

One example of this research is a study by Lovaas, Schaeffer, and Simmons (1965) in which punishment was used to decrease self-stimulatory and self-destructive behavior in schizophrenic children. The subjects were identical twins who evidenced no social responsiveness, were not toilet trained, spent up to three-fourths of their time in rocking and other self-stimulatory behavior, and often engaged in temper tantrums. The children were seen individually in a room in which the floors were wired so that shock could be administered to their feet. Every time the child engaged in self-stimulation or temper tantrums he received a shock. At the same time the experimenter said "No," thereby pairing the word "No" with shock. The experimenter also said "Come here" to the child, and if this request was not complied with the child received a shock. Shocks were administered in three sessions, discontinued, and then readministered.

Figure 6-3 shows the results of treatment. Both children displayed almost no self-stimulatory or self-destructive behavior for nine months after treatment. Physical contact increased markedly and stayed high for the same period of time. A single noncontingent shock almost a year later reinstated the prior training. Lovaas and his associates also found that the word "No" could become a successful negative reinforcer for these children.

There is some evidence, therefore, that punishment can be effective in altering maladaptive behavior. The use of punishment seems especially helpful in cases where behavior is highly resistant to extinction and where anxiety does not appear to be the major motivational force in maintaining the maladaptive behavior. In those cases where anxiety has a central role, desensitization procedures appear to be more useful.

Imitation and Vicarious Learning

Jones (1924), in her early study of the treatment of phobic children, demonstrated that fear could be reduced by having other children behave in a nonanxious manner in the presence of the phobic object. A similar finding was reported by Masserman (1943), who demonstrated that the presence of nonneurotic cats acting as models facilitated the learning of adaptive responses on the part of neurotic cats. These early leads, however, were not followed up, even by behavior therapists, until relatively recently.

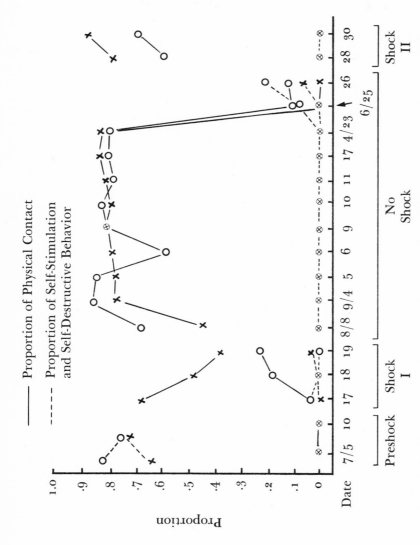

Figure 6-3. Proportion of time spent in self-stimulation, self-destructive behavior, and physical contact by two autistic children (X and O) receiving shock treatment over one-year period (from Lovaas, Schaeffer, and Simmons, 1965).

VICARIOUS MODELING.   Bandura and his associates have begun a systematic experimental program to determine the role of the model in the extinction of inappropriate behavior and the induction of appropriate behavior. In this research subjects with strong phobic reactions have been exposed to models who displayed approach responses to feared objects. Before and after exposure to the model subjects are tested for behavioral change. Subsequent tests are conducted to determine if the change generalizes to similar stimuli and if it endures after formal therapeutic conditions have been discontinued.

In one such study Bandura, Grusec, and Menlove (1967) exposed children who exhibited strong fear of dogs to a peer interacting fearlessly with a dog. This was done in a number of sessions, and the fear-provoking character of the model's behavior was gradually increased from session to session by relaxing the physical restraints on the dog, by varying the directness and intimacy of the model's responses, and by extending the duration of the interaction between the model and the dog. The children's approach behavior was measured toward two different dogs (the experimental animal and an unfamiliar dog) after the treatment program and one month later. Approach behavior was assessed by requiring a graded sequence of interactions with the dog. Children were asked, for example, to approach and pet the dog, release it from its pen, take its leash off, and finally to spend some time alone with the dog in its pen. The greater the number of these responses the child was able to make, the higher the approach score.

Bandura and his associates found that children who had been exposed to the peer-model were capable of significantly more approach responses than a control group of phobic children that had had no such experience. In addition, two-thirds of the children receiving the modeling treatment were eventually able to remain alone with the dog in its pen, while none of the control subjects were capable of the terminal response. For the children in the modeling group the effects generalized to the other dog and endured one month after the program had been completed.

In a similar study Bandura and Menlove (1968) investigated variables that were expected to facilitate vicarious extinction of conditioned emotionality by symbolic modeling procedures. They had three groups of children who were markedly fearful of dogs watch a series of films under different conditions: The first group (single-modeling) saw a model display progressively more intimate interactions with a single dog, the second group (multiple-modeling) saw a variety of models interacting nonanxiously with numerous dogs varying in size and fearsomeness, and the third group (control) saw movies containing no dogs. Both the single-modeling and the multiple-modeling techniques reduced the children's avoidance behavior (as measured by graded approach responses), but only in the multiple-modeling treatment were the children's fears weakened sufficiently to enable them to perform the most threatening approach behavior (being left alone in the pen with the dog). In both modeling conditions generalization was obtained, and the behavior was essentially unchanged in a follow-up test one month later.

Bandura and Menlove (1968) noted that a comparison of the results of their study with those of the Bandura, Grusec, and Menlove (1967) study suggests that symbolic modeling (via film demonstration) is a less powerful means of eliminating avoidance responses than live demonstrations. In the Bandura and Menlove study the single-modeling, symbolic technique was effective in reducing avoidance behavior, but it did not weaken the children's fears to the extent of allowing them to perform the terminal approach behavior. The diminished efficacy of the symbolic method was offset, however, by the use of more models and more aversive stimulus objects in the multiple-modeling condition. Presumably the most powerful technique would be the use of the multiple-modeling procedure in a live demonstration.

In addition to eliminating phobic disorders, modeling techniques have been employed to *enhance* social behavior. Thus O'Connor (1969) found that modeling procedures increased the amount of social interaction engaged in by social-isolate preschool children. In this study children who displayed marked social withdrawal watched a film depicting increasingly more active social interactions between children with positive consequences resulting from the interactions. When compared to a control group with similar withdrawal tendencies, the children who had seen the film displayed significant changes in their level of social interaction.

Bandura and his associates conceptualized the effects of modeling on extinction in terms of a *dual-process theory of avoidance behavior*. According to this view stimuli acquire, through their temporal contiguity with aversive experiences, the capacity to produce arousal reactions that have both central and autonomic components. Subsequently instrumental avoidance responses are conditioned to these arousal-correlated stimuli. If conditioned arousal reactions are extinguished, both the motivation and the internal controlling stimuli for avoidance responses are removed. It was Bandura's contention that conditioned emotional reactivity can be extinguished on a vicarious basis by having observers witness a model encounter aversive stimuli without experiencing any adverse consequences. Moreover, this extinction process was thought to occur primarily through the workings of central mechanisms rather than through the autonomic system as is generally supposed (Bandura & Rosenthal, 1966).

MODELING AND PARTICIPATION.   In much of social learning the observer does not merely watch a model perform, he also participates in some way or other. Frequently models and observers interact. Parents serve as models for their children, but they also *help* the child make appropriate responses and reward the child's attempts. Bandura and his coworkers have recently begun to investigate the efficacy of the combination of modeling and participation procedures in producing behavioral change.

Bandura, Blanchard, and Ritter (1969) compared modeling and participation procedures with modeling alone and with desensitization techniques. In their study adult and adolescent subjects with snake phobias were divided into four groups. One group of subjects (symbolic modeling) observed a graduated film depicting young children, adolescents, and adults engaging in fear-provoking interactions with a large king snake. Subjects were trained in relaxation techniques and could stop the film whenever it aroused their anxiety. When this happened they were to make relaxation responses and re-run the film until they could watch the particular scene without anxiety. They then went on to the next scene in the sequence. They continued this procedure until they could watch the whole film without anxiety.

A second group of subjects received modeling-participation treatment. They watched a therapist handle a snake and were aided, through demonstration, in performing progressively more approach responses toward the snake. The therapist himself would perform each response and then help the subject touch, stroke, and hold the snake's body with a gloved hand and then bare hands, until the subject could hold the snake in his lap without assistance. Each step of this process was realized gradually according to the apprehensiveness and anxiety of the subject.

Subjects in the third group received the standard form of desensitization therapy (Wolpe, 1958). They were trained in deep relaxation and were instructed to imagine snake scenes involving increasing amounts of aversiveness. They continued imagining each scene until it created no anxiety for them. Treatment was continued until the subjects' anxiety reactions were completely extinguished. As a control, Bandura and his associates included a fourth group that received no treatment of any sort.

When the various groups were compared, live modeling and participation was found to be far superior to the other methods in inducing change in behavior. Comparison of the number of approach responses made by subjects prior to treatment with the number of approach responses made after treatment revealed the modeling-participation technique to be dramatically effective. Symbolic modeling and desensitization were also effective when compared to the no-treatment (control) condition (Figure 6-4).

To further demonstrate the effectiveness of the modeling-participation procedure Bandura and his associates treated all subjects who
failed to achieve terminal performance (defined by the subject's
holding the snake in his lap), including controls, with this method. In
every case snake phobia extinguished in a few sessions. A one-month
follow-up assessment showed that this effect was maintained and generalized to real-life situations.

Lovaas (1967) also reported success using a modeling-participation
procedure. He found that with schizophrenic children mere verbal
modeling cues, even when highly discriminable, were not sufficient to
induce behavioral change. When both modeling and participation
methods were employed, however, the children learned the appropriate responses. In this research each correct response was rewarded
and incorrect responses were followed by verbal and physical aids that
were gradually faded on succeeding trials. Thus if the child was told
to take a toy from a box and responded appropriately, he was rewarded; if not, he was given the same instructions and aided by the

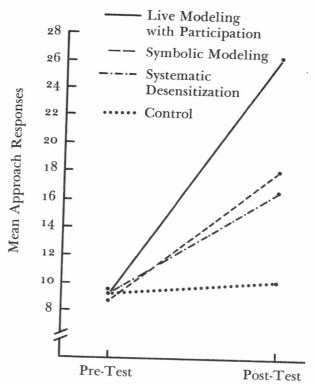

Figure 6-4. Mean number of approach responses performed by subjects before and
after receiving various treatments (from Bandura, Blanchard, and Ritter, 1969).

experimenter in making the correct motor responses. Eventually children were able to describe the motor behavior verbally and to generalize particular verbal responses to a variety of situations.

Similar research has been conducted with retardates and speech-deficient children (e.g., Cook & Adams, 1966; Straughan, Potter, & Hamilton, 1965). These studies employed a combination of modeling procedures and positive reinforcement for imitation of correct responses. The success of such methods may depend on the extent to which parents can be trained to serve as models and sources of reinforcement (Straughan, 1964; Whaler, Winkel, Peterson, & Morrison, 1965).

It would appear that imitation and modeling procedures are highly effective in bringing about therapeutic change. More research is needed to determine the mechanisms by which these results are achieved and to specify precisely what kinds of behavioral disorders are best treated by these methods. The range of behavioral deficits and socially inappropriate responses to which imitation and modeling procedures have been applied is still rather limited and more data are needed before the general therapeutic effectiveness of these methods can be assessed. In view of the remarkable success reported with these procedures, especially the modeling-participation technique, there should be no lack of research in the future.

THEORETICAL AND EMPIRICAL ISSUES

The work of the behavior therapists and their claims of success have been sharply criticized by psychologists with more traditional approaches to psychotherapy. This is not surprising since the behavior therapists have challenged some of the most commonly accepted traditional beliefs about therapy. Behavior therapists deny that the historical and developmental sequence of the patient's life must be explored if his present behavior is to be changed. They do not attempt to unravel the various strands of causality that supposedly tie present behavior to childhood events. Instead, they start with the patient's behavior as a given and work from there.

In addition, behavior therapists are concerned only with the disordered behavior. They do not attempt to treat the "whole" person. Instead they attempt to remove particular behavioral patterns that interfere with successful personal and social adjustment. They deny that the overt symptomatic behavior is a manifestation of a more fundamental pathogenic process. For behavior therapists there is no underlying pathology; removing the symptoms (inappropriate responses) removes the disorder.

General Theoretical Issues

The exchange between the behavior therapists and their critics has been a lively one. The critics have attacked the behavior therapists' approach on both theoretical and empirical grounds. On the theoretical level the main criticisms concern the use to which learning theory is put by behavior therapists and the behavior therapists' understanding of the nature of neurosis. In both cases the critics argue that the theoretical underpinnings of behavior therapy are inadequate and incorrect. We shall discuss these theoretical topics first and then turn to empirical issues.

LEARNING THEORY AND BEHAVIOR THERAPY.   The first theoretical criticism is directed at the use to which behavior therapists put learning-theory concepts. The behavior therapists have argued that their methods derive from laboratory research and from laws of learning established through careful experimentation. Their critics contend that there is no agreement as to what the laws of learning are and that, even if there were, more is involved in behavior therapy that can be explained on the basis of S-R learning principles.

To take one example: In Wolpe's (1958) systematic desensitization technique patients are presented with anxiety-arousing "stimuli" in a hierarchically organized manner. They are to visualize these stimuli during periods of silence that last up to one minute. Presumably, the stimuli evoke a response of anxiety that can then be counterconditioned by relaxation.

The critics have argued, however, that what happens is actually not that simple. By interviewing six patients being treated by the method of systematic desensitization, Weitzman (1967) obtained evidence that patients do not maintain static visualizations of the scene described by the therapist but report a flow of visual images involving transformations of images quite removed in their contents from the intended stimulus. These transformations and elaborations are under the control of the patient's internal, psychological processes. They are frequently *dynamically rich* and may even lead the patient to insight into the nature of his disorder. Weitzman argued that such data preclude the simplistic view that only a stimulus-response connection is being affected by desensitization therapy.

In fact, Weitzman has taken the position that it is possible to provide analytic interpretations of behavior therapy. That is, rather than basing the effects of behavior therapy upon a theory derived from principles of learning, Weitzman would understand the effects of techniques such as systematic desensitization on the basis of traditional analytic theories. For example, it is possible to view systematic desensitization as a process whereby reality-oriented binding of cathexes follows upon the inhibition of anxiety signals through the induction of deep relaxation. While such an analysis would follow orthodox Freudian lines, Jungian interpretations or Sullivanian interpretations are also possible. Admittedly, these theoretical interpretations would leave out much that is important from a dynamic point of view (such as the transference relationship); nevertheless Weitzman felt that such interpretations should be attempted in order to provide a model of psychotherapy that would *incorporate* behavior techniques such as systematic desensitization.

Breger and McGaugh (1965) have also argued that more is involved in behavior therapy than the advocates of a learning-theory interpretation are willing to admit. They contended that a great variety of activities (including many that occur in traditional therapy) go on in the course of behavior therapy, especially during the initial interview sessions. During these sessions the therapist elicits from the patient the list of anxiety-arousing situations and explains the techniques that he will employ. In doing so, he provides a positive environment for the patient to discuss his problems, gives explanations about the unadaptiveness of anxiety and symptoms, and offers hypotheses of various sorts. There is evidence from interview transcripts that such activities on the part of the therapist can in themselves be therapeutically effective. Since this is the case, Breger and McGaugh have argued that a more adequate model is needed than traditional S-R learning theory.

The model they suggested derives from a cognitive view of learning. Breger and McGaugh regarded learning as a process whereby information about the environment is acquired, stored, and categorized and whereby the individual adopts *strategies* for dealing with the environment. In the therapeutic situation it becomes apparent to the patient that his old strategies and responses are ineffective. He learns new strategies and responses because the environment is structured to allow this new learning. The therapist helps in the process by pointing out defective strategies and prompting new learning. Such a view of the therapeutic process, Breger and McGaugh argued, has greater generality than an S-R approach to therapy. By placing emphasis upon the cognitive aspects of therapy, Breger and McGaugh felt that they were closer to what actually transpires in the interaction between therapist and patient. Like Weitzman, they argued that their model incorporated all that was involved in behavior therapy (at least desensitization techniques) and explained a great deal more as well.

The cognitive model, like the psychoanalytic model espoused by Weitzman, has not been warmly received by psychologists committed to behavioral methods—and for many of the same reasons. Neither approach has proven to be superior to behavior therapy. In fact, the behavior therapists argue that the reverse is true. In addition, most behavior therapists feel that the preference for cognitive terms over S-R terms is misplaced. The advantage of S-R theory, they argue, is that it provides a precise, empirically testable terminology. While the theory has its deficiencies, it is at least subject to experimental verification. To speak of strategies, programs, plans, ideas, and the like does not contribute toward clarifying empirical issues. On the contrary, it has the effect, at least in the behaviorist's eyes, of impeding effective experimental analysis by imposing unnecessary and cumbersome translations between what is observed and what is inferred (Wiest, 1967).

Behavior therapists prefer an S-R learning-theory approach because such an approach has shown itself to be pragmatically useful. The main techniques of behavior therapy (desensitization, operant conditioning, aversive treatment, etc.) were derived solely or very largely from principles of learning. To reinterpret these techniques in nonbehavioral terms would be retrogressive. For the behavior therapists learning theory has proven its value because the methods derived from the theory work in therapeutic practice.

THE NATURE OF NEUROSIS.   As we have seen, the behavior therapists believe that neuroses are conditioned responses or habits that interfere with successful personal and social adjustment. They deny the distinction between symptoms and underlying factors and argue that in removing the symptoms (which are typically equated with behaviors that can be objectively observed) one removes the neurosis.

More dynamically oriented clinicians refuse to accept this identification of the symptom with the neurosis. To make such an identification one must describe neuroses in terms of specific symptoms. This may work for phobias, tics, and bedwetting, but it does not work as well for neurotic depression, obsessional disorders, and the kinds of persistent interpersonal entanglements that characterize so many neurotics (Breger & McGaugh, 1965). In such cases the psychodynamicist sees an integrated neurotic pattern, including the neurotic's characteristic ways of interacting with other people, intrapersonal modes of functioning, and certain behavioral symptoms. This pattern also includes characteristic modes of thinking and perceiving, secondary gains accruing to neurotic behavior, characteristic modes of fantasy and dreaming, and so forth.

The critics contend, therefore, that behavior therapists *oversimplify* neurosis and neurotic behavior. The theoretical foundation from which the behavior therapist operates leads to an inadequate and superficial view of the nature of clinical disorders. As a result, behavior therapists have restricted their attention almost entirely to neuroses that involve specific symptoms. They have avoided more complex neurotic patterns or, in those few cases where they have attempted to deal with more complicated phenomena, they have smuggled in dynamic concepts to account for the data.

Rachman and Eysenck (1966) have countered this argument by

pointing out that behavior therapists have been interested in neuroses involving specific symptoms mainly because in such cases responses can be accurately measured (and thus specific predictions can be tested). It is possible to count the rate at which tics occur, the strength of phobias, the number of bedwettings per week, and so forth. These measures can then be employed as dependent variables, and the effect of modifications in the independent variables can be assessed. It is this methodological concern, and not the wish to avoid the theoretical problem of generality, that has led behavior therapists to restrict themselves to neuroses that involve specific symptoms.

Other behavior therapists would argue that their methods, far from being limited in generality, are *more* effective for a *broader* range of behavior disorders than traditional dynamic techniques have proven to be. Thus behavior therapists have reported success in treating disorders either excluded from traditional treatment because of poor prognosis (e.g., alcoholics, chronic schizophrenics, delinquents) or not responsive to dynamically oriented treatment (e.g., autistic behavior, withdrawal symptoms, sexual perversions). In view of the relatively recent application of behavior methods, proponents of behavior therapy argue that their techniques have scored remarkably well. This brings us to the empirical side of the argument between behavior therapists and their critics.

The Problem of Symptom Substitution

The main empirical issue has been whether behavior therapy works. This can be rephrased: Will removal of symptoms without attention to underlying causes of the symptoms lead to the formation of new symptoms? The behavior therapists argue that dynamically oriented therapists are committed to the assumption that symptom substitution must follow a course of treatment that removes the symptom by treating it directly, without altering the underlying source of the symptom. On the contrary, the behavior therapists assume that removing the behavior eliminates the disorder; there is no "symptom substitution."

THE BEHAVIORISTS' CLAIMS OF SUCCESS.   As we have seen, Wolpe (1958) claimed that desensitization techniques were not only more effective than traditional psychotherapy but also more efficient. In a series of 210 cases he found that 90 percent were improved or cured after an average of 30 sessions. Wolpe (1960) reported the same percentage of patients were improved in follow-up studies of 122 patients treated with behavioral techniques. In a survey of follow-up studies (Wolpe, 1962) only four relapses were found among 249 patients.

Other proponents of behavior therapy have also reported success with behavior methods and no evidence of "symptom substitution" in follow-up studies (e.g., Ullmann & Krasner, 1965; Yates, 1958a, 1958b). In a review of behavior therapy research, Grossberg (1964) concluded that the evidence for successful and long-lasting treatment by behavior methods was "overwhelming." Follow-up studies seldom indicated additional behavior problems or relapses after cure. In fact, in only two cases (Lazarus & Rachman, 1957; Meyer & Gelder, 1963) of hundreds surveyed were additional behavior problems manifested.

The success claimed by behavior therapists contrasts sharply with that obtained by traditional methods. In a study by the American Psychoanalytic Association (Brody, 1962), for example, 60 percent of the patients analyzed were "cured" or "greatly improved." These patients were treated an average of four times a week for three to four years (i.e., about 700 sessions). Behavior therapists report success in over 90 percent of the cases they treat, and the average number of interviews is usually about 30 (Wolpe, 1960).

On the face of it this appears to justify the claims of behavior therapists (e.g., Eysenck, 1960; Lazarus, 1961) that their methods are far superior to traditional methods. Such an inference is not justified, however, unless it can be shown that the *degree of severity* was the same for patients treated by behavior therapy techniques and other methods of psychotherapy. This points to the need for studies involving proper controls, not simply the comparison of percent improved. Some efforts in this direction have been made.

Eysenck (1967), for example, reported the results of research in which 37 children were divided into two groups one of which received behavior therapy (desensitization training) and the other traditional psychotherapy. The children were suffering from all types of disorders except brain damage and psychosis, and a five-point rating scale was used to establish the severity of each child's disorder. Psychiatrists, who did not know to which group a child had been assigned, did the ratings. Children were rated after treatment and again ten months later. Seventy-five percent of the children who had received behavior therapy were rated cured at the close of treatment, as compared with only 35 percent of those who received psychotherapy. At the time of the ten-month follow-up, 85 percent of those who had received behavior therapy were rated cured, but only 29 percent of those in the psychotherapy group received the same rating. In a control group, which received no treatment, only 18 percent were found to be cured ten months later. Since behavior therapy and psychotherapy sessions were conducted by the same person (an experienced psychotherapist who was trained in behavior therapy for purposes of the study), these effects cannot be attributed to differences between therapists.

The study is open to criticism, however, since the two groups, those receiving behavior therapy and those receiving traditional psychotherapy, were not matched for degree of severity at the beginning of treatment. The children in the behavior therapy group were rated as more seriously ill initially—which would appear to lend even more support to the behavior therapist's claims of success. It does, however, introduce a methodological artifact, since the children in the psychotherapy group began with a higher clinical-status rating and were therefore less likely to increase their score to the point necessary to denote cure. Eysenck noted the possibility of such a ceiling effect, but pointed out that the percentage of cures resulting from psychotherapy in the experiment did not differ from that usually obtained in the clinics involved in the study.

Another problem concerns the method of rating clinical improvement. In Eysenck's study, as in many of the earlier studies, judgments of improvement were based upon therapists' evaluations. Since therapists' evaluations are of questionable validity, claims of success based upon such judgments may be unwarranted. To justify behavior methods, therefore, better research designs were needed—especially studies employing groups *matched for severity* and assessed through *objective criterion measures.*

Recently a number of studies have appeared in which the effectiveness of various techniques has been compared with matched samples and objective methods for assessing psychological change. Gordon Paul, for example, has conducted a program of research in which he investigated various methods of treating speech students suffering from stage fright. In one of the first of these studies (Paul, 1966), 67 subject were assigned to four matched groups: systematic desensitization treatment, insight-oriented psychotherapy, attention-placebo treatment (non-therapy oriented meetings between patient and therapist), and no treatment. Four measures of anxiety were administered before and after treatment: observable manifestations of anxiety during public speaking as rated by a trained observer, the subject's own ratings of their experienced anxiety, pulse ratings, and palmar sweat ratings. Ratings made before and after treatment demonstrated that the group receiving behavior therapy showed the greatest average reduction of anxiety on all four criteria (Figure 6-5).

In follow-up measures taken six weeks later the improvement obtained by desensitization procedures was maintained with no evidence of "symptom substitution." No differences were found between effects produced by different therapists, nor was improvement predictable from major personality variables. It should be noted that the five therapists employed in this study were psychotherapists trained in behavior therapy specifically for purposes of this research—who continued to prefer psychotherapy and its associated doctrines after the research was concluded.

Two years later Paul (1967) readministered the test battery he had given his subjects to determine the long-term effects of the various

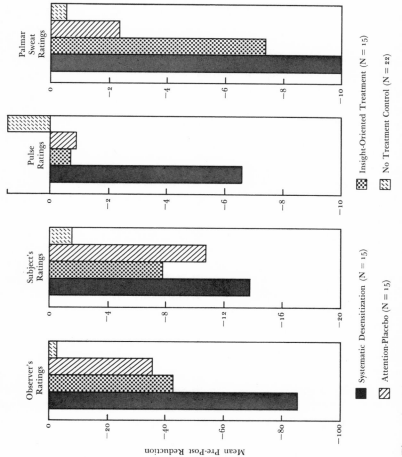

Figure 6-5. Mean reduction in measures of anxiety from pretreatment to post-treatment stress conditions (from Paul, 1966).

treatments. Systematic desensitization resulted in the greatest significant improvement (88%), followed by insight-oriented psychotherapy and attention-placebo (50% each) and untreated controls (22%). No evidence of relapse or symptom substitution was obtained.

Paul and Shannon (1966) investigated the effectiveness of different treatment procedures with patients suffering from chronic anxiety. Their methods included the four employed in the Paul (1966) study, as well as group desensitization procedures. Again pre- and post-test measures were taken to assess anxiety. Both individual and group desensitization procedures proved more effective than insight-oriented psychotherapy and nonspecific attention-placebo techniques. There were no significant differences in the effects of individual desensitization and group desensitization. Paul and Shannon also found that the academic performance (grade-point average) of subjects given behavior therapy improved, as compared to a no-treatment control group, suggesting that the specific reduction in anxiety achieved in the experiment may have generalized to other life situations.

In a follow-up study two years later Paul (1968) found a maintenance of improvement obtained earlier for group desensitization. Examination of test battery scores revealed that improvement was greater for group desensitization (80%) and individual desensitization (89%) procedures than for insight-oriented psychotherapy or attention-placebo treatment (53% each). Untreated controls showed improvement in 27 percent of the cases. When measures of academic performance were taken, the difference between subjects given behavior therapy and a no-treatment control group was found to be the same as the differences obtained immediately after treatment.

Paul (1967, 1968) found no evidence for symptom substitution. Indeed, Paul's (1968) data revealed high frequencies of participation in group discussions, social activities, clubs, and organizations for subjects in behavior therapy groups. Subjects who were previously chronically anxious reported greater self-confidence, greater relaxation, greater ease with people. Instead of symptom substitution, therefore, Paul found that the performance gain achieved by behavior methods during therapy was maintained with little loss. Follow-up studies by Bandura and his associates (Bandura, Blanchard, & Ritter, 1969; Bandura, Grusec, & Menlove, 1967; Bandura & Menlove, 1968) also indicated that the gain achieved through behavior methods (modeling) persists.

To summarize: Behavior therapists claim, first of all, that their methods are effective and efficient. Behavior therapy is more successful than traditional psychotherapy and takes less time. As evidence, behavior therapists cite comparative data as to percentage cured by both methods and, more recently, the findings of studies in which the two procedures are compared with matched samples. To counter the argument that removing the symptom does not cure the patient, behavior therapists cite results of follow-up studies that provide no evidence for "symptom substitution."

CONFLICTING EVIDENCE. In spite of the behavior therapists' lack of success in finding symptom substitution, many psychologists remain convinced that the removal of symptoms inevitably leads to the formation of new symptoms because the "underlying cause" has not been eliminated. Bookbinder (1962), for example, argued that depth psychology, by treating the neurotic predisposition and reorganizing the individual's character structure rather than removing specific symptoms, produces more permanent effects than behavior therapy. The psychotherapist is concerned with *neuroticism* (character structure) while the behavior therapist is concerned with *neurosis* (a particular symptom). Merely treating the symptom leaves the character structure unaffected.

Bookbinder recast his argument in learning-theory terms. The basic point of disagreement, he contended, is whether a patient has only one or a repertoire of anxiety-reducing responses. Bookbinder cited evidence indicating that patients have many anxiety-reducing responses and that, at least in some instances, the final responses in the repertoire represent psychotic reactions. Thus in more serious cases, the probability of symptom substitution is greater. For this reason, he argued, behavior therapists have had little success with schizophrenic episodes, severe depressions, suicidal and homicidal tendencies, and physical symptoms of a life and death nature.

Evidence for symptom substitution comes, for the most part, from studies involving hypnotic removal of symptoms. Seitz (1953) used the technique of serial symptom substitution, hypnotically blocking a symptom to see what the substitute would be. He found that the patient emitted a series of physical symptoms (torticollis, vomiting, headaches) and, when there were blocked, developed a homicidal psychotic reaction. Rosen (1953) obtained similar results, and Spiegel (1967) argued that symptom removal (by hypnosis) may result in reactive symptoms if failure is expected by therapist and patient. Holland (1967) also cited evidence that hypnotic removal of symptoms is frequently followed by new symptoms. Even in cases where hypnosis was not used, Fenichel (1945) reported that aversive suppression of symptoms has been followed by new symptom formation. He gave the example of the suppression of war neurosis by electric shock. After the neurotic behavior in question was eliminated, new symptoms appeared.

In a reply to Bookbinder, Yates (1962) agreed that a hierarchy of anxiety-reducing responses is a possibility (one that would fit well into a learning-theory explanation). He did not, however, feel that the existence of a hierarchy of differential response strength was supported by available evidence. Nevertheless, some data in favor of such a hierarchy were presented by Ullmann and Krasner (1965) in a case history involving a child at a summer camp. The child displayed a series of maladaptive responses including self-punishing behavior, tantrums, public nudity, stealing food, smearing feces, and, finally, piling shoes on other children. As each response was eliminated, another would take its place until the entire hierarchy of maladaptive responses had been extinguished. A psychoanalytically oriented psychologist would see this as evidence of symptom substitution. Behavior therapists, such as Ullmann and Krasner, deny this, as they do not accept the notion of "symptom."

REFORMULATIONS.   There have been two rather paradoxical reactions to the debate over symptom substitution. On the part of the behavior therapists there is a growing tendency to accept the possibility that eliminating the original maladaptive response *does not* necessarily cure the patient. It then becomes necessary to show that this failure can be explained in behavioristic terms. On the part of psychotherapists with a dynamic orientation, there is an increased acceptance of the possibility that eliminating the original maladaptive response *does* cure the patient. It then becomes necessary to show that this success can be explained in dynamic terms.

To a considerable degree the symptom-substitution controversy concerns the acceptance (by dynamically oriented psychotherapists) and the rejection (by behavior therapists) of the medical model of behavior. Behaviorists have not been willing to accept the dynamicists' assertion that an "underlying cause" (disease) exists of which the "symptom" is the external manifestation. Instead they deny the notion of an "underlying cause," regard the "symptom" as a maladaptive response, and attempt to remove this maladaptive response directly, arguing that in so doing they remove the behavior disorder in its entirety.

While this appears to be a feasible assumption in many cases, there is evidence that in some instances removing the maladaptive response does not cure the patient. Other maladaptive responses may appear in place of the response that was removed. Behavior therapists have therefore begun to accept the possibility that, once an undesirable response is eliminated, other undesirable responses can be emitted before adaptive behavior occurs. It then is necessary to successively eliminate the new maladaptive responses.

Goldiamond (1965), for example, described a case in which a woman assumed a fetal position for three days after an argument with her husband. Although the patient was restored to mobility by directed treatment of the maladaptive response, Goldiamond cautioned that the more general deficiency remained. That is, unless the patient learned more appropriate means of controlling her husband's behavior, the emergence of new childish and maladaptive responses would be relatively likely.

Symonds (1965) faced a similar problem in the case of a preschool girl who exhibited a series of maladaptive behaviors. As these behaviors were successively eliminated, new maladaptive responses developed. Once again the evidence seemed to indicate that responses are hierarchically organized and that eliminating those responses that are higher in the hierarchy raises the frequency of responses lower in the hierarchy.

Such a formulation is not new to learning theory. Dollard and Miller (1950) described the conditions under which such a hierarchy might be formed. They pointed out that the order of responses in the hierarchy could be altered through learning. In this conceptualization, as well as in the notion of a hierarchy of anxiety-reducing responses (Bookbinder, 1962; Yates, 1962), the group of responses is maintained by the same reinforcers. Cahoon (1968) has suggested that a group of responses can also be related in terms of common conditions of discriminative stimulus control. In this way, "symptom substitution" can be explained by arguing that the same stimuli that previously maintained maladaptive responses may, upon the elimination of the original maladaptive behavior, come to control other maladaptive responses. A similar position was espoused by Ulrich, Stachnik, and Mabry (1966).

In short, behavior therapists reject the medical model and the implication that the appearance of new maladaptive behavior indicates an "underlying cause" of the behavioral disorder. Instead, they would argue that a set of responses, hierarchically ordered, is bound together by a common reinforcing stimulus or common discriminative stimuli. The purpose of therapy is to eliminate those responses in the hierarchy that are maladaptive until new, appropriate responses appear. For behavior therapists the notion of "symptom substitution" is an instance of inappropriate terminology that obscures an important phenomenon—namely, the possibility of a set of maladaptive responses, acquired through learning, each of which must be eliminated in stepwise fashion before appropriate social behavior occurs.

For their part psychotherapists with a dynamic orientation are faced with impressive evidence that in some cases symptom substitution does not occur. Behavior therapy has proven to be an effective means not only of removing symptoms but of achieving *permanent cure*. Some psychodynamically oriented psychologists have attempted to show that these findings are not incompatible with dynamic theory. Weitzman (1967), for example, argued that analytic theory is not necessarily committed to a notion of symptom substitution and that the data from studies using behavioral techniques, especially systematic desensitization, can be explained in terms of analytic theory.

Thus analytic theory assumes that the ego depends for its development on the greater efficiency of secondary, versus primary, process. Secondary process leads to increasing mastery of object relations and the binding of libidinal energies in the service of the emerging ego. Since the removal of a symptom typically involves an increased mastery of object relations (less anxiety, greater ability to express love, hostility), the result is an increment in the bound energy available to ego functioning. Even if the dynamic source of the original symptom formation remains unaffected, the increase in bound energy may lead to an increase in the effectiveness of repressive cathexes. Consequently no further symptoms would be expected to appear.

Weitzman's analysis, regardless of its validity, points to the growing acceptance on the part of dynamically oriented psychologists of the claims of success advanced by behavior therapists. Weitzman and others who share a traditional orientation have argued that the most satisfactory theoretical framework for explaining the processes involved in systematic desensitization and other behavior therapy methods is an analytic (or cognitive) one. The behavior therapists, on the other hand, prefer the economy of a learning-theory interpretation. This difference of opinion is a theme that has recurred in the course of this chapter, and it will be our first topic of discussion in the following section.

EVALUATION

The debate over behavior therapy centers largely on the preference for different models of behavior. On the one hand, traditional approaches to psychotherapy are based on an analytic or cognitive model. Emphasis is placed on internal events, psychological processes, cognitive mechanisms. In contrast, behavior therapists prefer a learning model with its emphasis on overt behavior, stimuli and responses, reinforcement contingencies, and so forth. Some commentators have argued that this represents an instance of "paradigm clash" and that the controversy will be resolved only when one model proves to be superior empirically. We shall discuss this thesis first and then turn to an evaluation of the contribution of learning theory and behavior therapy to psychotherapy.

Paradigm Clash

In Chapter Five we discussed Kuhn's (1962) notion of paradigm clash in science—a situation in which two essentially different paradigms come into conflict with each other. No theoretical resolution is possible since the two paradigms begin with different metatheoretical assumptions that dictate the methods to be used, the data that are relevant, and the manner of relating the data to theoretical concepts. The suggestion has been made (Katahn & Koplin, 1968) that the controversy over behavior therapy represents an instance of paradigm clash.

According to this view, cognitive and learning models of psychotherapy differ fundamentally, to the extent that differences between them cannot be resolved. Cognitive and psychoanalytically oriented psychologists are concerned with understanding and explaining behavior, while behaviorists are more concerned with control and predictive efficiency. The analytic or cognitive model focuses on internal, dynamic events, while the behaviorist emphasizes the objective description of environmental events. The concepts employed also differ in fundamental ways. The notions of "cathexis," "strategies," "libidinal energy," and so forth are on a different level of abstraction than are the behaviorist's concepts "stimulus," "response," and "reinforcement." It is often impossible to compare theoretical concepts for this reason. Cognitive concepts may be closer to the experience of the behaving subject, but the behaviorist's concepts are closer to the data.

Kuhn (1962) argued that when a paradigm clash occurs, there is no way of deciding on logical grounds that one paradigm is to be accepted and the other rejected. Arguments at this level are doomed from the start because the proponents of each paradigm have different perceptions of the domain in question. Methods, concepts, and theory differ; even empirical data are interpreted in different ways. In the present instance, for example, what the psychoanalyst means by "cure" may be something quite different from what the behavior therapist means by the term.

Ultimately, according to the paradigm-clash interpretation, one paradigm will survive and the other will not. Intensive research using the two paradigms will, in the end, lead to the dominance of one paradigm over the other. This dominance will be based on utility and productivity: The more useful and productive paradigm will survive. Instead of attempting to resolve theoretical quarrels, therefore, proponents of each model should concern themselves strictly with empirical matters. The theories are irreconcilable; in the long run one will survive because it proves more useful.

If such an interpretation is valid, behavior therapists will have to demonstrate that their methods are more effective than traditional methods. This means that the methods of behavior therapy will have to be applied to the whole range of disorders treated by traditional techniques of psychotherapy. In addition, behavior methods will have to prove successful in treating disorders irresponsive to traditional methods of treatment. Many behavior therapists are convinced that they can succeed in this enterprise. Some would argue that they already have. We shall return to this issue shortly.

There is an alternative to the paradigm-clash interpretation, however. As we have seen in Chapter Five, some psychologists, such as Campbell (1963), foresee a higher-level integration of behavioristic and cognitive theories. According to this view, the conflict between cognitive and behavior theory will be resolved, not by the dominance of one model over the other, but by the incorporation of both models into a more inclusive theoretical framework. If such an interpretation is correct, there will be an eventual unification of theory in psychology.

At the moment there is little evidence that such a development is occurring in theory and research on psychotherapy. Instead, psychologists in this area seem to be largely concerned with justifying the merits of their own theoretical model and downplaying the value of opposing models. Rather than searching for a more inclusive theoretical framework that incorporates their methods as well as traditional approaches, advocates of behavior therapy such as Wolpe and Eysenck have been vigorously doctrinaire in their rejection of traditional approaches. Perhaps this is due to an initial need to justify novel approaches at the expense of existing methods, and possibly the future will witness a compatible merging of cognitive and behavior theories.

If the trend in other domains of psychology is an indication of what will happen in this area, the expectation of theoretical unification does not appear farfetched. As we have seen in preceding chapters, many psychologists with a learning-theory orientation have worked out mediational theories to handle internal (cognitive) events. These theoretical developments are most in evidence among the behavior therapists in Bandura's conceptualization of symbolic extinction through modeling. According to Bandura's dual-process theory, extinction is a function of central (cognitive) mechanisms. Presumably these mechanisms are the same as those internal representational responses thought to mediate vicarious learning generally (Chapter Four). Such a conceptualization gives cognitive processes their due without losing the rigor of behavioral analysis. If theoretical unification is indeed to be achieved, further formulations along these lines will have to be attempted and substantiated.

Psychotherapy and Learning Theory

A frequent criticism of behavior therapy is that there are serious theoretical inconsistencies and inadequacies. The behavior therapists, the criticism runs, supposedly base their techniques on learning theory, but in practice they violate many of the canons of such an approach. They often deal with covert and implicit behavior. In systematic desensitization, for example, critics have argued that imagistic behavior plays a central role and that a great part of such therapy involves activity more akin to traditional psychotherapy than to laboratory research on learning.

In addition, early behavior therapists (Eysenck, 1960; Wolpe, 1958) accepted a Hullian drive-reduction model of learning that had already been rejected by many learning theorists. Rather than updating their model, the now antiquated general theory of learning was retained and no account taken of recent developments in research on learning. For some time, therefore, theory has lagged behind research. In their eagerness to show that their methods work, a number of the behavior therapists have given lip service to learning theory but failed to show how theory and method interpenetrate.

More recently, however, behavior therapists have begun to take developments in research on learning into account and have attempted to update the theoretical underpinnings of behavior therapy. In line with general developments in research, there has been less concern with all-inclusive theories and more emphasis on specific learning phenomena (extinction, avoidance learning, counter-conditioning) and with the variables that affect these processes. In addition, some investigators, such as Bandura and his associates, have concentrated exclusively on one particular learning paradigm and on the way in which that paradigm and the learning principles that underlie it can be applied to psychotherapy.

Of all the behavior therapists the Skinnerians have been the most consistent in their application of learning principles. In contrast to Wolpe, Eysenck, and other behavior therapists who relied heavily on the Hullian drive-reduction model and who postulated a classically conditioned anxiety response as the core of neurosis, the Skinnerians ignored the emotional (drive) factor and focused exclusively on objective behavior. They regarded treatment as the explicit shaping of behavioral repertoires, with no thought to hypothetical inner states. Psychotherapy was viewed as a particular influence process within the broader context of studies of behavior control.

The results obtained through Skinnerian procedures have occasionally been quite dramatic. This is true especially of research with autistic children and chronic schizophrenics. In these cases, however, the therapist is dealing with the lowest possible degree of socialization. Personality and character are least developed, and the individual is least removed from the "animal" level. It has been argued that behavior methods derived from research with animals (such as operant techniques) should find effective application here but will be less effective with more complicated pathology (Mowrer, 1965).

This is reminiscent of the argument of dynamically oriented therapists that behavior therapy does not affect character structure and therefore is not effective in the treatment of complicated character defects and faulty interpersonal strategies that bring people to the hospital in the first place. The methods of behavior therapy are too limited, critics argue, to deal with severe depressions, suicidal and homicidal tendencies, thought disorders, and interpersonal entanglements. This brings us to the final, and critical, issue—how successful is behavior therapy as a form of treatment.

The Contribution of Behavior Therapy

In spite of the criticisms it has received and its own limitations, there can be little doubt that behavior therapy has made an important contribution to the field of clinical psychology. Behavior therapists have taken a problem-oriented approach to therapy. They have focused on limited portions of behavior and have attempted to make their analysis of the problems explicit and concrete. This in itself is an important contribution. Moreover, behavior therapists have emphasized the point that the therapist must have definite and specific objectives in mind in treating a patient. Some alternative behavior pattern must be chosen to take the place of the undesirable behavior. This emphasis upon the outcome of therapy is one of the strengths of the behavior therapy approach.

Behavior therapy has also led to innovations in technique. The behavior therapist will try almost anything that has a possibility of working to the patient's benefit. This flexibility has proven to be a healthy antidote to the rigidity of technique that characterized much of traditional psychotherapy. The behavior therapists have preferred to avoid committing themselves to individual techniques. The emphasis for them is on outcome, not technique.

For all their flexibility, however, the behavior therapists are united in their commitment to a search for explicit, systematic operations that the therapist can perform to produce particular and specific effects in the patient's behavior. The strategy they employ is derived from the laboratory. Different procedures are attempted with different symptoms and with different types of patients in order to determine the method that works best with each type of disorder. Presumably, by manipulating the treatment conditions in this way, systematic knowledge can be obtained.

Another contribution of behavior therapy techniques is in the area of measurement. Research on the effectiveness of psychotherapy requires the development of measurement procedures that are repeatable and verifiable. Unless such measures exist, there is no way of assessing the patient's response to treatment. The behavior therapist begins by using the patient's presenting complaints as the criterion for evaluating his response to treatment. Various measurement procedures have been developed for assessing the strength of anxiety, the amount of hallucinations, the intensity of a phobia, and so forth. Since the behavior therapist is chiefly concerned with objective behavior, he can often use objective means to assess the severity of an illness—e.g., counting the number of times a child has a temper tantrum in the course of a day or the number of tics a patient emits over a period of time. Once these measures are taken it becomes possible to assess the outcome of treatment.

The proper assessment of behavior change necessarily involves some consideration of long-term effects. Here again behavior therapists have made an important contribution by their efforts to demonstrate the persistence of the effects of behavior therapy and the lack of symptom substitution. Considerable care and attention have gone into the design of follow-up studies, and in some cases (e.g., Paul, 1967, 1968) subject loss has been held to a minimum. This emphasis upon the importance of follow-up studies cannot be ignored in future research on psychotherapy.

Needless to say, many of the criticisms leveled at behavior therapy are justified. In early studies faulty research designs were employed and the results contaminated by various sources of bias. Often comparisons between patients treated by behavior therapy and by other methods of psychotherapy were not justified because of differences in the two populations. Frequently patients were not matched on the basis of degree of severity of their disorders. In fact, one might ask whether it is possible to compare treatments across patients in actual clinical settings. No two patients are treated precisely alike even by the same therapist using a single technique. A unique set of circumstances surrounds each patient making comparison difficult.

Nevertheless, behavior therapists have been remarkably successful. A large number of well-controlled studies now exist in the literature demonstrating the effectiveness of behavior methods in treating a wide range of behavior disorders. In fact, as we have seen, behavior therapists have had success where traditional approaches usually fail— for example, with chronic schizophrenics, delinquents, and autistic children.

But what of other, more "complicated" disorders—such as those involving obsessional thought patterns, severe depression, or suicidal or homicidal impulses? Dynamically oriented therapists argue that in treating disorders of this sort their techniques are most effective, while those of the behavior therapists are least effective. In such cases the pathology is deeply rooted and affects the whole character structure of the individual. It is not merely a question of aberrant behavior; there is a general breakdown in cognitive functioning. The individual has lost contact with reality and engages in increasingly bizarre and idiosyncratic patterns of thought and action. According to the dynamicist, superficial application of behavior techniques inevitably proves ineffectual. More analytic methods are needed to come to grips with fundamental personality processes.

The behavior therapist does not accept this argument. If certain disorders have proven difficult to treat with behavior methods it is not because they are more fundamental or involve deeper personality processes. It is rather because they are ill-defined phenomena, not easily reduced to specific forms of behavior. Behavior therapists are concerned with behavior. To speak of obsessional thought patterns, depression, and destructive impulses has meaning to them only insofar as these disorders involve overt responses. Once these overt responses are identified, behavioral techniques can be applied to eliminate them and to introduce more appropriate responses in their place.

Essentially it is a question, once again, of acceptance of the medical model of behavior. Where the dynamically oriented therapist sees "pathology," the behavior therapist sees "behavior disorder." The behavior therapist argues that all so-called "complicated" intra- and inter-personal disorders are susceptible to treatment through behavioral methods. It is simply a question of identifying the maladaptive responses and the reinforcement contingencies that control these responses. There is nothing more to the disorder than the behavior. The dynamically oriented therapist, on the other hand, insists that it makes sense to speak of pathology. The patient with self-destructive impulses is no less sick because these impulses are not given overt expression. Nor does one cure a suicidal patient by eliminating the verbal expression of his self-destructive impulses. A deeper, more penetrating method of treatment is needed to remove the underlying pathology.

Research may resolve this debate in favor of one approach or the other. It is also possible that integrative, higher-order theories will be developed and that these theories will generate new methods incorporating the best features of present methods. But whatever the outcome, the application of learning theory and the principles of learning have been more productive and more successful in the area of therapy than in any other single domain. The excitement produced by this approach has not abated. A great deal remains to be done, but in view of the enthusiasm evidenced by so many investigators it seems likely that behavior therapy will receive even more attention in the next few decades than it has during the past decade.

7

Interpersonal Behavior

IN a theoretical paper on personality and social behavior, Robert Sears (1951) argued that an adequate social psychology requires the analysis of dyadic and interpersonal as well as monadic units. At the time he was writing, psychology had been almost exclusively concerned with a monadic behavior theory. Since then an enormous amount of research has been conducted in the study of interpersonal behavior. A good deal of this research has been discussed elsewhere in this book. In this chapter, we shall be concerned with research in the two areas of interaction explicitly mentioned by Sears: the analysis of psychological processes resulting from highly particularized constellations of interpersonal relations—i.e., the parent-child relationship central to the process of socialization—and the analysis of variables that affect the behavior of individuals in small groups. We shall also discuss research in the area of impression formation and interpersonal judgments. In keeping with the orientation of this book, we shall focus on approaches to these areas where learning theory is centrally employed.

SOCIALIZATION AND THE CONTROL OF BEHAVIOR

Previously we have discussed various aspects of the socialization process such as language development, attitude formation, and the transmission of behavioral patterns through imitation. In all of these processes familial and extra-familial influences contribute to regulating and controlling the social behavior of the child. The language the child speaks, the opinions he holds, the behaviors he engages in are all largely determined by the social environment. Here we shall discuss attempts on the part of psychologists with a learning-theory orientation to investigate how this control is achieved.

As we have seen in the preceding chapter, those in a position of control over other people possess numerous resources for exercising that control. Nevertheless, the process of socialization differs considerably from the process of therapy. In the therapeutic situation attempts are made to change behavioral patterns that are well developed and highly resistant to change. In the process of socialization, parents and other agents try to correct and modify behavior that is neither well developed nor highly resistant to change. Consequently, while the mechanisms are largely the same, less extreme measures are employed in the socialization process.

External Control

A distinction will be made here between external and internal sources of control. External sources are outside of the individual, whereas internal sources refer to self-administered determinants of control. Initially, external sources of control predominate, and only gradually does the child develop self-control.

POSITIVE SOCIAL REINFORCEMENT.   The most obvious source of external control is the use by socializing agents of rewarding or punishing resources to control the child's behavior. Aronfreed (1968) has noted that although positive and negative reinforcements can be separately conceptualized, they are highly *interdependent* in actual socialization episodes. The carrot and the stick are often employed with reference to the same act (Dollard & Miller, 1950; Miller, 1959). When positive reinforcement is withdrawn from the child, the resulting frustration has effects on his behavior much like the effects of punishment or anxiety. This reciprocal relationship between positive and negative components makes it difficult in any specific instance to assess their respective contributions to behavior control.

Nevertheless, a large number of studies have been conducted in an effort to determine the effects of positive reinforcement on the behavior of children. Since these studies have been concerned generally with the socialization process, the types of reinforcement employed are usually similar to those that occur in normal socialization. Thus positive reinforcement may take the form of praise or approval of the child's behavior, or it may be conveyed by more subtle changes in adult behavior. These responses may be relatively small in magnitude and may involve nods, changes in facial expression, posture, tone of voice, and so forth. Children have proven to be remarkably adept at learning under such conditions.

The reinforcement history of the child is an obvious factor affecting his susceptibility to social control. If the child has developed strong dependent habits, he will tend to be more responsive to reinforcement than if his dependent habits are weak (Ferguson, 1961). Children who have a history of failure are more likely to be influenced by social reinforcement from others (Gelfand, 1962; Lesser & Abelson, 1959). Endsley (1960) found that children who sought praise frequently from their teachers performed better on a learning task in which social reinforcements were administered than did children who sought praise relatively seldom. The child's history of institutionalization also affects responsiveness to social reinforcement (Stevenson & Cruse, 1961; Stevenson & Fahel, 1961).

In addition, the immediate circumstances surrounding the behavior have been found to influence the child's susceptibility to social reinforcement. If the child has been deprived of a particular type of reinforcement for some time before its introduction, the value of that reinforcement may be enhanced. Gewirtz and Baer (1958) tested different groups of children under three experimental conditions: after a twenty-minute isolation period (deprivation), after interaction involving twenty minutes of free play with a responding adult (satiation), and in a condition that involved neither deprivation nor satiation. When social reinforcement (in the form of "good" or "fine") was administered for correct responses in a learning task, the children in the deprivation group were found to learn most rapidly. The satiation group showed the poorest learning (Figure 7-1).

Gewirtz and Baer (1958) interpreted these results as indicating that *social drives* can be established through social reinforcer deprivation and that they function in a way similar to appetitive drives. Social deprivation primes the child to be receptive to social reinforcement just as hunger makes him receptive to food. Other interpretations, however, are possible. Walters and Karal (1960) argued that the differences between deprived and satiated groups in the Gewirtz and Baer study could be attributed to the emotional *arousal* produced by isolation in the deprivation condition. Evidence in support of this

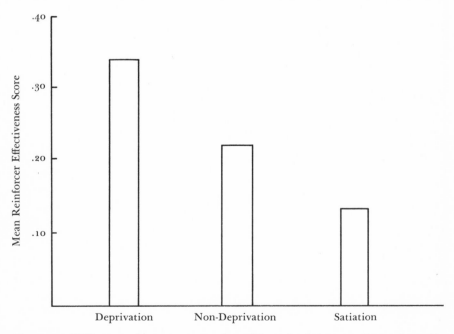

Figure 7-1. Differences between means for subjects in three experimental conditions (34 subjects in each group). Scores indicate the effectiveness of reinforcement on learning (from Gewirtz and Baer, 1958).

contention has been obtained by a number of investigators (e.g., Paivio, 1960; Walters & Parke, 1964; Walters & Ray, 1960). Paivio (1960) argued that the effect of isolation was to increase the apprehension aroused in the subject by the experimenter's attitude or instructions.

Another interpretation has been proposed by Hartup and Himeno (1959), who found that children subjected to a prior isolation period demonstrated more aggression than children who had experienced prior interaction with the experimenter. They regarded this as evidence that social isolation can have a frustrative effect and that it does not always act as a social drive that motivates the child to be responsive to social reinforcers. Instead, they proposed that social isolation can have *both* deprivation effects and frustration effects, depending on the nature of the situation.

Further evidence for the importance of the immediate circumstances surrounding behavior comes from a study comparing the consequences of reinforcement and non-reinforcement (Stevenson & Hill, 1965). After success in a marble game, children performed better under positive social reinforcement (supportive statements) than under non-reinforcement. After failure, however, their performance was lower under positive reinforcement than after non-reinforcement. Under certain circumstances, therefore, the administration of positive reinforcements can be shown to be a relatively poor method for modifying behavior.

This is especially true when the behaviors in question are high in the child's response hierarchy. Dependent and aggressive responses, for example, often have a relatively high probability of occurrence. Attempts to alter these response patterns by positive reinforcement may prove to be unrealistic. In such cases other methods of control may be required.

To summarize, research on the effects of positive reinforcement has shown this method of control to be greatly affected by the child's history of reinforcement and by situational factors. Social reinforcement in the form of praise and approval for the child's behavior is most effective when such reinforcement is highly valued by the child because of past experience. One condition that might lead the child to place a high value on reinforcement through praise and approval is social isolation. Yet the effects of social isolation are not invariably the same. The frustration involved in being separated from others for a period of time may generate aggressive responses that offset the positive effect of social reinforcement. In general, since reinforcement is itself a stimulus event, it is affected by the stimulus context and what has gone before. Praise and approval may have different meanings to the subject under different conditions, and various kinds of approval may have significantly different reinforcement effects. Continuing research in this area has produced a greater awareness of the complexities involved.

THE ROLE OF THE MODEL.   Since we have discussed imitative and observational learning at some length in Chapter Four, we shall deal briefly with these topics here. It is obvious that such processes exert a considerable influence in the control of behavior that occurs during socialization. Here again, the child's *reinforcement history* is an important factor in determining the effectiveness of imitative and observational techniques. If the child has a history of failure, including negative reinforcement for independent behavior, he will be likely to pattern his responses on those of a model (Gelfand, 1962). Imitative behavior can be more readily elicited in high-dependent children than in low-dependent children (Bandura & Huston, 1961; Ross, 1966). There is also some evidence that the child's disposition to reproduce the behavior or judgments of a model depends to a greater extent on the correspondence between the model's level of nurturance and the level to which the child has become adapted than on the sheer amount of nurturance the child receives from the model (Stein & Wright, 1964).

The effectiveness of imitative learning has been demonstrated in studies of aggression, dependency, and sexual behavior (Bandura & Walters, 1963). In other studies, it has been shown that observation of the behavior of others can influence the child's evaluative or linguistic responses (Bandura & Harris, 1966; Bandura & McDonald, 1963). Modeling procedures have also proven effective with autistic children (Lovaas *et al.*, 1966) and phobic children (Bandura, Grusec, & Menlove, 1967).

The suppression of relatively prepotent responses has been achieved through observation of the *punitive outcome* of the model's behavior in studies by Bandura (1965b) and by Walters and his associates (Walters & Parke, 1964; Walters, Parke, & Cane, 1965). In the Bandura (1965b) study, for example, three film sequences were shown to groups of children. In all cases, the adult model was depicted as behaving aggressively toward an inflated rubber doll, but the consequences of the aggression varied. In one condition, children saw the model punished for aggression; in another condition, the model was rewarded; and in the third condition, no outcome was depicted. Children in the model-punished condition showed less subsequent aggressive behavior in a test situation than did children who saw the model rewarded or neither punished nor rewarded.

In the studies by Walters and his associates, children who saw a model punished for a deviation broke a similar prohibition less often, less readily, and for shorter periods of time than did children who saw the model rewarded or neither rewarded nor punished. These results, therefore, are consistent with those of Bandura and indicate that observation of the behavior of another person and its outcome can suppress response tendencies in the observer, especially when the outcome involves punishment to the model.

The importance of punishment was further demonstrated in a study by Bandura, Ross, and Ross (1963b) in which it was found that children were more likely to imitate models who dispensed *both* rewards and punishments than they were to imitate models who were merely rewarding. This challenges a straightforward hedonic notion of socialization (the love-is-enough approach), and suggests that punishment has an important function in the control of the child's behavior.

THE PROBLEM OF PUNISHMENT.   Punishment is obviously a potent source of behavior modification in the socialization of the child. Punishment makes it possible to suppress undesirable behavior patterns and reinforce more desirable competing responses. Much social training involves such suppression. For example, the responses of a young child may become unacceptable as the child grows older and consequently require inhibition. Or behavior that is acceptable in older children and adults may be undesirable in young children. Similarly, responses that the child is allowed to make in one situation may be unacceptable in other situations. In each of these cases, the goal of socialization training is to suppress the current behavior and to teach the child new responses more appropriate for the given situation (Bandura & Walters, 1963).

The effectiveness of punishment in controlling behavior was questioned as a result of early studies (e.g., Estes, 1944; Liddell, 1944; Masserman, 1943). In these studies, the evidence seemed to indicate that punishment had only a *temporary* suppressive effect on behavior and actually *disrupted* adaptive behavior. Some learning theorists argued that punishment was an undesirable form of control that could have traumatic emotional consequences (e.g., Skinner, 1938; Thorndike, 1932).

The early research can be challenged, however, for not representing the conditions under which much of human socialization occurs. In most of the early studies, animals were placed in an instrumental learning situation under conditions of strong motivation. They were then punished for performing instrumental responses directed at reducing strong appetitive or aversive drives. Often there were no alternative responses available to the organism. Consequently, it is not surprising that their behavior was disrupted and maladaptive.

Under different conditions, the evidence indicates that consistent and intense aversive stimulation can effectively suppress undesirable behavior, especially if carefully applied (Church, 1963; Solomon, 1964). In fact, as Solomon (1964) has noted, it is possible to vary the conditions under which punishment is administered in such a way as to obtain almost any outcomes from complete suppression to strong enhancement of behavior. Experimental studies with animals have demonstrated that variations in such parameters as the intensity, frequency, and timing of punishment can lead to dramatically different consequences in behavior. There is no justification for concluding that the effects of punishment are inevitably temporary and disruptive. Instead, under appropriate conditions, punishment can have *permanent* and *adaptive* results.

Investigations with children in social-learning situations have also shown punishment to be a highly effective means of control. Studies with children differ from animal studies, however, in that the punishments employed typically reproduce the conditions under which socialization normally occurs in our culture. For this reason, the usual forms of punishment employed in these studies have been verbal disapproval, indications of displeasure, and other mildly aversive stimuli.

Bandura and Walters (1963) hypothesized that the effectiveness of punishment on the behavior of children is a function primarily of the *displeasure of the agent* and only secondarily of the pain-producing characteristics of the punishment. Since the agent of punishment has typically been the source of rewards, punishment at his hands is effective because it signifies the withdrawal of rewards.

Parke and Walters (1967) attempted to test this hypothesis by having two groups of subjects, one of which consisted of six- to eight-year-old boys who experienced positive interaction with the experimenter on two successive days. In these sessions the experimenter played with them and encouraged them by warmly expressing approval of their efforts in play activities. For the other group, the experimenter merely sat in the same room without interacting with the boys. In the training trials, the boys were required to choose one of a pair of toys some of which they were previously told were for another boy. Whenever the subjects reached for or touched a toy for another boy, he received a combination of physical and verbal punishments. After the training, the child was left alone for a fifteen-minute period in a room with the punishment-associated toys. The number of times each subject touched the toys, the latency of his first deviation, and the duration of his deviations were recorded by observers seated behind a one-way mirror.

The results supported the Bandura and Walters hypothesis. Children who had experienced positive interaction with the agent of punishment showed significantly greater resistance to deviation than subjects who had only impersonal contact. The hypothesis is also supported by data from the work of Sears, Maccoby, and Levin (1957) which indicated that punishment (spanking) was found to be an effective instrument of discipline by mothers rated as warm and affectionate.

In their studies, Parke and Walters (1967) also manipulated the *intensity* of punishment in an effort to determine the effect of this variable on the control of behavior. In general, a high-intensity physical punishment (a 96-decibel tone) was more effective than a low-intensity (68-decibel tone) punishment in inhibiting behavior. In certain circumstances, however, a low-intensity physical punishment was more effective. Thus in one experiment Parke and Walters found that a low-intensity punishment, when combined with a late rather than an early administration of punishment, had considerable suppressive effect. In this condition the effect of punishment (administered after the child was actually holding the forbidden toy) appeared to be less emotional or fear-provoking than when it was given early (when the child reached for the prohibited toy). Punishment in the early condition seems to maximize anxiety (Aronfreed, 1966; Aronfreed & Reber, 1965), whereas punishment in the late condition seems to have a cognitive function—possibly acting as a cue to focus the child's attention on the disapproved activity and to signal the agent's disapproval.

Aronfreed and Leff (1963) also found that low-intensity punishment could be more effective than high-intensity punishment under certain circumstances. In their study, six- to seven-year-old boys were required to choose between two small toys roughly comparable in attractiveness but differing along certain stimulus dimensions. In a simple discrimination situation, the child was punished for choosing red toys instead of yellow ones. In a more complex discrimination situation, the child was punished for choosing toys that had an active internal mechanism rather than toys that represented passive containers. Intensity of punishment was manipulated in both situations by a combination of verbal approval, deprivation of candy, and the sounding of a buzzer. More response inhibition was obtained among subjects in the simple discrimination task who had experienced more intense forms of punishment. In the complex task, however, response inhibition was greatest among subjects who experienced the milder punishments. Aronfreed and Leff attributed this to the higher level of anxiety that exists under high-punishment conditions and that thereby interferes with adaptive behavior.

Since punishment can produce conditioned anxiety that motivates undesirable patterns of behavior, including avoidance of the agents of punishment or hostility toward them, it has often been criticized as a method of child training. In a discussion of this issue, Walters and Parke (1967) have contended that while objections of this sort have some validity, there is considerable evidence that the suppressive effect of punishment can be sufficiently powerful to permit ample time for strengthening alternative pro-social responses. Moreover, they felt that in real-life situations, the undesirable effects may be rarer than experimental outcomes lead one to believe. That is, the agent of socialization does not punish all of the child's behavior; in fact, he is likely to reward a large proportion of it. Consequently, avoidance and hostile reactions to punishment are less typical outcomes since the relationship between the child and the socializing agents is generally a positive one.

Furthermore, as the child develops the requisite verbal skills, it becomes possible for him to identify a particular response as one of a forbidden class of responses. Parents need not punish the child each and every time he transgresses, but merely have to teach him that a given response is one of a prohibited class. Subsequently the child, through the mediation of verbal responses, will inhibit his tendency to perform responses that are within this class. Such learning requires the capacity to identify discriminative cues, including those involved in the observation of punishments administered to siblings or other children for particular behaviors.

In short, research indicates that punishment can be an effective means of controlling behavior when carefully applied. A number of investigators have suggested that the effects of punishment are more closely related to the attendant withdrawal of attention or affectional responses than they are to physical pain as such. Support for this contention comes from the finding that the more nuturant the agent of punishment, the more effective punishment is. Additional support is obtained from studies in which, under certain conditions, low-intensity punishments are found to be more effective than high-intensity punishments. In such cases punishment seems to focus the child's attention on disapproved activity and to signal disapproval on the part of the agent of socialization. Since weaker, less intense forms of punishment—particularly verbal reproaches—are more common than stronger, pain-inducing punishments in normal socialization, the most important effects of punishment may be discriminative and cognitive, rather than affective and emotional.

Internal Control

As he grows older, the child spends less time in the presence of his parents and other socializing agents, yet many of the response patterns he has learned through their training persist. Rather than depending on rewards and punishments administered by external agents, his behavior comes under internal or self-control. A number of theoretical alternatives exist to account for the process of acquiring self-control. Concepts such as introjection, internalization, the superego, conscience, and so on, have been widely used by psycho-analytically oriented theorists and others. Learning theorists, on the other hand, have usually avoided these constructs because of their surplus meaning. Instead, they have attempted to identify behavioral instances of self-control and to examine systematically the variables that affect such behavior.

SELF-CONTROL THROUGH SELF-CRITICAL RESPONSES.   One behavioral manifestation of self-control is resistance to deviation in the absence of agents of socialization. Research has indicated that a variety of conditions of learning can be employed to induce self-control of this sort. These include the direct application of reward or punishment to the child's behavior (e.g., Aronfreed & Reber, 1965; Parke & Walters, 1967) as well as observation of the consequences of the behavior of others (e.g., Bandura & Kupers, 1965; Walters & Parke, 1964; Walters, Parke, & Cane, 1965).

It then becomes necessary to explain how it is that these effects are achieved. The theorist is faced with the problem of explaining how past rewards, punishments, or observation of others affect present behavior. Most learning theorists have resorted to mediational concepts and have attempted to bridge the gap between external control and internal control through mediational responses. An example of such an approach is Aronfreed's (1964) work with self-critical responses.

According to Aronfreed, self-control is achieved because self-critical responses are associated with external punishment in such a way as to make their occurrence contiguous with the *attenuation of anxiety*. Once a child has had enough exposure to punishment for a particular transgression, he will begin to experience anxiety in anticipation of punishment. Components of punishment can therefore acquire value as signals for the termination of the child's anticipatory anxiety. Since socializing agents often include in their punishment verbalizations critical of the child's behavior, these criticisms can acquire anxiety-reducing value for the child as a result of temporal contiguity with reduction of the child's anticipatory anxiety. When the child reproduces the criticism in response to a subsequent transgression, even in the absence of socializing agents, a component of punishment is preferred to the experience of anxiety and takes on reinforcing properties.

Self-criticism in Aronfreed's view is representative of a class of responses that are acquired without occurring overtly or having discriminable effects on external reinforcing events. Instead, they are acquired because their cue properties are repeatedly presented through the external social behavior of a model in a temporal position that enables them to serve as *signals* for the reduction of an anticipatory state of anxiety. The child's subsequent emission of these responses is immediately self-reinforcing on their first occurrence.

In an experimental test of the acquisition of self-critical responses, Aronfreed (1964) employed a paradigm of socialization designed to specify the conditions under which children would acquire the use of the label "blue" to refer to their own punished behavior. The subjects (nine- and ten-year-old girls) were asked to guess which of four hidden dolls was looking at her. The girls were punished, verbally and with deprivation of candy, according to an unpredictable sequence. Thus they had no cues to identify the punished behavior before it occurred. Whenever a response occurred that was to be punished, however, a buzzer went off. Part of the agent's punitive reaction was the use of the label "blue" to refer to the child's behavior.

In the test situation, the children were again required to make guesses, but now when the buzzer went off the experimenter simply asked what had happened. The verbal replies of the girls indicated that the label "blue" was acquired to refer to transgressions. Moreover, it proved to be highly resistant to extinction over a series of non-punished trials. In contrast, the label "red," which was not associated with punishment, was not reproduced by the children even when it was used in a paradigm in which the agent had assumed a relatively nurturant role. Aronfreed saw this as evidence that the self-critical response was not simply the result of a disposition to imitate the verbalizations of the experimental agent, but had in fact acquired an intrinsic reinforcement value governed by the arousal of anxiety induced by punishment.

Aronfreed's explanation of self-control is based, therefore, on the acquisition of self-critical responses that have acquired secondary reinforcement value and that mediate behavior in the absence of agents of punishment. Other theorists (e.g., Bandura, 1969; Walters & Parke, 1967) have given anxiety a less central role and have stressed the importance of complex cognitive processes that mediate self-control behavior. Bandura's theory of observational learning, for example, places emphasis on internal representational responses that mediate overt behavior (Chapter Four). These mediational responses convey information to the observer about the characteristics of appropriate responses and permit the observer to make *judgments* as to whether a given response should be performed. They thereby mediate the form that behavior takes and allow for self-control in the absence of agents of punishment.

For many psychologists reliance on cognitive and emotional mediating events is unpalatable. Yet in spite of the resistance of Skinnerians and other learning theorists who prefer to do without such constructs, it seems likely that a great deal of attention will be given to the role of mediating processes in future theory and research on self-control in the absence of agents of socialization.

SELF-IMPOSED DELAY OF REWARD. Another behavioral manifestation of self-control is self-imposed delay of reward. In experimental paradigms investigating this phenomenon, subjects are typically given the choice of an immediate small reward or a delayed larger reward. Evidence for self-control is obtained when the subject can postpone immediate gratification in order to achieve a larger reward subsequently. This research has been comprehensively reviewed by Mischel (1966), a leading investigator in this area. It will suffice here merely to indicate some points of contact between this research and social-learning theory.

In contrast to Aronfreed's (1964, 1968) position according to which self-controlling responses are acquired through direct aversive stimulation, Mischel and his associates have based their conception of delay-of-reward behavior on a social-learning theory in which the probability for the occurrence of the behavior is a function of the subjective *expectancy* that it will lead to particular consequences in a given situation and the *reinforcement value* of those consequences (Rotter, 1954). Expectancies are regarded as a function both of direct experience with outcomes obtained in similar situations and of observational learning through which the individual observes the consequences obtained by models for particular behaviors.

According to this position, whether a child chooses an immediate outcome or larger delayed outcome depends on the relative strengths of the expectancy and reward values associated with each outcome. As the subjective value and the expectancy associated with a reward increase, the probability of its being chosen increases. Thus, when the probability associated with a delayed outcome was increased, children were found more likely to choose delayed, larger rewards (Mischel & Grusec, 1967). Similarly, when a larger reward was contingent upon successful work on a task like one on which the subject previously succeeded, it was chosen more frequently than when it was contingent upon success on a task like one on which the subject had previously failed (Mischel & Staub, 1965).

Further evidence for the importance of the relationship between expectancy and reward value was obtained in a study by Mischel and Masters (1966) in which children were subjected to frustration by having a movie they were watching interrupted close to its climax on the pretext of an electrical failure. The subjects in three different treatment conditions were told either that the failure could be repaired ($p = 1$), that there was a fifty-fifty chance it would be repaired ($p = .5$), or that there was no chance it could be repaired ($p = 0$). A control group watched the film without interruption. The children rated the movie before seeing it, after the interruption, and after the film was finished. The results showed that the value of the delayed reward was affected by the expectancy for its ultimate attainment.

When the probability of seeing the interrupted film was stated as zero, its rated value, even after the film was completed, increased significantly more than when p was .5 or 1 (Figure 7-2). Mischel and Masters interpreted these findings as indicating that in our culture unattainable positive outcomes may be more valued than those that are attainable and that, in fact, the unattainability of a particular outcome enhances its perceived desirability.

As Mischel (1966) has noted, these results have clear implications for understanding responses to imposed delay of reward. If an unattainable reward is perceived as more desirable, persons who, because of past history, expect that delayed or blocked rewards are lost irrevocably will respond quite differently from those who anticipate their ultimate attainment. The individual who has learned that blocked goals tend to be unattainable remains on the unhappy treadmill, expecting that what he wants cannot be obtained and overevaluating what he cannot have. In contrast, the person who has learned that frustrated goals ultimately tend to become available may respond with equanimity to delay of reward.

Research by Mischel (1958, 1961) with children in West Indian subcultures indicated that the socialization procedures to which these

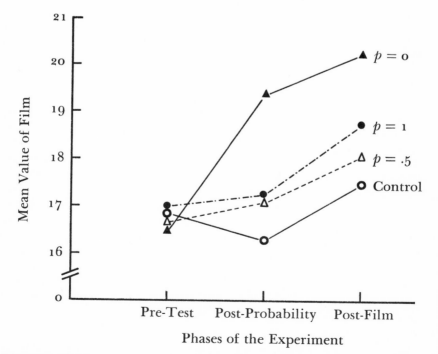

Figure 7-2. Subjects' ratings of film at each phase of the experiment (from Mischel and Masters, 1966).

children were subjected determined their tolerance of delay and their exercise of active control over the occurrence of reward. Other studies have also demonstrated that choices of delayed rewards are a function of the child's more generalized expectations of being able to predict successfully and control the available rewards in his environment. Metzner (1963), for example, found that children made voluntary choices of delayed rewards more frequently when their own performance would control the occurrence of the reward than they did when they would be required simply to wait for the reward. Bandura and Mischel (1965) found that an adult's verbalization of the relative predictability and value of immediate and delayed rewards produced shifts in the child's initial preference. Evidence from other studies (e.g., Mischel, 1966) also indicates that the child's ability to impose upon himself a delay of reward is a reflection of subjective expectancies about available rewards.

Mischel and Grusec (1967) and Grusec (1968) investigated children's ability to tolerate immediate punishment in order to avoid larger delayed punishments. The findings were consistent with the conceptualization of choice behavior as a function of reinforcement value and expectancy. As the probability associated with the delayed outcome increased, children were more likely to choose immediate smaller punishments. No relationship was obtained, however, between reward and punishment choices. That is, the evidence from both studies suggested that "ability to delay" is not a unitary trait and that the antecedents of reward and punishment choice behavior are different. While reinforcement value and expectancy are determinants of both kinds of choice, it appears that there are different antecedents when reward is involved than when punishment is involved (Grusec, 1968; Mischel, Grusec, & Masters, 1969).

INTERNAL VERSUS EXTERNAL CONTROL OF REINFORCEMENT.   Brief mention should be made at this point of Rotter's (1966) distinction between internal versus external control of reinforcement. This distinction relates to the individual's perception of a *causal relationship* between his own behavior and reward. When an event is perceived by the individual as the result of luck, chance, fate, as under the control of some powerful others, or as unpredictable because of the great complexity of the forces surrounding him, then the attribution of causality is external to the person himself. On the other hand, when the person perceives that the event is contingent upon his own behavior or his own relatively permanent characteristics, then the attribution of causality is to personal forces and control is said to be internal.

According to Rotter's (1954) social-learning theory, a reinforcement acts to strengthen the expectancy that a particular behavior or event will be followed by a reinforcement in the future. As the child develops and acquires more experience, he learns to differentiate those events that are causally related to preceding events and those that are not. If the reinforcement is seen as not contingent upon the subject's own behavior, its occurrence should not increase an expectancy as much as when it is seen as contingent. Rotter (1966) has speculated that individual differences in reinforcement history determine the degree to which reinforcement will be attributed to personal actions.

Research on internal versus external control of reinforcement has been reviewed by Rotter (1966) and Lefcourt (1966). Much of this research involves the use of the *Internal-External Control (I-C) scale* developed to measure individual differences in a generalized expectancy or belief in external control as a psychological variable (Rotter, 1966). For the most part, research has supported Rotter's theoretical predictions and indicated that the effects of external reinforcement on behavior in various task settings are systematically influenced by the individual's expectations about the extent to which the occurrence of reinforcement will be determined by his own behavior.

Little is known at this time, however, about the way in which individual differences in the perception of internal versus external control of reinforcement develop. Rotter (1966) hypothesized that expectancies generalize from a specific situation to a series of situations that are perceived as related or similar. Consequently, *generalized expectancies* are established regarding the nature of the causal relationship between one's own behavior and its consequences. These generalized expectancies result in characteristically different responses in situations culturally categorized as chance-determined versus skill-determined and may act to produce individual differences within a specific condition. Precisely what aspects of the socialization process involve the development of these generalized expectancies remains to be explored in future research.

SELF-REINFORCEMENT. One other approach to internal control has promoted a good deal of research. In this case, the behavioral manifestation of internal control is the imposition of self-regulatory standards of performance. That is, much social behavior occurs in the absence of external reinforcement and depends on self-generated reinforcement. People judge their behavior according to certain standards of self-evaluation and administer self-reward or self-punishment depending on whether their performance matches or fails to come up to self-prescribed standards. Rather than being directly the consequence of direct reinforcement, therefore, behavior is often controlled by internal, self-administered reinforcement.

One question to which researchers have directed their attention is how self-reinforcement processes are established and modified. Kanfer and his associates, for example, have studied a number of variables that affect the acquisition and characteristics of self-reinforcement responses. In their research, subjects perform a task in which there are *no objective standards for measuring successful performance*. The subject is free to administer to himself a token, point, or a prize depending on his judgment as to the adequacy of his response. The controlling variables for administering reinforcement stimuli are assumed to lie in the repertoire of discriminative stimuli in the subject's public and private behaviors. This approach to internal control, as understood by Kanfer and his associates (Kanfer, Bradley, & Marston, 1962; Kanfer & Duerfeldt, 1967a, 1967b, 1968; Marston, 1965), is essentially Skinnerian: The hope is that a parsimonious account can be given for self-control by showing that self-reinforcing operations parallel the effects of external reinforcement.

In their research with adult subjects, Kanfer and his associates have demonstrated that the rate of self-reinforcement is a function of such variables as rate of prior external reinforcement and the subject's confidence in task performance. Self-reinforcement has been found to reflect the subject's pretraining and to follow a fairly constant response pattern over various tasks. It is modifiable by social reinforcement and may take the form of negative as well as positive self-reinforcement.

These results are generally consistent with Kanfer's theoretical assumptions and point to the conditions under which ambiguous performance is self-defined as accurate. This is, however, only one aspect of self-reinforcement behavior. In many, perhaps most, social situations self-reinforcement occurs in circumstances where performance effects are not ambiguous but clearly discernible. People know how they have performed, but do not know how to *evaluate* their performance. Researchers have therefore attempted to define situations in which the tasks produce unambiguous performances that have no self-evaluative consequences.

One example is research by Bandura and Kupers (1964) in which children were exposed to a model performing a task and adopting either a high performance standard or a relatively low criterion of self-reinforcement. Whenever the model attained or exceed the self-imposed criterion, he rewarded himself and expressed positive self-evaluations. When he did not attain the criterion, he denied himself the reward and made self-critical remarks. Later the child performed the task alone (a bowling game) and received a predetermined set of scores. The dependent variable was the extent to which the child rewarded himself for his achievement.

Bandura and Kupers (1964) found that children adopted the pattern of reinforcement that they had observed the model employ. That is, lacking information as to how to evaluate his performance, the child followed the example of the model. When the model set a high standard of self-reinforcement, children were found to set a high standard and to reward themselves sparingly. When the model's standard was relatively low, children were found to consider low achievements worthy of reward and reinforced themselves generously (Figure 7-3).

These findings are supported by other studies. Mischel and Liebert (1966), for example, found that children imposed a stringent reward criterion on themselves when trained by an agent who was also self-stringent. They were less likely to do so if the agent was himself more lenient. Similar findings were reported by McMains and Liebert (1968) and Liebert and Ora (1968).

Bandura and Perloff (1967) found that under conditions of self-monitored reward—where children selected their own achievement standards and rewarded themselves whenever they attained this self-prescribed level of performance—no children chose the lowest score (which required least effort on the task). Instead, half of the children in this condition chose the highest achievement level as the minimal performance meriting self-reward. Since there was no social surveillance in this experiment, it would seem that the children had internalized in the course of socialization stringent reward criteria. Apparently, they preferred to deny themselves rewards if these rewards involved minimal effort. In terms of Rotter's (1954) social-learning theory, rewards involving more effort appear to have a higher subjective value.

In short, research on self-reinforcement has been increasingly concerned with understanding the conditions that lead to the acquisition and modification of standard-setting behavior. That is, investigators have studied how a self-prescribed standard of behavior is acquired and subsequently serves as a criterion for evaluation of the adequacy of one's performance. Such research is of importance because the processes that underlie evaluative behavior in a performance task are thought to be the same as the processes that underlie evaluative behavior in normal social interaction. That is, from a learning-theory point of view, those processes that govern the acquisition of evaluative standards on an achievement task govern the acquisition of the evaluative standards that regulate social conduct generally.

MORAL STANDARDS.   This brings us to the question of moral behavior. One of the most important methods of internal control over behavior is that achieved through moral standards. Developmental psychologists (e.g., Piaget, 1948) typically assume that moral judgments develop in accord with maturational processes and that the child progresses through a series of stages during which his moral judgments assume qualitatively different forms. Learning theorists, on the other hand, view moral judgments as responses learned like

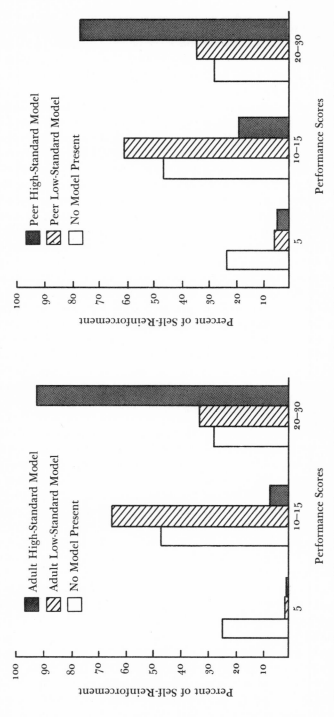

Figure 7-3. Frequency with which children rewarded themselves at three performance levels after observing models reinforce themselves either according to a high standard (score of 20 points) or a low criterion (10-point score) of achievement. Control subjects had no prior exposure to models. The figure on the left depicts the patterns of self-reward for children who observed adult models; the figure on the right presents the distribution of self-reward for children who were exposed to peer models (from Bandura and Kupers, 1964).

other responses. It follows that moral judgments can be altered when the contingencies governing learning are modified and that moral judgments are less age-specific than developmental psychologists had supposed.

In a test of this prediction, Bandura and McDonald (1963) employed an imitative learning (modeling) procedure to alter specific aspects of children's moral judgments. A series of pairs of stories that contrasted a well-intentioned act that resulted in considerable material damage with an ill-intentioned act that resulted in minor consequences was used to assess the child's orientation as to *objective* and *subjective* dimensions of morality (Piaget, 1948). In the experimental session the subjects responded alternately with a preinstructed adult. Each was read a different pair of stories in turn through a set of 24 pairs. By having the model respond in a way opposed to the child's initial style, Bandura and McDonald were able to demonstrate significant shifts from the child's initial orientation.

These findings have been replicated and the modification in style of moral judgment has been sustained over a period of two weeks (Cowan et al., 1969). Other studies, in which different techniques were employed to produce change, have demonstrated significant and enduring alterations in the style of moral judgments of grade-school children (Crowley, 1968) and adolescents (LeFurgy & Woloshin, 1969). The evidence, therefore, appears to support the learning-theory assumption that moral judgments are more modifiable and less age-specific than developmental theorists assumed.

As might be expected, this research has stimulated considerable controversy. In spite of the fact that their data replicated the findings obtained by Bandura and McDonald, Cowan and his associates (1969) questioned the adequacy of a learning-theory account of the development of moral judgments. Among other things, they argued that the data could not be explained on the basis of imitative learning. In their study, as in the Bandura and McDonald study, children had no opportunity to imitate the response of the model, since the child and the model always responded to items differing in content. Cowan and his associates felt that it was therefore not legitimate to use imitative learning as a prime explanatory concept.

As Bandura (1969) noted, however, imitative behavior need not be limited to copying or mimicry. Evidence from a number of studies (Bandura & Harris, 1965; Bandura & Mischel, 1965) indicates that observers are capable of responding in a way consistent with a model's *disposition* even though the observer never witnessed the model behave in the presence of particular stimuli. Bandura accounted for this higher-order form of modeling on the basis of vicarious discrimination training (Bandura & Harris, 1966) whereby the responses containing the relevant principle are reinforced while those lacking the relevant principle are consistently not rewarded. Presumably such behavior is mediated by symbolic representational responses.

If such a mediational explanation is to prove a viable one, a number of questions must be answered. How, for example, do children formulate the principles that govern their moral judgments? How is the ability to "abstract" relevant information from the behavior of others acquired? What are the variables that affect vicarious discrimination learning? How do the child's attributes—such as developmental status and personality characteristics—affect his capacity to make moral judgments?

The interest of psychologists with a learning-theory orientation in the question of moral behavior is relatively recent. Research in this area has only begun, although a number of learning-theory explanations have been proposed to account for the development of moral standards. In addition to Bandura's theory of observational learning, Aronfreed (1968, 1969) has proposed a mediational theory that stresses the role of cognitive and affective mediating processes. Generalized imitation, as discussed by Gewirtz (1969; Gewirtz & Stingle, 1968), has also been used to provide a learning-theory explanation for identification and the learning of moral values. The theory that succeeds in answering empirical questions such as those mentioned above can be expected to attain the greatest longevity.

THE ROLE OF GUILT IN INTERNAL CONTROL.   One mediating event that traditionally has been given prominence in discussions of internal control is the experience of guilt. Mowrer (1960b), for example, regarded guilt as a unique aspect of human socialization. It was, he felt, of central importance for understanding the phenomenon of *conscience*—the internalized sense of right and wrong. Hill (1960), in his presentation of a learning-theory approach to the acquisition of values, regarded guilt as one of the criteria of conscience and attempted to specify its behavioral correlates. Bandura and Walters (1963) and Aronfreed (1968) have discussed guilt in the context of self-critical and self-punitive responses.

Proponents of learning-theory approaches to self-control have, however, been cautious about having recourse to such concepts as guilt and conscience in accounting for self-control. Hill's (1960) discussion of these concepts represented an explicit attempt to translate them into behavioral terms and thereby integrate learning and personality theories. According to Hill, guilt and conscience can be reduced to a learning process in which the child makes a verbal response that is in effect an instruction to himself not to repeat a wrongdoing. The next time temptation comes he is likely to make this verbal response. If he succumbs to temptation, he will tend to confess before being caught and thereby avoid the temporary loss of parental affection. After repeated occasions of transgression, the child will learn the verbal response not simply to escape from parental disfavor after a transgression, but also to avoid transgressing entirely.

To define guilt solely in these terms, however, is to ignore the evidence of introspection and common usage which suggest that the experience of guilt involves anxiety aroused by the transgression and the evaluative cognition associated with it (Aronfreed, 1964). Unfortunately, it is often difficult to specify with precision behavioral reactions characteristic of guilt. Fear and shame are frequently intertwined with guilt, and it is usually impossible to separate the unique aspect of each. One could argue, for example, that guilt tends to be restricted to behavior that is primarily under the control of voluntary neural mediation, whereas fear and shame are likely to be the dominant affective reactions to behavior that is more dependent on involuntary neural mediation. On the more overtly behavioral level, it might be that a response predominantly associated with fear or shame is the response of attempting to conceal the fact of a transgression, whereas some restitutive act would be more likely to be correlated with guilt. But are various processes of self-control, such as self-criticism and self-punishment, due to guilt, shame, or fear? The answer would seem to depend on the circumstances involved in any concrete instance (Aronfreed, 1968).

The role of such internal, mediating processes in socialization is further obscured by research that indicates that identical physiological arousal (drug-induced) is interpreted differently by different subjects depending on previous learning and the person's perception of the situation (Schachter, 1964; Schachter & Singer, 1962). Thus there seems to be no correlation between physiological state and emotional state. Nor is it possible to determine with certainty the affective state an individual is experiencing solely on the basis of situational factors and overt behavior. Consequently, affective states such as guilt, shame, and fear, must be viewed as fundamentally *phenomenological* constructs. Attempts may be made to operationalize these affective states on the basis of verbal behavior, but their essential quality and the role they play in the socialization process have not, at least at the present time, been successfully analyzed.

To summarize, in this section we have seen that an intensification of interest in the process of socialization has led to increasingly refined learning-theory analyses. Rather than restricting their attention to the effects of external reinforcement and punishment, many investigators with a learning-theory orientation have become concerned with self-regulatory mechanisms: with the self-control achieved through self-reinforcement, through delay of gratification, through self-imposed standards of achievements, and through moral standards of conduct. These processes are seen to underlie much social behavior.

Theoretical explanations have stressed the role played by internal mediating mechanisms conceptualized predominately as cognitive (Bandura, 1969) or affective (Aronfreed, 1968). Traditional factors, such as guilt or shame or the notion of conscience, are looked upon with suspicion because of the difficulty of specifying these processes in behavioral terms.

JUDGMENT OF SELF AND OTHERS

During the socialization of the child, parents and others initially employ positive reinforcements and punishments in exercising control. Eventually, as the child spends more and more time out of the sphere of their influence, it becomes necessary for him to exercise his own control over socially undesirable responses. He learns to inhibit previously punished behavior, to make self-critical responses, and even to apply high standards to his own performance. Self-evaluative responses also develop with respect to oneself as an individual. We shall now turn to this question—namely, how individuals form judgments about themselves—and then examine research dealing with the way in which they form judgments about others.

Self-Judgments

In interacting with other people, the individual is constantly reinforced, positively and negatively, by them. He is praised, blamed, admired, reproached. His actions are rewarded or punished. On the basis of the feedback he derives from the environment, he forms an estimate of himself, of his own worth, and of the worth of specific behaviors.

EVALUATIVE REINFORCEMENT.   Hill (1968) has proposed that the feedback the individual receives from the social environment as to his worth and the worth of his behavior be called "evaluative reinforcement." The probability of certain responses is increased as a function of interaction with other people. Several interpretations are possible as to the specific mechanisms involved.

According to one view, for example, stimuli acquire evaluative meaning through their prior association with primary drives, especially pain. That is, negative evaluative stimuli are initially paired with primary aversive stimuli and thereby become conditioned, aversive stimuli. Proponents of this position (Dollard & Miller, 1950; Sears, Maccoby, & Levin, 1957) regarded evaluative stimuli as learned aversive drives which, like other aversive drive states, are unpleasant and motivate the individual to engage in behavior that reduces their strength.

A related view places more emphasis on the mediating role of anxiety (Brown, 1953, 1961). According to this interpretation, certain words, facial expressions, and actions become aversive because they arouse anxiety (which itself is a learned drive acquired through previous associations with pain). The child will be able to make evaluations about himself and his behavior because certain cues (signs of distress) are anxiety-provoking.

Another interpretation regards evaluative reinforcers as secondary reinforcers (Skinner, 1953) that acquire reinforcing properties through being paired with primary reinforcers. Or they may be seen as discriminative stimuli that signal positive or negative reinforcement (Hill, 1968). According to this last interpretation, evaluations are not reinforcers at all but signal the availability of reinforcement.

None of the various interpretations has solid empirical support and, while all are tenable hypotheses, more research is needed before any one interpretation can be accepted. Nonetheless, whatever the specific mechanism, learning theorists see evaluative reinforcers to be acquired through interaction with other people. If those around the child place a positive value on the label "artistic," the child will most likely incorporate this evaluation and judge artistic behavior in a positive manner. Similarly, agents of socialization teach the child that "mature" and "intelligent" have positive evaluative meaning and that certain behaviors deserve or do not deserve these labels. In this way, the child develops an impression of himself and makes judgments about his own actions.

Through evaluative reinforcement, therefore, the individual acquires a whole repertoire of verbal responses descriptive of his own behavior and its effects on others. If the child strikes another child, for example, an adult may respond by telling the child that this behavior is "cruel" and "bad." Subsequently, since "cruel" and "bad" have acquired negative evaluative meanings, they act as behavior-produced stimuli generating such responses as "I was cruel" and "I was bad." Such verbal responses, learned through evaluative reinforcement applied by the verbal community to specific behaviors, are centrally involved in what is called the "self-concept" (Staats & Staats, 1963).

SELF-APPRAISAL.   The concept of "self," of course, has quite specific meaning when used by proponents of a learning-theory, behavioral position. Skinner's definition is widely cited—namely, the self is "simply a device for representing a functionally unified system of responses" (1953, p. 285). The individual's attitude toward himself is part of this total system, and consists specifically of those responses that have acquired evaluative significance and have been applied to one's own characteristic behavior patterns.

The "self" then is a social product. As the child grows, he learns about himself. He becomes aware of his talents and his weaknesses, his likelihood of succeeding or failing in given situations, his physical and social attractiveness, his characteristic reactions. Such learning involves discriminative training and verbal behavior. The child acquires the capacity to apply evaluative reinforcers to his own behavior and he discriminates situations in which a given behavior is "good" and those situations in which it is "bad."

"Self"-learning, in this sense, never ends and is never perfect. New behavioral possibilities are always available and the individual must constantly make new discriminations. Success or failure in important enterprises have consequences for self-appraisal. Old response patterns are abandoned and new ones are learned. A number of life-transitions may occur, involving wholesale behavioral changes. Graduation from college, for example, may mean that a totally new system of responses has to be learned. The individual's appraisal of himself may be drastically altered. Behavior that has been positively evaluated in the course of the college career may now be negatively evaluated.

Such transitions highlight the importance of *situational determinants* of self-evaluation. Thus even in the normal course of events, behavior that is positively evaluated in one situation is not in another. Those responses appropriate in one setting are inappropriate in another. The complexity of human social behavior is reflected in the fact that most adults have learned, through differential reinforcement and extinction, behavior repertoires appropriate to different social situations. The individual's ability to move from one behavior repertoire to another on the basis of external, discriminative stimuli is an important factor in self-appraisal. The more skillful he is in adapting to circumstances, the more his behavior will be reinforced and the more favorable his self-evaluation.

A corollary of the approach to the "self" taken by most proponents of a learning-theory viewpoint is that a person possessing no verbal behavior of any sort would not have a "self" (Keller & Schoenfeld, 1950). Nor is self-appraisal possible without verbal behavior. Evaluative verbal responses are discriminatively conditioned to occur in the presence of certain stimuli or as a consequence of the individual's own behavior or behavior tendencies. They have been learned through contact with the verbal community and have acquired their evaluative significance because of reinforcement received from agents of socialization. Without such experience, a "concept of self" is impossible.

At this date, however, learning-theory analysis of the self and of self-appraisal remains essentially theoretical. Bem's (1967a) theory of self-perception, discussed in Chapter Five, represents an important recent development which has also provided some indirect empirical support for the "radical behaviorist" view of self-perception (Bandler,

Mandaras, & Bem, 1968; Bem, 1965). Bem's approach, it will be recalled, placed emphasis on the role of controlling stimuli available both to the individual himself and to members of the verbal community. Self-descriptive statements in this formulation are frequently based on cues available to an outside observer. It may be possible, therefore, to learn a great deal more than is known now about the determinants of self-appraisal by focusing on controlling stimulus events. Systematic research of this sort, however, has not yet been undertaken.

Judgments of Others

Besides forming judgments about himself, the individual will inevitably form judgments about other people. As he grows older, he comes into contact with more and more people. Some of these people he will immediately be attracted to, while some will arouse antipathy. In other cases, he will form no judgments until he has prolonged experience with the individual. Psychologists have been interested in the question of interpersonal judgment for some time now. Research has centered on two topics: impression formation and interpersonal liking.

IMPRESSION FORMATION.   Early psychological research on impression formation was concerned with how people recognize and identify emotions in others and how they form judgments about personality (Bruner & Tagiuri, 1954). While interest in these problems continues, the use of multidimensional scaling procedures (Cline, 1964; Jackson, Messick, & Solley, 1957; Osgood, Suci, & Tannenbaum, 1957; Rosenberg, Nelson, & Vivekananthan, 1968) has opened up new vistas for experimental exploration. A review of these developments has been presented by Tagiuri (1969).

One of the interesting issues in research on impression formation from a learning-theory point of view concerns the effect of *order of presentation*. In his classical experiment, Asch (1946) found that if socially desirable traits were presented first and then socially undesirable ones, subjects were more likely to form positive impressions; if the order in which the traits were presented was reversed, subjects were likely to form negative impressions. In both cases, therefore, primacy effects predominated. Luchins (1957) reported similar results. In his experiments, subjects were presented with two one-paragraph descriptions of an adolescent boy, one of which portrayed the boy as behaving in an extroverted manner, the other showing him as introverted. Subjects read first one paragraph and then the other, after which they indicated their impression of the boy by filling out various questionnaires. Again, the subjects' impressions were largely determined by the first block of information received.

Both Asch and Luchins interpreted these findings as indicating that items early in the sequence provided a context into which subsequent items are assimilated.

From a learning-theory viewpoint, such an explanation is rather vague and not entirely satisfactory. It implies that the first block of information somehow "sets up a direction that exerts a continuous effect on the later terms" (Asch, 1952, p. 212). Anderson and Hubert (1963), however, have demonstrated that the effects of primacy can be markedly reduced by having subjects recall adjective lists as well as forming impressions. In one of their conditions they even obtained a recency effect. Their data suggest that the critical factor is not a "context" established by initial items but simply that in such situations subjects do not attend as much to later items.

This interpretation is supported by research by Luchins (1958) in which he asked subjects to record their impressions twice, once after reading the first paragraph describing the stimulus person and again after reading both paragraphs. Impressions recorded after the first paragraph were necessarily closely related to the information in that paragraph. However, impressions recorded after both paragraphs did not indicate a primacy effect. Instead, subjects were found to change the content of their impressions abruptly in order to have them correspond to the information in the second paragraph. It would appear, therefore, that when measures are taken to assure that subjects will *attend* to later information, their impressions will reflect this information as well as earlier information.

Aside from this work on order of presentation there has been little systematic use of learning theory. Theoretical analyses of impression formation have had predominantly a cognitive flavor. Crockett (1965) has employed the notion of cognitive complexity, Fishbein (1963; Triandis & Fishbein, 1963) has related research results to cognitive consistency theory. Other approaches have also been primarily cognitive in orientation (e.g., Heider, 1958; Newcomb, 1958). Some attempts have been made to discuss impression formation in terms of general social-learning theory (Blake, 1958; Jones & Thibaut, 1958), but for the most part these approaches are exploratory and not at all exhaustive. A systematic theoretical analysis of research on impression formation in learning-theory terms has not yet been proposed.

A good deal of research has gone into determining the stimulus components of the judgmental process (e.g., Ekman, 1964; Hastorf, 1964; Jones & Davis, 1965; Pepitone, 1958). For the most part this research has indicated that almost any cues, direct or indirect, will be employed in interpersonal judgments. These cues derive both from the stimulus person and from the situation. There is considerable agreement among judges as to the value or "meaning" of particular stimuli. Nevertheless, the judgment that a person makes on the basis of stimulus information appears to involve more than the sum of the component parts. Some higher-order integration appears to occur. Presumably, an analysis of this process could be made employing learning-theory principles, but for the most part investigators have preferred to have recourse to cognitive (or perceptual) explanations.

INTERPERSONAL ATTRACTION.   In contract, research and theory on one particular aspect of interpersonal judgment—namely, the dimension of attraction—has been largely influenced by learning theory. The basic principle underlying work in this area is that two people will interact with each other to the extent that reciprocal rewards follow from their interaction. As we have seen, such a principle can be found in the social-learning theories of Homans (1961), Thibaut and Kelley (1959), and even Hull (1952). Its application to the specific area of interpersonal attraction can be credited primarily to Newcomb (1953, 1956). Elaboration and systematic investigation, however, were the work mainly of Byrne and his associates.

Byrne (1961) drew on Newcomb's analysis and proposed that attraction between people is a function of the extent to which reciprocal rewards are present in their interaction. He speculated that the effect of perceived similarity in attitudes would be increased liking because such similarity would be rewarding. The assumption underlying this contention is that in our culture people have well established, learned drives to be logical and to make a correct report of the environment (Dollard & Miller, 1950). People who are deficient in these respects are generally negatively evaluated. Since it is primarily through *consensual validation* that we determine whether someone else is logical or correct in interpreting environmental events, it follows that when another person offers us validation by indicating that his perceptions and attitudes are congruent with ours, the interaction is rewarding and hence the relationship is likely to be a positive one. When the other person indicates dissimilarity in perception and attitudes, the interaction is punishing, and a negative relationship is likely to be established.

To test the hypothesis that similarity in attitudes leads to interpersonal liking, Byrne (1961) administered an attitude scale to his subjects and two weeks later informed them they were to participate in a study of interpersonal prediction in which they were to see how much they could learn about members of another college class who had also been given the attitude scale. They were to form their judgments on the basis of how these "strangers" scored on the attitude scale. Actually, responses on the questionnaires were manipulated on the basis of the subject's own responses to achieve varying degrees of similarity. In accordance with his predictions, Byrne found that subjects who were given questionnaire data similar to their own, consistently evaluated the "stranger" more positively than did subjects given responses indicating dissimilar attitudes.

Byrne and Nelson (1965) attempted to proceed beyond these empirical findings and to build a theory of interpersonal attraction by specifying with more precision the relationship between stimuli that evoke differential attraction responses and interpersonal liking. In their study, students were asked to read an attitude scale purportedly filled out by an anonymous stranger and to evaluate him on a number of variables including attraction. Once again, the subjects themselves had previously filled out the questionnaire and so it was possible to vary the proportion of similar attitudes. Four levels of proportion were used, and the functional relationship between proportion of similar attitudes and attraction was found to be a linear one. Byrne and Nelson therefore proposed a tentative "law of attraction" where the attraction toward X is assumed to be a *positive linear function* of the proportion of positive reinforcements received from him (Figure 7-4). Byrne and Clore (1966) also found a positive linear relationship between the reported similarity of attitudes of the stranger to one's own and attraction. They found that the function held for three modes of presenting the stranger.

Byrne and Griffitt (1966) attempted to investigate the generality of the law of attraction by using elementary and secondary school chil-

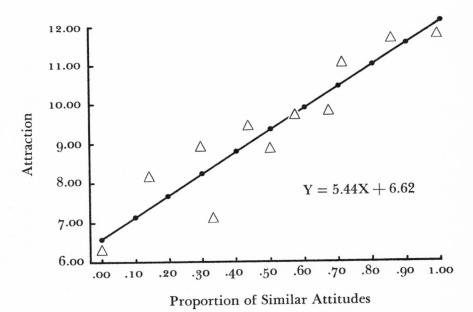

$$Y = 5.44X + 6.62$$

Proportion of Similar Attitudes

Figure 7-4. Attraction toward a stimulus person as a function of proportion of similar attitudes. The straight line function is based on 11 points representing the findings of a number of studies by Byrne and his associates (from Byrne and Forquist, 1961).

dren. Once again subjects were asked to respond to an attitude scale purportedly filled out by a stranger and then to indicate their attraction toward this stranger. At each age level, from age nine to seventeen, as degree of similarity increased, degree of attraction increased. The functions found from the data for older children, grades eight to twelve, and younger children, grades four to eight, were not appreciably different from the function reported for college students (Byrne & Clore, 1966). No developmental differences were found. Byrne and Griffitt concluded that the reinforcing effects of consensual validation are operative at least by age nine.

In a further study of the generality of the law of attraction Byrne, Griffitt, and Stefaniak (1967) employed personality characteristics rather than attitude statements as the source of reinforcement. They gave their subjects responses of a stranger to the Repression-Sensitization scale (Byrne, Barry, & Nelson, 1963). The stranger responded as the subject did to 20 percent, 50 percent, or 80 percent of the items. On a subsequent experiment, the stranger's responses did not correspond at all, corresponded in half the cases, or in all the cases to those of the subject himself. In both experiments, a linear relationship was obtained between degree of similarity and attraction, and the functions did not depart significantly from those obtained in studies in which responses on an attitude scale were used as the measure of similarity.

One difficulty with studies dealing with personality similarity and attraction, however, is that by creating a "stranger" differing from the subject along the personality dimension, it becomes highly likely that the experimenter has created a stimulus person differing to the same extent along the *likableness* dimension. That is, the subject is likely to choose likable traits as self-descriptive. If this is true, then the stimulus person will vary concomitantly in the possession of likable characteristics. A more similar "stranger" will be more likable, while a less similar "stranger" will be less so. There should be some demonstration that the stimulus person's similarity to the subject, over and above his possession of likable characteristics, affects the subject's appraisal.

There is some evidence, however, that when degree of likableness is controlled, the relationship between personality similarity and attraction is considerably weakened. In fact, McLaughlin (1970) failed to find a significant relationship between similarity and attraction when self-descriptive adjectives that had served as the basis for manipulating the similarity dimension were rated for likableness (Anderson, 1968) and these values were used as a control in an analysis of covariance design. It may be, therefore, that the typical finding of a positive relationship between personality similarity and attraction is largely a function of likableness.

Such results do not, of course, invalidate Byrne's theoretical contentions. They merely suggest that one of the reasons why similar attributes are more reinforcing to the individual may be that they are more likable and more socially desirable. When a stimulus person is dissimilar to the subject, he will also tend to possess traits that are less likable and less socially desirable. Consequently, the subject will be less attracted to him.

A number of studies have been conducted that indicate that *variations* in the general law of attraction are possible. Byrne and Rhamey (1965), for example, conducted an experiment in which the stranger was said to have evaluated the subject in the same manner as the subject was about to evaluate him. This information was given to the subject who therefore formed an opinion about the stranger both on the basis of what the stranger had said about him and on the basis of the stranger's responses on an attitude scale. If the stranger had given a positive evaluation of the subject, this was found to enhance significantly the subject's rating of the stranger (as compared to a control group that made its judgments solely on the basis of attitude responses). If the stranger's ratings were negative, the subject's ratings were significantly depressed. Byrne and Rhamey concluded that the equation for the law of attraction should include a weighting factor to take into account reinforcement magnitude. Presumably, a positive evaluation from the stranger in addition to similar attitude responses constitutes a reinforcement of greater magnitude than similar attitude responses alone.

In another study, Byrne and McGraw (1964) found that the fact that the stranger was a Negro did not affect the law of attraction when low-prejudice subjects were used. With high-prejudice subjects, however, the direct linear relationship between similarity and attraction was not obtained. High-prejudice subjects were found to respond positively to a Negro stranger only if the stranger was exactly similar to themselves in attitudes. If not, their response tended to be one of indifference or even dislike.

Novak and Lerner (1968) have shown that, under certain circumstances, people will be more likely to reject than accept someone similar to themselves. In their study, the stranger was presented as either similar or dissimilar to the subject on the basis of information from attitude scales. For half of the subjects in each condition, the stranger was further presented as emotionally disturbed, while for the other half he was presented as normal. Subjects were found to rate an emotionally disturbed stranger as less attractive than a normal stranger, although in both cases the similar stranger was rated more favorably than the dissimilar. When subjects were asked about their willingness to interact with the stranger, the data indicated a willingness to interact with similar normal strangers, but not with similar disturbed strangers. In fact, subjects were more willing to interact with a disturbed stranger who was dissimilar to them than they were to interact with one similar to them. Apparently, in Byrne's terms, the belief that another person is emotionally disturbed constitutes a negative reinforcement that is especially effective if that person is perceived as similar to oneself.

In this section we have discussed learning-theory approaches to the formation of judgments about self and others. From a learning-theory point of view such judgments are consequences of social exchange and the reinforcing consequences of social interaction. The individual forms his self-judgments on the basis of his experience with other people and learns to value what "significant others" (socializing agents and peers) value. Judgments of other people are largely a function of reinforcing consequences: It is more reinforcing to find other people who share one's own attitudes, values, and personality characteristics. Consequently the individual is more positively attracted to other people who are similar to him in these characteristics. He judges them more favorably—as a rule—than others who are different from him.

GROUP INTERACTION

Interpersonal attraction frequently involves more than two persons. Often mutual liking and attraction lead to increasing amounts of interaction among a group of people. The psychology of group behavior has many aspects, but learning-theory analyses of group processes have been concerned mainly with the conditions that lead to liking among group members and with the results that follow mutual attraction. The assumption is made that the greater the mutual attraction between the members, the greater the cohesiveness of the group. We shall discuss theory and research bearing on the issue of group cohesiveness and then turn to some of the effects of cohesiveness on group behavior.

Group Cohesiveness

Learning-theory analyses of group processes place central emphasis on the role of reinforcement in interpersonal behavior. The more reinforcing a behavior is to group members, the more likely it is to occur. In group interaction, however, the relationship between reinforcement and behavior is considerably more complex than it is in one- or even two-person situations. In a group, giving reinforcement to one person may require punishing other persons. Consequently, the use of principles of learning requires taking into account variables that may modify or even offset typical effects. Relatively complex social-learning theories have been proposed that deal explicitly with the effects of reward on group processes and group cohesiveness, and we shall review these briefly before turning to empirical research.

REWARDS AND COSTS.   In Chapter One we discussed the social learning theories of George Homans (1961) and Thibaut and Kelley (1959). In both cases analysis of social interaction was carried out in terms of rewards and costs. For Homans, rewards consisted of what was received in an exchange, less costs incurred. Costs referred to what was given up in an exchange, such as giving up the rewards obtainable in another exchange, or the risks involved in the exchange itself. In any social interaction, each person hopes to receive his fair share of the rewards ("distributive justice").

One of the assumptions of Homans' theory is that the activity (overt behavior) and sentiments (overt behavior representing attitudes and feelings) that an individual emits in response to another person is *valuable* to that other person. The more valuable a person's activities and sentiments are to others, the greater the esteem in which he is held. It is hypothesized that persons provide more value to one another to the extent that they have the same orientation or the same background. Group cohesiveness is a function of the values of the different rewards available to members of the group, and thus the more valuable the activities and sentiments of group members for each individual member, the greater the cohesiveness.

The leader of the group earns his authority by acquiring esteem, and he acquires esteem by rewarding others. Since, however, the man holding authority most probably has imposed costs on others by use of punishment or simply by depriving them of the rewards associated with leadership, the sentiments that develop toward him are likely to be ambivalent.

Thibaut and Kelley (1959) introduced the additional concept of *control*. The extent to which one person controls another is determined by the degree to which he can affect the outcome of another's behavior. Status is a function of control, and higher-status persons are preferred because they have greater extrinsic means for rewarding others. In fact, mere association or contiguity with such persons may provide reward.

Group members are attracted to each other, according to Thibaut and Kelley, because of the relationship between rewards and costs. If rewards can be maximized and costs minimized, then more attraction is likely to occur between members and group cohesiveness is likely to be great. This is most probable when value similarity exists, because individuals are in need of support in value areas and the perception of similarity is therefore rewarding. Value support has "learned reinforcement value" (1959, p. 42).

Thibaut and Kelley noted that although certain events may have some absolute evaluative significance, persons generally evaluate events in relative terms. The evaluative standards that a person applies to the outcomes of interactions in terms of rewards and costs are based largely on past experience and present motivation. This base line for comparison Thibaut and Kelley called the *comparison level* (CL). The CL is the reference point for behavior at any given instance. Those behaviors that are above the CL are positively evaluated, while those below are negatively evaluated. Since, however, the CL varies in accordance with experience, considerable individual differences can exist. A person who feels that he is competent and has high self-esteem will generally have a higher CL than a person who feels inferior.

In interpersonal behavior, the person's attraction to others will depend upon the evaluation of his outcomes in relation to his CL. It is further hypothesized that those outcomes for which the individual feels himself responsible will have a greater effect in determining the CL than those which the person feels were directed at him by chance or fate. Thus the CL will undergo modification when the person perceives that others are behaving toward him because of his actions. His behavior involves some costs, and he will consequently demand more from others under these circumstances than if he feels that their behavior toward him is spontaneous and not prompted by anything that he himself has done.

Other learning-theory explanations of group cohesiveness have also been proposed. Essentially all of these theories employ the principle of reinforcement, although with some variations. Lott (1961), for example, has argued that the primary condition for the development of mutual attraction between members of a group is the attainment of goals or reception of rewards in one another's presence. The more frequently a particular group member is associated with the achievement of goals, the greater the strength of the positive attitudes developed toward him.

Newcomb (1956) has presented a similar theory in which he postulated that the reinforcement one member receives from another is the major determinant of attraction toward him. Similar attitudes are more rewarding, and individuals are thought to have lower thresholds for interaction with persons who offer greater likelihood of reward. It is possible, however, for persons who do not share a great number of similar attitudes to acquire positive feelings toward each other if they are forced to interact for long periods of time in close propinquity. Under such conditions, reinforcing responses will be more frequently given than punishing responses, and the two parties will learn to emphasize those attitudes that they hold in common and to de-emphasize those that separate them. In the absence of forced proximity, however, individuals will choose to interact with others who are perceived as agreeing with them, especially on important and relevant issues (Newcomb, 1958).

Pepitone (1958) has taken a reinforcement-theory approach to the question of the attractiveness of people, but he has argued that it is not satisfactory simply to assume that attraction results from reinforcement or need satisfaction. Such a statement is too general, he argued, and merely restates the problem at a higher level of abstraction. What must be known is what particular factors produce change in attraction. Pepitone proposed that interpersonal relations are composed of valued acts and that the value assigned to an act depends on certain dimensions of "social causality." These include: (1) responsibility, or the perception of causality, (2) intentionality, or the intention of the actor, and (3) justifiability, or the question of whether the act deviates from some valued expectancy. Each of these has a predictable relationship with attraction.

MUTUAL ATTRACTION.   Empirical research has clearly demonstrated the *effectiveness* of rewards on interpersonal attraction. Solomon (1960), for instance, found that subjects who communicated with partners through electric switches developed greater liking toward those partners whose game strategy provided them with maximal gain. Other studies also have shown that persons are more positively evaluated when they help group members realize their goals (e.g., Berkowitz, 1957; Horwitz, 1958; Stotland & Hillmer, 1962). In general, research has supported theories of social exchange: People value others to the extent that their interaction is rewarding (e.g., Deutsch & Solomon, 1959; Howard & Berkowitz, 1958; Jones & Ratner, 1967).

Researchers have therefore attempted to define those conditions that *maximize* or *minimize* this effect. Kleiner (1960), for example, conducted an experiment in which a confederate of the experimenter was greatly instrumental in improving group performance. When the improvement produced a large reduction in threat of failure, measures of degree of liking and desirability of knowing the confederate were significantly greater than when threat reduction was small. Presumably, the reward derived from the confederate's contribution to group performance was greater in high-threat conditions. Other research has indicated that the reward derived from group participation is greater when the group is successful in realizing its goals than when the group fails (Heber & Heber, 1957; Hoffman, 1958).

Lott and Lott (1960) reported evidence in support of their contention that group attraction is related to the attainment of goals in one another's presence. They found that children who had been successful in a group game tended to choose a greater proportion of their fellow children on a sociometric test than did unsuccessful children. These findings were confirmed by James and Lott (1964).

Goal attainment therefore seems to emerge strongly as a factor that determines the reward value of the group to individual members. Yet the members reward one another in other ways. Thibaut and Kelley (1959), for example, stressed the importance of value support. Group interaction is rewarding because individuals find support in the group for their attitudes and opinions. Evidence for such a source of reward was obtained in a study by Hagstrom and Selvan (1965) in which ratings of group attraction were found to depend on both "social satisfaction" and "social cohesion." The first of these factors relates to attraction to the group as an *instrument of task perform-ance,* the second to attraction to the group as a *source of value sup-port.* Thus the group appears to have at least two sources of reinforcement at its disposal: It can reinforce the member by helping him realize his goals or by providing "consensual validity" (Byrne, 1961) to the member's values.

Pepitone (1958), as we have seen, has also been concerned with the sources of reinforcement involved in group behavior. In one of his studies (Pepitone & Kleiner, 1957) it was found that boys who had a fairly high expectation of winning a tournament of competitive activities increased in interpersonal liking significantly more over the course of the tournament than did boys who had a low expectation of winning. Pepitone (1958) interpreted these results as indicating that under conditions where team members had a high expectation of success, they tended to "thank" each other through the medium of sociometric choice for having brought it about. If responsibility had been attributed to some external source—such as "luck," the experimenter, or the other team—there would be no relationship between expectation of success and interpersonal liking. Further research conducted by Pepitone and his associates (Pepitone, 1964) has yielded results generally favorable to theoretical expectations.

A thorough review of the literature relating to group cohesiveness has been presented by Lott and Lott (1965). They discussed a number of the above-mentioned studies as well as other studies dealing with the consequences of reward (in the form of successful task completion) on group cohesiveness. They also discussed studies dealing with the effects of similar attitudes and values on interpersonal attraction and group cohesiveness. For the most part, the evidence indicates that reward (conceptualized either as successful task completion or con-sensual validation accruing from the perception of similar attitudes and values) leads to increased group cohesiveness.

Thus far we have restricted our attention to the effect of rein-forcement on interpersonal attraction and group cohesiveness. It should be noted, however, that reinforcement also affects other dimensions of group response and the response of individuals within the group. Bavelas and his associates (Bavelas, Hastorf, Gross, & Kite, 1965), for example, conducted a series of experiments in which they demonstrated that reinforcement via "feedback lights" was effective in altering verbal output among group members and their sociometric positions in four-man groups. Butler and Miller (1965) found that subjects who were more successful in rewarding or punishing others in the group received relatively more rewards and fewer punishments in the course of group interaction. Worthy, Gary, and Kahn (1969) conceptualized self-disclosure as a form of social reward and demonstrated that subjects tended to disclose more intimate information about themselves to other subjects from whom they had received more intimate information.

These last two studies provide empirical support for predictions based on principles of rewards and costs. The findings of Butler and Miller are in accord with the prediction of Thibaut and Kelley (1959) that individuals who exert more "control" in the group (who are more effective in determining the outcome of the behavior of others) are more favorably treated by group members. The research of Worthy and his associates supports Homans' (1961) prediction that people will behave in a manner that is in accord with "distributive justice" and that leads to a fair exchange between individuals.

Not all questions have been answered in this research, but some major theoretical predictions originating in reward-cost analyses of social exchange have been supported. Further validation comes from studies on laboratory game situations (Kelley, 1968). In general, the prediction that greater rewards are associated with greater interpersonal attraction and greater group cohesiveness stands up well. We shall turn now to a related empirical question—the effect of group cohesiveness on the behavior of members of the group. Here interpersonal attraction is not a dependent variable, but the independent variable in research.

Group Influence

The influence of the group on its members is determined to a considerable extent by the cohesiveness of the group. The more the members of the group like each other, the more influence the group can be expected to exert on individual members. The effects on behavior are not, however, immediately obvious.

EFFECTS OF INTERPERSONAL ATTRACTION.   One area of research interest has been *group performance*. There is some evidence that high interpersonal attraction among members facilitates task performance (Chapman & Campbell, 1957; Gardner & Thompson, 1956; Lott, 1961) and increases group productivity (Deutsch, 1960). Not all results, however, have been supportive (e.g., Fiedler, 1953; Hoffman & Maier, 1961). In fact, Stogdill (1959) has suggested that "the effort that is devoted to the development of integration might be conceived as a subtraction from the efforts that are devoted to productivity" (p. 269).

Other negative results have been obtained in research on the effect of intragroup attraction on learning. Yuker (1955) found no differences in recall for material presented to members of competitive groups (low intragroup attraction) and cooperative groups (high intragroup attraction). Shaw and Shaw (1962) found that second-grade children's ability to learn a list of spelling words correlated with group cohesiveness in the beginning of the period of interaction, but not in the end. In short, the evidence strongly suggests that several factors—such as the nature of the task, the strength of the bond between the members, and possibly others—affect the relationship between group attraction and group performance.

Besides task performance, researchers have been interested in the effect of intragroup attraction on *member conformity*. Thibaut and Kelley (1959) predicted that cohesiveness leads to an increase in the group's ability to make demands and the member's ability to resist demands. Ordinarily this would lead to increased conflict, but since group interaction is rewarding, members find ways to avoid conflict. Thus they may define a range of issues where conformity is expected, or they may yield to the authority of a leader.

In support of the Thibaut and Kelley prediction, the usual relationship obtained in studies of group attraction and conformity is a positive one (Lott & Lott, 1965). Lott and Lott (1961), for example, obtained a significant relationship between the degree of intermember attraction and conformity to a purported group standard with respect to an opinion question. Berkowitz (1957) had subjects work at a task under simulated group conditions and found that conformity to responses of partners on a task was a function of liking the partners.

There are some puzzling findings, however. In one study, (Schachter, Ellertson, McBride, & Gregory, 1951), it was found that people in high-cohesive groups followed group standards when there was little pressure to be productive to a greater extent than did people in low-cohesive groups. When pressure to be productive was increased, however, the cohesiveness variable made no difference. Festinger and Thibaut (1951) reported that the perception of similarity between members of a simulated group led to conformity of opinion regarding a football strategy problem but not regarding the treatment that should be given a hypothetical delinquent boy. Dittes and Kelley (1956) found that individuals who had either a very high or a very low acceptance as group members tended to conform less than those members with moderate acceptance.

It appears, therefore, that a number of variables—such as the external pressures, the nature of the issue, and the position of the member in the group—affect the extent to which intermember attraction determines conformity. The evidence suggests once again that the effects of interpersonal attraction on the behavior of group members is a complex function of a number of parameters. Theoretical precision, if it is to be achieved at all, will apparently be achieved at the price of simplicity.

REINFORCEMENT AND CONFORMITY.   Since a great deal of research has gone into the study of conformity we shall conclude this section by mentioning briefly some learning-theory analyses in this area. Besides interpersonal attraction other independent variables have been studied, such as the nature of the stimulus item, group size, and variations in pressure to conform (Asch, 1952; Blake & Mouton, 1961). Conformity has been shown to increase when it is necessary for the individual to rely on the responses of others in making his own response. The point has therefore been made that conformity is often psychologically and socially *economical* (Hollander & Willis, 1967).

This instrumental function of conformity behavior was stressed by Walker and Heyns (1962) who argued that conforming behavior is an instrumental act leading to need satisfaction and goal attainment and is therefore modifiable via reinforcement. While other variables are admittedly important, reinforcement from the social environment can be a critical factor in determining the amount and nature of conformity behavior. In experiments on conformity, a major source of social reinforcement has been *feedback* from the experimenter. Jones, Wells, and Torrey (1958) found that experimenter feedback in terms of contrived group consensus was highly effective in producing conformity when the importance of group accuracy was stressed. Feedback in terms of objective reality reduced conformity, although it did so to a lesser degree when group accuracy and conformity were emphasized. Other studies have shown that when the experimenter informs the subject of the accuracy of his responses prior to the subject's receiving conflicting information from other subjects, conformity to the group response is greatly reduced (Kelman, 1951; Luchins & Luchins, 1961). Endler and his associates (Endler, 1965, 1966; Endler & Hoy, 1967) have also shown that varying conditions of social reinforcement produces different degrees of conformity behavior.

In these studies, reinforcement has been conceptualized exclusively in terms of feedback from the experimenter. Other reinforcing processes, however, may be operative. Social-learning theory, especially the exchange theories of Homans (1961) and Thibaut and Kelley (1959), regards conformity as a social process in which positive reinforcement effects are produced through interaction with others. Conformity is either a *deserved reward* given to others to facilitate social exchange and to bring about rewarding exchanges in the future, or it is *payment in advance* for anticipated rewards.

Jones' (1964, 1965) work on "ingratiation" derived from such a frame of reference. According to Jones, conformity, especially opinion conformity, is often used as an ingratiation technique. It is employed instrumentally as a means for securing anticipated rewards. Jones and Jones (1964) found that those subjects who were most concerned with becoming attractive to the other person showed moderate conformity to the other's opinions, avoiding consistent agreement or disagreement. The subject apparently did not wish to seem either too compliant or too discrepant. Jones and Jones referred to this as the "self-presentation dilemma" in which the subject is attempting to maintain his integrity. In those cases where subjects did show a great deal of conformity, they tended to justify this behavior by reporting high confidence in their opinion and greater attraction to the target person.

Other investigations support the notion that conformity behavior often serves as a means for securing rewards. Davis and Forquist (1965) spoke of the "tactical" use of conformity in a study in which they reported that, although subordinates would disagree with their superior, they would evaluate the superior's arguments more favorably the more they depended on him to supply future rewards. In a study by Zeff and Iverson (1966) group members whose positions in a group were threatened by the prospect of being moved to an inferior group were found to conform to the other members' opinions to a greater extent than did group members who had the prospect of moving to a superior group. Jones, Gergen, Gumpert, and Thibaut (1965) found that, when the target person appeared to be susceptible to influence in his evaluation of the subject's performance, subjects used tactics of opinion conformity in an attempt to influence that evaluation.

Conformity behavior can be acquired, therefore, because of reinforcements that accrue directly from the behavior itself—as is the case in studies where experimenter feedback is employed as a reinforcing device—or because of reinforcements that can be expected to follow upon the behavior in the future—as is the case in the "ingratiation" studies. In addition, as we have seen, subjects may conform to group norms because of an attraction to group members based on consensual validation or experiences of past success. In such cases, the reinforcement is apparently intrinsic to the group process. Group interaction is in itself reinforcing.

In this section we have reviewed only a small portion of the vast amount of research that has been conducted in the area of group behavior. Table 7-1 provides an overview, although the relationships specified there between independent and dependent variables may be

Table 7-1
Some Results of Research Prompted by a
Learning-Theory Approach to Group Behavior

INDEPENDENT VARIABLE		DEPENDENT VARIABLE
Goal Attainment	⟶ (Increases)	Interpersonal Attraction (*Berkowitz, 1957; Horwitz, 1958; Lott & Lott, 1960; James & Lott, 1964; Stotland & Hillmer, 1962*)
Value Support and Positive Appraisal	⟶ (Increases)	Interpersonal Attraction (*Deutsch & Solomon, 1959; Hagstrom & Selvan, 1965; Jones, 1966; Jones & Ratner, 1967; Lott & Lott, 1965*)
Interpersonal Attraction	⟶ (Improves)	Group Performance (*Chapman & Campbell, 1957; Gardner & Thompson, 1956; Lott, 1961*)
Interpersonal Attraction	⟶ (Increases)	Member Conformity (*Berkowitz, 1957; Lott & Lott, 1961; Lott & Lott, 1965*)
Feedback (Direct Rewards)	(Increases or Decreases)	Member Conformity (*Endler, 1965, 1966; Jones et al., 1958; Kelman, 1951; Luchins & Luchins, 1961*)
Anticipated Rewards	(Increases or Decreases)	Member Conformity (*Jones, 1964, 1965; Jones et al., 1965; Jones & Jones, 1964; Zeff & Iverson, 1966*)

modified considerably by the introduction of additional variables.
Goal attainment and value consensus generally produce increased
attraction between group members. Learning theorists argue that this
is because goal attainment and value consensus are reinforcing to the
individual member. Interpersonal attraction is itself a source of reinforcement that leads to superior group performance and increased
member conformity. Other sources of reinforcement also bring about
conformity, especially feedback as to the success or accuracy of one's
responses and the expectation of rewards in the future.

EVALUATION AND CONCLUDING COMMENTS

The notion of interpersonal behavior employed in this chapter is
not significantly different from that used in the rest of this book. In
this chapter, we have directed our attention to theory and research

dealing with the socialization process, judgment of self and others, and group interaction. All the preceding chapters have been similarly concerned with phenomena that occur in the course of social interactions. Consequently, much of what we say here refers not simply to the learning-theory approaches we have discussed in this chapter but to learning-theory approaches to social behavior generally, as discussed throughout the book.

In spite of the differences between learning theorists, common elements exist that are shared by all variants of behaviorism. The principle of reinforcement, the use of conditioning models, associationistic learning—these features are central to all contemporary learning theories. Yet researchers have become increasingly aware of the need for extending and enlarging the capacities of the theory. In human social behavior a great deal occurs that cannot be explained simply by recourse to traditional learning principles. To take one example—investigations of the socialization process indicate that much of the child's learning occurs through observation of other people in the social environment. The work of Bandura and his associates on observational learning constitutes an important advance in learning-theory analyses of social behavior.

Another example concerns the traditional concept of *reinforcement*. It is now widely accepted that much behavior is determined not by external reinforcement as traditionally conceived but by internal self-reinforcement. That is, researchers have come to accept the possibility of the child's rewarding himself for certain behaviors in the absence of agents of socialization. Numerous studies of various aspects of self-control have confirmed the importance of these internal, self-regulatory processes.

Research has also shown that external forms of reinforcement in social settings may be quite complex. In the socialization process, for example, relatively subtle aspects of the parent-child relationship are apparently important determinants of behavior. Facial cues or gestures may acquire reinforcing potential, and it may be these cues rather than more overt behavioral responses on the part of the parent that control behavior.

Frequently, however, investigators have shown little interest in identifying conditions of reinforcement. In investigations of conformity behavior, for instance, it is usually assumed that conformity is instrumental to the attainment of future rewards. Yet there has been little systematic research into the question of what these rewards are. This type of usage is common in much of the research in a learning-theory framework. If hard pressed, the theorist would probably be able to spell out in abstract terms the definitional properties of a reinforcement, but as the term is used to explain social behavior it apparently includes an enormous range of stimuli, most of which are conditioned rather than unconditioned reinforcers.

This relates closely to another definitional problem involving basic terms. The concepts of *stimulus and response,* like the term reinforcement, are often used by advocates of a learning-theory position without definitional specification. Frequently no attempt is made to identify the properties of a stimulus or a response. This becomes apparent when one considers that for some theorists a person, as such, constitutes a stimulus event, whereas for other theorists each discrete response that the person makes—his verbal and motor responses, his physical characteristics, his mannerisms—all are viewed as stimuli that affect the behavior of others. In many cases, theorists seem to use stimulus-response language in an analogous rather than a literal sense. Extrapolations are made from laboratory experimentation where usage is relatively rigorous to social situations where usage is vague and imprecise.

There is, however, an increasing awareness of the dangers of extrapolation from laboratory experiments to human social behavior. In general, the tendency has been to derive behavioral explanations of social phenomena from the study of social behavior directly rather than to deduce the explanation from general learning theory. Theorists have preferred to work out laws of learning that apply specifically to the particular social phenomenon in question. Thus some investigators have conducted extensive studies of imitation and vicarious learning, others have focused on speech and language learning, while still others have devoted their attention to the effects of punishment. In each case, systematic investigation of the variables that affect the phenomenon in question have been conducted, often with considerable success. Continued efforts in this direction should lead to significant theoretical and empirical advances and should produce an understanding of the dynamics of social behavior in learning-theory terms that does not involve unwarranted generalizations or extrapolation from single-organism laboratory experiments.

Some of the research discussed in the present chapter exemplifies this tendency to focus on independent phenomena systematically. The study of self-reinforcement and standard-setting behavior, for instance, has led to clarification of processes crucial to socialization. Kanfer, Bandura, and their associates have displayed considerable experimental ingenuity in investigating the variables that affect self-reinforcement in complex social settings. The research of Byrne and his coworkers on the relationship between similarity and attraction is another case in point. By manipulating the conditions that produce a perception of similarity, these investigators have defined a "law of attraction" and have, in addition, determined conditions that alter the normal positive relationship between similarity and attraction.

In other cases, however, little systematic work has been conducted and learning theorists have been content to argue that their principles apply—without demonstrating empirically how they do. In part, this is because of the evasiveness of the phenomena in question—as in the case of self-appraisal and self-perception. In part, it is because of a tendency to use learning theory loosely without much concern about the operational precision of theoretical constructs. Much of the research on group behavior suffers from this deficiency. Investigators often use learning theory as a frame of reference, but basic terms, especially the term "reinforcement," mean all things to all men.

Two final issues should be mentioned. The first of these concerns the use of *mediating S-R events* to explain human symbolic processes. Not all theorists employ such mediating events, yet many advocates of a learning-theory approach to social behavior have had recourse to such hypothetical processes in an effort to explain internal representational and emotional events. At worst, chains of mediating stimuli and responses are postulated with little or no independent evidence and without attempting to relate these events to observations. At best, some means are provided for objectively indexing events and for predicting behavioral consequences. The typical case is somewhere in between these extremes. It seems likely that the fruitful (some would say legitimate) use of hypothetical mediating processes must wait until more is known about implicit verbal behavior and about the manner in which emotional experience is encoded. That is, what is needed is research directed explicitly at determining the fundamental paradigms for verbal behavior and emotional responsiveness.

A second issue relates to the apparent *lack of communication* among advocates of learning-theory approaches to social behavior. Each man goes his own way, with little attention to what others are doing. Perhaps more progress would be made if some attempts at cross-fertilization were made. This holds both for experimentation and theory construction. Confusion in research might be avoided if there were a greater concern with replication, at least in those aspects of research where replication is possible. In this way the effects obtained in one study can be compared with those in another study and differences can be attributed to alterations in independent variables only, and not to differences in experimental design, materials used, procedures employed, and so forth. In theory construction more effort should be made to attain conceptual consistency, especially in the use of basic terms, and to determine those situations where different theoretical predictions are made. In this way the number of theories can hopefully be narrowed down, with only those of established empirical validity surviving. Of course, it may prove impossible to rule out theoretical differences entirely. The same phenomenon can be conceptualized in many different ways, just as, to use Wiest's (1967) example, it is possible to conceptualize the falling of a leaf as reflecting its manifest destiny, its intention, or the will of God.

Theoretical differences will most likely persist, even within the ranks of those proposing learning-theory interpretations. For the Skinnerians, the postulation of mediating concepts is whistling in the dark. For others, such mediating concepts are absolutely necessary if some insight is to be obtained into the nature of language and verbal behavior. All agree, however, that the starting point must be publicly observable facts and that what one looks at and hopes to measure is behavior, not some private, inner state.

There are, of course, large gaps of ignorance concerning many of the causes of social behavior. Nevertheless a great deal of work has been done and is being done to reduce this ignorance by experimental analysis of the identifiable variables that control human behavior. In the course of this book we have seen numerous examples of important research with children and adult subjects in social settings. Yet in many areas this research represents merely a first approximation to major substantive issues, and serious difficulties remain. This is especially true of language and verbal behavior. Since overt verbal responses and covert (mediating) verbal responses are of such great importance for other forms of social behavior, learning theorists will have to give concentrated attention to this area if their theories are to withstand empirical scrutiny. How well they will respond to this challenge cannot be predicted. But if the history of learning theory in this country is any indication of what the future will be like, one can expect more controversy among theorists, more sophistication in research, and a growing increase in understanding.

REFERENCES

Adorno, T. W., Frenkel-Brunswik, E., Levinson, D. J., & Sanford, R. N. *The authoritarian personality*. New York: Harper, 1950.

Aiken, E. G. The effort variable in the acquisition, extinction, and spontaneous recovery of an instrumental response. *Journal of Experimental Psychology,* 1957, **43**, 47–51.

Allport, F. H. *Social psychology*. Cambridge, Mass.: Houghton-Mifflin, 1924.

Allport, G. W. The historical background of modern social psychology. In G. Lindzey & E. Aronson (Eds.), *The handbook of social psychology*. Vol. 1. 2nd ed. Reading, Mass.: Addison-Wesley, 1968. Pp. 1–80.

Allport, G. W., & Postman, L. *The psychology of rumor*. New York: Holt, 1947.

Anderson, N. Likableness ratings of 555 personality-trait names. *Journal of Personality and Social Psychology,* 1968, **9**, 262–279.

Anderson, N. H., & Hubert, S. Effects of concomitant verbal recall on order effects in personality impression formation. *Journal of Verbal Learning and Verbal Behavior,* 1963, **2**, 379–391.

Angermeier, W. F., Schaul, L. T., & James, W. T. Social conditioning in rats. *Journal of Comparative and Physiological Psychology,* 1959, **52**, 370–372.

Aronfreed, J. The origin of self-criticism. *Psychological Review,* 1964, **71**, 193–218.

Aronfreed, J. The internalization of social control through punishment: Experimental studies of the role of conditioning and the second signal system in the development of conscience. *Proceedings of the Eighteenth International Congress of Psychology*, Moscow, 1966.

Aronfreed, J. *Conduct and conscience*. New York: Academic Press, 1968.

Aronfreed, J. The concept of internalization. In D. A. Goslin (Ed.), *Handbook of socialization theory and research*. Chicago: Rand-McNally, 1969.

Aronfreed, J., & Leff, R. The effects of intensity of punishment and complexity of discrimination upon the learning of an internalized inhibition. Unpublished manuscript, University of Pennsylvania, 1963.

Aronfreed, J., & Reber, A. Internalized behavioral suppression and the timing of social punishment. *Journal of Personality and Social Psychology,* 1965, **1**, 3–16.

Aronson, E. The effect of effort on the attractiveness of rewarded and unrewarded stimuli. *Journal of Abnormal and Social Psychology,* 1961, **63**, 375–380.

Aronson, E. Effort, attractiveness, and the anticipation of reward: A reply to Lott's critique. *Journal of Abnormal and Social Psychology,* 1963, **67**, 522–525.

Asch, S. E. Forming impressions of personality. *Journal of Abnormal and Social Psychology,* 1946, **41**, 258–290.

Asch, S. E. *Social psychology*. Englewood Cliffs, New Jersey: Prentice-Hall, 1952.

Atthowe, J. M., & Krasner, L. A preliminary report on the application of contingent reinforcement procedures (token economy) on a "chronic" psychiatric ward. *Journal of Abnormal Psychology,* 1968, **73**, 37–43.

Ayllon, T., & Azrin, N. H. The measurement and reinforcement of behavior of psychotics. *Journal of Experimental Analysis of Behavior,* 1965, **8**, 357–383.

Baer, D. M., Peterson, R. I. & Sherman, J. A. The development of imitation by reinforcing behavioral similarity to a model. *Journal of the Experimental Analysis of Behavior,* 1967, **10**, 405–416.

Baer, D. M., & Sherman, J. A. Reinforcement control of generalized imitation in young children. *Journal of Experimental Child Psychology,* 1964, **1**, 37–49.

Bagby, E. The etiology of phobias. *Journal of Abnormal and Social Psychology,* 1922, **17**, 16–18.

Bagehot, W. *Physics and politics.* New York: Appleton, 1875.

Ban, T. A. *Conditioning and psychiatry.* Chicago: Aldine, 1964.

Bandler, R. J., Madaras, G. R., & Bem, D. J. Self-observation as a source of pain perception. *Journal of Personality and Social Psychology,* 1968, **9**, 205–209.

Bandura, A. Psychotherapy as a learning process. *Psychological Bulletin,* 1961, **58**, 143–159.

Bandura, A. Social learning through imitation. In M. R. Jones (Ed.), *Nebraska symposium on motivation.* Lincoln, Nebraska: University of Nebraska Press, 1962, Pp. 211–269.

Bandura, A. Vicarious processes. A case of no-trial learning. In H. Berkowitz (Ed.), *Advances in experimental social psychology.* Vol. 2. New York: Academic Press, 1965. Pp. 1–55. (a)

Bandura, A. Influence of models' reinforcement contingencies on the acquisition of imitative responses. *Journal of Personality and Social Psychology,* 1965, **1**, 589–595. (b)

Bandura, A. Social-learning theory of identificatory processes. In D. A. Goslin (Ed.), *Handbook of socialization theory and research.* Chicago: Rand-McNally, 1969. Pp. 213–262.

Bandura, A. *Principles of behavior modification.* New York: Holt, Rinehart, & Winston. 1969. (a)

Bandura, A., & Barab, P. G. Conditions governing nonreinforced imitation. Unpublished manuscript, Stanford University, 1969.

Bandura, A., Blanchard, E. B., & Ritter, B. J. Relative efficacy of modeling therapeutic changes for inducing behavioral, attitudinal, and affective changes. *Journal of Personality and Social Psychology,* 1969, **13**, 173–199.

Bandura, A., Grusec, J. E., & Menlove, F. L. Observational learning as a function of symbolization and incentive set. *Child Development,* 1966, **37**, 499–506.

Bandura, A., Grusec, J. E., & Menlove, F. L. Vicarious extinction of avoidance behavior. *Journal of Personality and Social Behavior,* 1967, **5**, 16–23.

Bandura, A., & Harris, M. B. Modification of syntactic style. *Journal of Experimental Child Psychology,* 1966, 4, 341–352.

Bandura, A., & Huston, A. C. Identification as a process of incidental learning. *Journal of Abnormal and Social Psychology,* 1961, **63**, 311–318.

Bandura, A., & Kupers, C. J. Transmission of patterns of self-reinforcement through modeling. *Journal of Abnormal and Social Psychology,* 1964, **69**, 1–9.

Bandura, A., & McDonald, F. J. The influence of social reinforcement and the behavior of models in shaping children's moral judgments. *Journal of Abnormal and Social Psychology,* 1963, **67**, 274–281.

Bandura, A., & Menlove, F. L. Factors determining vicarious extinction of avoidance behavior through symbolic modeling. *Journal of Personality and Social Psychology,* 1968, **8**, 99–108.

Bandura, A., & Mischel, W. Modification of self-imposed delay of reward through exposure to live and symbolic models. *Journal of Personality and Social Psychology,* 1965, **2**, 698–705.

Bandura, A., & Perloff, B. Relative efficacy of self-monitored and externally imposed reinforcement systems. *Journal of Personality and Social Psychology,* 1967, **7**, 111–116.

Bandura, A., & Rosenthal, T. L. Vicarious classical conditioning as a function of arousal level. *Journal of Personality and Social Psychology,* 1966, **3**, 54–62.

Bandura, A., Ross, D., & Ross, S. A. Transmission of aggression through imitation of aggressive models. *Journal of Abnormal and Social Psychology,* 1961, **63**, 575–582.

Bandura, A., Ross, D., & Ross, S. A. Imitation of film-mediated aggressive models. *Journal of Abnormal and Social Psychology*, 1963, **66**, 3–11. (a)

Bandura, A., Ross, D., & Ross, S. A. A comparative test of the status of envy, social power, and secondary reinforcement theories of identificatory learning. *Journal of Abnormal and Social Psychology*, 1963, **67**, 527–534. (b)

Bandura, A., Ross, D., & Ross, S. A. Vicarious reinforcement and imitative learning. *Journal of Abnormal and Social Psychology*, 1963, **67**, 601–607. (c)

Bandura, A., & Walters, R. H. *Social learning and personality development*. New York: Holt, Rinehart, & Winston, 1963.

Bavelas, A., Hastorf, A. H., Gross, A. E., & Kite, W. R. Experiments in the alteration of group structure. *Journal of Experimental Social Psychology*, 1965, **1**, 55–70.

Beach, F. A. The descent of instinct. *Psychological Review*, 1955, **62**, 401–410.

Beech, H. R. The symptomatic treatment of writer's cramp. In H. J. Eysenck (Ed.), *Behavior therapy and the neuroses*. New York: Pergamon Press, 1960.

Bem, D. J. An experimental analysis of self-persuasion. *Journal of Experimental Social Psychology*, 1965, **1**, 199–218.

Bem, D. J. Self-perception: An alternative interpretation of cognitive dissonance phenomena. *Psychological Review*, 1967, **74**, 183–200. (a)

Bem, D. J. The self as the object of judgment. Paper read at the American Psychological Association, Washington, D. C., 1967. (b)

Bem, D. J. & McConnell, H. K. Testing the self-perception explanation of dissonance phenomena: On the salience of premanipulation attitudes. *Journal of Personality and Social Psychology*, 1970, **14**, 23–31.

Berger, S. M. Incidental learning through vicarious reinforcement. *Psychological Reports*, 1961, **9**, 477–491.

Berger, S. M. Conditioning through vicarious instigation. *Psychological Review*, 1962, **69**, 450–466.

Berger, S. M. Observer practice and learning during exposure to a model. *Journal of Personality and Social Psychology*, 1966, **3**, 696–701.

Berger, S. M., & Lambert, W. W. Stimulus-response theory in contemporary social psychology. In G. Lindzey & E. Aronson (Eds.), *Handbook of social psychology*, Vol. 1, 2nd ed. Reading, Massachusetts: Addison-Wesley, 1968. Pp. 81–178.

Berkowitz, L. Liking for the group and the perceived merit of the group's behavior. *Journal of Abnormal and Social Psychology*, 1957, **54**, 353–357.

Berlyne, D. E. *Conflict, arousal, and curiosity*. New York: McGraw-Hill, 1960.

Berlyne, D. E. Emotional aspects of learning. *Annual Review of Psychology*, 1964, **15**, 115–142.

Berlyne, D. E. *Structure and direction in thinking*. New York: Wiley, 1965.

Bever, T. G. Associations to stimulus-response theories of language. In T. R. Dixon & D. L. Horton (Eds.), *Verbal behavior and general behavior*. Englewood Cliffs, New Jersey: Prentice-Hall, 1968. Pp. 478–494.

Bever, T. G., Fodor, J. A., & Weksel, W. On the acquisition of syntax: A critique of "contextual generalization." *Psychological Bulletin*, 1965, **72**, 467–482.

Bexton, W. H., Heron, W., & Scott, T. H. Effects of decreased variation in the sensory environment. *Canadian Journal of Psychology*, 1954, **8**, 70–76.

Blake, R. R. The other person in the situation. In R. Tagiuri & L. Petrullo (Eds.), *Person perception and interpersonal behavior*. Stanford, California: Stanford University Press, 1958. Pp. 229–242.

Blake, R. R., & Mouton, J. S. Conformity, resistance and conversion. In I. A. Berg & B. M. Bass (Eds.), *Conformity and deviation*. New York: Harper, 1961. Pp. 1–37.

Blodgett, H. C. The effect of the introduction of reward on the maze performance of rats. *University of California Publications in Psychology*, 1929, **4**, 113–134.

Boardman, W. K. Rusty: A brief behavior disorder. *Journal of Psychology*, 1962, **26**, 293–297.

Bookbinder, L. J. Simple conditioning vs. the dynamic approach to symptoms and symptom substitution: A reply to Yates. *Psychological Reports*, 1962, **10**, 71–77.

Bower, G. H., & Miller, N. E. Rewarding and punishing effects from stimulating the same place in the rat's brain. *Journal of Comparative and Physiological Psychology*, 1958, **51**, 669–674.

Braine, M. D. On learning the grammatical order of words. *Psychological Review*, 1963, **70**, 323–348.

Braine, M. D. On the basis of phrase structure: A reply to Bever, Fodor, and Weksel. *Psychological Bulletin*, 1965, **72**, 483–492.

Brawley, E. R., Harris, F. R., Allen, E., Fleming, R. S., & Peterson, R. F. Behavior modification of an autistic child. *Behavioral Science*, 1969, **14**, 87–97.

Breger, L., & McGaugh, J. L. Critique and reformulation of "learning-theory" approaches to psycho-therapy and neurosis. *Psychological Bulletin*, 1965, **63**, 338–358.

Brehm, J. W., & Cohen, A. R. Re-evaluation of choice alternatives as a function of their number and qualitative similarity. *Journal of Abnormal and Social Psychology*, 1959, **58**, 373–378.

Brehm, J. W., & Cohen, A. R. *Explorations in cognitive dissonance.* New York: Wiley, 1962.

Broadbent, D. E. *Perception and communication.* New York: Pergamon Press, 1958.

Brody, M. W. Prognosis and results of psychoanalysis. In J. H. Nodine & J. H. Moyer (Eds.), *Psychosomatic medicine.* Philadelphia: Lee & Febiger, 1962.

Brown, G. W., & Cohen, B. D. Avoidance and approach learning motivated by stimulation of identical hypothalamic loci. *American Journal of Physiology*, 1959, **197**, 153.

Brown, J. S. Problems presented by the concept of acquired drives. In Brown *et al., Nebraska symposium on motivation.* Lincoln, Nebraska: University of Nebraska Press, 1953. Pp. 1–21.

Brown, J. S. *The motivation of behavior.* New York: McGraw-Hill, 1961.

Brown, R. *Social psychology.* New York: The Free Press, 1965.

Bruner, J. S., & Tagiuri, R. The perception of people. In G. Lindzey (Ed.), *Handbook of social psychology.* Vol. 2. Cambridge, Massachusetts: Addison-Wesley, 1954. Pp. 634–654.

Buhler, C. *From birth to maturity.* London: Kegan Paul, Trench, Trubner, 1935.

Bush, R. R., & Mosteller, F. *Stochastic models for learning.* New York: Wiley, 1955.

Butler, D. C. & Miller, N. Power to reward and punish in social interaction. *Journal of Experimental Social Psychology*, 1965, **1**, 311–322.

Butler, R. A. Discrimination learning by rhesus monkeys to visual-exploration motivation. *Journal of Comparative and Physiological Psychology*, 1953, **46**, 95–98.

Butler, R. A. Discrimination learning in rhesus monkeys to auditory incentives. *Journal of Comparative and Physiological Psychology*, 1957, **50**, 239–241.

Byrne, D. Interpersonal attraction and attitude similarity. *Journal of Abnormal and Social Psychology*, 1961, **62**, 713–715.

Byrne, D., Barry, J., & Nelson, D. Relation of the revised Repression-Sensitization Scale to measures of self-description. *Psychological Reports*, 1963, **13**, 323–334.

Byrne, D., & Clore, G. L. Predicting interpersonal attraction towards strangers presented in three different stimulus modes. *Psychonomic Science,* 1966, **4**, 239–240.

Byrne, D., & Griffitt, W. A developmental investigation of the law of attraction. *Journal of Personality and Social Psychology,* 1966, **4**, 699–702.

Byrne, D., Griffitt, W., & Stefaniak, D. Attraction and similarity of personality characteristics. *Journal of Personality and Social Psychology,* 1967, **5**, 82–90.

Byrne, D., & McGraw, C. Interpersonal attraction towards Negroes. *Human Relations,* 1964, **17**, 201–213.

Byrne, D., & Nelson, D. Attraction as a linear function of proportion of positive reinforcements. *Journal of Personality and Social Psychology,* 1965, **1**, 659–663.

Byrne, D., & Rhamey, R. Magnitude of positive and negative reinforcements as a determinant of attraction. *Journal of Personality and Social Psychology,* 1965, **2**, 884–889.

Cahoon, D. D. Symptom substitution and the behavior therapies: A reappraisal. *Psychological Bulletin,* 1968, **69**, 149–156.

Campbell, D. T. Social attitudes and other acquired behavioral dispositions. In S. Koch (Ed.), *Psychology: A study of a science.* Vol. 6. New York: McGraw-Hill, 1963. Pp. 94–172.

Cantril, H. *The psychology of social movement.* New York: Wiley, 1941.

Carlsmith, J., Collins, B., & Helmreich, R. Studies in forced compliance: I. The effect of pressure for compliance on attitude change produced by face-to-face role playing and anonymous essay writing. *Journal of Personality and Social Psychology,* 1966, **4**, 1–13.

Cassem, N. H., & Kausler, D. H. The effects of stimulus association value and exposure duration of R-S learning. *Journal of Experimental Psychology,* 1962, **64**, 94.

Centers, R. A laboratory adaptation of the conventional procedure for the conditioning of verbal operants. *Journal of Abnormal and Social Psychology,* 1963, **67**, 334–339.

Chapanis, N. P., & Chapanis, A. Cognitive dissonance: Five years later. *Psychological Bulletin,* 1964, **61**, 1–22.

Chapman, L. J., & Campbell, D. T. An attempt to predict the performance of three-man teams from attitude measures. *Journal of Social Psychology,* 1957, **46**, 277–286.

Chomsky, N. *Syntactic structures.* The Hague: Mouton, 1957.

Chomsky, N. Review of B. F. Skinner, Verbal behavior. *Language,* 1959, **35**, 26–58.

Chomsky, N. Formal properties of grammars. In R. D. Luce, R. R. Bush, & E. Galanter (Eds.), *Handbook of mathematical psychology.* Vol. 2. New York: Wiley, 1963. Pp. 323–418.

Chomsky, N. *Aspects of the theory of syntax.* Cambridge, Massachusetts: MIT Press, 1965.

Chomsky, N. *Cartesian linguistics.* New York: Harper & Row, 1966.

Church, R. M. Emotional reactions of rats to the pain of others. *Journal of Comparative and Physiological Psychology,* 1959, **52**, 132–134.

Church, R. M. The varied effects of punishment on behavior. *Psychological Review,* 1963, **70**, 369–402.

Cline, V. B. Interpersonal perception. In B. A. Maher (Ed.), *Progress in experimental research in personality.* Vol. 1. New York: Academic Press, 1964. Pp. 221–284.

Cofer, C. N., & Appley, M. H. *Motivation: Theory and research.* New York: Wiley, 1964.

Cohen, A. Communication discrepancy and attitude change. *Journal of Personality,* 1959, **27**, 386–396.

Cohen, B. H. Role of awareness in meaning established by classical conditioning. *Journal of Experimental Psychology*, 1964, **67**, 373–378.

Cohen, H. L., Filipzak, J. A., Bis, J. J., & Cohen, J. E. *Contingencies applicable to the special education of delinquents.* Silver Springs, Maryland: Institute for Behavioral Research, 1966.

Cook, C., & Adams, H. E. Modification of verbal behavior in speech deficient children. *Behaviour Research and Therapy*, 1966, **4**, 265–271.

Cook, T. D., & Insko, C. A. Persistence of attitude change as a function of conclusion re-exposure: A laboratory-field experiment. *Journal of Personality and Social Psychology*, 1968, **9**, 322–328.

Corrozi, J. F., & Rosnow, R. L. Consonant and dissonant communications as positive and negative reinforcements in opinion change. *Journal of Personality and Social Psychology*, 1968, **8**, 27–30.

Cowan, P. A., Langer, J., Heavenrich, J., & Nathanson, M. Social learning theory and Piaget's cognitive theory of moral development. *Journal of Personality and Social Psychology*, 1969, **11**, 261–274.

Craig, K. D. Vicarious reinforcement and non-instrumental punishment in observational learning. *Journal of Personality and Social Psychology*, 1967, **7**, 172–176.

Crockett, W. H. Cognitive complexity and impression formation. In B. A. Maher. (Ed.), *Progress in experimental personality research.* Vol. 2. New York: Academic Press, 1965. Pp. 47–90.

Crowley, P. M. Effect of training upon objectivity of moral judgments in grade-school children. *Journal of Personality and Social Psychology*, 1968, **8**, 228–232.

Crutchfield, R. S. Conformity and character. *American Psychologist*, 1955, **10**, 191–198.

Davis, K. E., & Forquist, C. C. Perceived threat and determinants of the tactical use of conformity. *Journal of Experimental Social Psychology*, 1965, **1**, 219–236.

Davis, P. Discrimination without awareness in a psychophysical task. *Perceptual and Motor Skills*, 1964, **18**, 87–90.

Davison, G. C. Systematic desensitization as a counterconditioning process. *Journal of Abnormal Psychology*, 1968, **73**, 91–99.

Dean, S. J., & Hiesinger, L. Operant level, awareness, and the Greenspoon effect. *Psychological Reports*, 1964, **15**, 931–938.

de Charms, R., & Rosenbaum, M. E. The problem of vicarious experience. In D. Willner (Ed.), *Decisions, values, and groups.* Vol. 1. New York: Pergamon Press. Pp. 267–277.

Deese, J., & Hulse, S. H. *The psychology of learning.* 3rd ed. New York: McGraw-Hill, 1967.

De Nike, L. D. The temporal relationship between awareness and performance in verbal conditioning. *Journal of Experimental Psychology*, 1964, **68**, 521–529.

De Saussure, F. *Cours de linguistique generale.* Paris: Payot, 1916.

Deutsch, M. The effects of cooperation and competition upon group process. In D. Cartwright & A. Zander (Eds.), *Group dynamics: Research and theory.* 2nd ed. Evanston, Illinois: Row, Peterson, 1960. Pp. 414–448.

Deutsch, M., & Solomon, L. Reactions to evaluations by others as influenced by self evaluations. *Sociometry*, 1959, **22**, 93–112.

Di Lollo, V., & Berger, S. M. Effects of apparent pain in others on observer reaction time. *Journal of Personality and Social Psychology*, 1965, **2**, 573–575.

Dittes, J. E., & Kelley, H. H. Effects of different conditions of acceptance upon conformity to group norms. *Journal of Abnormal and Social Psychology*, 1956, **53**, 100–107.

Dixon, P. W., & Oakes, W. F. Effect of intertrial activity on the relationship between awareness and verbal operant conditioning. *Journal of Experimental Psychology,* 1965, **69,** 152–157.

Dixon, T. R., & Horton, D. L. (Eds.), *Verbal behavior and general behavior theory.* Englewood Cliffs, New Jersey: Prentice-Hall, 1968.

Dollard, J., & Miller, N. E. *Personality and psychotherapy.* New York: McGraw-Hill, 1950.

Doob, L. W. The behavior of attitudes. *Psychological Review,* 1947, **54,** 135–156.

Dulany, D. E. The place of hypotheses and intentions: An analysis of verbal control in verbal conditioning. In C. W. Eriksen (Ed.), *Behavior and awareness.* Durham, North Carolina: Duke University Press, 1962. Pp. 102–129.

Dunlap, K. *Habits, their making and unmaking.* New York: Liveright, 1932.

Ebbinghaus, H. *Memory.* New York: Teachers College, 1913. (Original, *Über das Gedächtnis,* Leipzig, 1885).

Ekman, P. A comparison of verbal and non-verbal behavior as reinforcing stimuli of opinion responses. Unpublished doctoral dissertation. Adelphi College, 1958.

Ekman, P. Body position, facial expression, and verbal behavior during interviews. *Journal of Abnormal and Social Psychology,* 1964, **68,** 295–301.

Elms, A., & Janis, I. Counternorm attitudes induced by consonant versus dissonant conditions of role-playing. *Journal of Experimental Research in Personality,* 1965, **1,** 50–60.

Endler, N. S. The effects of verbal reinforcement on conformity and deviant behavior. *Journal of Social Psychology,* 1965, **66,** 147–154.

Endler, N. S. Conformity as a function of different reinforcement schedules. *Journal of Personality and Social Psychology,* 1966, **4,** 175–180.

Endler, N. S., & Hoy, E. Conformity as related to reinforcement and social pressure. *Journal of Personality and Social Psychology,* 1967, **7,** 197–202.

Endsley, R. C. Dependency and performance by preschool children on a socially reinforced task. Unpublished M.A. thesis, State University of Iowa, 1960.

Eriksen, C. W. Figments, fantasies, and follies: A search for the subconscious mind. In C. W. Eriksen (Ed.), *Behavior and awareness.* Durham, North Carolina: Duke University Press, 1962. Pp. 3–26.

Estes, W. K. An experimental study of punishment. *Psychological Monographs,* 1944, **57,** No. 3 (Whole No. 263).

Estes, W. K. Learning theory and the new "mental chemistry." *Psychological Review,* 1960, **67,** 207–223.

Estes, W. K. Learning theory. *Annual Review of Psychology,* 1962, **13,** 107–144.

Eysenck, H. J. (Ed.), *Behaviour therapy and the neuroses.* New York: Pergamon Press, 1960.

Eysenck, H. J. New ways in psychotherapy. *Psychology Today,* 1967, **1,** 39–47.

Farber, I. E., The things people say to themselves. *American Psychologist,* 1963, **18,** 185–197.

Feldman, S. M., & Underwood, B. J. Stimulus recall following paired-associate learning. *Journal of Experimental Psychology,* 1957, **53,** 11–15.

Fenichel, O. *The psychoanalytic theory of neurosis.* New York: Norton, 1945.

Ferguson, P. E. The influence of isolation, anxiety, and dependency on reinforcer effectiveness. Unpublished M.A. thesis, University of Toronto, 1961.

Ferster, C. B. Positive reinforcement and behavioral defects of autistic children. *Child Development,* 1961, **32,** 437–456.

Ferster, C. B., & De Meyer, M. K. The development of performance in autistic children in an automatically controlled environment. *Journal of Chronic Diseases,* 1961, **13,** 312–345.

Ferster, C. B., & Skinner, B. F. *Schedules of reinforcement.* New York: Appleton-Century-Crofts, 1957.

Feshbach, S. The stimulating versus cathartic effects of a vicarious aggressive activity. *Journal of Abnormal and Social Psychology,* 1961, **63,** 381–385.

Festinger, L. *A theory of cognitive dissonance.* Stanford, California: Stanford University Press, 1957.

Festinger, L., & Carlsmith, J. M. Cognitive consequences of forced compliance. *Journal of Abnormal and Social Psychology,* 1959, **58,** 203–210.

Festinger, L., & Thibaut, J. Interpersonal communication in small groups. *Journal of Abnormal and Social Psychology,* 1951, **46,** 92–99.

Fiedler, F. E. The psychological distance dimension in interpersonal relations. *Journal of Personality,* 1953, **22,** 142–150.

Finley, J. R., & Staats, A. W. Evaluative meaning words as reinforcing stimuli. *Journal of Verbal Learning and Verbal Behavior,* 1967, **6,** 193–197.

Fishbein, M. An investigation of the relationship between beliefs about an object and the attitude toward that object. *Human Relations,* 1963, **16,** 233–239.

Fishman, H. C. A study of the efficiency of negative practice as a corrective for stammering. *Journal of Speech Disorders,* 1937, **2,** 67–72.

Fiske, D. W., & Maddi, S. R. *Functions of varied experience.* Homewood, Illinois: Dorsey Press, 1961.

Flanders, J. P. A review of research on imitative behavior. *Psychological Bulletin,* 1968, **69,** 316–337.

Fodor, J. A. Could meaning be an r_m? *Journal of Verbal Learning and Verbal Behavior,* 1965, 4, 73–81.

Franks, C. M. (Ed.), *Conditioning techniques in clinical practice and research.* New York: Springer, 1964.

Franks, C. M. (Ed.), *Behavior therapy: Appraisal and status.* New York: McGraw-Hill, 1969.

Freedman, J. L., & Sears, D. O. Selective exposure. In L. Berkowitz (Ed.), *Advances in experimental social psychology.* Vol. 2. New York: Academic Press, 1965. Pp. 57–97.

Freud, S. *A general introduction to psychoanalysis.* Garden City, New York: Garden City Publishing Co., 1920.

Fromkin, H. L. Reinforcement and effort expenditure: Predictions of "reinforcement theory" versus predictions of dissonance theory. *Journal of Personality and Social Behavior,* 1968, **9,** 347–352.

Gardner, E., & Thompson, G. *Social relations and morale in small groups.* New York: Appleton-Century-Crofts, 1956.

Garrett, M., Bever, T., & Fodor, J. The active use of grammar in speech perception. *Perception and Psychophysics,* 1966, **1,** 30–32.

Garrett, M., & Fodor, J. Psychological theories and linguistic constructs. In T. R. Dixon & D. L. Horton (Eds.), *Verbal behavior and general behavior theory.* Englewood Cliffs, New Jersey: Prentice-Hall, 1968. Pp. 451–477.

Gelfand, D. M. The influence of self-esteem on rate of verbal conditioning and social matching behavior. *Journal of Abnormal and Social Behavior,* 1962, **65,** 259–265.

Gerst, M. S. Symbolic coding operations in observational learning. Unpublished doctoral dissertation, Stanford University, 1968.

Gewirtz, J. L. The origins of social motivation and emotional attachment. In *Current trends in psychological theory.* Pittsburgh: University of Pittsburgh Press, 1960.

Gewirtz, J. L. Mechanisms of social learning. In D. A. Goslin (Ed.), *Handbook of socialization theory and research.* Chicago: Rand-McNally, 1969. Pp. 57–212.

Gewirtz, J. L., & Baer, D. M. Deprivation and satiation of social reinforcers as drive conditions. *Journal of Abnormal and Social Psychology,* 1958, **57**, 165–172.

Gewirtz, J. L., & Stingle, K. G. Learning of generalized imitation as the basis for identification. *Psychological Review,* 1968, **75**, 374–397.

Glucksberg, S. A self-made straw man. *Contemporary Psychology,* 1968, **13**, 624–625.

Goldiamond, I. Self-control procedures in personal behavior problems. *Psychological Reports,* 1965, **17**, 851–868.

Golightly, C., & Byrne, D. Attitude statements as positive and negative reinforcements. *Science,* 1964, **146**, 789–799.

Goulet, L. R. Verbal learning in children: Implications for developmental research. *Psychological Bulletin,* 1968, **69**, 359–376.

Greenspoon, J. The effect of verbal and nonverbal stimuli on the frequency of members of two verbal response classes. Unpublished doctoral dissertation, Indiana University, 1950.

Greenspoon, J. The reinforcing effect of two spoken words on the frequency of two responses. *American Journal of Psychology,* 1955, **68**, 409–416.

Greenwald, A. G. An amended learning model of persuasion. Paper read at American Psychological Association, Washington, D. C., 1967.

Greenwald, A. G. The open-mindedness of the counter-attitudinal role player. *Journal of Experimental Social Psychology,* 1969, **5**, 375–388.

Greenwald, A. G. The rejection phenomenon in attitude "transplant" by role playing. *Journal of Personality and Social Psychology,* in press.

Grossberg, J. M. Behavior therapy: A review. *Psychological Bulletin,* 1964, **62**, 73–88.

Grusec, J. E. Waiting for rewards and punishments: Effects of reinforcement value on choice. *Journal of Personality and Social Psychology,* 1968, **9**, 85–89.

Grusec, J. E., & Mischel, W. Model's characteristics as determinants of social learning. *Journal of Personality and Social Psychology,* 1966, 4, 211–215.

Guthrie, E. R. *The psychology of learning.* New York: Harper & Row, 1935.

Guthrie, E. R. *The psychology of learning.* Gloucester, Massachusetts: Smith, 1952. Rev. ed.

Guthrie, E. R. Association by contiguity. In S. Koch (Ed.), *Psychology: A study of a science.* Vol. 2. New York: McGraw-Hill, 1959. Pp. 158–195.

Guthrie, E. R., & Horton, G. P. *Cats in a puzzle box.* New York: Holt, Rinehart, & Winston, 1946.

Guthrie, E. R., & Powers, F. F. *Educational psychology.* New York: Ronald, 1950.

Hagstrom, W. O., & Selvin, H. C. Two dimensions of cohesiveness in small groups. *Sociometry,* 1965, **28**, 30–43.

Hall, J. F. *The psychology of learning.* Philadelphia: Lippincott, 1966.

Harlow, H. F. Learning and satiation of response in intrinsically motivated complex puzzle performance by monkeys. *Journal of Comparative and Physiological Psychology,* 1950, **43**, 289–294.

Harlow, H. F. Harlow, M. K., & Meyers, D. R. Learning motivated by a manipulation drive. *Journal of Experimental Psychology,* 1950, **40**, 228–234.

Hartup, W. W., & Himeno, Y. Social isolation vs. interaction with adults in relation to aggression in preschool children. *Journal of Abnormal and Social Psychology,* 1959, **59**, 17–22.

Hastorf, A. H. The perception and evaluation of behavior change. Paper presented at Western Psychological Association, Portland, Oregon, 1964.

Havelka, J. Problem-seeking behavior in rats. *Canadian Journal of Psychology,* 1956, **10,** 91–97.

Hebb, D. O. Drives and the C.N.S. (Conceptual nervous system). *Psychological Review,* 1955, **62,** 243–254.

Heber, R. F., & Heber, M. E. The effect of group failure and success on social status. *Journal of Educational Psychology,* 1957, **48,** 129–134.

Hefferline, R. F., & Keenan, B. Amplitude-induction gradient of a small-scale (covert) operant. *Journal of Experimental Analysis of Behavior,* 1963, **6,** 307–315.

Heider, F. Perceiving the other person. In R. Tagiuri & L. Petrullo (Eds.), *Person perception and interpersonal behavior.* Stanford, California: Stanford University Press, 1958. Pp. 22–26.

Helmreich, R., & Collins, B. E. Studies in forced compliance: Commitment and magnitude of inducement to comply as determinants of opinion change. *Journal of Personality and Social Psychology,* 1968, **10,** 75–81.

Hetherington, E. M., & Frankie, G. Effects of parental dominance, warmth, and conflict on imitation in children. *Journal of Personality and Social Psychology,* 1967, **6,** 119–125.

Hicks, D. J. Imitation and retention of film-mediated aggressive peer and adult models. *Journal of Personality and Social Psychology,* 1965, **2,** 97–100.

Hildum, D. C., & Brown, R. W. Verbal reinforcement and interviewer bias. *Journal of Abnormal and Social Psychology,* 1956, **53,** 108–111.

Hilgard, E. R., & Bower, G. H. *Theories of learning.* 3rd ed. New York: Appleton-Century-Crofts, 1966.

Hill, W. F. Learning theory and the acquisition of values. *Psychological Review,* 1960, **67,** 317–331.

Hill, W. F. *Learning: A survey of psychological interpretations.* San Francisco: Chandler, 1963.

Hill, W. F. Sources of evaluative reinforcement. *Psychological Bulletin,* 1968, **69,** 132–146.

Hoffman, L. R. Similarity of personality: A basis for interpersonal attraction? *Sociometry,* 1958, **21,** 300–308.

Hoffman, L. R., & Maier, N. R. F. Quality and acceptance of problem-solutions for members of homogeneous and heterogeneous groups. *Journal of Abnormal and Social Psychology,* 1961, **62,** 401–407.

Holland, B. C. Discussion. Appended to H. Spiegel, Is symptom removal dangerous? *American Journal of Psychiatry,* 1967, **10,** 1282–1283.

Holland, J. G., & Skinner, B. F. *The analysis of behavior.* New York: McGraw-Hill, 1961.

Hollander, E. P., & Willis, R. H. Some current issues in the psychology of conformity and nonconformity. *Psychological Bulletin,* 1967, **68,** 62–76.

Holt, E. B. *Animal drive and the learning process.* London: Williams & Norgate, 1931.

Homans, G. C. *Social behavior: Its elementary forms.* New York: Harcourt, Brace, & World, 1961.

Horwitz, M. The veridicality of liking and disliking. In R. Tagiuri & L. Petrullo (Eds.), *Person perception and interpersonal behavior.* Stanford, California: Stanford University Press, 1958. Pp. 191–209.

Hovland, C. I., Janis, I. L. & Kelley, H. H. *Communication and persuasion.* New Haven: Yale University Press, 1953.

Hovland, C., & Weiss, W. The influence of source credibility on communication effectiveness. *Public Opinion Quarterly,* 1951, **15,** 635–650.

Howard, R. C., & Berkowitz, L. Reactions to the evaluators of one's performance. *Journal of Personality,* 1958, **26,** 494–507.

Hull, C. L. *Principles of behavior.* New York: Appleton-Century-Crofts, 1943.
Hull, C. L. *A behavior system.* New Haven: Yale University Press, 1952.
Humphrey, G. Imitation and the conditional reflex. *Pedagogical Seminary,* 1921, **28,** 1–21.

Insko, C. A. Primacy versus recency in persuasion as a function of the timing of arguments and measures. *Journal of Abnormal and Social Psychology,* 1964, **69,** 381–391.
Insko, C. A. *Theories of attitude change.* New York: Appleton-Century-Crofts, 1967.
Insko, C. A., & Butzine, K. W. Rapport, awareness, and verbal reinforcement of attitude. *Journal of Personality and Social Psychology,* 1967, **6,** 225–228.
Insko, C. A., & Cialdini, R. B. A test of three interpretations of attitudinal verbal reinforcement. *Journal of Personality and Social Psychology,* 1969, **12,** 333–341.

Jackson, D. N., Messick, S., & Solley, C. M. A multidimensional scaling approach to the perception of personality. *Journal of Psychology,* 1957, **44,** 311–318.
Jacobson, E. *Progressive relaxation.* Chicago: University of Chicago Press, 1938.
James, A., & Lott, A. J. Reward frequency and formation of positive attitudes toward group members. *Journal of Social Psychology,* 1964, **62,** 111–115.
Janis, I. L., & Feshbach, S. Effects of fear-arousing communications. *Journal of Abnormal and Social Psychology,* 1953, **48,** 78–92.
Janis, I. L., & Gilmore, J. The influence of incentive conditions on the success of role playing in modifying attitudes. *Journal of Personality and Social Psychology,* 1965, **1,** 17–27.
Jenkins, J. J. The challenge to psychological theorists. In T. R. Dixon & D. L. Horton (Eds.), *Verbal behavior and general behavior.* Englewood Cliffs, New Jersey: Prentice-Hall, 1968. Pp. 538–549.
Jenkins, J. J., & Palermo, D. S. Mediation processes and acquisition of linguistic structure. In U. Bellugi & R. Brown (Eds.), *The acquisition of language, Monographs of social research and child development,* 1964, **29,** 141–169.
Johnson, H., & Steiner, I. Effort and subjective probability. *Journal of Personality and Social Psychology,* 1965, **1,** 365–368.
Jones, E. E. *Ingratiation: A social psychological approach.* New York: Appleton-Century-Crofts, 1964.
Jones, E. E. Conformity as a tactic of ingratiation. *Science,* 1965, **149,** 144–150.
Jones, E. E., & Davis, K. E. From acts to dispositions: The attribution process in person perception. In L. Berkowitz (Ed.), *Advances in experimental social psychology.* Vol. 2. New York: Academic Press, 1965. Pp. 219–266.
Jones, E. E., Gergen, K. J., Gumpert, P., & Thibaut, J. W. Some conditions affecting the use of ingratiation to influence performance evaluation. *Journal of Personality and Social Psychology,* 1965, **1,** 613–625.
Jones, E. E., & Thibaut, J. W. Interaction goals as bases of inference in interpersonal perception. In R. Tagiuri & L. Petrullo (Eds.), *Person perception and interpersonal behavior.* Stanford, California: Stanford University Press, 1958. Pp. 151–178.
Jones, E. E., Wells, H. H. & Torrey, R. Some effects of feedback from the experimenter on conformity behavior. *Journal of Abnormal and Social Psychology,* 1958, **57,** 207–213.
Jones, H. G. The behavioral treatment of enuresis nocturna. In H. J. Eysenck (Ed.), *Behavior therapy and the neurosis.* New York: Pergamon Press, 1960.
Jones, M. C. The elimination of children's fears. *Journal of Experimental Psychology,* 1924, **7,** 382–390.

Jones, R. G., & Jones, E. E. Optimum conformity as an ingratiation tactic. *Journal of Personality*, 1964, **32**, 436–458.

Jones, S. C. Some determinants of interpersonal evaluating behavior. *Journal of Personality and Social Behavior*, 1966, **3**, 397–403.

Jones, S. C., & Ratner, C. Commitment to self-appraisal and interpersonal evaluations. *Journal of Personality and Social Psychology*, 1967, **6**, 442–447.

Kagan, J. The concept of identification. *Psychological Review*, 1958, **65**, 296–305.

Kalish, H. I. Behavior therapy. In B. B. Wolman (Ed.), *Handbook of clinical psychology*. New York: McGraw-Hill, 1965. Pp. 1230–1253.

Kanfer, F. H., Bradley, M. M., & Marston, A. R. Self-reinforcement as a function of degree of learning. *Psychological Reports*, 1962, **10**, 885–886.

Kanfer, F. H., & Duerfeldt, P. H. Effects of pretraining on self-evaluation and self-reinforcement. *Journal of Personality and Social Psychology*, 1967, **7**, 164–168. (a)

Kanfer, F. H., & Duerfeldt, P. H. Motivational properties of self-reinforcement. *Perceptual and Motor Skills*, 1967, **25**, 237–246. (b)

Kanfer, F. H., & Duerfeldt, P. H. Comparison of self-reward and self-criticism as a function of types of prior external reinforcement. *Journal of Personality and Social Psychology*, 1968, **8**, 261–268.

Kanfer, F. H., & Marston, A. R. Human reinforcement: Vicarious and direct. *Journal of Experimental Psychology*, 1963, **65**, 292–296.

Katahn, M. & Koplin, J. H. Paradigm clash: Comments on "Some recent criticism of behaviorism and learning theory with special reference to Breger and McGaugh and to Chomsky." *Psychological Bulletin*, 1968, **69**, 147–148.

Kausler, D. H. *Readings in verbal behavior*. New York: Wiley, 1966.

Keller, F. S., & Schoenfeld, W. N. *Principles of psychology*. New York: Appleton-Century-Crofts, 1950.

Kelley, H. H. Interpersonal accommodation. *American Psychologist*, 1968, **23**, 399–410.

Kelman, H. C. Effects of success and failure on "suggestibility" in the autokinetic phenomenon. *Journal of Abnormal and Social Psychology*, 1950, **45**, 267–285.

Kelman, H. C., & Hovland, C. "Reinstatement" of the communicator in delayed measurement of opinion change. *Journal of Abnormal and Social Psychology*, 1953, **48**, 327–335.

Kendler, T. S., & Kendler, H. H. Reversal and nonreversal shifts in kindergarten children. *Journal of Experimental Psychology*, 1959, **58**, 56–60

Keppel, G. Verbal learning and memory. *Annual Review of Psychology*, 1968, **19**, 169–202.

Kessen, W., & Mandler, G. Anxiety, pain, and inhibition of distress. *Psychological Review*, 1961, **68**, 398–404.

Kimble, G. A. *Hilgard & Marquis, Conditioning and learning revised*. New York: Appleton-Century-Crofts, 1961.

King, B. T., & Janis, I. L. Comparison of the effectiveness of improvised vs. non-improvised role-playing in producing opinion change. *Human Relations*, 1956, **9**, 177–186.

King, G. F., Armitage, S. G., & Tilton, J. R. A therapeutic approach to schizophrenics of extreme pathology: An operant-interpersonal method. *Journal of Abnormal and Social Psychology*, 1960, **61**, 276–286.

Kleiner, R. J. The effects of threat reduction upon interpersonal attraction. *Journal of Personality*, 1960, **28**, 145–155.

Knight, R. P. Evaluation of the results of psychoanalytic therapy. *American Journal of Psychiatry*, 1941, **98**, 434.

Koch, S., & C. L. Hull. In W. Estes *et al., Modern learning theories.* New York: Appleton-Century-Crofts, 1954. Pp. 1–178.

Koch, S. Behavior as intrinsically regulated. In M. R. Jones (Ed.), *Nebraska symposium on motivation.* Lincoln, Nebraska: University of Nebraska Press, 1956. Pp. 42–87.

Kohlberg, L. A cognitive-developmental analysis of children's sex-role concepts and attitudes. In E. E. Maccoby (Ed.), *The development of sex differences.* Stanford, California: Stanford University Press, 1966. Pp. 82–173.

Krasner, L. Studies of the conditioning of verbal behavior. *Psychological Bulletin,* 1956, **55**, 148–171.

Krasner, L., Knowles, I. B., & Ullmann, L. P. Effect of verbal conditioning of attitudes on subsequent motor performance. *Journal of Personality and Social Psychology,* 1965, **1**, 407–412.

Krasner, L., Ullmann, L. P. & Fisher, D. Changes in performance as related to verbal conditioning of attitudes toward the examiner. *Perceptual and Motor Skills,* 1964, **19**, 811–816.

Kuhn, T. S. *The structure of scientific revolutions.* Chicago: University of Chicago Press, 1962.

Lana, R. E. Three theoretical interpretations of order effects in persuasive communication. *Psychological Bulletin,* 1964, **61**, 314–320.

Lang, P. J., & Lazovik, A. D. Experimental desensitization of a phobia. *Journal of Abnormal and Social Psychology,* 1963, **66**, 519–525.

Lang, P. J., Lazovik, A. D., & Reynolds, D. J. Desensitization, suggestibility, and pseudotherapy. *Journal of Abnormal Psychology,* 1965, **70**, 395–402.

Lanyon, R. I. Verbal conditioning and awareness in a sentence construction task. *American Journal of Psychology,* 1964, **77**, 472–475.

Lashley, K. The problem of serial order in behavior. In L. Jeffress (Ed.), *Cerebral mechanisms in behavior.* New York: Wiley, 1951. Pp. 112–136.

Lawrence, D. H. Learning. *Annual Review of Psychology,* 1958, **9**, 157–188.

Lawrence, D. H., & Festinger, L. *Deterrents and reinforcement: The psychology of insufficient reward.* Stanford, California: Stanford University Press, 1962.

Lazarus, A. A. Group therapy of phobic disorders by systematic desensitization. *Journal of Abnormal and Social Psychology,* 1961, **63**, 504–510.

Lazarus, A. A. The results of behavior therapy in 126 cases of severe neurosis. *Behaviour Research and Therapy,* 1963, **1**, 69–80.

Lazarus, A. A., & Rachman, S. The use of systematic desensitization in psychotherapy. *South African Medical Journal,* 1957, **31**, 934–937.

Lefcourt, H. M. Internal versus external control of reinforcement. *Psychological Bulletin,* 1966, **65**, 206–220.

LeFurgy, W. G., & Woloshin, G. W. Immediate and long-term effects of experimentally induced social influence in the modification of adolescents' moral judgments. *Journal of Personality and Social Psychology,* 1969, **12**, 104–110.

Lenneberg, E. Understanding language without ability to speak: A case report. *Journal of Abnormal and Social Psychology,* 1962, **65**, 419–425.

Lenneberg, E. A biological perspective of language. In E. H. Lenneberg (Ed.), *New directions in the study of language.* Cambridge, Massachusetts: MIT Press, 1964. Pp. 65–88.

Lependorf, S. The effects of incentive value and expectancy on dissonance resulting from attitude-discrepant behavior and disconfirmation of expectancy. Unpublished doctoral thesis, State University of New York, Buffalo, 1964.

Lesser, G. S., & Abelson, R. P. Personality correlates of persuasibility in children. In I. L. Janis & C. I. Hovland (Eds.), *Personality and persuasibility.* New Haven: Yale University Press, 1959. Pp. 187–206.

Lewis, D. J., & Duncan, C. P. Vicarious experience and partial reinforcement. *Journal of Abnormal and Social Psychology*, 1958, **57**, 321–326.

Liddell, H. S. Conditioned reflex method and experimental neurosis. In J. McV. Hunt (Ed.), *Personality and the behavior disorders*. Vol. 1. New York: Ronald Press, 1944. Pp. 389–412.

Liebert, R. M., & Ora, J. P. Children's adoption of self-rewarding patterns: Incentive level and method of transmission. *Child Development*, 1968, **39**, 537–544.

Linder, D. E., Cooper, J., & Jones, E. E. Decision freedom as a determinant of the role of incentive magnitude. *Journal of Personality and Social Psychology*, 1967, **6**, 245–254.

Lindley, R. H. Effects of controlled coding cues in short-term memory. *Journal of Experimental Psychology*, 1963, **66**, 180–187.

Lindsley, O. R. Operant conditioning methods applied to research in chronic schizophrenia. *Psychiatric Research Report*, 1956, **5**, 118–138.

Lindsley, O. R. Reduction in rate of vocal psychotic symptoms by differential positive reinforcement. *Journal of the Experimental Analysis of Behavior*, 1959, **2**, 269.

Liversedge, L. A., & Sylvester, J. D. Conditioning techniques in the treatment of writer's cramp. *Lancet*, 1955, **1**, 1147–1149.

Lott, A. J., & Lott, B. E. Group cohesiveness, communication level and conformity. *Journal of Abnormal and Social Psychology*, 1961, **62**, 408–412.

Lott, A. J., & Lott, B. E. Group cohesiveness as interpersonal attraction: A review of relationships with antecedent and consequent variables. *Psychological Bulletin*, 1965, **64**, 259–309.

Lott, B. E. Group cohesiveness: A learning phenomenon. *Journal of Social Psychology*, 1961, **55**, 275–286.

Lott, B. E. Secondary reinforcement and effort: Comment on Aronson's "The effect of effort on the attractiveness of rewarded and unrewarded stimuli." *Journal of Abnormal and Social Psychology*, 1963, **67**, 520–522. (a)

Lott, B. E. Rejoinder. *Journal of Abnormal and Social Psychology*, 1963, **67**, 525–526. (b)

Lott, B. E., & Lott, A. J. The formation of positive attitudes towards group members. *Journal of Abnormal and Social Psychology*, 1960, **61**, 297–300.

Lovaas, O. I. A program for the establishment of speech in psychotic children. In J. K. Wing (Ed.), *Early childhood autism*. Oxford: Pergamon Press, 1967.

Lovaas, O. I., Berberich, J. P., Perloff, B. F., & Schaeffer, B. Acquisition of imitative speech by schizophrenic children. *Science*, 1966, **161**, 705–707.

Lovaas, O. I., Schaeffer, B., & Simmons, J. A. Building social behavior in autistic children by use of electric shock. *Journal of Experimental Research in Personality*, 1965, **1**, 99–109.

Luchins, A. S. Experimental attempts to minimize the impact of first impressions. In C. I. Hovland *et al.* (Eds.), *The order of presentation in persuasion*. New Haven: Yale University Press, 1957. Pp. 62–75.

Luchins, A. S. Definitiveness of impression and primacy-recency in communications. *Journal of Social Psychology*, 1958, **48**, 275–290.

Luchins, A. S., & Luchins, E. H. On conformity with judgments of a majority or an authority. *Journal of Social Psychology*, 1961, **53**, 303–316.

Maltzman, I. Thinking: From a behavioristic point of view. *Psychological Review*, 1955, **62**, 275–286.

Maltzman, I. Awareness: Cognitive psychology vs. behaviorism. *Journal of Experimental Research on Personality*, 1966, **1**, 161–165.

Manis, M., & Ruppe, J. The carryover phenomenon: The persistence of reinforced behavior despite the absence of a conscious behavioral intention. *Journal of Personality and Social Psychology,* 1969, 11, 397–407.

Marshall, G. R. Toilet training of an autistic eight-year-old through conditioning therapy: A case report. *Behaviour Research and Therapy,* 1966, 4, 242–245.

Marston, A. R. Imitation, self-reinforcement, and reinforcement of another person. *Journal of Personality and Social Psychology,* 1965, 2, 255–261.

Marston, A. R., & Kanfer, F. H. Group size and number of vicarious reinforcements in verbal learning. *Journal of Experimental Psychology,* 1963, 65, 593–596.

Masserman, J. H. *Behavior and neurosis.* Chicago: University of Chicago Press, 1943.

Max, L. W. Breaking up a homosexual fixation by the conditioned reaction technique: A case study. *Psychological Bulletin,* 1935, 32, 734.

McDougall, W. *Introduction to social psychology.* London: Methuen, 1908.

McGeoch, J. A. *The psychology of human learning.* New York: David McKay, 1942.

McGeoch, J. A., & Irion, A. L. *The psychology of human learning.* 2nd ed. New York: Longmans, Green, 1952.

McGuire, W. J. Order of presentation as a factor in "conditioning" persuasiveness. In C. I. Hovland *et al.* (Eds.), *The order of presentation in persuasion.* New Haven: Yale University Press, 1957.

McGuire, W. J. Attitudes and opinions. *Annual Review of Psychology,* 1966, 17, 475–514.

McGuire, W. J. The nature of attitudes and attitude change. In G. Lindzey and E. Aronson (Eds.), *Handbook of social psychology.* Vol. 3. 2nd ed. Reading, Massachusetts: Addison-Wesley, 1969. Pp. 136–314.

McLaughlin, B. "Intentional" and "incidental" learning in human subjects: The role of instructions to learn and motivation. *Psychological Bulletin,* 1965, 63, 359–376.

McLaughlin, B. Similarity, recall, and appraisal of others. *Journal of Personality,* 1970, 38, 106–116.

McMains, M., & Liebert, R. M. Influence of discrepancies between successively modeled self-reward criteria on the adoption of a self-imposed standard. *Journal of Personality and Social Psychology,* 1968, 8, 166–171.

McNeill, D. On theories of language acquisition. In T. R. Dixon & D. L. Horton (Eds.), *Verbal behavior and general behavior theory.* Englewood Cliffs, New Jersey: Prentice-Hall, 1968. Pp. 406–420.

Mechanic, A. Effects of orienting task, practice, and incentive on simultaneous incidental and intentional learning. *Journal of Experimental Psychology,* 1962, 64, 393–399.

Metzner, R. Effects of work requirements in two types of delay of gratification situations. *Child Development,* 1963, 34, 809–816.

Meyer, V., & Gelder, M. G. Behavior therapy and phobic disorders. *British Journal of Psychiatry,* 1963, 109, 19–28.

Miller, G. A., Galanter, E., & Pribram, K. H. *Plans and the structure of behavior.* New York: Holt, 1960.

Miller, G. A., & McNeill, D. Psycholinguistics. In G. Lindzey & E. Aronson (Eds.), *The handbook of social psychology.* Vol. 3. 2nd ed. Reading, Massachusetts: Addison-Wesley, 1969.

Miller, N., & Campbell, D. T. Recency and primacy in persuasion as a function of the timing of speeches and measurements. *Journal of Abnormal and Social Psychology,* 1959, 59, 1–9.

Miller, N. E. Liberalization of basic S-R concepts: Extensions to conflict behavior, motivation, and social learning. In S. Koch (Ed.), *Psychology: A study of a science.* New York: McGraw-Hill, 1959. Pp. 196–292.

Miller, N. E., & Dollard, J. *Social learning and imitation.* New Haven: Yale University Press, 1941.

Miller, N. E., & Kessen, M. L. Reward effects of food via stomach fistula paired with those of food via mouth. *Journal of Comparative and Physiological Psychology,* 1952, **45,** 555–564.

Miron, M. J., & Osgood, C. E. The multivariate structure of qualification. In R. B. Cattell & K. R. Hammond (Eds.), *Handbook of multivariate experimental psychology.* Chicago: Rand-McNally, 1965.

Mischel, W. Preference for delayed reinforcement: An experimental study of cultural observation. *Journal of Abnormal and Social Psychology,* 1958, **56,** 57–61.

Mischel, W. Father-absence and delay of gratification: Cross-cultural comparisons. *Journal of Abnormal and Social Psychology,* 1961, **63,** 116–124.

Mischel, W. Theory and research on the antecedents of self-imposed delay of reward. In B. A. Maher (Ed.), *Progress in Experimental Personality Research.* Vol. 3. New York: Academic Press, 1966. Pp. 85–132.

Mischel, W., & Grusec, J. Determinants of the rehearsal and transmission of neutral aversive behaviors. *Journal of Personality and Social Psychology,* 1966, **3,** 45–53.

Mischel, W., & Grusec, J. Waiting for rewards and punishments: Effects of time and probability on choice. *Journal of Personality and Social Psychology,* 1967, **5,** 24–31.

Mischel, W., Grusec, J., & Masters, J. C. Effects of expected delay time on the subjective value of rewards and punishments. *Journal of Personality and Social Psychology,* 1969, **11,** 363–373.

Mischel, W., & Liebert, R. M. Effects of discrepancies between observed and imposed reward criteria on their acquisition and transmission. *Journal of Personality and Social Psychology,* 1966, **3,** 45–53.

Mischel, W., & Liebert, R. M. The role of power in the adoption of self-reward patterns. *Child Development,* 1967, **38,** 673–683.

Mischel, W., & Masters, J. C. Effects of probability of reward attainment on responses to frustration. *Journal of Personality and Social Psychology,* 1966, **3,** 390–396.

Mischel, W., & Staub, E. The effects of expectancy on waiting and working for larger rewards. *Journal of Personality and Social Psychology,* 1965, **2,** 625–633.

Montgomery, K. C. The role of exploratory drive in learning. *Journal of Comparative and Physiological Psychology,* 1954, **47,** 60–64.

Moore, N. Behavior therapy in bronchial asthma: A controlled study. *Journal of Psychosomatic Research,* 1965, **9,** 257–276.

Mowrer, O. H. On the dual nature of learning—a reinterpretation of "conditioning" and "problem-solving." *Harvard Educational Review,* 1947, **17,** 102–148.

Mowrer, O. H. *Learning theory and personality dynamics.* New York: Ronald, 1950.

Mowrer, O. H. The psychologist looks at language. *American Psychologist,* 1954, **9,** 660–694.

Mowrer, O. H. *Learning theory and behavior.* New York: Wiley, 1960. (a)

Mowrer, O. H. *Learning theory and the symbolic process.* New York: Wiley, 1960. (b)

Mowrer, O. H. Cognitive dissonance or counterconditioning? A reappraisal of certain behavioral "paradoxes." *Psychological Record,* 1963, **13,** 197–211.

Mowrer, O. H. Learning theory and behavior therapy. In B. B. Wolman (Ed.), *Handbook of clinical psychology.* New York: McGraw-Hill, 1965. Pp. 242–276.

Mowrer, O. H., & Mowrer, W. M. Enuresis: A method for its study and treatment. *American Journal of Orthopsychiatry*, 1938, **8**, 436–459.

Mueller, C. G., & Schoenfeld, W. N. Edwin R. Guthrie. In W. K. Estes *et al.*, *Modern learning theories*. New York: Appleton-Century-Crofts, 1954. Pp. 345–379.

Mussen, P., & Parker, A. L. Mother nurturance and girls' incidental imitative learning. *Journal of Personality and Social Psychology*, 1965, **2**, 461–464.

Newcomb, T. M. An approach to the study of communicative acts. *Psychological Review*, 1953, **60**, 393–404.

Newcomb, T. M. The prediction of interpersonal attraction. *American Psychologist*, 1956, **11**, 575–586.

Newcomb, T. M. The cognition of persons as cognizers. In R. Tagiuri & L. Petrullo (Eds.), *Person perception and interpersonal behavior*. Stanford, California: Stanford University Press, 1958. Pp. 179–190.

Novak, D. W., & Lerner, M. J. Rejection as a consequence of perceived similarity. *Journal of Personality and Social Psychology*, 1968, **9**, 147–152.

O'Connell, E. J., Jr. The effect of cooperative and competitive set on the learning of imitation and nonimitation. *Journal of Experimental Social Psychology*, 1965, **1**, 172–183.

O'Connor, R. D. Modification of symbolic withdrawal through symbolic modeling. *Journal of Applied Behavioral Analysis*, 1969, **2**, 15–22.

Olds, J. Self-stimulation of the brain. *Science*, 1958, **127**, 315–324.

Olds, J. Hypothalamic substrates of reward. *Physiological Review*, 1962, **42**, 554–604.

Olds, J., & Milner, P. Positive reinforcement produced by electrical stimulation of septal areas and other regions of the rat brain. *Journal of Comparative and Physiological Psychology*, 1954, **47**, 419–427.

Osgood, C. E. Studies on the generality of affective meaning systems. *American Psychologist*, 1962, **17**, 10–28.

Osgood, C. E. On understanding and creating sentences. *American Psychologist*, 1963, **18**, 735–751.

Osgood, C. E. Meaning cannot be an r_m? *Journal of Verbal Learning and Verbal Behavior*, 1966, **5**, 402–407.

Osgood, C. E. Toward a wedding of insufficiencies. In T. R. Dixon & D. L. Horton (Eds.), *Verbal behavior and general behavior theory*. Englewood Cliffs, New Jersey: Prentice-Hall, 1968. Pp. 495–519.

Osgood, C. E., Suci, G. J., & Tannenbaum, P. H. *The measurement of meaning*. Urbana, Illinois: University of Illinois Press, 1957.

Osgood, C. E., & Tannenbaum, P. H. The principle of congruity in the prediction of attitude change. *Psychological Review*, 1955, **62**, 42–55.

Ostrom, T. M. Physical effort and attitude change. Paper presented at the meeting of the American Psychological Association, New York, 1966.

Paivio, A. Audience influence, social isolation, and speech. *Journal of Abnormal and Social Psychology*, 1963, **67**, 247–353.

Parke, R. D., & Walters, R. H. Some factors influencing the efficacy of punishment training for inducing response inhibition. *Monographs of the Society for Research in Child Development*, 1967, **32**, No. 1 (Serial No. 109).

Paul, G. L. *Insight vs. desensitization in psychotherapy*. Stanford, California: Stanford University Press, 1966.

Paul, G. L. Insight versus desensitization in psychotherapy two years after termination. *Journal of Consulting Psychology*, 1967, **31**, 333–348.

Paul, G. L. Two-year follow-up of systematic desensitization in therapy groups. *Journal of Abnormal Psychology*, 1968, **73**, 119–130.

Paul, G. L., & Shannon, D. T. Treatment of anxiety through systematic desensitization in therapy groups. *Journal of Abnormal Psychology*, 1966, **71**, 124–135.

Pavlov, I. P. *Conditioned reflexes*. London: Oxford University Press, 1927.

Pavlov, I. P. The reply of a physiologist to psychologists. *Psychological Review* 1932, **39**, 91–127.

Pepitone, A. Attributions of causality, social attitudes, and cognitive matching process. In R. Tagiuri & L. Petrullo (Eds.), *Person perception and interpersonal behavior*. Stanford, California: Stanford University Press, 1958. Pp. 258–276.

Pepitone, A. *Attraction and hostility*. New York: Atherton, 1964.

Pepitone, A., & Kleiner, R. The effects of threat and frustration upon group cohesiveness. *Journal of Abnormal and Social Psychology*, 1957, **54**, 192–200.

Piaget, J. *The moral judgment of the child*. Glencoe, Illinois: The Free Press, 1948. (First English edition, London: Kegan Paul, 1932).

Piaget, J. *Play, dreams, and imitation in childhood*. New York: Norton, 1951.

Postman, L. Short-term memory and incidental learning. In A. W. Melton (Ed.), *Categories of human learning*. New York: Academic Press, 1964. Pp. 145–201.

Postman, L., Adams, P. O., & Bohm, A. M. Studies in incidental learning: V. Recall for order and associative clustering. *Journal of Experimental Psychology*, 1956, **51**, 334–342.

Postman, L., & Senders, V. L. Incidental learning and the generality of set. *Journal of Experimental Psychology*, 1946, **36**, 153–165.

Pubols, B. H., Jr. Constant versus variable delay of reinforcement. *Journal of Comparative and Physiological Psychology*, 1962, **55**, 52–56.

Rachman, S., & Eysenck, H. J. Reply to a "Critique and reformulation" of behavior therapy. *Psychological Bulletin*, 1966, **65**, 165–169.

Razran, G. H. S. Conditioning away social bias by the luncheon technique. *Psychological Bulletin*, 1938, **35**, 693.

Razran, G. H. S. Conditioned response changes in ratings and appraising sociopolitical slogans. *Psychological Bulletin*, 1940, **37**, 481.

Restle, F. A survey and classification of learning models. In R. R. Bush & W. K. Estes (Eds.), *Studies in mathematical learning theory*. Stanford, California: Stanford University Press, 1959. Pp. 415–428.

Reynolds, G. S. *A primer of operant conditioning*. Glenview, Illinois: Scott, Foresman, 1968.

Risley, T., & Wolf, M. M. Experimental manipulation of autistic behaviors and generalization into the home. In R. Ulrich, T. Stachnik, & J. Mabry (Eds.), *Control of human behavior*. Glenview, Illinois: Scott, Foresman, 1966. Pp. 193–198.

Roberts, W. W. Both rewarding and punishing effects from stimulation of posterior hypothalamus of the cat with the same electrode at the same intensity. *Journal of Comparative and Physiological Psychology*, 1958, **51**, 400–407.

Rosen, H. Discussion of Seitz' "Experiments in the substitution of symptoms by hypnosis." *Psychosomatic Medicine*, 1953, **15**, 422–424.

Rosenbaum, M. E. The effect of verbalization of correct response by performers and observers on retention. *Child Development*, 1967, **38**, 615–623.

Rosenbaum, M. E., & de Charms, R. Direct and vicarious reduction of hostility. *Journal of Abnormal and Social Psychology*, 1960, **60**, 105–111.

Rosenberg, M. When dissonance fails: On eliminating evaluative apprehension from attitude measurement. *Journal of Personality and Social Psychology*, 1965, **1**, 28–42.

Rosenberg, S., Nelson, C., & Vivekananthan, P. S. A multidimensional approach to the structure of personality impressions. *Journal of Personality and Social Psychology*, 1968, **9**, 283–294.

Rosenhan, D., & White, G. M. Observation and rehearsal as determinants of pro-social behavior. *Journal of Personality and Social Psychology*, 1967, **5**, 424–431.

Rosenkrans, M. A. Imitation in children as a function of perceived similarity to a social model and vicarious reinforcement. *Journal of Personality and Social Psychology*, 1967, **7**, 307–315.

Rosnow, R. L. Opinion change and order of presentation in experimentally manipulated anxiety and in natural familiarity with a topic. Unpublished doctoral dissertation. American University Press, 1962.

Rosnow, R. L. A delay-of-reinforcement effect in persuasive communication? *Journal of Social Psychology*, 1965, **67**, 39–43.

Rosnow, R. L. "Conditioning" the direction of opinion change in persuasive communication. *Journal of Social Psychology*, 1966, **69**, 291–303.

Rosnow, R. L., & Lana, R. E. Complementary and competing-order effects in opinion change. *Journal of Social Psychology*, 1965, **66**, 201–207.

Ross, D. Relationship between dependency, intentional learning, and incidental learning in preschool children. *Journal of Personality and Social Psychology*, 1966, 4, 374–381.

Rotter, J. B. *Social learning and clinical psychology*. Englewood Cliffs, New Jersey: Prentice-Hall, 1954.

Rotter, J. B. Generalized expectancies for internal versus external control of reinforcement. *Psychological Monograph*, 1966, **80**, No. 1 (Whole No. 609).

Schachter, S. The interaction of cognitive and physiological determinants of emotional states. In L. Berkowitz (Ed.), *Advances in experimental social psychology*. Vol. 1. New York: Academic Press, 1964. Pp. 49–80.

Schachter, S., Ellertson, N., McBride, D., & Gregory, D. An experimental study of cohesiveness and productivity. *Human Relations*, 1951, 4, 229–238.

Schachter, S., & Singer, J. E. Cognitive, social and physiological determinants of emotional states. *Psychological Review*, 1962, **69**, 379–399.

Schein, E. H. The effect of reward on adult imitative behavior. *Journal of Abnormal and Social Psychology*, 1954, **49**, 389–395.

Schultz, D. Primacy-recency within a sensory variation framework. *Psychological Record*, 1963, **13**, 129–139.

Schwitzgebel, R. Reduction of adolescent crime by research method. *Journal of Corrective Psychiatry and Social Therapy*, 1961, **7**, 212–215.

Schwitzgebel, R. *Streetcorner research*. Cambridge, Massachusetts: Harvard University Press, 1964.

Schwitzgebel, R., & Kolb, D. A. Inducing behavior change in adolescent delinquents. *Behaviour Research and Therapy*, 1964, **1**, 297–304.

Scott, W. A. Attitude change through reward of verbal behavior. *Journal of Abnormal and Social Psychology*, 1957, **55**, 72–75.

Scott, W. A. Cognitive consistency, response reinforcement, and attitude change. *Sociometry*, 1959, **22**, 219–229. (a)

Scott, W. A. Attitude acquisition by response reinforcement: Replication and extension. *Sociometry*, 1959, **22**, 328–335. (b)

Scriven, M. A. A study of radical behaviorism. In H. Feigl & M. Scriven (Eds.), *Minnesota studies in the philosophy of science*. Vol. 1. Minneapolis: University of Minnesota Press, 1956. Pp. 88–130.

Sears, R. R. A theoretical framework for personality and social behavior. *American Psychologist*, 1951, **6**, 476–483.

Sears, R. R., Maccoby, E. & Levin, H. *Patterns of child rearing.* Evanston, Illinois: Row, Peterson, 1957.

Seitz, P. F. D. Experiments in the substitution of symptoms by hypnosis: II. *Psychosomatic Medicine,* 1953, **15**, 405–422.

Shaw, F. J. A stimulus-response analysis of repression and insight in psychotherapy. *Psychological Review,* 1946, **53**, 36–42.

Shaw, M. E., & Shaw, L. M. Some effects of sociometric grouping upon learning in a second grade classroom. *Journal of Social Psychology,* 1962, **57**, 453–458.

Sheffield, F. D. Theoretical considerations in the learning of complex sequential tasks from demonstration and practice. In A. A. Lumsdaine (Ed.), *Student response to programmed instruction: A symposium.* Washington, D. C.: National Academy of Science-National Research Council, 1961. Pp. 13–32.

Sheffield, F. D. A drive-induction theory of reinforcement. In R. N. Haber (Ed.), *Current research in motivation.* New York: Holt, Rinehart, & Winston, 1966.

Sheffield, F. D., Roby, T. B., & Campbell, B. A. Drive reduction versus consummatory behavior as determinants of reinforcement. *Journal of Comparative and Physiological Psychology,* 1954, **47**, 349–354.

Sherrington, C. S. *The integrative action of the nervous system.* New Haven: Yale University Press, 1947 (1906).

Shoben, E. J. Psychotherapy as a problem in learning theory. *Psychological Bulletin,* 1949, **46**, 366–392.

Siegel, A. W., & Stevenson, H. W. Incidental learning: A developmental study. *Child Development,* 1966, **37**, 811–817.

Singer, R. D. Verbal conditioning and generalization of prodemocratic responses. *Journal of Abnormal and Social Psychology,* 1961, **63**, 43–46.

Skinner, B. F. *The behavior of organisms.* New York: Appleton-Century-Crofts, 1938.

Skinner, B. F. *Walden two.* New York: Macmillan, 1948.

Skinner, B. F. Are theories of learning necessary? *Psychological Review,* 1950, **57**, 193–216.

Skinner, B. F. *Science and human behavior.* New York: Macmillan, 1953.

Skinner, B. F. What is psychotic behavior? In *Theory and treatment of psychosis: Some newer aspects.* St. Louis: Washington University Studies, 1956.

Skinner, B. F. *Verbal behavior.* New York: Appleton-Century-Crofts, 1957.

Skinner, B. F. A case history in scientific method. In S. Koch (Ed.), *Psychology: A study of a science.* Vol. 2. New York: McGraw-Hill, 1959. Pp. 359–379.

Skinner, B. F. Operant behavior. In W. K. Honig (Ed.), *Operant behavior: Areas of research and application.* New York: Appleton-Century-Crofts, 1966. Pp. 12–32.

Slack, C. W. Experimenter-subject psychotherapy: A new method of introducing intensive office treatment for unreachable cases. *Mental Hygiene,* 1960, **44**, 238–256.

Smith, S., & Guthrie, E. R. *General psychology in terms of behavior.* New York: Appleton-Century, 1921.

Smith, S., & Guthrie, E. R. Exhibitionism. *Journal of Abnormal and Social Psychology,* 1922, **17**, 206–209.

Solomon, R. L. The influence of some types of power relationships and game strategies upon the development of interpersonal trust. *Journal of Abnormal and Social Psychology,* 1960, **61**, 223–230.

Solomon, R. L. Punishment. *American Psychologist,* 1964, **19**, 239–253.

Spence, K. W. *Behavior theory and conditioning.* New Haven: Yale University Press, 1956.

Spiegel, H. Is symptom removal dangerous? *American Journal of Psychiatry,* 1967, **10**, 1279–1282.

Spielberger, C. D. The role of awareness in verbal conditioning. In C. W. Eriksen (Ed.), *Behavior and awareness*. Durham, North Carolina: Duke University Press, 1962. Pp. 73–101.

Spielberger, C. D. Theoretical and epistemological issues in verbal conditioning. In S. Rosenberg (Ed.), *Directions in psycholinguistics*. New York: Macmillan, 1965. Pp. 149–200.

Spielberger, C. D., Southard, L. D., & Hodges, W. F. Effects of awareness and threat of shock on verbal conditioning. *Journal of Experimental Psychology*, 1966, **72**, 434–438.

Spinoza, B. Tractatus de intellectus emendatione. In R. H. M. Elwes (Ed. & tr.), *The chief works of Benedict de Spinoza*. New York: Dial Press, 1928 (1677).

Staats, A. W. Verbal habit-families, concepts, and the operant conditioning of word classes. *Psychological Review*, 1961, **68**, 190–204.

Staats, A. W. Outline of an integrated learning theory of attitude formation and function. In M. Fishbein (Ed.), *Readings in attitude theory and measurement*. New York: Wiley, 1967.

Staats, A. W. *Learning, language, and cognition*. New York: Holt, Rinehart, & Winston, 1968.

Staats, A. W., & Staats, C. K. Attitudes established by classical conditioning. *Journal of Abnormal and Social Psychology*, 1958, **57**, 37–40.

Staats, A. W., Staats, C. K. *Complex human behavior: A systematic extension of learning principles*. New York: Holt, Rinehart, & Winston, 1963.

Staats, A. W., Staats, C. K., & Crawford, H. L. First-order conditioning of meaning and the parallel conditioning of GSR. *Journal of General Psychology*, 1962, **67**, 159–167.

Staats, A. W., Staats, C. K., & Heard, W. G. Denotative meaning established by classical conditioning. Tech. Rep. No. 13 Contract No. Nonr-2794 (OZ) between the Office of Naval Research and Arizona State University, 1959.

Stein, A. H., & Wright, J. C. Imitative learning under conditions of nurturance and nurturance withdrawal. *Child Development*, 1964, **35**, 927–938.

Stevenson, H. W., & Cruse, D. B. The effectiveness of social reinforcement with normal and feebleminded children. *Journal of Personality*, 1961, **29**, 124–135.

Stevenson, H. W., & Fahel, L. S. The effect of social reinforcement on the performance of institutionalized and noninstitutionalized normal and feebleminded children. *Journal of Personality*, 1961, **29**, 136–147.

Stevenson, H. W., & Hill, K. T. The effects of social reinforcement and nonreinforcement following success and failure. *Journal of Personality*, 1965, **33**, 418–427.

Stoghill, R. *Individual behavior and group achievement*. New York: Oxford University Press, 1959.

Stotland, E., & Hillmer, M. Identification, authoritarian defensiveness, and self-esteem. *Journal of Abnormal and Social Psychology*, 1962, **64**, 334–342.

Straughan, J. H. Treatment with child and mother in the playroom. *Behaviour Research and Therapy*, 1964, **2**, 37–41.

Straughan, J. H., Potter, W. K., & Hamilton, S. H. The behavioral treatment of an elective mute. *Journal of Child Psychology and Psychiatry*, 1965, **6**, 125–130.

Sylvester, J. D., & Liversedge, L. A. Conditioning and the occupational cramps. In H. J. Eysenck (Ed.), *Behavior therapy and the neurosis*. New York: Pergamon Press, 1960.

Symonds, P. M. Classroom discipline. In J. M. Seidman (Ed.), *Readings in educational psychology*. 2nd ed. Boston: Houghton-Mifflin, 1965.

Taffel, C. Anxiety and the conditioning of verbal behavior. *Journal of Abnormal and Social Psychology*, 1955, **51**, 496–501.

Tagiuri, R. Person perception. In G. Lindzey & E. Aronson (Eds.), *Handbook of social psychology.* Vol. 3. Reading, Massachusetts: Addison-Wesley, 1969. Pp. 395–449.

Tarde, G. *The laws of imitation.* (transl.) New York: Holt, 1903.

Tate, B. G., & Baroff, G. S. Aversive control of self-injurious behavior in a psychotic boy. *Behaviour Research and Therapy,* 1966, **4,** 281–287.

Taylor, J. A. A personality scale of manifest anxiety. *Journal of Abnormal and Social Psychology,* 1953, **48,** 285–298.

Terman, L. M., & Merrill, M. A. *Measuring intelligence.* Boston: Houghton-Mifflin, 1937.

Thibaut, J. W. An experimental study of the cohesiveness of underprivileged groups. *Human Relations,* 1950, **3,** 251–278.

Thibaut, J. W., & Kelley, H. H. *The social psychology of groups.* New York: Wiley, 1959.

Thorndike, E. L. Animal intelligence: An experimental study of the associative processes in animals. *Psychological Review, Monograph Supplement,* 1898, **2,** No. 8.

Thorndike, E. L. *The psychology of learning.* New York: Teachers College, 1913.

Thorndike, E. L. *The fundamentals of learning.* New York: Teachers College, 1932.

Thorpe, W. H. Comparative psychology, *Annual Review of Psychology,* 1961, **12,** 27–50.

Tolman, E. C. *Purposive behavior in animals and men.* New York: Appleton-Century, 1932.

Tolman, E. C. *Drives toward war.* New York: Appleton-Century, 1946.

Tolman, E. C. Cognitive maps in rats and men. *Psychological Review,* 1948, **55,** 189–208.

Tolman, E. C. Principles of purposive behavior. In S. Koch (Ed.), *Psychology: A study of a science.* Vol. 2. New York: McGraw-Hill, 1959. Pp. 92–157.

Tolman, E. C., & Honzik, C. H. Introduction and removal of reward and maze performance in rats. *University of California Publications in Psychology,* 1930, **4,** 257–275.

Tolstoy, L. The history of yesterday. *Complete works, Jubilee edition.* Moscow-Leningrad: 1935 (1851).

Triandis, H. C., & Fishbein, M. Cognitive interaction in person perception. *Journal of Abnormal and Social Psychology,* 1963, **67,** 446–453.

Ullmann. L. P., & Krasner, L. (Eds.), *Case studies in behavior modification.* New York: Holt, Rinehart, & Winston, 1965.

Ullmann, L. P., & Krasner, L. *A psychological approach to abnormal behavior.* Englewood Cliffs, New Jersey: Prentice-Hall, 1969.

Ulrich, R., Stachnik, T., & Mabry, J. (Eds.) *Control of human behavior.* Chicago: Scott, Foresman, 1966.

Underwood, B. J. *Psychological research.* New York: Appleton-Century-Crofts, 1957.

Underwood, B. J., & Keppel, G. One-trial learning? *Journal of Verbal Learning and Verbal Behavior,* 1962, **1,** 1–13.

Verplanck, W. S. The control of the content of conversation: Reinforcement of statements of opinion. *Journal of Abnormal and Social Psychology,* 1955, **51,** 668–676.

Walters, R. H., & Karal, P. Social deprivation and verbal behavior. *Journal of Personality,* 1960, **28,** 89–107.

Walters, R. H., & Parke, R. D. Influence of response consequences to a social model on resistance to deviation. *Journal of Experimental Child Psychology*, 1964, **1**, 269–280.

Walters, R. H., & Parke, R. D. The role of distance receptors in the development of social responsiveness. In L. P. Lipsitt & C. C. Spiker (Eds.), *Advances in child development and behavior*. Vol. 2. New York: Academic Press, 1965. Pp. 59–96.

Walters, R. H., & Parke, R. D. The influence of punishment and related disciplinary techniques on the social behavior of children: Theory and empirical findings. In B. A. Maher (Ed.), *Progress in experimental personality research*. Vol. 4. New York: Academic Press, 1967. Pp. 179–228.

Walters, R. H., Parke, R. D., & Cane, V. A. Timing of punishment and the observation of consequences to others as determinants of response inhibition. *Journal of Experimental Child Psychology*, 1965, **2**, 10-30.

Walters, R. H., & Ray, E. Anxiety, social isolation, and reinforcer effectiveness. *Journal of Personality*, 1960, **28**, 358–367.

Watson, J. B. *Behavior: An introduction to comparative psychology*. New York: Holt, Rinehart, & Winston, 1914.

Watson, J. B. *Behaviorism*. Chicago: University of Chicago Press, 1924.

Watson, J. B. What the nursery has to say about instincts. *Pedagogical Seminary*, 1925, **32**, 293–326.

Watson, J. B. *The ways of behaviorism*. New York: Harper, 1928.

Watson, J. B., & Rayner, R. Conditioned emotional reaction. *Journal of Experimental Psychology*, 1920, **3**, 1–4.

Watts, W. A. Relative persistence of opinion change induced by active compared to passive participation. *Journal of Personality and Social Psychology*, 1967, **5**, 4–15.

Watts, W. A., & McGuire, W. J. Persistence of induced opinion change and retention of inducing message content. *Journal of Abnormal and Social Psychology*, 1964, **68**, 233–241.

Weinrich, V. Travels through semantic space. *Word*, 1958, **14**, 346–366.

Weiss, R. F. Persuasion and the acquisition of attitudes: Models from conditioning and selective learning. *Psychological Reports*, 1962, **11**, 709–732.

Weiss, R. F. A delay of argument gradient in the instrumental conditioning of attitudes. *Psychonomic Science*, 1967, **8**, 457–458.

Weiss, R. F., & Pasamanich, B. Number of exposures to persuasive communication in the instrumental conditioning of attitudes. *Journal of Social Psychology*, 1964, **63**, 373–382.

Weiss, R. F., Rawson, H. E., & Pasamanich, B. Argument strength, delay of argument and anxiety in the "conditioning" and "selective learning" of attitudes. *Journal of Abnormal and Social Psychology*, 1963, **67**, 157–165.

Weitzman, B. Behavior therapy and psychotherapy. *Psychological Review*, 1967, **74**, 300–317.

Whaler, R. G., Winkel, G. H., Peterson, R. F., & Morrison, D. C. Mothers as behavior therapists for their own children. *Behaviour Research and Therapy*, 1965, **3**, 113–124.

White, R. W. *Ego and reality in psychoanalytic theory*. New York: International University Press, 1963.

Whiting, J. W. M. Resource mediation and learning by identification. In I. Iscoe & H. W. Stevenson (Eds.), *Personality development in children*. Austin, Texas: University of Texas Press, 1960. Pp. 112–126.

Wiest, W. M. Some recent criticisms of behaviorism and learning theory with special reference to Breger and McGaugh and to Chomsky. *Psychological Bulletin*, 1967, **67**, 214–225.

Wilson, W. C. Imitation and and the learning of incidental cues by pre-school children. *Child Development*, 1958, **29**, 393–397.

Wolberg, L. R. *The technique of psychotherapy*. New York: Grune & Stratton, 1954.

Wolf, M. M., Risley, T., & Mees, H. Application of operant conditioning procedures to the behavior problems of an autistic child. *Behaviour Research and Therapy*, 1964, **1**, 305–312.

Wolfe, J. B. Effectiveness of token rewards for chimpanzees. *Comparative Psychological Monographs*, 1936, **12**, No. 60.

Wolpe, J. *Psychotherapy by reciprocal inhibition*. Stanford, California: Stanford University Press, 1958.

Wolpe, J. The experimental foundation of some new psychotherapeutic methods. In A. J. Bachrach (Ed.), *Experimental foundations of clinical psychology*. New York: Basic Books, 1962.

Wolpe, J. For phobia: The hair of the hound. *Psychology Today*, 1969, **3**, 34–37.

Worthington, A. G. Generalization phenomena associated with previous pairings of UCS (shock) and subliminal visual stimuli. *Journal of Personality and Social Psychology*, 1966, **3**, 634–640.

Worthy, M., Gary, A. L., & Kahn, G. M. Self-disclosure as an exchange process. *Journal of Personality and Social Psychology*, 1969, **13**, 59–63.

Yates, A. J. The application of learning theory to the treatment of tics. *Journal of Abnormal and Social Psychology*, 1958, **56**, 175–182. (a)

Yates, A. J. Symptoms and symptom substitution. *Psychological Review*, 1958, **65**, 371–374. (b)

Yates, A. J. A comment on Bookbinder's critique of "Symptoms and symptom substitution." *Psychological Reports*, 1962, **11**, 102.

Yerkes, R. M., & Dodson, J. D. The relation of strength of stimulus to rapidity of habit-formation. *Journal of Comparative and Neurological Psychology*, 1908, **18**, 459–482.

Yuker, H. E. Group atmosphere and memory. *Journal of Abnormal and Social Psychology*, 1955, **51**, 17–23.

Zeff, L. H., & Iverson, M. A. Opinion conformity in groups under status threat. *Journal of Personality and Social Psychology*, 1966, **3**, 383–389.

Zimbardo, P. The effect of effort and improvisation on self-persuasion produced by role-playing. *Journal of Experimental Social Psychology*, 1965, **1**, 103–120.

Zimmerman, J., & Hanford, P. V. Sustaining behavior with conditioned reinforcement as the only response-produced consequence. *Psychological Reports*, 1966, **19**, 391–401.

Name Index

Subject Index

Acquired behavioral dispositions, 166
Aggressive behavior, imitation of, 155–156, 159, 163–164, 255
Associationism, 4–5, 7, 10, 30, 104–105, 113–114
Attentional processes, imitation and, 137–138, 153, 163
Attitude:
  change, 177–204
  cognitive content of, 202–204
  conditioning of, 167–174
  definition of, 166
  development of, 167–177
  dual-process acquisition theory, 171–174
  instrumental learning of, 170–171
  operant learning of, 174–176
Autism, 222, 224, 225, 226, 247
Avoidance training, 184
Awareness, 60–64

Backward learning, 50, 78
Behavior therapy, 208–250
Belief, 94–95

Chaining model of language acquisition, 104–105
Choice and attitude change, 190, 197–198
Classical conditioning, 4, 5, 19, 30, 50–54, 67, 96–97, 118, 128, 129, 135–136, 146, 154, 167–170, 172, 174, 216–221
Cognitive theory, 5, 17, 18, 34, 35, 47, 79–80, 117, 142, 161, 206–207, 234, 244–246, 276, 277
Commitment and attitude change, 190, 191
Communicator credibility and attitude change, 178–180
Comparison level, 43, 283
Concept learning, 6
Conditioned affectivity (see Emotional learning)
Conditioned inhibition, 193
Conditioned reflex, 8
Conditioned reinforcement, 149, 161
Conflict theory, 29, 211–212
Conformity, 180, 287–290

Conscience, 33–34, 142, 270
Consensual validation, 277, 285
Consistency, drive for, 198, 276
Contextual generalization, 111–114, 121–124
Contiguity, conditioning by, 10, 30, 73–74, 133, 134, 136–137, 146, 154, 155, 161–162
Control of behavior:
  external, 252–259
  internal, 259–272
Counterattitudinal advocacy and attitude change, 187–191, 196–198, 200

Delay of punishment, 264
Delay of reinforcement, 171
Delay of reward, 262–264
Dependence and imitation, 152, 255
Discrimination learning, psychotherapy as, 211–215
Discriminative stimuli, 84, 132, 143, 145, 159
Displacement, 197
Dissonance theory, 187–199
Distributive justice, 45, 282
Drive, 13, 24, 69–71, 130

Education, 11–12
Effort expenditure and attitude change, 191–194
Emotional learning, 8, 27–28, 31, 135, 145, 153, 154, 209–210
  extinction of emotional response, 8–9, 210–211
  verbal learning, 96–97
Empathetic learning, 133, 153
Enuresis, 210–211, 222
Equivalence:
  response, 106–115
  stimulus, 106, 115
Ethology, 77
Evaluative reinforcement, 272–273
Exchange theory, 44–46
Exhibitionism, 209–210
Expectancy, 35, 262
Experimentation, 77

Fear, 15, 30